George Brent

Ireland's Gift to Hollywood
and its Leading Ladies

by

Scott O'Brien

Also by Scott O'Brien:

Kay Francis – I Can't Wait to be Forgotten (**2006**)

Classic Images Magazine – "**Best Books of 2006**" **Laura Wagner** – "O'Brien has a way with words as he beautifully examines Kay's films. He skillfully uses Kay's own diary to paint a picture of an independent woman ahead of her time."

Virginia Bruce – *Under My Skin* (**2008**)

Daeida Magazine – **David Ybarra (editor)** – "*Under My Skin* ... is a well-researched, tactful, and skilled examination into the tragedy of a talented, beautiful and popular figure in film history, desperate to fall in love and stay in love at any cost. Highly recommended."

Ann Harding – *Cinema's Gallant Lady* (**2010**)

San Francisco Gate – **Mick LaSalle** – "I'm especially impressed that Scott O'Brien has managed to come up with a thick, fact-filled, smart and very readable biography of this *enormous* talent. Harding deserves to be known, and the public deserves to know her."

Ruth Chatterton – *Actress, Aviator, Author* (**2013**)

Huffington Post – **Thomas Gladys** – "**Best Film Books of 2013**"

George Brent

Ireland's Gift to Hollywood
and its Leading Ladies

A biography by

Scott O'Brien

Published in the USA by:
BearManor Media
P O Box 71426
Albany, Georgia 31708
www.bearmanormedia.com

ISBN   978-1-59393-599-3 (paperback)

Printed in the United States of America.

Book & cover design by Darlene and Dan Swanson of Van-garde Imagery, Inc.

Contents

1948 — Debonair George Brent basked in the luminosity of his leading ladies

George Brent

By Jeanine Basinger

My first experience of George Brent on screen was in a movie that is still one of my favorites: the 1944 *Experiment Perilous*, directed by Jacques Tourneur, and pairing Brent with the exquisite Hedy Lamarr at the peak of her beauty. Not only does Brent rescue Lamarr from her abusive husband (Paul Lukas), securing in my eyes a "knight in shining armor" status, but he also narrates the movie in his melodious and soothing voice. Imagine my surprise when barely two years later I found him trying to kill the shy Dorothy McGuire (playing a mute) in *Spiral Staircase* ... or when I came across him in a colorful MGM musical playing Jane Powell's suave father! Right from the beginning of my awareness of George Brent, I learned something that is often forgotten about him: he was much more than a prop for Bette Davis! He could be a hero, or he could be evil. That was George Brent's greatest asset: he could fit in where needed.

Brent was the type of leading man who the Hollywood studio system couldn't function without. He was handsome, solid, reliable, and utterly believable as a real man on screen. Over six feet tall, and in his youth slim and athletic looking, he was what a female moviegoer wanted in a man: dependable, but with, as Preston Sturges might have put it, "a little sex."

He was sophisticated but comfortable; he was debonair, but not too deb-onair; funny, but also serious. Above all, he would not overwhelm his co-stars, and that made him indispensable as a leading man for Hollywood's great female actresses. He could <u>support</u>, and yet still be the desired or dominant male. (It's very revealing that as a young man he was around the Abbey theatre, a repertoire company.) Actors who can support while playing the lead are a rare breed, and George Brent was one of the best.

Brent's most common "type" was a role we don't see much of today: the dream man, who would appear in a woman's life and provide her with whatever it was she most needed—money, sex, escape, love, or a medical cure. He was born to play in movies that were known as "women's films." Female fans loved him, and it's no secret that real life women adored him too. I am happy that someone decided to tell Brent's full story, and based on his earlier biographical books on Ruth Chatterton, Virginia Bruce, and Ann Harding, I think Scott O'Brien is the perfect person to be Brent's Boswell. I look forward to reading the truth about the actor I remember telling Barbara Stanwyck in *My Reputation* that life was out there for her if she wanted it … all she had to do was reach out and take it. George Brent gave American women the news they wanted to hear.

Jeanine Basinger – Wesleyan University
Corwin-Fuller Professor of Film Studies
Chair, Film Studies Department
Curator, Cinema Archives

In top-hat and tails,
Brent exuded gentlemanly
charm (WB) c. 1937
(below) "Horses are more
interesting than people,"
admitted Brent, the lone wolf.

Introduction

I was brought up on the belief that my life is my own to live and that, except where it crosses other lives, it is my own affair entirely," George Brent asserted. "I resent questions from people who have no business asking or knowing about my life before they came into it."[1] Brent's reputation as a lone wolf who refused to talk about his past made him a marked man in Hollywood. Reporters considered him bad copy. What was behind Brent's reticence? Why all the mystery surrounding his roots, his childhood, his parents whom he claimed to be dead? Were there emotional wounds that he simply wanted to forget? A reluctant Brent, along with the Warner Bros. publicity department, created a back story for the actor peppered with plausible lies that would appeal to the fans: a college education in Dublin; a player for the famous Abbey Theatre; a revolutionary for the IRA who escaped Ireland with a price on his head.[2] The challenge for a biographer is to separate fact from fiction. Not an unusual prospect when writing about a Hollywood star from the distant past.

George Brent's solid, gentlemanly charm as an actor is often dismissed as being repetitive, passive, and—unfairly—wooden. He was a handsome, virile romantic lead, but not so dominating a screen presence that he deflected focus from his glamorous leading ladies. For two decades,

Brent remained a popular choice of Hollywood's top female stars. Bette Davis, who costarred with Brent in eleven films, explained that he didn't hog the limelight. This, coupled with the fact that she had a long-time crush on him, which culminated in an affair, added to their onscreen simpatico. Greta Garbo requested Brent for her love interest in *The Painted Veil*. Evidently her heart throbbed for Brent offscreen as well. The two spent a great deal of time together. Brent went so far as to build a massive wall around his Toluca Lake residence so he and Garbo could play tennis and swim in privacy.[3] The press began referring to him as "the male Garbo." When asked about her, Brent would offer brusque assessments, such as, "She is beyond analyzing because of her genius."[4] Brent's home studio, Warner Brothers, capitalized on the popular screen team of Brent and Kay Francis, the studio's reigning queen. Author James Robert Parish included the duo's six films together in his 1974 publication, *Hollywood's Great Love Teams*. "In their day," wrote Parish, "Francis-Brent were regarded by the bulk of steady filmgoers as the height of refined, upper class romantics."[5] After completing *Living on Velvet* (1935), Brent's reputation as a ladies man translated into a one-night stand with Miss Francis, who enjoyed detailing her affairs in a diary now held at Wesleyan University.[6]

Jeanine Basinger, who wrote the foreword for this biography, had remarked in 1993, "If I had to pick one actor as Mr. Woman's Film, it would be George Brent. He's really quite wonderful-elegant, low-keyed, understated. He's quietly there, holding down his corner."[7] While Basinger noted that he lacked the "electric" quality of an Errol Flynn, Brent's list of A-list actress costars was impressive: Claudette Colbert, Loretta Young, Jean Arthur, Myrna Loy, Ginger Rogers, Olivia de Havilland, Joan Fontaine, Mary Astor, Madeleine Carroll, Joan Bennett, Constance Bennett, Hedy Lamarr, Merle Oberon, Virginia Bruce, Lucille Ball, and Jane Russell. He married two of his leading ladies: Ruth Chatterton and Ann Sheridan. In 1978, Brent was coaxed out of retirement by his old director Irving Rapper (*The Gay Sisters*) for a cameo role in *Born Again,* a film based on a book by Watergate mastermind Charles Colson. Brent agreed to be interviewed at the time, and singled out Barbara Stanwyck as his favorite costar. The two made five films together. "She was the most human, the most unassuming person in the world," he reminisced. "A very kind person. There's not a malicious bone in Barbara Stanwyck's body."[8] However, while Brent offered his opinions on leading ladies, the man himself remained a mystery.

In 1935, feature writer Dick Mook took on the unhappy assignment of interviewing Brent on the Warner set of *The Goose and the Gander.* Mook slumped into a chair next to Kay Francis who took pity on him. "I let myself in for an interview with George," he muttered. "And there's no story there. At least, not as far as I'm concerned. ... I can't get anything out of him."[9] "He's a liar, a pest and a nitwit," Francis agreed, trying to cheer the reporter up. "Liar?" repeated Mook. "One of the biggest," Kay calmly confirmed. "He'll promise anything under the sun ... but he thinks no more of breaking his word than he does of tying his scarf." Francis registered a common complaint around Hollywood that Brent never showed up at dinner parties to which he enthusiastically accepted invitations. "You said he was a pest?" inquired Mook. "One of the worst," declared Kay. "He has a passion for tickling people. If a person is ticklish, God help them when George is around!" (Cameraman Wesley Anderson readily confirmed this accusation against Brent, who had a reputation as a prankster.) Francis then zeroed in on Brent's real problem. "I think George is probably the cagiest person I've ever known," she said. "He's so close-mouthed that if he spoke out of the right side of his mouth the left side wouldn't know what he'd said. I think underneath he's one of the most cautious people imaginable. I don't know anyone who knows what

George is really like. I think he knows—but he isn't telling."[10] Writer Dan Camp was even blunter regarding his interviews with Brent. "He's told me, many a time, to go straight plumb to hell when I asked him about women," Camp stated. "And when I'd switch to the other subject—Hollywood—he'd tell me to go to hell again."[11]

Brent's fourth wife, actress Ann Sheridan, elaborated on Brent's penchant for privacy—his shrinking from familiarity. "George suffers from a shyness that is out of this world," Sheridan revealed shortly before their 1943 divorce. "I used to think he was pretending when he said he didn't like people, but after I married him I discovered that it was really a phobia. Someone at the studio would invite us to dinner, and George would accept with the utmost charm. But by the time we'd gotten home ... George would've talked himself into a state of abject misery. We'd end up staying home."[12] Studio employees were also puzzled by Mr. Brent. "George always looks on the black side," complained one crew member. "He seems to think that life is trying to give him a rotten deal. Whereas, we all think that life has been pretty good to him. He has no reason to complain. Imagine, a yacht, a plane, a bank account, Garbo, Davis and Sheridan, all in one lifetime!"[13]

Before we unravel the life of George Patrick Brendan Nolan, who later rechristened himself George Brent, let's allow the man to *explain himself.* In 1938, Brent offered an astute, reasonable assessment regarding his demand for privacy in an article he titled:

Brent – without a shirt, and generally uncommunicative.

Without a Shirt

When I was a youngster in Ireland, my grandfather used to read to me from his place in the chimney corner, and one of his favorite ways of ending the evening's entertainment was to quote these lines:

> *The loss of wealth is loss of dirt,*
> *All sages in all times assert;*
> *The happy man's without a shirt.*

I found the verse again not long ago in Bartlett's Quotations at a time when I'd begun to understand how fundamentally right John Heywood, who wrote it, and my grandfather, who quoted it, really were.

Like almost every other actor, I've had a full share of ups and downs of fortune. I find that I remember some of the lean financial periods with more pleasure than I recall the prosperous ones. Much as we desire it, continued success throughout life would result in a very dull existence, but like everyone else except the poets and my grandfather, I dread failure and poverty. I wouldn't like to be without a shirt—even though I profess to believe what my grandfather read to me. I wish I had the courage of my convictions. The Irish were not meant to be a contented race and I'm no different from the rest of them.

Ever since I can remember I have been periodically fed up with things as they are and itching to move on or go to work to change them. I know that no one man can hope to change Hollywood and I've no idea how I would like to have it changed, if I could, but I do know that a few weeks or months in the desert make the place seem much more bearable. Lately I've been spend-

ing a part of my time in the desert. Not in a so-called desert resort, but out in the real desert where both the sand and the people are unspoiled. I'm learning how much peace of mind one can find and how little everything else counts. Also, I spend most of the daylight hours without a shirt.

I had to come to Hollywood three times before I got any kind of a tumble here that seemed to promise any permanent screen success. Clark Gable, with whom I worked or competed on the stage, came to Hollywood and became a success while I was still cooling my heels in producers' offices. My eyes gave me trouble and for a little while I wasn't sure that both my career and my life were not to be blighted by blindness.

"The happy man's without a shirt!" That may be true, but the happy man is not the one without eyes or without objectives in life—not in this generation at least. My grandfather's philosophy doesn't hold up too well in the face of such dismal prospects. I suffered all the tortures of the damned, but I learned to keep my own counsel and to live in the present without too much concern over the past or the future. People have occasionally complained to me that I do not take them into my confidence, that I do not tell them my life story on first or second meeting. A few hectic months in Ireland during the stormy after-the-war period, when no man knew what other man he could trust, taught me the value of being generally uncommunicative.

I resent questions from people who have no business asking or knowing about my life before they came into it. I want to be friendly but not to the extent that I have no privacy, no solitude when I want it and no life of my own away from the idly curious. This, I have been told, will make me a marked man in Hollywood.

∞

Brent offered several clues to his past while explaining himself. Coupled with the extensive archival resources now available, separating fact from fiction in the telling of George Brent's story becomes a feasible task. I was encouraged by Irish filmmaker Brian Reddin to pursue writing about Brent. In the summer of 2012, Reddin was filming an Irish TV documentary that focused on the actor's life, *Reabhloidithe Hollywood* (2013). As I prepped for an interview with Reddin, I helped unravel Brent's return to Ireland in early 1921. Based on my and Reddin's detective work, we determined that young George Nolan's connection to Dublin University and the Abbey Theatre was either non-existent, or peripheral, at best. His participation in Ireland's War of Independence was not a farfetched plight for a vagabond sixteen-year-old with a great deal of pluck. The story you are about to read is a long overdue tribute to George Brent the actor, and a revealing look into his heretofore private world.

George Patrick Brendan Nolan (c. 1905) against the background of Ballinasloe, Ireland (Courtesy of Photoquest) The photo was used by The Los Angeles Evening Herald Express as part of their Hollywood Babies series (October 1934)

1

Ballinasloe Laddybuck

In late summer 1932, George Brent told the reputable Gladys Hall (founding member of the Hollywood Women's Press Club) that only three people in the world were "really significant and important" to him: his sister Kathleen; her husband Victor Watson, editor for *The New York Daily Mirror*; and actress Ruth Chatterton, who he had recently married. As usual, Brent was reticent to talk about his past. Studio publicity filled in those details. He played along with all the hype in order to avoid leading, uncomfortable questions. "People," said Brent, "never really care about you. When you are down, there is no one to help or to care. When you are up, there are—back-slappers. Next to being pitied, back-slapping is the most odious thing that can be done."[14] In 1930, an eminent eye specialist had told Brent that he was going blind. "My first instinct was—suicide," he told Hall. "I kept thinking, 'Have I worked so hard all these years—for *this*?' You achieve a certain philosophy if you survive the first shock of the thing. You retreat to your mind and find that you have scenes and faces to live with." Brent went to the east coast, had an operation, and convalesced at the home of his sister. "For weeks while I sat there in bandaged darkness … I knew the feelings of a blind man." Brent, born George Patrick Nolan on March 15, 1904, in Ballinasloe, Ireland, offered details of his childhood from a blind man's point of view.[15]

I seemed to 'see' mostly the days when I was a boy back home in Ireland. An unhappy kid, living with relatives who didn't seem to understand the kind of kid I was, painfully shy and painfully sensitive, trying my best to hide it. My father, a newspaperman, had died when I was two. I 'saw' myself as a boy running barefoot over the bogs in the early morning. My memory … had eyes. I could 'see' the Autumn mornings when we went out, my Uncle and I, to round up the sheep that were lambing in the fields. I remembered their mournful, questioning eyes, the soft sounds they made. I could smell the sweet, warm smell of the milk I fed the babies out of nursing bottles—forgetting, then, that I was a shy and not very happy little boy, conscious only that I was doing the best I could for creatures in distress.

Faces and memories in the darkness start a train of thought. I thought of the different kinds of love. And it is not the kind based on sex appeal. There is too much stress laid on physical attraction. I should say that at least seventy-five percent of love should be mental, should be companionship and sympathy. It is the most devastating thing in life—this physical attraction and the havoc it brings. I know—because I went through that sort of thing, too. I married it. And I went through Hell for nearly two years, although the marriage itself lasted less than six months.

I came to America for the first time when I was eleven. And that memory remained with me, too, though I hadn't thought about it for many years. I could see the dark waters and the averted and voiceless faces of my fellow-passengers, watching for the deadly periscope.

George Nolan was accompanied on this voyage, departing from Liverpool, by his sister Kathleen. It was September 11, 1915. England was at war. Germany had begun submarine warfare in February of that year. On May 7, the British liner *Lusitania* was sunk by a German U-Boat. George and Kathleen, who was fourteen, had every reason for panic until they arrived safely in New York on the *S.S. Philadelphia*, September 20.[16]

Missing from Brent's childhood reminiscences was any mention of his other siblings and the truth about his mother and father, who he claimed were dead.[17] George was the youngest of five children. His birth certificate details that his father, John Nolan, a shopkeeper, and his wife, Mary McGuinness Nolan, lived on Main Street in Ballinasloe.[18] The couple had married in 1892.[19] The following year their daughter Mary was born. John ("Jack") Nolan was born in 1896. He was followed by two more daughters: Lucile ("Lucy") born in 1898, and Kathleen, 1901.

Irish Filmmaker Brian Reddin helped clear up the mystery and Hollywood spin surrounding George Brent's family. While shooting a documentary on the actor and confronting Brent's different versions of his youth, Reddin collected some facts and drew some logical conclusions based on what he had discovered. Reddin pointed out, "From what I have unearthed, Brent's father worked as both a shopkeeper and a postal worker. He appears to have been quite negligent as a father, because George's mother left him and immigrated to New York [1905] along with [the two oldest] of George's siblings."[20] George was brought up by his grandfather on a farm and his mother sent for him and his sister Kathleen in 1915.[21] Brent's father did not die when Brent was two. John Nolan remained in Ireland. "I think his father was a heavy drinker and the family fell apart," Reddin elaborated. "Certainly his father was alive and living in Ballinasloe in 1911 according to the Irish census. Locals tell me he was still alive when George left for the States in 1915, but nobody seems to know what happened to him after that. I imagine that father and son did not have a good relationship."[22]

The 1911 Irish census also indicated that George and his elder sister Lucy lived with their maternal uncle Richard McGuinness in Cloonfad, due east of Ballinasloe, near Shannonbridge.[23] This was at the homestead of Michael McGuinness, George's grandfather. Richard was the uncle with whom George tended sheep. In November 1913, George's mother sent her daughter Mary back to Ireland to fetch Lucy and bring her to New York. On the ship manifest Lucy and Mary both confirmed that her Grandfather Michael McGuinness, of Cloonfad, was their nearest relative in Ireland.[24]

Brent's fond memories and admiration for his philosophical Grandfather McGuinness was unusual turf for him to talk about. Rarely did he mention his boyhood in Ballinasloe or Cloonfad. A young lad abandoned by his mother (when he was barely one-year old)—it's easy to understand why Brent described himself as being "unhappy ... painfully shy" surrounded by people who "didn't seem to understand." Columnist James Reid observed in 1940 that as a youngster George got used to being on his own, not expecting favors from anybody. "That goes a long way," Reid emphasized, "toward explaining why [George] is a Lone Wolf today."[25]

George's connection to the land during those first eleven years helped him forget. The area of East Galway and South Roscommon was predominantly agricultural. His childhood chores included putting away peat for winter fuel, digging potatoes, tending the sheep, and other duties that came up, such as feeding hogs, milking cows, and caring for horses. The district of Ballinasloe, built on a major ford over the River Suck, was a short distance from the River Shannon, in which the impulsive five-year-old lad nearly drowned. "I was swimming in the river Shannon," Brent explained. "I got beyond my depth, went down for the third time." One boy grabbed Nolan by his thick black hair and pulled him back to life. "Perhaps my luck," George joked, "made me overconfident and cocky about tempting fate."[26]

Clonfad, Ireland. Childhood home of George Nolan and his grandfather Michael McGuinness. (courtesy of Brian Reddin) (below) In nearby Shannonbridge, the popular pub Killeen has a signed photograph of George Brent (insert), the native lad who became a movie star.

Ballinasloe was also host to one of Europe's oldest horse fairs each October. The town was renowned for show jumping and equestrian activity. This explains one of Brent's lifelong passions. "I have always loved horses," he would say. "I was raised on a farm in Ireland, so racing is in my blood."[27] In 1966, Brent would return to Ireland and live in the outskirts of Dublin—a couple of hours away from director John Huston. Huston had relocated there during the investigations of the House Un-American Activities Committee. He went so far as to renounce his U.S. citizenship and become an Irish citizen. George's reason for returning to Ireland was to breed race horses. "Ireland is a great country for raising horses and racing them," he said at the time. "And that is my main occupation now."[28] His return to the old sod didn't last long. While the prize broodmares and yearlings that accompanied him took well to the Irish grasses, Brent did not. "It was the wettest and coldest winter I have ever endured," he admitted. "I couldn't take it. It was different when I was young; then, I'd bounce back every day."[29]

When George and Kathleen arrived in New York in 1915, they found their mother very much alive. In fact, she had paid for their passage. The Passenger List detailed that the 4' 8" Nolan boy had black hair and brown (hazel) eyes. Brother and sister were designated as going to live with Mrs. M. Nolan, their mother, at 302 West 90th Street. (Warner publicity stories would later state that he and Kathleen went to live with an aunt.) It wasn't exactly a "family reunited." George moved in with three adult strangers: his mother, age thirty-nine; his sister Mary, twenty-two, who was employed as a telephone operator; and Lucy, seventeen, a checker. His elder brother John, twenty, had recently enlisted in the U.S. Army.[30] For whatever reason, the only sibling that Brent was ever inclined to acknowledge was his sister Kathleen. In fact, after he signed his Warner Brothers' contract in December 1931, and was handed a questionnaire, Brent skipped over all the questions regarding his relatives and ancestors.[31]

When it came to his education, Brent's main ambition was to "get out of school as soon as possible."[32] If anything, he was self-educated. It took a skull fracture during a basketball game to finally pull him out of the classroom as well as out of commission. He "hovered between life and death for some time" before recovery.[33] He wasn't discouraged by this turn of events. Instead, he was bent on earning money and having adventures. He mentioned working on farms in northern New York—picking fruit for a cent a basket. "By the time I was sixteen," he claimed, "I was working in a bank in the day time and going to school at night. I was preparing to study law. It looked like such a long hard pull ahead before I could hope to begin to practice, especially since I must earn my own way. That I had to do. There was something stubborn inside me which demanded that I be independent. But my craving for action got the better of me. . . ."[34]

The bulk of George Nolan's education came from books. A voracious reader since childhood, he used to steal candles to read by at night. "The books I read—stacks and stacks of them!" he declared. Brent admitted that it may have contributed to his eventual eye troubles. "The enormous amount of night reading I had done, trying to learn, trying to be something ... I didn't regret it." There was yet another distraction for the strapping youth. Girls. One in particular. Brent admitted to a romantic episode with a red-haired colleen when he was fifteen. Hers was one of the faces that came back to him during his bout with near blindness. "I believe we underestimate youth," he said in the summer of 1932, "and the sufferings and permanence of the emotions of youth. We are liable to say, 'Oh, he's young. He'll get over it.' Not necessarily. *I never have.* I haven't seen her for years. I believe she is in London. She's a writer."[35]

In the January 1920 U.S. Census, fifteen-year-old George was listed as attending school. He lived with his now "widowed" mother and sister Lucy, a model, at a rental on West Seventy-Seventh Street in Manhattan.[36] There was also a two-year-old nephew in tow. George's eldest sister, Mary, wed Robert Fletcher around 1917.[37] For whatever reason, young Robert Jr. was being raised by Grandmother Nolan. Possibly, Mary had lost her husband during the war.[38] Kathleen had acquired a job as New York's first female news photographer for the *New York American* and now went by the name "Peggy" Nolan. It was under these circumstances that young George's craving for action finally found resolve.

George had become an avid reader of *Pearson's Magazine* and was spellbound by the lectures of Irish radical Frank Harris, who was the magazine's editor.[39] Harris, a man in his mid-sixties, lectured on "Individualism" at the magazine's headquarters on Fifth Avenue. Although a liberal, Harris was opposed to socialism/collectivism, thinking it would destroy individual effort in the arts, letters, science, and industry. His audience consisted mostly of eager young men and women, like George, who became "virtual disciples of the passion driven prophet."[40] Born in Galway in 1856, Harris grew up hating his father. His mother became a distant figure. As a runaway youth, Harris's life read like adventure fiction. At sixteen, he arrived in New York where he found a girlfriend. By day, he worked on the construction of the Brooklyn Bridge, and by night, according to Harris's autobiography, there were even greater accomplishments in the bedroom. He then headed to the frontier west, where he became pals with "Wild Bill" Hickok. (Jack Lemmon portrayed Harris in the 1958 film *Cowboy*.) While in Kansas, Harris studied law and was admitted to the bar. He abandoned law and decided to go to Europe. In 1883, he became editor for *The London Evening News*. Known for his booming, resonant voice and talking about subjects that were utterly taboo, Harris created a great deal of dead silence among his listeners. During a luncheon at London's posh Café Royal, Harris bellowed, "Homosexuality? No, I know nothing of the joys of homosexuality. My friend Oscar can no doubt tell you all about that. But I must say that if Shakespeare asked me, I would have to submit."[41] When Harris boasted that he'd gotten himself invited to every great house in London, Wilde made the famous rejoinder "But never more than once, Frank."[42] When Harris died in 1931, one obituary surmised, "He may have got more out of life if he had been less of a rolling stone."[43]

George absorbed the doctrines of Frank Harris like a sponge. The lectures fired his imagination. The nearly six-foot 175-pound sixteen-year-old wanted to do things, rather than just listen. He mentioned a young priest who urged him to work for "The Cause" back in Ireland. Grandfather McGuinness had planted the seeds of radicalism in his grandson long ago.[44] McGuinness, "who was ready to knock down an Englishman any time he saw one," had driven the point home in his grandson. A childhood fantasy also fueled George's desire to return home. During a 1939 interview with Alice Pardoe West, George described his grandfather's "old stone house with fabulously thick walls and perilously steep slate roofs, surrounded by acres of grazing land ... right in the heart of Ireland." "I used to pretend that the old house was a fort," laughed Brent, "and that I had been left there alone to defend it to my last breath against a host of invading British. And boy, did I defend it!"[45] West observed that "a passionate love of country had been instilled in the man." Not that young George wasn't aware of the ugly side of war. "I was a youngster of nine or ten," he recalled. "A soldier came home from the War—a stranger with a strangely terrible face. One day, suddenly, he opened his coat and showed me his breast and his shirt—*alive with lice.* I had never seen a sight so horrible. Somehow, I saw the whole War in that man's misery and ignominy."[46] Regardless, the teenager lost no time in gathering up his small savings and setting sail. Crusading for Ireland's independence promised plenty of action.

Return to Ireland, 1921, "The Troubles"

Now days are dragon-ridden, the nightmare
Rides upon sleep: a drunken soldiery
Can leave the mother, murdered at her door,
To crawl in her own blood, and go scot-free. . . .

Violence upon the roads: violence of horses;
Some few have handsome riders. . . .[47]

These excerpts from a poem by Ireland's beloved William Butler Yeats describe the atmosphere in which young George Nolan immersed himself once he returned to native soil. "Cast a cold eye on life, on death ...," cautioned Yeats. It was this ideal that Nolan would carry with him long after "The Troubles" became history.

On January 29, 1921, George sailed second class on the *S.S. Carmania* arriving in Liverpool February 7.[48] Some stories say he stayed with a cousin in London before heading to the University in Dublin. In 1934, columnist Buck Herzog went so far as to say that Brent was requested to leave the University after he knocked out an English professor "with a straight jab to the jaw."[49] Brent stated numerous times that he didn't like school or being confined indoors. Filmmaker Reddin confirms that Brent would have been too young and "would never have been accepted into a third level college."[50] In 1940, Brent told census takers that he had four years of college to his credit. It's very doubtful that he went beyond the tenth grade. As reporter Herbert Cruikshank said about Brent, "You're never quite certain whether or not this Ballinasloe laddybuck is passing out the blarney."[51] Young Nolan's involvement with Dublin's Abbey Theatre was minimal, at best, even though Brent declared, "It was theatre at its best. And, how we loved it! Not the 'box-office' thing or the 'surefire' thing—but the good thing, the artistic."[52] Brian Reddin discovered that the Abbey archive has no record of Nolan performing there. "They kept record of everyone who walked on that stage," says Reddin. "But, he could have been allowed to observe rehearsals and do odd jobs. All we have is Brent's word—and we know how reliable that is!"[53] In the early 1970s, Brent told biographer Don Stanke that his participation was limited to observing the other players and getting an occasional "walk on."[54] "I was just a kid," Brent admitted on another occasion, "but they let me have little parts and it got into my blood."[55]

It was said that Brent descended from a long line of Irishmen who served with the British Armies. He stated that his father had lived in Calcutta for many years as an army officer.[56] "I was supposed to be a soldier," he told columnist Alice L. Tildesley in 1932, "but I hated the regularity of army life." What did appeal to him was the irregularity and excitement of being selected as a dispatcher for guerilla warfare leader Michael Collins. Collins was among the signatories of the peace treaty that brought forth the Irish Free State. "I did everything intensely and furiously," Brent admitted. "When the chance to join the Irish revolution as a dispatch carrier for Michael Collins came my way, I leaped to accept the invitation to danger, adventure and thrills."[57] Brent's admiration for Collins was deep. "Our leader, Collins," he said, "was a magnificent man, and fired us all with determination to do or die for him. He himself was eventually killed, and with him went great genius. He had real heroic spirit."[58] Inevitably, the closest that George Nolan got to the British Army was opposing it— and fulfilling his childhood fantasy. "I didn't realize the price I might have to pay," said Brent. "I was told that I'd face the firing squad if caught, but that just made it seem more like a great lark and glorious fun."[59]

Ireland's War of Independence was conducted on both a small and large scale between the Irish Republican Army (IRA) and the state forces of the United Kingdom, such as The Black and Tans (known for their brutality) and the regular British Army. There were assassinations and reprisals on both sides. Collins used the services of numerous teenagers as dispatchers to carry messages between himself and fellow rebels. Dispatching was a position that usually lasted about six to eight weeks. There was always the risk of being recognized and trailed. Tales abound of George's adventures. The war intensified during the early months of 1921. The streets weren't safe and were open to the fire of British snipers. By May, the battle was being fought bitterly. IRA volunteers in Dublin carried out 107 attacks on British forces in the city alone.[60] There was always the threat of being interrogated, beaten—in some cases executed.

One report told of young Nolan being arrested by the Black and Tans while hiding documents in his abundance of hair.[61] His youthful zest for excitement was amplified beyond his wildest dreams. Brent didn't often offer details regarding the dangers involved, but in 1938, he opened up to one of the more courageous journalists, Gwen Dew. Before she was captured by the Japanese at the outset of World War II, Dew had already seen plenty of action herself. She had heard about Brent's thrilling past and wanted some hard, cold facts. She got them. Brent spoke plainly,

> *I was a courier and I took secret dispatches from Dublin to Glasgow. Was it dangerous? Yes. We couldn't tell who was an opposition spy, waiting to steal our dispatches, and make serious trouble for us. I disguised myself as an American tourist, who was apparently wandering from town to town, from Ireland to Scotland and back. Sometimes, with important papers tucked inside my clothes, I rode in the same carriages with soldiers who were looking for me. Sometimes I walked miles with actual warfare going on around me. It was mostly guerrilla warfare, but it was not uncommon to be bombed, and I saw death strike around me many times. The soldiers put wire tops over the trucks in which we sometimes rode. If a bomb hit this before it exploded, it would bounce off into the road, and then go off. We were lucky more than once!*
>
> *If you will recall the Irish Rebellion, you will remember that it was a time of intense feeling, of hatred, and a determination to kill anyone who wasn't on your side. This wasn't a playtime in which an enemy was sent to jail or reprimanded. If you were caught, you were executed. That was all there was to it. The Irish don't fool when they are fighting, you know!*[62]

The crusading American journalist Lowell Thomas wrote that Brent had used the Abbey Theatre as a cover for his work with *Sinn Fein* (Irish Republican Army). Brent had a tendency to fall asleep during rehearsals due to the fact he was up most of the night carrying messages between outlying command posts. His behavior aroused suspicion. Thomas detailed,

> *Finally, the British sent a squad of soldiers to arrest Brent. The soldiers were told to get to the Players and "arrest the man who is sleeping there." By a quirk of fortune worthy of Hollywood, another member of the cast happened to be asleep that day— while Brent was awake enough to escape attention. So, as soon as Brent saw the soldiers arrest the sleeping actor, he realized that the Tommies were really after him—and made a prompt escape.*[63]

Thomas, unable to leave well enough alone, stretched the truth to say that Brent had also mined gold fields of South Africa before his return to the U.S. Or, could it have been the Kimberley Diamond mines? During his screen career, Warner Brothers' ballyhoo boys would get enough facts out of Brent to dole out a number of fantastic tales. Occasionally, he would simply say, "Why don't you just write whatever you want to about me? You know what people like to read."[64]

Make no mistake. Dispatchers, like young Nolan, played a vital role in the revolution. Their messages were relayed by foot, bicycle and, for long distances, motorbike. They traveled from Dublin to Belfast and Glasgow, Scotland. In George's case, when he finally felt that his trail was "too hot," he slipped down from Scotland to Land's End, England. There was an empty freighter off the Cornish coast. In essence, he smuggled himself aboard. In 1942, Brent offered details regarding his so-called "escape:"

> *One of my most exciting moments, was when I escaped out of Ireland into England, and then hired a leaky motor boat to take me out to a tramp freighter bound for America. But it was the jump from the boat to the rope ladder that hung over the freighter's side, that was risky … and then after I made it, I had to face the captain. But I was lucky again, for the fellow happened to be an acquaintance and had a liking for any Irishman in distress. So that ended my career in the old country.*[65]

Brent elaborated to Gwen Dew as to the specific incident that triggered his decision to leave:

> *I was dining in a little hotel in Glasgow. The waiter fussed rather unnecessarily about my table. Finally he leaned over to fill my glass of water, and as quietly as possible said, 'Is everything in order in your room, sir?' Suddenly I realized that this wasn't an idle query, and I went as quietly as possible to my room. From my dispatch case I removed all incriminating papers, and hid them.*

Brent's words confirm exactly what he told reporter Thornton Sargent three years earlier. When he returned a second time to his room the contents of his bag were strewn upon the floor. "The dressers were open and the whole room upset," Brent had stated. "My heart stopped for a moment, as I realized I had missed the firing squad by half an hour. Had the British agents made their search that much sooner I would surely have been caught."[66] "I've never known who that waiter was," said Brent, "but he saved my life. It soon became evident that I was suspected, and that my every move was watched. And so my usefulness to headquarters was naturally lessened. I had to leave the country in a great hurry, not very far ahead of those who were searching for me."[67]

There are other, less reliable versions of George's last minute flight; for instance, that there was a price on his head—and perhaps there was. By the time he headed back to the United States, a truce, the Anglo-Irish Treaty, had been signed on July 11, 1921. In December, the treaty partitioned Ireland into a largely Protestant North and an overwhelmingly Catholic South, which became known as "The Irish Free State." Young Nolan was back on U.S. soil on August 22, after sailing on the Canadian steamship *Bilbster* to Montreal, and boarding the D&H Railroad to Rouses Point, New York.[68] He claimed that his last foreign residence was France, lied about his age, stating that he was twenty-two, and listed his profession as "Seaman." Seventeen-year-old Nolan declared that he was headed to New York City where he would live permanently with his sister Kathleen.[69]

In the fall of 2012, Irish news correspondent Barry Lally, in an article titled "The Story of Three Georges," elaborated on how the "myth-making powers of Tinseltown's spindoctors" had convoluted the story of George Brent and his participation in the War of Independence. Indeed there was a George Nolan who was a member of "A" Company of the 4th Battalion, Dublin Brigade, during the 1916 Easter Rising. Our George had just turned twelve. "However," writes Lally, "another fortuitous discovery was made, which took care of that little problem. A George Nolan (of whom nothing else is apparently known) was born near Shannonbridge in 1899, and by conflating the three Georges the PR boys [at Warner] contrived . . . a plausible tale."[70] Lally agrees with filmmaker Brian Reddin that among the thousands of unrecorded young couriers for the IRA, sixteen-year-old Nolan was a likely candidate. In retrospect, young George had dodged bullets and risked his life nightly while carrying out orders. In 2012, Brent's son Barry explained to filmmaker Reddin that his father's youthful concern for what was going on back home in Ireland was a reflection of his search for stability. "He felt so strongly about Ireland," said Barry, "and keeping a cohesiveness there."[71] Remembering those days at the age of sixty-eight (1972), Brent shook his head. "This thing goes back two hundred years or more. There's no way of settling it. It's crazy, they'll keep on fighting, the Catholics against the Protestants, the Irish against the English."[72] In U.S. census reports, Brent always indicated that he was born in the "Irish Free State."[73]

In 1940, Brent countered that his youthful return to Ireland was all a mistake. "I should have stayed here and gone on with the law," he said thoughtfully. "That was what I was cut out for, really . . . and if I had it to do again, I'm sure I'd stay. Of course, if I had I'd have missed the most thrilling years of my life. And I'm pretty sure I should never have thought of becoming an actor."[74] In 1938, Brent referred to his return to Ireland in 1921 as being only "a few hectic months."[75] Unlike the radical Frank Harris, young George Nolan's rolling stone from February–August 1921 was brief but significant. He packed enough action and adventure in that small amount of time to inspire a great deal of hyperbole in the years that followed. As George Brent, the actor, would acknowledge, it also left an underlying, indelible distrust of strangers for the remainder of his life.

On at least two occasions, George reconnected with former pals from his rebel days. While in New York in the spring of 1939, he looked up Irish pub owner Tim Costello, who owned a notorious watering hole located on Third Avenue. Tim, born in County Offaly in 1895, had also been a dispatch runner.[76] Costello's Bar was a sanctuary for famous writers: Hemingway, Steinbeck, James Thurber, and John O'Hara. Brent was joined by his sister Kathleen and Ralph Bellamy for the occasion. Together, they bellied up to the long mahogany bar to reminisce with Costello and enjoy some of the smoothest Irish whiskey they had ever tasted.[77] In the fall of

1939 while filming *The Fighting 69ᵗʰ* Brent was pleased to learn that the film's technical advisor was none other than John T. Prout. Prout was a training officer for the IRA (1919–1921), as well as a World War I officer in the 165ᵗʰ infantry, on which the film was based.[78]

In the aftermath of George Nolan's adventure and brief glimpse at the Abbey players, something was triggered. He brought back with him "the smell of the greasepaint, the roar of the crowd." By December 1921, he had found his niche. It all began when theatrical legend and director Guthrie McClintic signed George Nolan for a minor role in A. A. Milne's *The Dover Road*.

2

Hillbilly Dumps and Broadway (1921–1930)

I've played mining towns and little hillbilly dumps where the audiences catcall, throw things, and spoil your best emotional scenes," recalled Brent in 1932. "But after that you go on acting, even if the roof falls in."[79] George Nolan's auspicious stage debut was on Broadway—he'd have to wait a few years before reaching the dim lights of hillbilly dumps. Opening December 23, 1921, at the Bijou Theatre, *The Dover Road* was a huge success during its ten-month run. A. A. Milne's fey, three-act comedy focused on an eloping couple from London with plans to embark on a romantic interlude in Paris. They are waylaid at a charming country home on the road to Dover. Much to their surprise, they learn that the eloper's *real* wife and *her* young lover are among the guests. The lead actor, Charles Cherry, played the eccentric host who schemes to prevent everyone from making "silly asses" of themselves. Nolan was cast as one of Cherry's two butlers. His three lines were repetitions of "Yes, Mr. Dominic." George was also allowed to serve the whiskey. This he did for 305 performances. The eighteen-year-old served more whiskey on *The Dover Road* tour. Following a four-week run at Chicago's Playhouse, the cast headed to Boston where the play closed December 30, 1922.

George went along with the publicity hype associated with his new trade. New York's *Evening Telegram* noted, "George Nolan who acts the role of the other servitor hails from Dublin University."[80] One critic praised that *The Dover Road* had "a fine polish" and "the nicety of expression peculiar to the English"—a tall order for a young Irish lad who had just spent six months immersed in everything *anti*-British.[81] The success of the play helped rank Guthrie McClintic as one of New York's prominent director-producers. McClintic had recently married Katharine Cornell, regarded as one of the great stage actresses of the twentieth century. George Nolan's first theatrical opportunity allowed him to spend a year surrounded by experts. He absorbed technique and the fundamentals of being on stage.

Early 1923 found Nolan with a Brooklyn stock company at Gotham Theatre. He had a minor role as an Arab, Ben Ali, in *The Sheik's Love*. The play's drawing power depended solely on its title. Sheiks were in. Rudolph Valentino had seen to that. One of the nicer critics called it "a weird melodrama of the desert," which provided the players "no great opportunities."[82] In the late summer, producer George Gatts signed Nolan for a road tour of *The Unwanted Child*, which one critic labeled "anti-abortion propaganda" that was crudely written and amateurishly acted.[83] George played a young husband with a wandering eye. He had to wait until New Year's 1924 for a more promising offer.

Abie's Irish Rose

One of the rumors that confronted George Brent, the movie star, was that he had married at the age of twenty while on tour playing a philandering Jewish boy in *Abie's Irish Rose*. In 1935, George asked columnist Jack

1926. Sheet music featuring George B. Nolan, age twenty-one. Photo was taken during his *Abie's Irish Rose* tour and prior to his nose operation.

Grant, "Did you know that I am the father to twins?" The surprised Grant shook his head. "Neither did I," George continued, "until Hollywood told me." Once started, George waxed loquacious:

> *Having only recently heard the story myself, I may not do it justice. The locale, I hear, was Indianapolis. I was playing the role of Abie in Abie's Irish Rose when the romance began. An Indianapolis society girl attended the opening night performance and becoming enamored—my fatal beauty of course, a meeting was arranged. The girl proved so cute and cunning—and it is also inferred—so wealthy that I married her forthwith. Our married*

life together was very brief. A scant two months. Unable to endure
my brutalities—probably I was extremely cruel following her dis-
inheritance, even beating her as many say I did—she returned
home to her forgiving family. Her father had the marriage an-
nulled and her mother helped her prepare for the Blessed Event.
The stork brought twins—bouncing baby girls.[84]

Brent went on to explain that denials of the preposterous tale were useless. Gossip in Hollywood was a fine art. He knew how the game was played. "I prefer to be amused," George concluded. "I might point to several impossibilities in the story. But there I would be left—pointing."

It's true that *Abie's Irish Rose* played Indianapolis in the summer of 1924 for eight weeks at the Capitol Theatre. It turns out that Nolan spent his spare time, not making babies, but puttering around the golf course. George, now billed as "George B. Nolan," and fellow actor Billy Fay, who played his on-stage father, became pals and rented rooms in a private home.[85] Other boarders included saxophonist George Johnson, who performed at the Casino Gardens with the Wolverines, a Midwestern jazz ensemble featuring the legendary Bix Beiderbecke on cornet. In 1947, Johnson recalled playing golf with twenty-year-old Nolan. Joined by banjo player Bob Gillette and drummer Vic Moore, the two actors and three musicians spent more time on the golf course than they did entertaining "live" audiences. "All summer we played from never less than thirty-six to sometimes seventy-two holes a day," recalled Johnson. "We lost track of Nolan and Fay after we left Indianapolis. You can imagine my surprise nine years later, while attending a movie, when the familiar face of George B. Nolan appeared on the screen." "I often wonder," said Johnson, "if he enjoys life as much as he used to when he made $150 a week."[86] Johnson added that at the time all Nolan had to worry about was a "nasty slice."

No doubt Brent, the film star, enjoyed his hefty salary, despite being an easy target for gossip. "The more prominent we are in the profession," deduced George, "the easier we are to hit. Hollywood reminds me of a huge shooting gallery."[87] The only explanation that Brent could offer regarding the tall tale of his baby twin girls during the run of *Abie's Irish Rose* had to do with the play itself. "As you doubtless remember," said Brent, "the feud between the Irish and Jewish families comes to an end when Abie and Rose have twins, one of whom is named Rebecca and the other Patrick."[88]

Anne Nichols's *Abie's Irish Rose* ran for over 2,300 performances following its 1922 premier—the longest run in Broadway history. New York critics loathed it but audiences lapped it up. The touring company, in which Nolan starred, held the record as the longest running tour until *Hello Dolly! Abie* . . . was filled with humor and complication. It told of a Jewish boy, Abraham Levy, and a Catholic girl, Rosemary Murphy. The couple decide to throw away all family tradition and elope. They are married by a Protestant minister. Then, in order to keep their horrified families happy, their union is reinforced with both a Jewish and Catholic ceremony. The cast managed to keep the fun at a boiling point for three acts. On one occasion George fell off stage and broke his arm. Everyone marveled as he got back up to the stage, and went on with the show.[89] "George Nolan as Abie is a charming youth," wrote a critic for Omaha's *World-Herald*, "but he is not Jewish in the least. He has a slight naiveté that is very attractive."[90] It was offbeat casting for the romantic leads. Peggy Parry, who played George's Irish-Catholic sweetheart, was from Utah. For some critics, the heart of the play was the quiet scene between the Jewish rabbi and the Catholic priest—both who had ministered to dying boys of different faiths during the World War. They discuss the absurdities of mankind's prejudice as well as the unnecessary obstacles that stand in the way of Abie and Rosemary's happiness.

The *Abie* tour played for numerous extended runs: thirteen weeks in Cincinnati; twelve weeks in Baltimore and Washington, D.C.; fifteen weeks in Kansas City—by May 1925, George had chalked up 1,105 performances.[91] While playing in Omaha, he told a reporter that his troupe was different from the rest. "We do not have the theatrical atmosphere about us off stage," he remarked. "The fact is we are more domesticated than those players who are touring all the time. The apparent artificiality that comes with constant acting and associating with the actor folk, gradually wears off."[92] George felt that he grew "roots" in every city he was planted. He took interest in "civic matters," which no doubt included teeing off whenever possible. He also exercised his saddle horse along bridle paths in local city parks.

Playing Abraham Levy increased Nolan's hopes for real recognition. He stayed with the role and collected his $150 a week salary for two years. Before the end of its run *Abie's Irish Rose* had become a cliché. Rodgers and Hart's hit tune "Manhattan" included the lines, "Our future babies we'll take to *Abie's Irish Rose*. I hope they'll live to see it close." The play's author raked in over a million dollars. The money George saved while touring with *Abie* . . . was carefully put aside. He was making big plans. It remains somewhat of a mystery as to what he was up to in 1926. Some have confused him with George Brant, a tenor, who appeared in such musical productions as *The Nightingale* and *The Golden Dawn* (1927). However, in the summers of 1926–'27, George Nolan actually realized his dream of having his own stock company, first in Nashville, North Carolina, and then in the industrial town of Pawtucket, Rhode Island.

During the three months that Nolan's troupe played Pawtucket he staged and acted in twelve plays at the Star Theatre. It was a dream realized but short lived. The local textile workers showed little interest. Top admission was 60 cents ($7.90 in 2014). To drum up business George offered free kisses to any lucky woman who bought a box of concessionaire candy containing a white slip of paper.[93] His smooch fest apparently didn't fare well. At the end of the summer George returned to New York with only $1.47 in his pocket.[94] "I lost my shirt in Pawtucket," said Brent. "It may have been valuable experience and perhaps it reduced the size of my head a trifle—but if I had it to do over again, I'd certainly skip it."[95]

For a short time, George was employed as treasurer of Broadway's Strand Theatre. He put aside enough cash (legitimately) to open a new stock company in Northampton, Massachusetts.[96] On September 5, his Academy Players made a strong start with John Golden's romance *Seventh Heaven*. George played Chico, an optimistic sewer worker in the streets of Paris, who dreams of a better life. It would turn out to be his favorite stage role. The role of Diane, Chico's love interest, a young prostitute, was played by Helen Louise Lewis. A critic for the *Springfield Weekly Republican* thought Lewis "sincere" but focused on the brilliance of Nolan's portrayal, saying "George B. Nolan as Chico, leaped into the favor of the audience almost as suddenly as he made his first appearance."[97] The review respected Nolan's ambition—his stock companies in Pawtucket and another short-lived venture in the rural town of Nashville, North Carolina. Also mentioned was his previous tour in Mary Rinehart's complex murder mystery *The Bat*.

One thing emerged from Brent's stay in Northampton that he *did not* like talking about: his marriage to leading lady Helen Louise Lewis. *Variety* noted that the ceremony for the couple took place on October 20, 1927, at Hartford, Connecticut.[98] The groom registered as "George Brent Nolan." The honeymooners celebrated their nuptials by rehearsing for their next play, *Stella Dallas*. George played Richard Grosvenor, the young suitor of Stella's daughter Laurel, played by the new Mrs. Nolan. This was followed by the romantic comedy *Loose Ankles* in which Helen played a wealthy socialite who wants to be "compromised" and create a scandal. George's character volunteers to help. *Loose Ankles* celebrated loose talk and loose morals. Some critics called it "smut."

In December, Mr. and Mrs. Nolan announced that they would be leaving the Academy Players. George was tired of being "frozen up" each winter. They went to Florida where rent was low and the weather warm. George took along his young protégé Jimmy Linehan. He had known Jimmy's mother. When the boy finished high school George took him under his wing and gave him his chance on stage. The Nolans opened the season at the Plaza Theatre in St. Petersburg. The company proved a popular success. It was hard work. The daily routine consisted of rehearsals every morning at 10 o'clock to prepare for the following week's bill. George later claimed, "I could learn twenty-five pages in an hour of fast scrutiny."[99]

St. Petersburg was old turf for Helen Louise Lewis and the audience gave her a warm welcome back. *Up in Mabel's Room* scored a big success. George was singled out for praise. "George Nolan was at his best last night," said one critic. "It was rather a strenuous part … he had to dive under the bed many times and remain there for long periods. He did the part in a way that could not be improved upon."[100] Diving under beds and buying pink lingerie for a wife who suspects it's for someone else kept audiences howling for a week. Two weeks later all eyes were on George as he romped around in his BVD's for *The Girl in the Limousine. In The Family Upstairs*, it was a gray-haired, bespectacled George Nolan who received raves from the *St. Petersburg Times*. "Nolan makes the elder Mr. Heller a character we will long remember. Never in his life did he do a more forceful piece of acting than last night. Nolan plays a big part in making *The Family Upstairs* … a riot from start to finish."[101]

George and Helen continued the season while staying at the Royal Palm Hotel. They costarred in such popular plays as *Tiger Rose, Peg O' My Heart, The Patsy*, and *Dancing Mothers*. The Boston Braves showed up for a performance of *The Girl in the Limousine*—the entire team. News reports jested that it was part of baseball's pre-season training. On April 6, Plaza Players were gone. It was reported that "Mr. and Mrs. Nolan left in their automobile" going directly to New York. It was a memorable trip. As George maneuvered through the rain slicked gumbo roads typical of the silty soil in the Georgia hills, he saw a young African-American boy frantically waving his arms and yelling "Stop!" "I slammed on my breaks and skidded to a stop," he recalled, "only six feet from a railroad. Just a second later a passenger train screamed by."

March 1928 – Publicity news photos of George and his wife Helen Louise Lewis during their run at the Plaza Street Players in St. Petersburg, Florida.

Watching the train disappear left George with a peculiar "but grand and glorious feeling." "I gave the youngster a dollar," said George, "and drove on. That particular day, that's all I valued, my life."[102] His brush with death proved to be pivotal. It put a lot of things in perspective—like his unhappy marriage to Helen. Before long, the couple went their separate ways. By fall, Helen Louise Lewis was back in her home state of Ohio, without George, starring in the appropriately titled *Love 'Em and Leave 'Em*.

Helen Louise Lewis

By 1972, Brent claimed he could not remember the name of his first wife, referring to her as "Molly."[103] He did admit that the marriage only lasted about six months. The rest of the details remained a mystery.

Helen Louise Lewis was performing on stage by 1913. A 1915 advertisement in *The New York Clipper* listed the red-haired twenty-year-old ingénue as being 5' 1", 111 pounds, and seeking stock or repertory engagements. At that time, eleven-year-old George Nolan was adjusting to his new life in New York. Helen's mother, Gertie Lewis, was also an actress. Gertie had caused quite a scandal in 1903 after making headlines when a Baptist minister refused the actress's offer to sing her acclaimed rendition of "The Holy City" in his church. After quoting Corinthians "touch not the unclean things," he told reporters, "'The Holy City' should only be sung by holy people."[104] Had the minister known that Gertie was a twice-wed divorcee he doubtless would have thrown in a little hellfire to protect what he called the "tender consciences" of his flock.

Gertie wasn't exactly a doting mother. She divorced Mr. Campbell, Helen's father, and let her parents, Mr. and Mrs. William T. Lewis (a photographer) in Zanesville, Ohio, raise her daughter.[105] Helen admired her actress mother who she saw only occasionally. But following her mother's death in 1909, it was Helen's Uncle Jack, an actor-manager, who took Helen under his wing until producer David Belasco signed her under his management.[106]

Helen's versatility as an actress was perfect for playing leads in stock companies. One of her hits was Belasco's 1921 road revival of the melodrama *Tiger Rose*. One critic praised, "Miss Lewis has that fiery imagination which raises her, at moments, to the point where her work ceases to be acting and becomes poetry. She will go far."[107] By the age of thirty-two, Helen had had plenty of stage experience to prepare her and young Nolan for the joys and woes of matrimony. She had played in *Wedding Bells, Grounds for Divorce* (both with Ralph Bellamy) and *Which One Shall I Marry?* The actress was cautious about people with whom she became intimate. "I always look at the curve of a person's mouth the minute I meet him or her," she stated in one interview. "If the mouth drags down at the corners I don't bother to cultivate the acquaintance. If, however, the mouth curls up I know I am meeting a cheerful optimist and that to know him will be a pleasure."[108]

Ruth Biery, one of the stable of top Hollywood writers, said that Brent's "much older" first wife "lent an encouraging hand; told him he would be a great actor."[109] The Nolan-Lewis team costarred in well over two dozen plays. It was inevitable that George would learn something from Helen Louise Lewis. However, it was only a matter of months into their marriage before the curves of George Nolan's tail, as well as his mouth, were dragging "down at the corners." "I went through Hell," Brent recalled. From what he had to say, much of the havoc in their relationship came from Helen's sexual demands. George wanted the emphasis to be on love and companionship.[110] Their divorce wasn't finalized until 1930 in Los Angeles.[111]

In the fall of 1928, George played in two Broadway productions. He was among the gamblers in the risqué frolic *Night Hostess* at the Martin Beck Theatre. A young Katharine Hepburn, using the alias Katherine Burns, shared the stage playing a prostitute. After years of denying her participation in the play, Hepburn finally admitted to TV host Dick Cavett that she did indeed play what she called a "wicked fascinator." It was her first opportunity on Broadway.[112] Hepburn didn't last long. She got sacked by the producer for looking "too wholesome."[113] George, faring better, left the cast by his own accord for a featured role in *The K Guy*—a comedy about Hollywood. Playing a handsome Western movie star, Nolan was among a dozen characters that typified life in a poverty row film studio. Following tryouts in New Rochelle, Syracuse, and Trenton, the play opened October 15 at the Biltmore where, as one critic noted, it "misfired." After eight performances *The K Guy* closed. Nolan headed to Milwaukee to join the Sherman Brown Players. He also toyed with the idea of using the name George Brent.

In Milwaukee, the newly christened George Brent played second lead in George M. Cohan's *Elmer the Great.* It was all about a not-too-bright baseball player who is tempted to throw the "big game." Russell Hicks took the role of Elmer when it opened at the Pabst Theater. Brent played his manager. *The Milwaukee Journal* praised, "Contributing to the authenticity of the comedy is George Brent . . . an exceedingly neat piece of work."[114] Producer Sherman Brown pulled out his bankroll to splurge on a series of guest stars. Brent's shining moment arrived while costarring with old-timer Henrietta Crosman in the Saxon Kling play *Crashing Through*. He played Chris, a good-looking riveter, who sits seventy-two stories aloft on a dangling beam, which crashes through the ceiling of a witty dowager (Crosman). Her granddaughter falls even harder for Chris, but he is taken aback by her progressive ideas. She calls marriage an outdated institution. The *Milwaukee Sentinel* raved, "Mr. Brent was a handsome and most thoroughly convincing young lad. To Miss Crossman and to George Brent must go the honors . . . for they made Mr. Kling's opus almost believable."[115] Brent and Crosman would cross paths again in 1935, costarring as mother and son in the film *The Right to Live*. Sherman Brown's hope that big names would draw big crowds failed to fill the coffers.[116] It would be Brown's last season. Talking pictures were in. Stock was doomed, and so was vaudeville, but no one seemed to notice.

When Brent talked about his "five stock companies" and "over 300 roles" he indicated that his stay at Denver's reputable summer theater, Elitch Gardens, was the most rewarding. In the summer of 1929, under the direction of Melville Burke, Brent's fellow cast members included future film players Madge Evans and Victor Jory.[117] As leading man at Elitch, Brent participated in seventeen productions. Ethel Barrymore attended one of his performances and thought him "out of the ordinary."[118] Barrymore's presence remained a vivid memory. "That raking, unforgettable nose of hers," recalled George, "that look of serious, intense concentration on her face. The way she always looks when she's watching a play."[119] When not on stage, Brent took time out to party with such fancy steppers as newsmen Gene Fowler and H. Allen Smith. "Boy! What times we used to have," Brent would say. "Man, those guys took time to live! Sometimes I wonder how I lived through some of those sessions. Why, there was one that lasted about 16 days. . . ."[120]

Arnold Gurtler, stage manager at Elitch, suggested that George have a nose operation. Gutler's son, Jack, reminisced in 1982, "If you look at pictures of George Brent when he played at the Gardens and then at later pictures, you'll notice he took Dad's advice."[121] Brent's new stage name and nose made a significant difference. The latter would boost his potential as a screen star in the near future.

While Wall Street crashed, Brent landed a role in the comedy *Seven Year Leave*. He played a ladies' man who tempts a married woman during a yachting party. She welcomes what she calls an "experiment in lewdness" while her husband is away in Spain studying the lives of saints. One critic chalked up thirty laughs during the spectacle. It folded before its intended Broadway debut.[122] Avoiding another potential flop in *She's No Lady,* Brent bowed out during rehearsals. The comedy starred Lynne Overman as a female impersonator. One critic called it "tripe"—a cheap replay of *Charley's Aunt.* Instead of serving tripe, George bought himself a bouquet of flowers.

Brent had his own way of handling numerous career disappointments. A young acquaintance of his sister Kathleen said that whenever George "reached the bottom of his luck; he bought a bunch of flowers and just looked at them."[123] She also thought George "was the best of brothers." Whenever possible, Kathleen was there for George during his

Brent's sister, Kathleen
Nolan (c. 1928)
(Courtesy of Ian Watson)

career ups and downs. While he had toured in *The Dover Road* in 1922, she left her job as a news photographer and ventured to Hollywood. She married the good-looking Rumanian film director, Marcel De Sano. De Sano, an acclaimed war hero, had a promising, if slender, talent. He was also emotionally unstable. During their marriage, De Sano gained a reputation for bowing out of important film projects starring Mary Pickford, Lon Chaney, John Gilbert and Garbo—all because of his anxieties. Kathleen and Marcel had a son named Marcel Jr., who went by "Patrick."[124] The couple divorced in the summer of 1926. Two years later, Kathleen returned to New York and married her former boss, veteran Hearst editor Victor Watson. Watson, also known for paranoia, called upon his psychiatrist to stand in as best man.[125] George was comfortable with his new brother-in-law and fond of his nephew Patrick, whom Watson adopted.

In January 1930, Brent took what he thought to be a step in the right direction. He signed on to play a philandering novelist in *Those We Love*—scheduled to open on Broadway in February. George Abbott, who would receive numerous Grammy Awards for such hits as *The Pajama Game*, co-authored and directed. In Abbott's eye-dabber, Brent offered a sensitive portrayal of a married man who is caught in an innocent flirtation that mushrooms into a full-fledged affair. A critic for the *Daily Star* felt the play deserved attention, saying, "George Brent played along naturally, extending himself only at the right moments."[126] A reviewer for the *Brooklyn Daily Eagle* commented, "Only the fine acting of Armina Marshall and George Brent saved its performance from boring the audience last night."[127] During the Brooklyn run, Brent had second thoughts. On Tuesday evening, February 11, news reports indicated that Brent was "stricken suddenly" and replaced by Abbott himself. Two days later, it was announced that Brent had been added to the cast of the aptly titled, *Love, Honor and Betray.*

George's theatrical agent, Jane Broder, was considered to be one of the best and most respected in New York. In order to secure Brent's career, Broder encouraged him to sign a contact with legendary producer Al Woods. Woods helped jump-start the careers of many of Brent's contemporaries and future costars such as Claudette Colbert, Kay Francis, and Joan Blondell. Brent considered Woods's *Love, Honor and Betray* a real career break. It starred veteran Alice Brady and featured future Hollywood talent such as Clark Gable, Glenda Farrell, and Robert Williams. Brent stated that Brady was "grand to work with, if she likes you."[128] She liked George. Initially, Woods's bold satire on sex was titled *The Fatal Woman* and opened in Atlantic City. A critic for *Variety* thought Brady "very good" and the three-act play had a "moderate Broadway chance."[129]

1930 – *Love, Honor and Betray* with Alice Brady and Glenda Farrell

Each act took place at a cemetery where the ghosts of three men compare notes about their luckless affair with a selfish woman. Brady devours each man as he tells his sad story. Glenda Farrell played Brady's daughter. She is romanced by the family chauffeur, played by Brent—who had ignored the advances of her insatiable mother, Miss Brady.

When *Love, Honor and Betray* opened on Broadway, *The New York Times* said that the acting lacked "the sting of satire."[130] Critic Arthur Pollock enjoyed the novelty of the play, thought Gable, as the lover, "had his moments," but approved mostly of Brent and Farrell, who "stood out by virtue of their moderation."[131] Pollock thought that Brady was "completely lost." "Never has she appeared to be so bad an actress," he complained. During the play's run, George introduced Clark Gable to Arnold Gurtler, who was casting players for Elitch Gardens. Following Gable's interview, Gurtler jotted into his casting notes: "Don't interview again. Ears too big."[132] *Love, Honor and Betray* folded on April 19. By then, George Brent was living in Los Angeles.

Before leaving New York, Brent had an offer from Fox studios. His three-year contract with Al Woods wouldn't start until September 1930.[133] Fox executive Winfield Sheehan kept an office at New York's Hotel Savoy. Sheehan engaged a number of new faces for the screen, including George Brent and Humphrey Bogart.[134] Brent was suggested for the lead in *The Man Who Came Back* and signed a six-month contract. He would play a prodigal son who is cut off from family fortunes and shanghaied to China. Alcohol, opium, and general depravity were also in the mix. Excited, Brent packed his bags, left *Love, Honor and Betray*, and headed to Hollywood. He was told to grow a heavy beard. Fox wanted to test his onscreen mettle in a lavish two-hour Western that Raoul Walsh was directing. On April 10, *Film Daily* mentioned that Brent, "accompanied by the beard he raised for a role in Fox's *The Big Trail*," had arrived on the Movietone lot.[135]

Brent soon learned that he had lost the role in *The Man Who Came Back* to Charles Farrell, an established Fox star. Brent wasn't alone. Humphrey Bogart had also been promised the part. Sheehan's bait had lured Brent and Bogart westward; it wasn't long before both men scurried back to New York. George Brent's anticipated screen debut amounted to nothing more than standing next to the rear end of a horse. He was given no lines. On screen, the heavy-bearded newcomer looked more than a little lost. But, the rear end in question didn't belong to just any old horse. It was being ridden by a clean-shaven newcomer by the name of Marion "Duke" Morrison, who director Walsh rechristened "John Wayne."

After being lost amid "20,000 extras" in *The Big Trail,* a film that wouldn't be released until fall, Brent was having second thoughts about Hollywood. While staying as a guest at the home of fellow actor William Harrigan, Brent had told census takers that he was a "Motion Picture Actor." [136] Now, he wasn't sure. So, he returned to New York and was consoled by his agent Jane Broder. Together, they tried to find something for him to do on stage until his contract with Al Woods took effect. To Brent's surprise, he suddenly found himself scheduling a last-minute return flight to the west coast in early July. While aboard United Air Lines, he wrote a letter to Broder explaining,

> *Dear Jane,*
>
>   *Right now the plane is doing exactly one-hundred-and-forty miles an hour—pitch black underneath. Am going to do a Canadian mounted picture. They called me from the west day before yesterday and here I am. I want to thank you lots for your kindness to me while I was in New York. Maybe next time [we'll find] a part that is right for me*

So long for now Jane, and good luck.
Most Sincerely, George Brent[137]

On August 15, after completing two features at Fox, Brent cabled Broder in New York. "WILL STAY HERE … DO ALL YOU CAN TO GET MY RELEASE FROM WOODS … EVERYTHING OK … LOVE, GEORGE."[138] Al Woods wasn't happy. On August 5 he had sent the actor a reminder that he needed to be back in New York by September 1. Apparently, Fox was impressed with George's work. "For some time the studio has been trying to get Woods to relinquish his claim on the actor," reported *Variety*, "but the legit producer is holding out."[139] Did Jane Broder iron things out with Al Woods? Was Brent's fling with Tinseltown ruining his future chances on Broadway? After two more insignificant roles, the disappointed actor discovered that Fox had dropped him from their payroll.

It would be another year before George Brent established any kind of security in Hollywood. In the meantime, making matters worse, he was told he was going blind.

Fair Warning (Fox 1931) Bad guy Brent, next to Louise Huntington, aims for action. (below) Hero George O'Brien about to fill Brent with lead.

3

"I Was a Stooge for Charlie Chan and Rin Tin Tin"

George Brent didn't mince words when he summed up his early film career. "I was a stooge for Charlie Chan and Rin Tin Tin," he would say.[140] In the Rin Tin Tin serial *Lightning Warrior*, natives performed a death dance around George while he was tied to a stake. Forewarned, Brent had one ear to the ground to return to Broadway. That's when fate stepped in. Cinema queen Ruth Chatterton, after seeing Brent in a Warner screen test, declared, "Where has *he* been all my life?"[141] Afterwards, "La Chatterton" raised her stellar wand and Brent's screen career became a foregone conclusion.

Brent's films at Fox garnered him little attention. *Under Suspicion,* the Canadian Mountie picture that brought him back to Hollywood, was an operetta. It starred baritone J. Harold Murray warbling love songs to ladylove Lois Moran. The rival for Ms. Moran's affections was played by Brent—Murray's superior officer. Critics concurred that the film's real marvel was cinematographer George Schneiderman's gorgeous on location scenery in Canada's Jasper National Park. Most reviews thought the film story "weak." "Of suspense there is none," said critic Red Kann. "The

acting is extremely indifferent."[142] He complained that Murray kept singing throughout the sixty-six minute feature "for no good reason." *Variety*
added, "The only time the hero does not sing is when he is sliding down a
cliff." The *Chicago Daily Tribune* pointed out, "George Brent as the villain
is the worm he's meant to be."[143] Brent played another bad worm in the
George O'Brien western *Fair Warning*, which was shot on location around
Mt. Whitney. O'Brien was the man-idol of small boys and churned out
five Western releases in 1930. "It's a cinch to please the kid trade," said
Variety. Brent led a gang of desperados known for their bloody barroom
brawls. *Motion Picture News* mentioned, "George Brent, who began his
stage career with a company in Dublin, is the villain who regrets his evil
life, splits with the gang and is shot at the finish."[144]

In October 1930, Brent was seen celebrating his new career at Hollywood's popular Brown Derby with his sister Kathleen and her husband,
Victor Watson.[145] However, Brent's next two releases, *Once a Sinner* and
Charlie Chan Carries On, afforded him even less opportunity. The message
of . . . *Sinner* was that smart women never tell their husbands if they've
engaged in premarital sex. *Film Daily* found the film "flat and unconvincing." Dorothy Mackaill, the woman who sowed a single wild oat, gave a
sincere performance but couldn't overcome the film's trite message. The
film established Joel McCrea, who played a television inventor, as one of
Hollywood's popular leading men. It also reunited Brent with his mentor
from *The Dover Road*, director Guthrie McClintic. A critic for the *Boston
Herald* felt McClintic's smooth direction induced natural performances
from his players. None of the reviews mentioned Brent, whose inconse-
quential character bore the name James Brent. George fared a bit better
in *Charlie Chan Carries On*. Playing one of the suspects aboard an ocean
liner, he brags about his exploits as a captain in the British Army. But under interrogation, he admits, "Well, I was just . . . romancing a bit." "Were
you ever *in* the Army?" an inspector asks. "Well, no, the title is really hon-

orary."[146] When Chan (Warner Oland) arrives on the scene, Brent's character insists that he's being framed for several murders. Critics enjoyed the film's mix of suspense and Chan's philosophical wisecracks in his first bona fide "talking picture." Again, Brent's minor role was not mentioned in reviews. On this sour note, he was dropped by Fox studios, although he had been mentioned for their upcoming film *Skyline.*

George & Gilda

In 1930–'31, while Brent toyed with becoming a film actor, he spent time romancing shimmy queen Gilda Gray. Even though she was living on the east coast, their names were frequently linked in gossip columns. Gilda did pay George a visit in Los Angeles. Publisher Billy Fawcett (*True Confessions*) threw a breakfast bash on December 21, 1930, inviting Gilda and her designated actor "boyfriend" Brent. The two partook in several rounds of ham and eggs while listening to hobo author Jim Tully talk about his exploits. After returning to New York on December 30, Gilda announced to the press that George was lined up to become her third husband.[147] Rumors of their impending marriage continued after George signed a ten-week contract with Universal in March. Erich von Stroheim was preparing a talkie remake of his 1919 hit *Blind Husbands.* Von Stroheim talked of using color and wide-screen in order to fully embrace film as a third dimension art.[148] He selected Brent for the lead in this project.[149] Brent was among many who made a series of tests for the coveted role. Unfortunately, the film was cancelled. Instead, Brent found himself stuck in the farce *Ex-Bad Boy.* It starred Robert Armstrong, trying to impress his hometown sweetheart (Jean Arthur) that he's a tough guy—a man of the world. So, he zeroes in on Brent, who plays the boastful fiancé of movie star Letta Lardo (Lola Lane), and beats him to a pulp. *Film Daily* found the sixty-seven minute feature slow-moving. The *Chicago Daily*

Ex-Bad Boy (Universal 1931) Bully Brent acts tough for
Spencer Charters and Robert Armstrong

Tribune labeled it "amiable idiocy . . . good for several laughs," and promised, "You won't get brain fag from it."[150]

A battered and bruised Brent was then rushed into *Homicide Squad*.
On June 4 came the curious report from *Hollywood Daily Citizen* that he
had left the production and had flown to New York "to reach the sick-
bed of his mother."[151] This brief mention of Brent's mother was unusual.
After he became a star, Brent always insisted that his mother had died
before he came to the United States. It could be that his 1930 bedside
visit with his mother caused a deeper rift between the two. It would be
years before Mary Nolan passed away. By June 15, Brent was back on the
sound stage of *Homicide Squad*. Fifth billed, he played the son of a police
chief (Noah Beery) and was killed off in the first reel. Only John Scott
of the *Los Angeles Times* commented on his performance. "George Brent

rates more than ordinary mention," wrote Scott. "As the boy with a strong heart who invades the very den of the public enemy and is shot down for his efforts, Brent is poised, impassive and convincing."[152] No one else seemed to notice or care. To make matters worse, Brent was told he was going blind. He returned once more to New York, this time to stay with his sister Kathleen and her husband. The couple resided in Pawling, a quaint village nestled in the foothills of the Berkshires. It was the perfect place for George to recuperate, ponder his next step … and reconnect with Gilda Gray.

Before cameras had rolled on *Ex-Bad Boy*, Gilda Gray was denying her previously announced nuptials with Brent. A Polish immigrant, Gray had worked steadily since her first marriage in 1912.[153] Her raw energy gained her notoriety in 1919 when she introduced her version of the shimmy-shake in vaudeville. She claimed she borrowed her dance moves from the Native Americans. "I studied the shimmy out in Yellowstone Park a couple of summers ago," she explained. "I saw a bunch of Sioux Indians doing it and I got dead stuck on it."[154] A hard worker, Gilda knew how to hold an audience's attention. American popular cultural critic, Gilbert Seldes, made the observation that on stage Gilda virtually "trembled herself into a state of ecstasy."[155]

Shimmy Queen Gilda Gray
feeling no pain (c. 1930)

She made over a million dollars in vaudeville and films during the 1920s. She also chalked up a couple of marriages. By the time she cooed her way into Brent's life, she had an eighteen-year-old son she was putting through military school.[156] Gray had had many lovers. Her second husband, who was also her business manager, accused her of misconduct with numerous men in their highly publicized 1928 divorce.[157] She, in turn, called him an "ungrateful drunkard."[158]

In the summer of 1931, a few days after Brent returned to the east coast, thirty-five-year-old Gilda Gray had shimmied herself into a coma— literally. She wasn't expected to live.[159] Wires and letters poured in from across the country, but it was George's attentions that made all the differ-ence. He was her most frequent visitor at New York's Hotel Warwick. She admitted later, "Daily flowers arrived from the darkly handsome George Brent. I recall George sitting beside my bed, talking of his screen aspira-tions and his warm brown eyes and love of life were like new blood in my veins."[160] In turn, Gilda encouraged George to pursue his film career, despite his disappointments, and do whatever screen tests were neces-sary. While George dealt with his eye problems (severe conjunctivitis), he considered what Gilda Gray had to say.

Adhering to doctor's orders, George bathed his eyes in Epsom salts. The solution, absorbed into cotton bandages, was applied in hour-long sessions, along with oxide of mercury near the eyelashes.[161] His infection was so severe that it took a few months to cure. "A hell of a mess," ob-served Brent, who had to limit his reading long after recovery.[162] "I was broke, though," he admitted, "so I barged out here to Hollywood again." He was feeling despondent and didn't want to impose upon his sister any longer. Mascot Pictures, a poverty row studio, had tempted George with the lead in a twelve-part serial starring Rin Tin Tin. There were no other prospects. He was tired of not staying long enough in one place to es-tablish a real career. "You can't vibrate back and forth across the country like a blooming homing pigeon and hope to get yourself settled at either end," he observed. George spent what little money he had left on a plane ticket back to California.[163] According to Gilda Gray, George asked her to come with him. She wasn't up to it. "Don't wait for me," she told him. "Go darling . . . it's your big chance. I sense it."[164] Walter Winchell had already reported that George and Gilda's "youknowwhat" had "gone sour."[165] Not that Gilda had changed her mind about Brent. She would show up in Hollywood after his career took a surprise and promising turn.

Arriving on the west coast October 15, Brent submerged his talent into becoming an action hero in *The Lightning Warrior*. The serial involved a mysterious, cloaked figure known as The Wolf Man, who was menacing a remote mining community. Producer Nat Levine selected Brent to play Alan Scott because he thought Brent had the makings of a fine actor.[166] Brent had the right attitude and look—except when disguised in full headdress as a dancing Indian. The real acting was left to junior hero Frankie Darro as the orphaned boy of a mine owner. Brent came across as a fine horseman, although his stunt work was done by Kermit Maynard (younger brother of Western star Ken Maynard) and Yakima Canutt. The aging canine star, Rin Tin Tin, also demanded the use of doubles (including a stuffed wolf dog). Uneven direction and a far-fetched plot didn't get in the way of creating excitement for the kiddies who came to see Rin Tin Tin in his film swan song. He died the following summer.[167] *The Lightning Warrior* is considered by many fans of the genre to be among the best cliff-hangers ever produced.

As his film career came to another standstill, Brent found relaxation by playing tennis at Charlie Chaplin's. Brent's attractive costar in *The Lightning Warrior*, Georgia Hale, had the run of Chaplin's estate while "The Little Tramp" was in Europe. Hale was intimately involved with

Chaplin at the time. In her memoirs, Hale said that she played a lot of tennis with Brent and he was "a good player."[168] When not playing tennis, Brent grabbed any acting opportunity that came along. He made so many screen tests that they seemed like a joke. After lining himself up with an agent he was asked to shoot a routine screen test at Warner Brothers. Brent recalled,

> I was supposed to help out another guy who was making the test. I was living out of one suitcase in those days. You went out for every job that came your way. Anyway, screen tests are cold potatoes, so I downed a shot of whisky before I left the apartment. I didn't care, it wasn't my test. Just before we shot it—Dieterle directed it, I think—I started to get a glow on. I stopped shaking. It was the steadiest performance I ever gave.[169]

It wasn't long before Brent received orders to visit the new queen of the Warner lot, Ruth Chatterton, in her bungalow. She had seen his test. When George arrived, he got the once-over. "Talk about embarrassing moments!" he said. "I felt like take-me-home for $1.98. We talked a little, but to tell the truth the first thing I remember her saying is, 'I suppose they want me to have a look at you.' I tried to be nonchalant and said, 'Ha-ha I supposed so, too.' The next few seconds seemed an awfully long time, but finally: 'Well, you look all right to me!' "[170] Chatterton approved and Brent signed a seven-year contract at $250 weekly. "I was flat broke," said Brent, "It was a heaven-sent deal."[171] Brent's new Warner contract was signed in December 1931. He was assigned to be Ruth Chatterton's new leading man.

The studio also cast Brent in *So Big*, a truncated version of the Pulitzer Prize-winning novel by Edna Ferber. In this film, shot first, Barbara Stanwyck played the farm widow Selina, who struggles to eke out a living and instill in her son an appreciation for beauty and hard work. Selina's ideals rub off on Roelf, a neighbor boy, who grows up to become a famous sculptor (Brent). Her son, on the other hand, gives up his career as an architect for easy money, selling bonds. Although her youthful voice failed to change as her character aged, Stanwyck carried the film emotionally with an honest and heartfelt naiveté. Director William Wellman emphasized the rough edges of Ferber's book with wry humor and a tug at the heart. The town prostitute registers more benevolence than the local preacher. Selina's self-absorbed son becomes convinced that buying things is as good as creating them—helping to underscore Ferber's message that those who seek only money are never satisfied.

During production of *So Big*, Warner publicity touted that Brent was the studio's "Clark Gable." The big buildup fell flat after the preview. "George Brent is acceptable," said critic Norbert Lusk, "but fails to reveal anything to warrant the excitement of his employers."[172] Considering

So Big (WB 1932) Brent's Warner debut placed him with two frequent co-stars: Bette Davis and Barbara Stanwyck

Brent's allotted time on screen (seven minutes) there wasn't an opportunity to reveal much of anything, but some felt that Brent overshadowed Hardie Albright, who played the son. "George Brent as the grown up Roelf, does excellent and understanding work," observed another critic.[173] From the moment Roelf returns to sweep Selina into his arms, their happy reunion evokes a reluctant tear. Theirs was a tender fulfillment that carried the message "we all belong to one another." Even so, it must have come as a surprise that Brent received second billing. Ruth Chatterton was using her influence to push his career forward. When director Tay Garnett saw a special showing of *So Big* on the Warner lot, he announced that Brent was his choice for the male lead opposite Kay Francis in *One Way Passage*.[174] Unfortunately for George, the role went to William Powell. *One Way Passage* made many of the "Top 10 Lists" for 1932.

New Warner contract player Bette Davis, who along with Brent was being groomed for screen stardom, shows up during the last scenes of *So Big*. She played a modern version of Selina, echoing the same ideals. It's been said that Stanwyck and Davis didn't exactly hit it off during filming. When Davis blew her lines, Stanwyck grew impatient. "It all makes me so jittery," Davis complained. Stanwyck fired back, "You make *yourself jittery*! Try to fit into things!"[175] Lyle Talbot, who worked with Stanwyck and Davis, commented on the latter, "I always felt her mind was solely on herself and the effect she was producing."[176] Years later, Stanwyck was blunt about Davis with biographer Lawrence J. Quirk. "She had a kind of creative ruthlessness that made her success inevitable," observed Stanwyck.[177] In February 1932, Davis joined Brent and Ruth Chatterton for the film *The Rich Are Always With Us*. In this, Davis had a happier experience. She maintained the greatest admiration for the legendary Chatterton, who had had an enviable career on Broadway.

The Rich Are Always With Us (WB 1932) George cuddles Ruth following their famous cigarette scene. (below) Adrienne Dore eavesdrops on lovebirds Brent and Chatterton.

The chemistry between George Brent and Ruth Chatterton was obvious to everyone on the set of *The Rich Are Always With Us*. Brent got the jitters when filming began. Newly under contract herself, with a hefty salary, Chatterton was definitely the stellar favorite on the lot—she had prestige written all over her. "First day on the set," said Brent, "I spilled a cup of coffee. Ruth knocked a prop cordial into her lap, and between us we upset a glass of water. When a couple of troupers indulge in such shenanigans, there's something unusual afoot. This time it was love. And it hit me hard. I had an idea that Ruth felt a little the same way. During the rest of the picture we were both in the clouds. It wasn't hard to play the romantic scenes. There weren't enough of them to suit us."[178] When the first day of shooting wrapped, a reporter cornered Ruth, who gushed, "[Brent] is the best leading man I have worked with in Hollywood. He gave me the most perfect day I have had since coming to the screen."[179]

The Rich Are Always With Us allowed Chatterton to bring depth and shading to a snappy, modern, if unimportant story. Her scenes with Brent have the warm chemistry one would expect under the circumstances. Playing the richest woman in the world, with a philandering husband, placed Chatterton in familiar screen territory, along with the fresh-faced talents of Brent and Bette Davis. Davis said she was terrified of playing with Chatterton and never forgot the first day of shooting. "Miss Chatterton swept on like Juno," Davis recalled. "I had never seen a real star entrance in my life. I was properly dazzled. Such authority! Such glamour! She was absolutely luminous."[180] In her first scene with Chatterton, Davis appears agitated. She enters a restaurant where Chatterton and Brent are having an intimate tête-à-tête. Davis was so flustered she couldn't get her lines out. The cameras stopped. She looked at Chatterton and blurted, "I'm so damned scared of you I'm speechless!"[181] This broke the ice and Davis was surprised to find Chatterton sympathetic. "She was most helpful in her scenes with me after that," recalled Davis.[182] "Miss Chatterton and I were friends from then on. I will always consider her one of the great actresses of her day."[183]

In *The Rich Are Always With Us*, Ruth played Caroline Grannard, a woman trying to remain true to her unfaithful husband (John Miljan). Her struggle includes strolls through moonlit gardens with news correspondent Julian Tierney (Brent). After a speedy Paris divorce, Caroline begs him, "Please kiss me into needing you." Julian obliges. They face a series of obligatory misunderstandings before being reconciled in holy matrimony inside a hospital. It was a happy, if over-the-top, finish. Bette

Davis, in her trademark, edgy performance, played Caroline's best friend Malbro. Malbro wants Julian for herself but can't get to first base with him. Life was reflecting art. Davis had seen Brent on stage in New York and developed what she called an "all-time crush."[184] She remembered watching helplessly as he fell in love with Chatterton during the filming of *The Rich Are Always With Us.* Davis consoled herself by marrying a former school chum, Harmon Nelson, soon after the film's release.

Al Green's direction and the polish of Ernest Haller's photography helped compensate for any shortcomings in *The Rich Are Always With Us.* Critic Norbert Lusk raved about Brent this time, saying, "George Brent is keyed perfectly to the requirements of the correspondent. He is graceful, civilized and effortless."[185] *The New York Times* nodded, "George Brent, who portrays Julian, does capitally."[186] Many critics noticed a new spontaneity in Chatterton and the love scenes "memorable." Los Angeles critic Elizabeth Yeaman shared Ruth's enthusiasm for Brent, cheering, "This new screen actor justifies all the advance 'raves.' As an actor, he is far more polished and subtle than Gable ever dreamed of being. Furthermore, Miss Chatterton responds to his charm noticeably and her best scenes are with Brent."[187] Yeaman had trouble accepting Bette Davis as a "social equal" to "nicely bred people" such as Brent and Chatterton. "Bette Davis is prone to overact," smacked Yeaman. "She appears cheap because of her manner more than anything else." Davis comes across as anxious. It may have fit the character, as Julian complains that Malbro is "always making a nuisance of herself." Midway into the film, Davis appears more at ease during a snappy three-way phone conversation in which she reassures Caroline, who is calling from Paris, that Julian only stays home and smokes opium. Any charm that Davis lacks is compensated for by the natural chic of Chatterton and Brent. Their flirtatious give-and-take during a balcony scene is one of the film's delights. Brent persists in trying to kiss her.

"Haven't you any morals at all?" she asks after rebuffing him.

Joan Blondell and Brent confront Holmes Herbert
in *Miss Pinkerton* (WB 1932)

"Well," he answers, "they began to ache when I was sixteen. So, I had them pulled out."

After gushing about "new screen rave" George Brent, a review in *Screenland* went on to say, "Ruth Chatterton has acquired a new sparkle. Watch their love scenes—very hot! It's La Chatterton's best one for a long time."[188] Released in the heart of the Depression, it is a stretch to imagine poor folk lining up to see what troubled the rich—who, after all, helped create the economic mess in the first place. Perhaps it was therapeutic to watch millionaires suffer. *The Rich Are Always With Us* should also be remembered for the scene in which Brent and Chatterton spend a long, hard night on a chaise lounge. He puts two cigarettes in his mouth, lights them—one for Chatterton and one for himself. While they enjoy a smoke, she tells him about a woman who kept her lover hidden in an attic for two years. "That's how I feel about you," she says playfully. "Don't want anyone to look at you, or know anything about you." "Would you mind if I took a walk now and then?" he asks. "You might get run over," she answers. "Of course, I could take you out on a leash." After a pause, Brent smiles, "Yes! I'd like that!" The catchy cigarette idea was duplicated ten years later between Paul Henreid and Bette Davis in *Now Voyager*.

Brent was rushed into a third Warner film costarring Joan Blondell. Reportedly, Blondell had wandered onto the set of *The Rich Are Always With Us* and after five minutes turned excitedly to the publicity man with her and asked, "*Who* is that man? Is he under contract here?" Five days later George was assigned the lead in her picture Miss Pinkerton. Blondell had the title role as a nurse who helps Brent, a detective, solve a couple of murders. It was routine hokum, designed for chills and laughs. Film historian William K. Everson felt that "Brent's suppressed frustration [made] for a better contrast than when [Blondell's] cohort was James Cagney, whose pepper and wisecracks matched her own."[189] Everson's assessment was generous. Blondell attempted to give the dialogue her usual snap, but the screenplay fell flat. The onscreen chemistry between Brent and Blondell is easily forgotten. The Los Angeles Examiner felt that Brent held his own even though "he plays almost his entire role without removing his hat."[190] "And he has such nice hair, too," pouted the review.

In *Week-End Marriage*, based on a Faith Baldwin novel, fourth-billed Brent was on screen for six minutes—less screen time than he had in *So Big*. In the lead, Loretta Young does a marvelous job with a hopelessly dated story. She plays a successful career woman whose marriage is in trouble. When her husband becomes bedridden, her physician blames her, lecturing that women who stay home and avoid careers build good marriages. Guilt ridden, Young is compelled to lie (doctor's orders) to her useless, intoxicated, philandering husband (Norman Foster). She tells him how helpless she is and puts on the symbolic apron. The real message in *Week-End Marriage* is that women need to lie and sacrifice their careers in order to build a better America. *Film Daily* called it "wholesome." The critic for *Motion Picture* accurately deduced that the film solved "nothing," while noting that Brent was "lost in a brief bit."[191]

Upon the film's release, Brent and Young were selected to go on a promotional tour for *Week-End Marriage*. They were frequently seen lunching together while rehearsing their stage act for the tour. Gossips indicated that the two were an item, but their meetings, according to Brent, were "merely business." His heart was elsewhere. He had fallen in love with Chatterton, who was married to actor Ralph Forbes. The couple frequently invited George over for dinner. The happy trio was often seen out socially. It wasn't long before Brent took Forbes aside one evening. "Ralph," he said quietly, "I'll have to stop coming here. I can't come to your house again." When Forbes inquired as to the reason, Brent replied, "Because, I'm irrevocably in love with your wife."[192] Ralph shook his hand, saying that he appreciated George's honest, straightforward admission. Brent's revelation didn't cause an upheaval. For several years, Ruth and Ralph recognized that their marriage had evolved into friendship. Ironically, after *The Rich Are Always With Us* was completed, Ruth cast Ralph, whose screen career had slumped, in a play that she was directing titled *Let Us Divorce*. He played a priggish barrister—a role that fit him like a glove. George often drove to watch their rehearsals in Santa Barbara. "Insiders" said that on one occasion George was visiting the couple in their hotel room while Ralph was going over his lines. Ruth went over to her husband and asked for permission to marry George. "Yes, yes," he was purported to have said. "Certainly. But don't disturb me while I'm getting my lines."[193]

In June 1932, George, Ruth, and Ralph all went their separate ways. George began his promotional tour with Loretta Young, Ruth sailed for Europe, and Ralph went to Reno to file for divorce. And who should shimmy her way into Tinseltown but Gilda Gray. She was touring in "Gilda Gray's Ubangi Revue" as the "priestess of primitive rhythm." To fortify her savage gyrations it was rumored that she chowed down raw meat sandwiches prior to each performance.[194] It wasn't long before Gilda heard gossip about the pre-divorce engagement of Brent and Chatterton. A reporter asked for her reaction. Gray gave a hearty laugh and sighed,

Week-End Marriage (WB 1932) Loretta Young and Brent enliven a hopelessly outdated plot. (below) *They Call it Sin* (WB 1932) with David Manners and Loretta Young.

"Well, we live and learn!"[195] In hindsight, it was Brent's good fortune not to marry Gilda. She was making a concerted effort to have her stepfather committed to an old folks home. "My father and I have never been able to get along," she told reporters. "It will serve him right!"[196]

Prior to leaving Hollywood for his vaudeville tour, Brent was added to the cast of a second Loretta Young feature, *They Call It Sin*. For being second billed, Brent seemed strangely absent. Young, looking absolutely luminous, played a small-town girl who follows her heart to the big bad city and the arms of a New York businessman (David Manners), who ends up marrying someone else. Manners had twice the screen time as Brent, who played his best friend, a physician. Brent had one good line. Advising Manners about his love life, Brent said, "If you're going to insist on being a jackass, I'm going to turn your case over to a veterinary." The other good line went to Una Merkel, who played Young's sidekick. Merkel goes up to a bar, approaches Brent, and asks, "Do you know anything about poets?" "A little," Brent replies. "What nationality was Robert Burns?" "Scotch," he answers. "That's what *I'll* have!" smirks Merkel. When the disillusioned Young falls into the arms of Brent at the *finis*—it comes across as being a tacked on, if happy, ending. While *They Call It Sin* didn't indulge in moralizing, *The New York Times* summed it up as being "unimportant" and "tedious."[197] Critics paid little or no attention to the Brent-Young combination in spite of their definite onscreen simpatico. Offscreen, Young had developed a serious crush on her costar.

While on tour, George and Loretta performed a ten minute sketch titled "The Honeymoon." They spent a week in Washington, D.C., and a week in Philadelphia. Loretta's mother chaperoned. When their "Honeymoon" arrived in New York City, Brent checked into the swank Hotel Pierre seventeen floors above Central Park. Writer James Roy Fuller paid a visit to the rising star for a breakfast interview. Fuller noticed several well-used ashtrays on a cocktail table (Brent admitted to smoking three to five packs of cigarettes a day) as well as a pair of brown goggles. George was still having eye trouble. He talked about his tour, which played to packed houses. He put on the brown goggles, explaining, "The studio lights hurt my eyes. The heat is terrific, and it's a strain going through a scene, even if it lasts only two or three minutes. You hear about whoopee in Hollywood—why, when you get up at six in the morning and go through that all day, when night comes it's whoopee to bed."[198] George had been advised not to strain his eyes but couldn't resist reading William Faulkner's recent release, *Sanctuary*. It was about a "fast girl" from a fictional Southern town who is raped and ends up in a Memphis brothel.[199] Brent hoped that Faulkner's next book would "retain the original charm of the author's style."[200] When Fuller asked about Ruth, and if they were indeed engaged, Brent answered, "So, well? Ask Miss Chatterton when she comes back." Brent's press agent warned Fuller that if he pursued the subject any further he would jump out the window.

Now a hot property, Brent had many requests for interviews. It gave him the opportunity to talk about filmmaking. "It's creative work, in its way," he observed. "Of course, it is not on the plane of painting great pictures, or writing fine books—but it does have a manner of satisfying to some degree the artistic itch of people ungifted in other arts."[201] Brent liked to talk about his love of horses, polo and steeplechase riding. He mentioned swimming and tennis. He had no interest in politics or governmental problems. He wanted to make money. To see the world. He disliked vulgarity and people who infringed upon his privacy. "Brent's gravity and his habit of gentle speech—without any brogue," wrote scenarist Charles Grayson, "belie George's intense nervousness. At the studio he invariably lunches alone, as in his present high-strung state he cannot eat and talk at the same time without suffering from nervous

June 1932. On their "Honeymoon"
promotional tour, George told love-struck
Loretta Young that he was on the verge of
marrying Ruth Chatterton.

indigestion. He lost ten pounds, making *So Big*."[202] When asked about marriage, Brent disposed of the subject by saying, "Yes. I was married once—when I was nineteen. It only lasted a month and it's one of those things I don't talk about."[203]

It wasn't until *after* Chatterton returned from Europe that Brent felt free to wax poetic about his feelings for her. The difference in their ages (Chatterton was thirty-nine) had left many a young damsel wondering. Of younger women, Brent said, "Of course they're charming kids, every one of 'em. But for the love of Saint Kevin, what would a man do with one as a wife? She'd be in your lap—figuratively and literally—from dawn 'til dark. You'd not be able to call your soul your own." "Their attractions are for the very young," he emphasized, "or the very old. I'm not in either category."[204] Brent spelled out his feelings for Ruth plainly. "In Ruth," he said, "I've found every single thing a man might seek in a woman. So far as I'm concerned she has everything. Beauty, of course. And a mentality that shines with the brilliance of a silver dollar in the sun. She's not the all-possessive clinging-vine type. And she has real honor in the masculine sense of the word." Brent praised Chatterton's "natural dignity," culture and innate refinement. "There's no vulgarity, no rough stuff, on the set of a Chatterton picture," he noted. "There's not a studio employee who doesn't swear by her. I've yet to meet anyone she hasn't treated with courtesy."

According to Hollywood writer Jerry Lane, Loretta Young was smitten with Brent during filmmaking and while back East on tour. Her eyes danced whenever she talked about him. After they gave their final stage performance in St. Louis, Brent took her out for supper and confided, "Loretta, I'm going to marry Miss Chatterton—if she'll have me." When tears welled up in Loretta's eyes, Brent was shocked. He thought they were just pals. "Sorry George," she apologized, "I didn't understand. The best of luck to you—always."[205] Brent was going to need it.

While George had resisted the charms and attention of nineteen-year-old Loretta Young, Ruth Chatterton, unbeknownst to anyone, was engaged in a secret rendezvous with a handsome Bureau Chief for the Associated Press. He was covering the political crisis in Spain, and his name was Rex Smith.

At home, Ruth "gliding" into her second marriage

4

George & Ruth & Ralph

"A modern version of *ménage a trois"*

(Adela Rogers St. Johns)

In June 1932, Warner publicity announced George Brent's first film as a lead star: *20,000 Years in Sing-Sing.* It was based on the best seller by Lewis E. Lawes, warden for the infamous maximum security prison.[206] In an important dramatic role, Brent would play a troublemaker who faces the electric chair. It was scheduled for a November release and would co-star Ann Dvorak. In mid-July it was revealed that Lawes had approved Spencer Tracy for the lead. In August, while Warner camera crews filmed around the prison in Ossining, New York, Brent was close by doing his vaudeville shtick with Loretta Young. *20,000 Years in Sing-Sing* provided Spencer Tracy a breakthrough performance and established his career as a strong male lead. Brent, on the other hand, continued in supporting roles helping to illuminate the studio's leading ladies. Instead of showing any real interest in George Brent, the actor, the film colony focused on the curious relationship of the new trio about town: George, Ruth, and Ralph.

Since their wedding in 1924, Ruth Chatterton and Ralph Forbes indulged in what they referred to as "vacations from marriage." They would go their separate ways for several months and then happily reunite. Ruth and Ralph had a deep and abiding affection for each other and would remain devoted friends until Ralph passed away in 1951. The point being, George was not seen as an intrusion on their happiness. George and Ralph became the best of friends. When asked about George and a potential breakup of her marriage, Ruth, in exasperation, blurted, "I don't even bother to deny any more that I'm divorcing Ralph. I've been doing it for three years now."[207]

Ralph Forbes, who would always jest that he had been "hag-ridden" his whole life, had a great time in Reno the summer of 1932. "I'm as devoted to Miss Chatterton as if she were my sister," he beamed to the reporters that surrounded him in the "Divorce Capital of America."[208] Publicist Scoop Conlon and his wife joined Forbes. They spent a lot of time playing poker. During their six-week stay Ralph was in his element. When he wasn't gambling he was telling ribald yarns around the campfire, citing Shakespeare and Kipling to an appreciative group of wildly assorted Americans. Brent, of course, was on his East coast promotion for *Week-End Marriage.* He had arranged his schedule so that when Ruth's boat docked in August, he would be there to greet her with open arms. In the meantime, Ruth was in the arms of a well-built, red-haired, and attractive thirty-four-year-old reporter in Madrid.

In 1931, news reporter Rex Smith attended a party at Ruth and Ralph's sumptuous home. He mentioned to Ruth his assignment covering news in politically unstable Spain. She spontaneously suggested a rendezvous in Madrid. Rex liked the idea. "All right," Ruth told him, "I'll meet you in the Trocadero [one year] from tonight."[209] They promised never again to mention their secret plan. Smith's second wife, Jessie Royce Landis, revealed later, "Many people know this story. In fact, it was taken as the basis of a film in which Irene Dunne and Charles Boyer starred."[210] Landis was referring to director Leo McCarey's film classic, *Love Affair* (1939). Before Ruth left for Europe, she had practically turned the studio upside down in order to keep her date with Rex on June 22.[211] Ruth returned from Europe on August 11. She had indulged in a nice long fling and was ready for marriage number two.

There was a big to-do on August 13, 1932, when Ruth and George married less than twenty-four hours after her divorce. They motored up to Westchester County where Justice Winfred C. Allen performed the ceremony at high noon. Brent gave his real age of twenty-eight, while Ruth lopped off five years to instantly become thirty-four. Two of Chatterton's actress friends, Frances Starr and Virginia Hammond, were witnesses. The wedding party then celebrated at the home of actor William Courtney in Rye, New York. "Too happy for words" is all the bride had to say as she and Brent headed for New York City in the late afternoon.[212] On August 15, the couple attended the wedding of Frances Starr to banker R. Golden Donaldson at Starr's posh Savoy-Plaza Hotel apartment. Two days later, Mr. and Mrs. Brent and a retinue of servants boarded a private car attached to a westbound train for Hollywood.

The honeymooners stayed in Ruth's swanky bungalow on the Warner lot. It was there they threw their first big party—a southern dinner with fried chicken prepared in the smart kitchenette; a table set for ten in the green carpeted dining room; the atmosphere enhanced by the glow from two blazing fireplaces. Guests included Ruth's mother, Tilly; Helen Hayes and husband Charles MacArthur; and Ruth's new director, William Wellman. Ruth was well aware of Brent's unhappy first marriage. "He was thoroughly disillusioned about women," she admitted, "disliked them, distrusted them." Ruth felt that she and Brent had something "sound and permanent." "We both love to travel," she said. "He wants to show me the

Purchase Price (**WB 1933**) **with Barbara Stanwyck**

Ireland that is his. We both love music. A large part of our evenings now, either at home in Beverly Hills or here in the studio bungalow, we listen to symphonies and opera on the radio or the phonograph. Neither of us wants children. I never have felt the maternal urge—an offshoot, perhaps, of my original shrinking from things that tie. We are the same kind of people."[213] Writer Gladys Hall put it succinctly when she commented that Ruth "stepped as smoothly . . . from first marriage to second as she might step in her own drawing-room, from one rug to another."[214]

Ralph Forbes continued to be part of the Chatterton-Brent equation. He dropped in frequently to dine with them. He also tagged along for theater outings. The trio became a much-talked-about triangle. Adela Rogers St. Johns referred to them as a "modern version" of *ménage a trios.*[215]

Prior to his marriage, Brent had completed a total of seven films at Warners. Cecil B. DeMille made a concerted effort to borrow him for the male lead in *Sign of the Cross.* Brent was too much in demand on the Warner lot. The prestige of being cast in a DeMille production would have given Brent enviable visibility. Instead, he was assigned to an oddity titled *The Purchase Price.* In this, Barbara Stanwyck played a torch singer who escapes a "naughty nightclub" and the clutches of a bootlegger (Lyle Talbot). She becomes the want-ad bride of a Dakota farmer (Brent). The implausible tale demanded that Stanwyck's character find spiritual uplift in milking cows and contemplating wheat. The *New York Times* opined, "One of the weirdest scenarios within the memory of man."[216] Brent claimed to have put a lot of effort into his role. He blew his lines nineteen times during one scene. "I dried up," said Brent. "When you get that way the only thing to do is to stop working."[217] He admitted that *The Purchase Price* was his worst picture for 1932. Critics agreed. Norbert Lusk commented, "George Brent plays the farmer as a lout with sniffles, probably to demonstrate his versatility as an actor. But the experiment fails and Mr. Brent convinces us that he is more at ease in the airy nothingness of Miss Chatterton's classes in drawing room deportment."[218] Brent's characterization was awkward. It was Stanwyck's performance that made the film palatable. Director William Wellman provided his trademark touches of crude down-home folk and a salty appreciation for the risqué. While on the train to meet future husband Brent, Stanwyck sits next to other brides-to-be who are giddily gobbling bananas. Wellman got some undeniably good scenes from the Stanwyck-Brent duo, but the film lacked focus and suffered the consequences.

Warner had also capitalized on the "steam" generated by the Chatterton-Brent duo in a film adapted from the novel *Children of Pleasure,* produced prior to their marriage. Rechristened *The Crash,* the story revolved around the lives of money-obsessed individuals and the Wall Street tumble of '29. Adorned in twenty-two Orry-Kelly gowns, Ruth played Linda Gault, a woman who seduced wealthy men for stock market tips. Her husband, Geoffrey (Brent), uses her as bait to make a killing on

On the Warner set with Mr. and Mrs. Brent (Courtesy of Brian Reddin)

Wall Street. He's little more than a pimp who seems fonder of liquor than his wife. "What's the matter with us anyway?" he asks her. "The more money we make, the more wretched we are." Unable to solicit a desired tip at a crucial moment, Linda makes up a lie to tell Geoffrey. As a result, they lose everything. Afraid of poverty, Linda goes to Bermuda and tries to drink herself to death but falls for an Australian sheep rancher (Paul Cavanaugh) instead. Director William Dieterle, or perhaps Ruth, had the idea of showing a close-up of a book the rancher is reading, Aldous Huxley's *Antic Hay*, all about the self-absorbed elite. The book was highly controversial, considered immoral, banned in Australia, burned in Cairo. *The Crash*, with its own selfish, unscrupulous characters, concludes with Linda and Geoffrey reuniting for a happy, if unlikely, conclusion. If nothing else, the bold, pre-Code flavor of this film makes it worth watching.

Critic Elizabeth Yeaman referred to the husband-wife team in *The Crash* as "human parasites . . . cautious cheaters on the fence, ready to jump on whichever side seems most profitable."[219] Chatterton and Brent offered convincing performances of unsympathetic characters, but was the story a good choice? Ruth's maturity belied dialogue that emphasized her youthful charm. Brent wasn't given much to do. *The New York Times* made no mention of his performance. Norbert Lusk said, "George Brent is singularly lackluster, his expression rarely changing from negative indifference."[220] Yeaman deduced that *The Crash* was an "ill chosen" vehicle. She was right. *The Crash* failed with audiences. Critics mentioned the lack of spontaneity in the fifty-eight-minute feature, blaming Dieterle. *Film Daily* suggested to theater owners, "Ballyhoo the Chatterton-Brent romance, and go light on the picture."[221]

Ruth Chatterton

By the time George Brent married Ruth Chatterton, she had been a household name since her acclaimed 1912 Broadway debut in *The Rainbow*. The play's producer and costar, Henry Miller, was completely smitten with his "new discovery." Following a successful run, Miller-Chatterton took the play on a cross-country tour that lasted over a year. Chatterton's box office smashes also included *Daddy Long-Legs* and *Come Out of the Kitchen*. It was her remarkable success that afforded Miller the opportunity to build a shrine to himself: The Henry Miller Theatre. Miller not only struck gold with Chatterton he also found her to be a most grateful pupil and mistress. The thirty-three years difference in age didn't pose a problem until Ruth became designated as an actress-manager. She had matured. She began staging her own productions and investing her own money in projects. Her deep affection for Miller made it all the more difficult in the fall of 1924, when she fell in love with her young costar in the *Magnolia Lady*—British actor Ralph Forbes. Miller was furious at this turn of events and stormed out of Chatterton's life. As Broadway legend George M. Cohan put it, "He was crazy about Ruthie, Miller was."[222]

Following her marriage to Forbes, Chatterton teamed in several plays with him, none of them successful. By 1926, she succumbed to performing dramatic sketches in vaudeville. Forbes, on the other hand, signed an MGM contract following his stand-out role in the critically acclaimed *Beau Geste* (1926). It would be two years before German actor Emil Jannings came to Ruth's rescue, offering her a lead in *Sins of the Fathers* (1928). Paramount put her under contract and everyone watched as Chatterton's popularity soared. She surpassed Clara Bow at the box office and was nominated twice for an Academy Award as Best Actress. Chatterton knew she was back on top.

Ruth Chatterton was born December 24, 1892, in New York City. Her father, Walter Smith Chatterton, like his father before him, married into money. A poor father figure, he was unreliable and declared several bankruptcies before separating from Ruth's mother in 1907. Lilian Reed Chatterton came from a stable, well-to-do background. Lilian's father, Andrew Reed, was a ship builder. While Ruth was growing up she and her parents lived in a Fordham Heights estate with Lilian's parents. Any security that Ruth had as a girl was provided by her Grandfather Reed.

Ruth had little to do with her father, especially after he wrote her a scathing letter regarding her decision to go on stage at the age of sixteen. Accompanied by her mother, Ruth performed in stock companies in Washington, D.C., Milwaukee, and Worcester. Following Grandfather Reed's death, Lilian lived on a $10 weekly annuity. Mother and daughter scrimped by, until that fateful moment in March 1912, when Ruth stepped onto the empty stage of Broadway's Liberty Theatre. It was her first performance in *The Rainbow*. Ruth stood silently, waiting for her cue. For some strange reason the audience rocked the theater with a welcoming ovation. Their reaction, the thunder of applause, forever afterward gave Chatterton pause. In 1955, she reflected back to that moment and said, "I've never understood it. I hadn't done a thing. Some magnetic

George referees while inebriated Bebe Daniels accuses Ruby Keeler of "sh-peeking through the keekhole" in the blockbuster *42nd Street* (WB 1933)

quality apparently reached the audience. I was lucky."[223] With George Brent, however, Ruth Chatterton's luck would be short-lived.

In September 1932, shortly after their marriage, Brent was cast as Ruth's love interest in William Wellman's *Frisco Jenny*. Wisely, the studio pulled him out of that project—his character was killed off in the first fifteen minutes. Instead, Brent was given third billing in *42nd Street*. In 2006, the film ranked thirteenth in the American Film Institute's list of best musicals. Upon the film's 1933 release, some felt that Brent walked through his role. Years later, he admitted, "I felt lost in that film. It was no place for me, but they told me I had to do it, and 'they' were boss."[224] Brent played Pat Denning, an out-of-work actor and boy-toy for musical star Dorothy Brock (Bebe Daniels). Whenever he shows up, Brock gives him the high sign to get lost. It's obvious that she prefers the company of a sugar daddy (Guy Kibbee) who is backing her new show. Brent's character isn't a complete loser. He refuses money from Brock when she takes pity on him. "Not another nickel," he tells her, adding that he's had a "sudden attack of manhood." After Brock breaks her ankle and leaves the show, the fresh faces of Ruby Keeler and Dick Powell take over. Critics offered nothing but rave reviews for *42nd Street*. Dance director Busby Berkeley's inventive musical numbers dazzled audiences. *The New York Times* called it "the liveliest and most tuneful musical to come out of Hollywood." The film introduced a popular music score and created a box office sensation. Amid all the brouhaha, reviews rarely mentioned Brent. However, in a cast of hard-boiled characters, his masculine charm infused the film with easygoing warmth. *Liberty* magazine noted that Brent did "much to inject pleasure into the fast-moving and kaleidoscopic film."

Upon completing his role in *42nd Street* Brent was offered the lead in Paramount's *Luxury Liner*. Touted as "The Grand Hotel of the Ocean," it looked like the break Brent had been waiting for. After reading the script, he felt that the picture would propel his career forward. Unfortunately, his performance in *Luxury Liner* sank like the Titanic. Critics were unanimous. "George Brent might have been a robot for all the personality and feeling he exhibited," said the *Hollywood Reporter*.[225] "George Brent is not at his best," echoed *The New York Times*. The script itself was tedious and other cast members appeared to be walking through their parts. The superb acting of Vivienne Osborne, who played Brent's erring wife, gave *Luxury Liner* its only shot of adrenaline. The other bright spot was Alice White gold-digging her way from steerage to first class and back again.

When someone suggested Brent might get ahead faster if he went to the right parties, he gave it a try. "It didn't take me long to discover that Thalberg and Goldwyn always went off by themselves to play backgammon," Brent recalled. "The other giants of the industry broke up into two's and three's—always the same two's and three's. Meanwhile, here I was a stranger, stranded with some other strangers. It was fairly obvious that I was wasting my time. What I was like off the screen didn't mean a thing."[226]

∞

Popular team - Kay Francis and George Brent in The Keyhole (WB 1933)

Some of Brent's films he would have preferred not to make. "We had to do them," he said, "whether we liked them or not because of that contract. It was very much like being in bondage."[227] Six days a week, from sunrise and often ending at midnight, took its toll. He admitted to being dependable, yet somehow strangely lackluster in "one asinine story after another." "Lord what muck!" he complained.[228] He felt he was being oversold and blamed the factory atmosphere. "You go into a role before you've finished the last, and you're never sure just what character you're playing. The dry mechanics of this thing are getting me down!"[229] The first day of each shoot the cast and crew would make small talk and tell jokes to break the tension. Brent laughed about it years later. "What we needed was a court jester," he recalled. "That getting-to-know-each-other period before the start of a picture helped tremendously."

Brent's luck improved when he was teamed for the first time with Kay Francis. Francis aroused a nuance from Brent that was fresh and appealing. In *The Keyhole*, these two impeccably mannered screen personalities had a relaxed, attractive style that jelled. They would costar in a total of six films. *The Keyhole* had Brent playing a New York detective who is hired to trail a woman (Francis) who is suspected of being unfaithful by her wealthy, much older husband (Henry Kolker). Part of detective Brent's assignment is to make love to her in Havana. He does and, eventually, she reciprocates. As the camera dotes on them, the duo strikes a playful note, which flames into a romance that is tangible. At the finish, husband Kolker realizes what a fool he was—inadvertently playing cupid to this love match. Scenes are juxtaposed with the frothy antics of Glenda Farrell's blonde shill and Allen Jenkins as Brent's numbskull assistant. *Film Daily* commented, "Kay Francis is gorgeous and makes the film entertaining through sheer personality."[230] A Los Angeles critic praised, "George Brent brings a certain magnetism to the role of the detective."[231] The *Los Angeles Examiner* review agreed, "George Brent has one of the best roles assigned him in many months."[232]

Prior to the release of *The Keyhole*, Warners accepted president-elect Franklin Delano Roosevelt's invitation for an array of studio stars to attend his inauguration on March 4. Brent joined Ruby Keeler, Bebe Daniels, Joe E. Brown, Tom Mix, Warner Baxter, Bette Davis, Leo Carrillo, Lyle Talbot, Ginger Rogers, and Una Merkel on a cross-country train known as the *42nd Street Special*. They left from Hollywood on February 21, 1933, and made stops in thirteen cities. There were luncheons with local dignitaries, parades that attracted up to 300,000 people, and radio interviews. Lyle Talbot recalled, "Bette Davis never knew where we were. She'd speak from the platform and say, 'It's great to be here in Cleveland,' and we'd be in Detroit."[233]

After Brent returned from his *42nd Street* junket, he and Ruth enthusiastically studied house plans, sketches, and blueprints. They were planning a new home—but, before they dug any deeper into the idea, they took off on a belated honeymoon to Europe. George got released from

In 1934, novelist Homer Croy wrote that Ralph
Forbes and George were "Damon and Pythias to
each other." George told Croy, "There is no man
I'd rather see or with whom I'd rather be."

doing *Mary Stevens, M.D.*, with Kay Francis, and the couple sailed from
New York on the *Europa* on March 23. Ralph Forbes did not tag along
this time. While Brent enjoyed Ralph's company, he later admitted that
enough was enough. Forbes would regularly show up for breakfast. Brent
claimed that Forbes even had a permanent place reserved in their boudoir. Ruth insisted on keeping a photo of Ralph on her nightstand.

Instead of Ralph Forbes, George and Ruth were joined by Ronald
Colman on their continental tour. The trio took a motor trip through
Spain. Colman told intimates that Ruth was the only woman who had ever
won his confidence. Chatterton was indirectly responsible for his success.
She had arranged with Henry Miller for Colman to play her hot-blooded
young lover in the 1922 stage success *La Tendresse*. As a result, film director Henry King saw Colman's performance and offered him the male
lead in Lillian Gish's *The White Sister*. The role secured Colman's future

in films. Brent, most likely, welcomed Colman aboard. Ruth would have someone else to talk to. She loved the art of conversation and would often stay up until the wee hours talking about ideas and what was going on in the world. George preferred to give his mind a rest and enjoy a brief respite from a talkative wife. Naturally, the three stars were stimulated by their surroundings. They attended bullfights in Spain and hobnobbed with Ruth's occasional paramour, Rex Smith, who was a bullfight enthusiast. Rex took them to a bull ranch where Chatterton was game to enter the ring. Ruth had the thrill of being chased by a couple of sexually mature, even-horned, two-year-old bulls. "Juan Belmonte, the great fighter, laughed heartily," said Ruth. "Of course, I was right to run, and the top of my car was a safer place."[234] Belmonte is still considered by many to be the greatest matador of all time. Matador Brent also made a few passes at the vicious young bulls, laughing when they grazed his side. The white-goateed owner of the ranch cheered, "Thees Señor Brent has what you call thee *guts*. . . ."[235]

Colman tagged along to Paris, where the trio sent a risqué "French postcard" to Hollywood columnist Louella Parsons.[236] Ruth later commented that she never knew Colman to be so "miserable." Unlike Ruth and George, it was obvious that Colman had no desire to "get away from it all."[237] There was talk of Chatterton doing a film in England. The press reported that she focused instead on seeing England, Germany, and George's Ireland. In 2013, Irish filmmaker Brian Reddin said he could find no mention in the Irish press of their visit to the Emerald Isle. This may explain why they later planned to visit Ireland the following spring. While in Germany, the couple was less enthusiastic about what was going on—the hypnotic appeal of Hitler, his rhetoric, and its effect on the German people. "I have never belonged to anything, not even a country club," Ruth would recall. "I don't like mass stuff. I was in Germany in '32 and '33 and I saw that man coming up, and I said, 'Look out, look out, look out. . . .'"[238]

Lilly Turner (WB 1933) Frank McHugh, in a standout performance,
joined the Chatterton-Brent team

Mr. and Mrs. Brent left for New York from Southampton on the *S.S.
Berengaria* on May 27. George was listed as an "Actor" and Ruth a "Cinema Artist." Upon arriving back in Hollywood, Ruth was confined to bed
with a serious case of bronchitis. Dr. William E. Branch reported that
it was a relapse. Ruth had been ill in Italy, and again on her way home
from Europe. Branch went so far as to indicate that she had a "nervous
breakdown."[239] For a cure, Ruth and George headed for the hills of San
Bernardino. Once there, they followed Dr. Henry (Hal) Bieler's recommended diet: no salt, no sugar, and plenty of green vegetables. They
claimed that it did them a world of good. Gloria Swanson was a lifelong
advocate of Bieler's idea that "food is your best medicine." When they returned home, George's sister, Kathleen, visiting from New York, joined in
the regimen and stayed around to help Mr. and Mrs. Brent celebrate their
first wedding anniversary on August 13.

In the summer of 1933, Warner Bros. released the third Chatterton-Brent film (completed shortly before they left for Europe). *Lilly Turner* was a screen adaptation of a play by Philip Dunning and George Abbott. Hoping to follow the success of *Frisco Jenny,* Warners put director William Wellman in charge of the production. His son, William Wellman, Jr., recalled, "Ruth Chatterton was very independent and very strong. A lot of directors didn't want to work with her. My father liked the independent woman, the strong woman who could hang out with the guys."[240] In 2013, I chatted with Wellman Jr. at a film festival in San Francisco. "My father thought George Brent was alright," said Wellman, "but he and Ruth *really* connected."[241] Along with Warners' stock characters Frank McHugh, Guy Kibbee, and Robert Barrat, the cast created an engaging ensemble. While most of the action occurs in seedy surroundings, the characters come across as human. Critics were hard on the film. *The Hollywood Reporter* put the curse on it, saying that it could "only be classed as garbage. The good work of a fine cast … no way compensates for the unsavory pall which hangs over *Lilly Turner.* Lilly strikes a fair average by repulsing as many men as she sleeps with."[242] As the film had no moral, it was a perfect target for the moralistic.

On screen, Chatterton played a carnival prop, a cooch dancer, about to have a baby. When her husband's *real* wife shows up, we learn that he's a bigamist. "You mean … I'm not married?" Lilly asks. The woman shakes her head, "Tough luck girlie. I know just how you feel." Frank McHugh does a memorable job as Dan, a booze-loving barker who comes to Lilly's rescue. They marry the day before she's going to deliver. Lilly loses her baby, but her troubles have just begun. She and Dan join up with a bogus medicine show run by Doc McGill (Guy Kibbee). Midway into the film, George Brent arrives to give a good account of himself as Bob, an unemployed engineer who fills in for Fritz, the medicine show's volatile "Strong Man" (Robert Barrat), who has been hauled away to a mental institution. The film's happy interlude has Lilly and Bob fall in love. Dan's devotion to

Pre-Code favorite *Baby Face* (WB 1933),
with Barbara Stanwyck

booze has kept him from consummating his marriage to Lilly, let alone recognizing that she is in love with someone else. Wellman's trademark dashes of humor give the film buoyancy. The ending isn't exactly what you would expect. Lilly bids a fond adieu to Bob and remains loyal to drunken, debilitated Dan, who had helped her out of a jam when she was in a tight spot. As *Film Daily's* review of *Lilly Turner* emphasized, "It is not family fare."[243]

Amid a slew of negative reviews, the *Los Angeles Examiner* thought *Lilly Turner* "swell entertainment. Ruth Chatterton . . . handled her dramatic scenes with intensity, her love scenes with tenderness. Frank McHugh turns in a humorous performance that coaxes the picture right into his vest pocket. You may find it hokey, but you won't be bored."[244] Helping to keep the film afloat, George Brent's Irish grin and quiet sincerity were a definite plus. His love scenes with Chatterton are among the film's best. Los Angeles critic Eleanor Barnes wrote, "Brent … takes over the duties of sweetheart and strong man. He does the former more convincingly than the latter."[245] For *Lilly Turner*, Brent missed out on being in the third most popular film of the year, *Gold Diggers of 1933*. He was replaced by Warren William.

Baby Face, Brent's third film with Barbara Stanwyck, had been completed in January but ran into postproduction problems. Producer Darryl F. Zanuck (who wrote the story using the pseudonym Mark Canfield) shot a new ending. Censors still rejected it. Further cuts and rewrites for *Baby Face* finally permitted its general release in July. Following a preview, *Film Daily* synopsized, "Rather hot yarn of how a luscious lass makes her way in the world by trading on her charms. George Brent is the ultimate hero."[246] "Don't take the children to *Baby Face*," warned another critic. The film opens with Stanwyck's no-good father pimping her off to speakeasy patrons in the slums. From there, we watch her climb the corporate ladder—on her back. Playing a bank president, Brent becomes the target for gold digger Lily (Stanwyck). Her seductive charm soon finds Brent, "the ultimate hero," keeping new wife Lily supplied with jewelry, furs, and cash. When the bank is in trouble, he is indicted. On screen, Stanwyck's tough, calculating face is amazing to watch. She makes her conniving character understandable. As for Brent, he displays just enough savoir faire to make Stanwyck's Lily realize that she is not her bank account. As a concession to censorship the two ultimately find happiness in the very same factory slums from which Lily had escaped. If there was any message, it was simply that men are at the mercy of their libido. "Three cheers for sin!" enthused the review in *Liberty* magazine.

After almost two years of hard work, Warner Bros. refused to elevate George Brent to star status. He was still considered a featured player. Regardless, as author James Robert Parish pointed out, Brent "began acting like the 'star' he thought he was fast becoming."[247] Perhaps he had reason. Samuel Goldwyn put a bid on Brent's services for his sumptuous pro-

From Headquarters (WB 1933) Brent in one of his top-
notch roles with Margaret Lindsay and Eugene Pallette

duction *Nana*.[248] Warner refused. In place of Goldwyn, Brent was given
another role in one of his wife's films, *Female*. This was followed by director William Dieterle's overlooked gem, *From Headquarters*, a pioneer-
ing effort with visual flourish that focused on the intricacies of forensics,
as well as lead star Brent, who played a detective. *Photoplay* declared it a
"cracking good mystery about murder. It maintains bullet-like speed and
suspense right to the end."[249] Brent offers what is easily one of his better
performances. He is focused, authentic, and engaging in his portrayal of
a love-torn investigator. The fact his former sweetheart is implicated in
the murder gives him emotional edge while he stays cued to his job. In
Los Angeles, the *Evening Herald Express* raved, "George Brent . . . gives
a splendid account of himself."[250] Brent found director Dieterle to be "a
good man and easy to work with."[251]

RKO then requested Brent's services for the Katharine Hepburn film
Spitfire. Warners agreed. *Film Daily* reported that Brent and Hepburn
had left for location shooting in Hemet, California.[252] For some reason
Warners pulled him out of the Hepburn film and told him to travel to
Stockton, California, for on-location shooting of *Mandalay*—a film that

Chatterton turned down. Kay Francis had taken over the star role. Tired of being jerked around, Brent refused. He stated that the role of the alcoholic doctor in *Mandalay* would "injure and degrade him."[253] Brent had his eye on doing *Massacre*, a film that championed the ongoing plight of Native Americans and exposed how government agencies and corporate interests exploit native peoples.[254] The role of the crusading, college-educated Sioux Indian went into the able hands of Richard Barthelmess. Brent was also disappointed about not doing the Hepburn film and put in a claim to refuse assignments or quit. "I appeared in consecutive roles that any half-witted ham could have played," he fumed.[255] It would be seven months before George Brent was given another film assignment. In the meantime, he pioneered in fighting the mighty Warner machine. "The actors who raise hell now and then," argued Brent, "seem to get along better than those who try to be agreeable."[256] His one-man strike mirrored that of James Cagney (whose salary issues were justified based on the huge returns his films generated at the box office). In October 1933, Brent was on suspension, although he continued to report to work. On December 18, he walked. He was off salary. Brent then sought a settlement of his contract so he could freelance.[257] Brent aired his grievances publicly and bluntly told his friend, columnist Jack Grant,

> *What am I to do? I'm tied with a contract as firmly and securely as a prisoner in dungeon chains. I am not being given anything worthwhile on the screen. I can't quit, for the contract covers stage and radio, too. If I was suspended for insubordination, I could be kept idle the balance of my natural life. The months of suspension are only tacked on to the end of the contract. I'd never be free and acting is the only profession in which I'm trained.*[258]

When Grant asked what Ruth had suggested, Brent snorted, "I've never asked her, and I never will. If I'm not man enough to work out my own salvation, I'd better chuck the whole business." As tension mounted at home, Ruth felt it wasn't her place to advise George, and she told Grant, "He is brooding over this contract thing, until he is nearly insane."[259]

By the end of 1933, Brent was in the doghouse
with Warners ... and his wife

5

The Male Garbo

After Brent was suspended by Warner Brothers, Ruth was bewildered by his behavior. He was unhappy, uncommunicative—wouldn't speak to her for days. She attempted to rally friends to cheer him up, but he was anything but cordial when they appeared at the doorstep. Occasionally, he was downright rude. In January 1934, Ruth went to Palm Springs for a month's rest. She suffered from a bad cold as well as a bad marriage. She said she was "richly tired" of Hollywood and all that went with it. In March, accompanied by her mother, Ruth boarded a train for New York.[260] During a stopover in Chicago she issued a statement, "Hollywood gossips seemingly resent married happiness. There is no strife in the Brent household."[261] In private, Ruth had promised herself a week to think things over. She wired George on March 26, saying that a separation was the only solution.[262] By then, George's sister Kathleen had arrived to help him settle into the Town House for a brief stay. When asked, George summed up his feelings thusly: "Two people in the same line of endeavor should not be married."[263]

Temporarily abandoning films, Ruth rekindled her passion for aviation. It proved to be therapeutic, and it significantly redefined her life. Ironically, Brent also took up aviation. He purchased a deep-cream-colored plane with red leather upholstery and began flying lessons to escape his career troubles. Brent told a reporter from Seattle, "I've been flying since 1925, when they were using condemned army crates and you could get a pilot's license with ten hours of soloing. I was playing stock in New England then."[264] "The first time I made a solo flight was the most thrilling moment of my life, bar none!"[265] It would be several months before Brent returned to films. Bette Davis recalled that during his suspension, Brent would pilot his plane over the studio sound stage, circling endlessly. Film crews were unable to shoot. This, no doubt, expedited Brent's return at full salary.[266] By late summer he was back at work, costarring with a kindred spirit: Greta Garbo. She epitomized the word "reclusive." It wasn't long before newshounds began calling George Brent "The Male Garbo."

Before George and Ruth left for Europe in 1933, Warners bought Donald Clarke's torrid novel, *Female*. In New York, the State Supreme Court had declared it "obscene." The content of Clarke's novel had to be thoroughly purged for the screen. Gutting the original story, screenwriters Gene Markey and Kathryn Scola, who had done the screenplay for *Baby Face*, kept only the idea of a woman executive who dallies with the affections of her male employees. Among Pre-Code aficionados, *Female* is considered the best Chatterton-Brent film. In *Female*, Ruth played Alison Drake—an automobile industry magnate. She doesn't mince words when explaining herself to an old school chum, "I'm going to travel the same open road that men have always traveled." Alison is single, all business, and has one hobby. She invites attractive male employees to her home, under the ruse of talking about business matters. Once there, she orders rounds of Russian vodka to fortify their libido—before rewarding them with a complimentary trip to her boudoir. *The New York Times* said *Female* was "produced with a sense of humor. Miss Chatterton acts with the necessary flair for the role. Mr. Brent does quite well."[267] Brent's character,

Jim Thorne, is a young engineer who piques Alison's interest. When she learns that he is a new employee, she tries her regular routine. He rebuffs her with, "I was engaged as an engineer, not a gigolo."

Alison Drake was an unusual character for 1933. She was a woman in a powerful professional role, indulging in routine sexual relationships. When Jim Thorne offers marriage, she refuses. "Don't let's spoil everything," she insists. Sex without matrimony suits her fine. Not until her company is in a financial crisis does she promise to head for the altar, telling Jim that he can resolve the crisis and run the firm. Of course, it's a cop-out that reflects the times. As the trailer for the film promises, "It takes a *real* man to tame this kind of female!" *Film Daily* found the film to be "snappy fun." At the Los Angeles preview, columnist Jimmy Starr

Refusing to be just another Chatterton
boy-toy in *Female* (WB1933)

called *Female* "a smart and sparkling comedy-drama. George Brent is particularly good as the strong, silent lover."[268] In 2000, author/critic Mick LaSalle observed, "Chatterton had not only the sex appeal, but the years, the force, and the brains to pull off such a role."[269]

Three directors worked on *Female*. When William Dieterle took ill, William Wellman completed the necessary exterior shots.[270] Jack Warner was still dissatisfied with one scene. Michael Curtiz re-shot the necessary footage and received sole credit. Brent later recalled that Curtiz was "a nice guy, but difficult to work with. He was a screamer and a shouter."[271] Chatterton-Brent still exude chemistry in their fourth and final screen outing. Within a couple of months after its release, the couple had gone their separate ways both professionally and privately.

It wouldn't be until the fall of 1934 that Ruth obtained an interlocutory decree in her divorce proceedings. She claimed that Brent had been "sulky, unreasonable, and domineering." Her testimony, "I lost twelve pounds the last week we lived together as man and wife," garnered the headline, "Ruth Chatterton, 12 Pounds Lighter, Is Given Divorce."[272] Ruth's secretary, Rita Gray, also took the stand to say, "Miss Chatterton was almost on the verge of a nervous breakdown and it was because of the way that Mr. Brent treated her."[273] One reporter deduced that the "black-haired, hazel-eyed Dublin chap … who was made a movie star by Miss Chatterton, took to domesticity like a bull in a china shop."[274] At least the reporter gave credit where credit was due. Brent's screen career had all but fizzled until Chatterton uttered her famous cry, "Where has *he* been … ?" While Brent referred to Chatterton as "one of the greatest living actresses," he relished being on his own again.[275] "I think any man likes his freedom once in a while," he grinned. "He can read his newspaper at the table; he doesn't have to dress for dinner. . . . *He doesn't have to talk when he gets home from the studio dead tired.*"[276]

During his suspension, Brent questioned the legitimacy of the studio extension clause, and he sued.[277] He lost his case. There had been talk of him returning to the stage. Producer Danny Wells wanted Brent for the male lead in *Biography*, opposite Alice Brady, at the Los Angeles Biltmore. Brent's contract forbade it. He was running low on funds. For his thirtieth birthday, Brent didn't exactly eat cake. He now had a plane to support and told reporters that there was no choice but to "eat crow" and go back to work. "I swallowed enough pride back there to float the Mauritania," he admitted afterward. "Maybe it'll agree with me."[278] Prior to returning to work, he entertained his sister Kathleen. They stepped out for dinner at the Derby and the Friday night fights at the Hollywood Stadium. The siblings also relaxed in Palm Springs. Brent began shooting his next film, *Housewife*, on April 11—seven months after completing *From Headquarters*.

Upon patching things up with Warner Bros., Brent moved from $250 to $1,000 a week, but roles continued to be unrewarding. Although first billed, Brent was highly displeased with *Housewife*. This film disappointment was best described by costar Bette Davis, "Dear God! What a hor-

Housewife (WB 1934) Davis and Brent in the throes of illicit love

ror!"[279] Brent played the spineless husband of Ann Dvorak, a super-effi-
cient wife, who pushes him toward success in the advertising game. She
does this by literally pouring a bottle of wine down his throat and sending
him out into the night to hustle a lucrative contract with a cosmetic mogul.
He succeeds. Brent returns home to announce, "You know honey? I just
discovered tonight what's been the matter with me for years. I don't drink
enough!" Affluence also goes to Brent's head. He rekindles a romance with
a former girlfriend (Davis). He is so distracted by illicit desire that he runs
over his son with the car. The boy survives as does the marriage. *Film Daily*
thought the story "flimsy." "Best work is done by Ann Dvorak as the in-
dustrious wife," said the review.[280] Davis had recently executed a bravura
performance in *Of Human Bondage*. In *Housewife* she swaggers in to do the
obvious. Like Brent, she was highly displeased with her lackluster assignment. In protest, Davis didn't show up the first week of filming. The studio
sent a few hostile telegrams reminding her that she had no choice in the
matter. During retirement, Brent put it bluntly, "Jack Warner used to refer
to us as 'the peons down on the set.' They were ruthless."[281]

It came as a surprise when Warner Bros. sent Brent over to MGM to costar with Myrna Loy in her first solo leading role. Brent was impressed
with what he saw. "At MGM," he recalled, "they didn't make pictures, they
re-made them. They took more time and if there was something about the
picture that wasn't liked, that portion would be re-done as many times
as necessary until it was considered perfect. MGM had style!"[282] His enthusiasm registered on screen. Brent exhibited new buoyancy and his
scenes with Loy are infectious. The script by Herman J. Mankiewicz has
the satirical wit and sophistication one would expect from the Academy
Award-winning scenarist.

In *Stamboul Quest*, Loy played Fräulein Doktor, a real life German spy who was credited with sending Mata Hari to her death. In her memoirs, Loy stated, "The Fräulein was still alive when I played her. She'd become a drug addict, lost her mind, and landed in a Swiss sanatorium." Loy enjoyed working with Brent. "He was a good actor, but rather difficult," she said, "—not difficult with me, but I'd see him asserting his independence from time to time, particularly when they kept changing the script. He did a lot of good work, but never became a really big star." [283] In turn, Brent had praises for Loy. "Myrna is a great scout," he said at the time. "She's human, and she's attractive. There is nothing upstage about her. I think she is beautiful. Add to that a jaunty air, a quick wit, and an authentic ability to act, and you have Myrna."[284] Brent considered *Stamboul Quest* an "outstanding film." He displayed his own authentic "jaunty air" with excellent results. It was an attribute that would be sorely lacking in some of his later work. Brent mentioned that *Stamboul Quest* was shot "on the cuff" (May–June 1934) due to the revised Production Code, effective that July. This may explain Loy's comment about Brent being "rather difficult" regarding the numerous script alterations.

Brent and Myrna Loy made an engaging team in *Stamboul Quest* (MGM 1934). Here with Edward Keane

Stamboul Quest opens with Loy's Fräulein Doktor residing at a Swiss convent. She has a far-off look in her eyes, disengaged from reality. Her story dissolves into flashback, which details her work in counter-espionage during the World War. Brent played a fast-talking American medical businessman who intrudes into the Fräulein's inscrutable world and softens her resistance to love. Initially, Loy is instructed to make sure the American is what he claims to be. She appears at a restaurant where he dines. She is haughty, glamorous, and enticing. Brent is hooked. He introduces himself and invites her to his hotel. "Do I look like a woman who would go to a stranger's room?" she asks. "If you did," he replies, "I wouldn't ask you." While they soak in the atmosphere of his suite, it becomes obvious he wants to make love. Loy is tempted but leaves while Brent retrieves one of the many bottles of champagne conveniently chilling in his bathtub. When Brent finally tracks the Fräulein down, he begs, "Please be glad to see me!" Together, they board a train to Constantinople and engage in more banter provided by Mankiewicz's clever script.

Before long, bombs fly around the Fräulein and her American beau. The attempt to keep her true identity from him is thwarted when he learns of her plans for "dinner until dawn" with a high-ranking Turkish officer. The Fräulein defends the use of her body (sex) as a weapon for war. When Brent attempts to leave without her, she has him arrested. Director Sam Wood does a splendid job as the film makes the transition from light intrigue to more serious matters. The film's climax has Fräulein Doktor duped into thinking she has sent her lover to the firing squad. The realization drives her stark staring mad—a mental state that inevitably places her into the convent where our story began. The original print ended there. MGM decided to soften the blow by having Brent arrive at the sanatorium to rescue the Fräulein.

Critic Norbert Lusk felt that Loy and Brent had never done better work than they did in *Stamboul Quest*. "Mr. Brent gives the most notable performance of his career," said Lusk. "Hitherto rather stolid, he gives a dizzily bright performance."[285] "George Brent was the surprise of the picture," noted another review. "He has never had a part so suitable."[286] *Stamboul Quest* was released prior to *Housewife* and made MGM a nice profit of $235,000.

On June 3, while Brent was shooting *Stamboul Quest*, his thirty-nine-year-old valet, John Kane, was held on suspicion of manslaughter. Kane was driving Brent's large roadster on the wrong side of the road over Cahuenga Pass. Following a collision, the blood-splattered roadster leaped over the curb and plunged fifty feet down a ravine. While Kane suffered only head injuries, a passenger in one of the other two cars was killed. Two weeks later, Charles E. Herbert and his wife sued Brent for $30,635 for injuries and damages.[287] This turn of events didn't surprise Brent. The actor was used to his valet not showing up. "I wait," said Brent, "knowing that sooner or later I'll get a telephone call to come down and bail him out."[288] Kane's saving grace was that he was Irish and devoted to Brent. They had known each other since George Nolan was on stage but separated briefly during Brent's marriage to Chatterton.[289] Brent explained later that Kane had called for him at the studio, but things were behind schedule. He told Kane to come back in an hour. The delay could have well saved Brent's life. Brent's penchant for having only the best money can buy subsided momentarily. He bought a little Ford coupe to replace his unsalvageable luxury car.

Four days after the accident, Brent was once again kept overtime at MGM. He was scheduled to fly with his flying instructor, Bob Riddell. By the time Brent arrived at the landing field, his eyes looked up to follow a silver speck in the sky. He was upset that he had been kept from being at the controls himself. When the plane motor sputtered, George froze in his tracks. He watched as the plane faltered and spun downward. The echo of the plane's impact thundered across the valley. Riddell and his student passenger were killed. "When Bob didn't come back," said Brent grimly, "I decided to give up flying. That crash did scare the hell out of me. It stunned me to know the man I had flown hours with, done loops with, laughed with, shouldn't have made a happy landing. And it made me feel kind of helpless to realize that except for an ironic twist of fate I'd have been in that plane with him."[290] Brent didn't quit. "When it's my time, I'll get it regardless of what I'm doing," he said philosophically. Asked if he was a fatalist, Brent answered, "You have to be if you fly."

Brent's success at MGM didn't change Warners' attitude about his status as a supporting player. He was immediately put into a vehicle designed to make a star out of pale blonde Jean Muir and billed below her. *Desirable* is about a veteran stage star (Verree Teasdale) who prefers to keep the existence of her attractive nineteen-year-old daughter (Muir) a secret, especially from Brent—who she wants for herself. Of this trio, Brent is the easiest to like—he's relaxed, warm, and displays *joie de vivre*. He is protective of the daughter who seems clueless about a lot of things. He becomes her self-appointed watchdog. *Motion Picture Daily* called Muir's performance "triumphant." The critic for the *Chicago Daily Tribune* was less enthusiastic, saying that Muir "invests every moment with a panting earnestness that becomes dreadfully wearing, and does most of her act-ing with her mouth."[291] The review thought Brent easily outshone Muir and added, "I have never liked Mr. Brent better." The Warner campaign to make Muir a star took a nosedive. Brent liked his role in *Desirable*. "It was a romantic lead—much as I dislike them," he said. "But it had comedy and lightness also."[292] Brent liked young Muir. When he wasn't exercis-ing and soaking in the spa at the Hollywood Mineral Baths, they were seen together around town. [293] He even took Muir up in his plane. Gossips hinted romance, but before long Brent was under the spell of Hollywood's reclusive Swede.

In July 1934, MGM paged Brent once again—per the request of Greta Garbo. Brent was apprehensive. "I'm flattered, of course," he admitted. "I'm nervous at the idea of playing with her. I never knew an actor set for a lead with her who wasn't in a panic before starting the picture."[294] *The Painted Veil* by W. Somerset Maugham managed to make adultery both intriguing and understandable. After all, it involved Garbo, darkened temples in China, a fortune teller predicting "radiant happiness and trouble profound," and a million dollar budget. It was exotica with erotic undertones. When Brent tells Garbo, "Why can't we be unhappy together"—as if it were the most wonderful thing in the world—viewers understood. The opening scene establishes Katrin (Garbo) as a restless Austrian on the verge of spinsterhood. When her father's associate Walter Fane (Herbert Marshall) proposes marriage, she sees not romance, but escape and adventure. His medical research is located in China. The newlyweds arrive in Hong Kong where Fane's associates, particularly Jack Townsend (Brent), a diplomatic attaché, acknowledge that Katrin is a "beautiful specimen." While the somber Fane battles a cholera epidemic, the upbeat Townsend offers his undivided attention to Fane's new wife—escorting her to curio shops and social events. Brent's masculine, impetuous charm is on par with Marshall's, but in a different key. The luminous Garbo, as expected, outshines them both.

Garbo and Brent team with compelling results. During a dusk-till-dawn festival celebrating the sun and moon gods, true feelings melt into a passionate embrace. It isn't long before Fane comes home midday to discover his wife's bedroom locked and Townsend's hat lying on a table outside the door. The love triangle is resolved when Fane, smoldering with jealousy, forces Katrin to accompany him inland where the epidemic is rampant. Once there, the film slows down to absorb death and dying closing in on them. Katrin learns to appreciate the full spectrum of her husband's work with those who are suffering. Her affair with Townsend looks small in comparison. She isn't so much redeemed as she is enlightened.

At the preview, audiences complained about the film's length. Brent's polo scenes (for which he did not use a double) were deleted, and some of the opening scenes were re-shot with new cast members (Beulah Bondi, who played Garbo's mother, was replaced by Bodil Rosing). When *The Painted Veil* was finally released, *The New York Times* praised that Garbo was "the most miraculous blend of personality and sheer dramatic talent that the screen has ever known. Mr. Brent, a clever and pleasing actor, makes an agreeable and intelligent chap of the lover."[295] *Modern Screen's* review added, "George Brent enacts the cad and, no offense, gives a thoroughly convincing performance." Brent added a dash of cocky conceit that befitted his character and impressed critics. "I am a heavy of sorts in my picture with Garbo" he stressed. "A heavy with some redeeming qualities. That is better than a straight lead in my opinion."[296] As far as working with Garbo, Brent said, "I got along perfectly with her. I had always felt that the greater the artist, the easier he is to work with. Greta Garbo certainly proved the theory as far as I am concerned."[297] In 1972, Brent told writer Fred Watkins, "Garbo was wonderful. She was the only actress I ever worked with who would stay next to the camera, while the camera was on you and keep reacting to you. Most of the time it was just a stand-in."[298]

While Brent was at MGM, Warner Bros. ran a contest to help select the star for their upcoming production of *Anthony Adverse*. The polls narrowed it down to George Brent, Leslie Howard, and Fredric March.[299] Los Angeles columnist Elizabeth Yeaman thought that Howard had the dreamy sensitiveness, but Brent had "the necessary physique and Irish temperament" that could be adapted to the role. "But is he subtle enough as an actor?" inquired Yeaman. She also noted in her column that Warners had more requests for the loan of Brent than any other actor.[300] His name had become box office thanks to MGM's exploitation of *The Painted Veil*… and a much publicized romance with Garbo.

After completing *The Painted Veil*, Brent relaxed near peaceful, slumbering, Toluca Lake (twelve miles northwest of Los Angeles) where he had purchased a cottage from Charles Farrell. George enjoyed spending his time reading the works of Hemingway and the late Irish nationalist Donn Byrne. He was especially pleased with his work at MGM and invited writer Franc Dillon for an interview. "I don't want to talk too soon," said Brent, "but I'm doing better than I've ever done before. In fact, for the first time since I came to Hollywood, I feel that I'm going places."[301] He walked Dillon around his bachelor pad. Simple furnishings—exquisite taste, comfortable and quiet. "Isn't it peaceful?" he smiled. "It's just for one person. You can see there's not room for two." Dillon dared ask about George marrying again. "If I do," he replied, "I hope someone hits me on the head with a baseball bat."

Brent was in the air every chance he got. He told Dillon that he got a kick out of simply flying down to San Diego for a soda. "You get up there where the air is clean and pure and you take a deep breath and then forget all about the studios and work!" Brent concentrated on saving his money and pointed out, "I have a business manager who collects my checks, pays my bills and allows me twenty-five dollars a week for pocket money. I have to buy my lunches, cigarettes, haircuts, picture shows, pay tips and other incidentals out of that. When I want extras I have to argue." He noted a few extras he had purchased—lamps, pillows, silver and glassware, and the little bar that he had put in. "You've no idea how much those things cost me in lung power," Brent laughed. His one extravagance was his airplane, "Desert Breeze," whose name was painted on the nose in red letters. Brent took Dillon out into the back yard, which edged along

Adulterers Garbo and Brent find
redemption in *The Painted Veil* (MGM 1934)

the rippling waters of the lake. "Isn't this heavenly?" he asked. "This is all I want. Just quiet and peace of mind." It wouldn't be long before George argued with his manager for yet another extra—a huge concrete wall behind the pepper trees surrounding his home. It was designed to keep peeping toms from spying on his most frequent visitor, Greta Garbo.

Garbo & Brent

The simpatico between Garbo and George Brent offscreen became a hot topic while filming *The Painted Veil*. Brent let it be known how adamant he was about maintaining his independence—ruling out romance. "I want more than anything to be completely free," he said, "legally and socially free … to be responsible for nobody but myself." He didn't talk about Garbo, and Garbo didn't talk at all. "It's a great combination," wagged one columnist.[302] Garbo withdrew favor from friends who offered interviews about her. Brent respected this and kept mum. With Garbo, Brent could enjoy companionship, just as he did with his pug dog Whiskey, and not be concerned with matrimony. "Brent's athleticism and introversion were much like—and compatible with—the Swede's," wrote Barry Paris in his well-documented 1995 study, *Garbo*.[303] Garbo would arrive at Brent's home heavily veiled and wearing dark glasses. She moved swiftly, looking neither left nor right before entering his front door. She liked the fact that Brent was a loner, not part of the social scene, and avoided crowds. Together they swam in his pool, canoed on the lake, and enjoyed tennis. Brent, who was a year older than Garbo, was taking lessons from Mushy Callahan, the junior welterweight. Garbo was game for donning gloves for an occasional bout with Brent's punching bag. If they went out to eat it was at the more secluded restaurants. They took drives along the coast highway in George's small coupe and frequently ventured to their favorite retreat in La Quinta—a private desert resort outside of Palm Springs. They were like two happy bachelors, which is how Garbo often described herself. "I will probably remain a bachelor all my life," she once declared.[304]

Sexually ambiguous, Garbo carried an air of androgyny. Her allure went beyond the physical. To what degree passion played into the Garbo-Brent relationship is uncertain. Her most publicized romance since arriving in the United States in 1925 was with costar John Gilbert. Their titillating onscreen ardor catapulted Garbo to stardom. They lived together intermittently. Indeed, Garbo had a way of fascinating both sexes. She had close friendships with women who were avowed lesbians, such as novelist Mercedes de Acosta. In 2005, Garbo's Swedish friend, actress Mimi Pollak, released letters from their sixty years of correspondence. In a 1930 letter, Garbo wrote her saying, "We cannot help our nature, as God has created it. But I have always thought you and I belonged together."[305] When Pollak gave birth to a son a few months later, Garbo cabled that she was "incredibly proud to be a father." During his retirement, Brent simply admitted that he was fascinated by Garbo.

Brent was atypical himself when it came to the opposite sex. "There are so many women in Hollywood that are empty-headed little dolls," he said. "They're pretty; they're fun—if you like that kind of fun. But they don't know anything, they can't talk intelligently about anything except gossip or the latest swing number and I'm not interested in either. I'm not desperate. I'm male, quite normal, with all human appetites and reactions."[306] Brent had previously stated that relationships based on physical attraction created havoc.

Brent's "Great Wall of Garbo" surrounding his residence provided no guarantees. Jack Oakie often visited scenarist Charles Binyon, who lived next door to Brent in Toluca Lake. Binyon informed him that Garbo was next door all the time. "I looked through the tall hedges," recalled Oakie in 1978. "I found myself face to face with that beautiful face as she stared right back at me. I did what any intelligent motion picture 'star' would do: I stood still, opened my mouth and remained silent." On another occasion, Oakie and Mary Brian were rowing across the lake and had to edge along Brent's property in order to dock. "There they were," said Oakie, "George and Garbo—sitting on the water's edge. [They] left as quickly and quietly as they could."[307] Myrna Loy, whose dressing room was right next to Garbo's on the MGM lot, found her to be a puzzlement. "I never knew what to do with her," said Loy. "She never encouraged anybody. In her dressing room she had a secret door put in for quick getaways. She [was] a very scared lady."[308]

Prior to filming *The Painted Veil*, Greta was threatening to return home to Sweden to devote her talent to the legitimate stage and raising potatoes. When it was disclosed that she would stay in Hollywood, everyone assumed it was because of Brent. Newshounds had a field day conjuring up headlines such as, "Ay Tank Ay Stay Here Now" and "Greta Garbo Wants to Be Alone, With George Brent."[309]

Instead of providing Brent a stand-out role after his successful turn at MGM, Warner Bros. put him in a somber affair titled *The Right to Live*. Granted, it was another W. Somerset Maugham story, but the film's central character Maurice Trent, a free-spirited aviator who ends up paraplegic, was given to Colin Clive. Clive's gallantry and neurotic anguish easily stole the show from the other players. Halfway through the film Brent, cast as Maurice's brother, shows up as a successful coffee grower visiting from Brazil. He predictably falls for his brother's wife (Josephine Hutchinson). The already despondent Maurice is pleased—more determined than ever to leave the world graciously. In the original play, Maurice's mother employs euthanasia to resolve her son's problems. On screen, Maurice seals his own doom with a bottle of sleeping pills. In essence, the film was about the right to die. His sacrifice allows his wife and brother to venture to Brazil guilt free. Although bold, frank, and effective, the film did little to boost Brent's career. "Generally speaking," he said at the time, "romantic leads are thankless roles. I am particularly unhappy in them. I flatten out, too stale, unless there is some humorous relief in the part."[310] Colin Clive, who was about to film the horror classic *The Bride of Frankenstein*, had a reputation for creating tension on the set of whatever film he was making. "Colin was a fine actor but he made everyone around him nervous—nervous as hell!" recalled Ian Hunter. When Bette Davis asked Brent his opinion of Clive as a potential suitor, he snickered, "[Colin] is a maniac who might cut your head off some night and plunk it on the icebox!" Davis laughed raucously and replied, "Maybe I'd cut his head off—how do you know?"[311]

Brent was compensated with his own aviator role in *Living On Velvet*. It was the first of three films in a row that he did with Kay Francis, produced between November 1934–April 1935. *Living on Velvet* held to director Frank Borzage's formula—the spirit behind reality. The emotional turmoil of Brent's character, Terry Parker, begins after a plane he is piloting crashes, killing his parents and sister. He becomes aimless and lives recklessly. He tells his friend Gibraltar (Warren William), "I really shouldn't have lived. I really died with them." He sees himself living on borrowed time . . . living on velvet, as he puts it. When Terry meets the attractive Amy Prentiss (Francis) things look promising. After their whirlwind marriage, Amy comes to realize that Terry's demons have a stronger hold on him than she does. "I haven't cured you of your trouble," she tells him. "Why, I haven't even made you happy." She leaves. It is difficult to take pity on either of them, especially after the self-absorbed Terry intentionally crashes his automobile. Amy comes to the rescue again, and her love finally manages to overshadow Terry's troubled past.

The pat, love-cures-all ending didn't please critics. *The New York Times* felt that despite all its bright qualities, the film dwindled "off to an unconvincing and rather meaningless ending." "Mr. Brent's performance is excellent," the review noted. "It is not the fault of the cast that the picture does not merit unqualified praise."[312] In a 1997 issue of *Film Comment*, Kent Jones noted that Borzage would bend plots inside-out to accommodate his view that to find love was to find one's true self. "Few meetings in the cinema," wrote Jones, "are as charged as Brent and Francis locking eyes in *Living on Velvet* . . . it's so forceful that it goes beyond the merely sexual."[313] One possible explanation for the contrived ending involves Warren William's status at Warner Bros. In the original story Brent's character dies, and Gibraltar ends up with Amy. As William's career was on a downslide, the script was revised to favor the Francis-Brent combination. *Variety* concluded that Brent gave "just the right impulsiveness" to his character. "Purely as acting," said the review, "it is commendable." Los Angeles critic Harrison Carroll pointed out Brent's "growing authority as an actor." "He creates a vivid portrait of the flyer," praised Carroll.[314] Francis herself commented, "George is pretty much like that character he played in *Living On Velvet.* There have been so many times in his life when,

Kay Francis tames reckless aviator Brent with love in
Living On Velvet (WB1935)

by all the laws of right and logic, he should have been killed and wasn't. I
think he feels he's living on borrowed time."[315]

After a ten-month idyll with Brent, Garbo still longed to return to
Sweden. According to author Barry Paris, Brent begged her not to go. She
was undeterred. Upon completing Tolstoy's *Anna Karenina* in May 1935,
Garbo departed for her homeland. Brent had his male secretary Carter
Gibson (nephew of director Alfred E. Green) travel east on the same train
to look after Garbo's comfort.[316] She was at ease with Gibson, familiar
with him, as he lived with Brent at Toluca Lake. Garbo was out of Brent's
sight for a year. For a while, she was escorted around Stockholm by the
confirmed bachelor and gay English playwright Noel Coward. News reports predicted an engagement. Behind the back of the press, Garbo and
Coward laughingly referred to each other as "my little bridegroom" and
"my little bride."[317] In the meantime, Brent pined away. At least he had
Gibson. Aside from being secretary, the tall, lanky, bespectacled Gibson
had been Brent's stand-in at Warner Bros. for over three years. The two

flew around together in Brent's plane and shared evening meals.[318] They flew to Agua Caliente for a brief vacation prior to Garbo's departure. Journalist W. Ward Marsh called the Brent-Gibson combination "one of the closest friendships in Hollywood."[319]

When Garbo returned to the U.S. in 1936, her relationship with Brent remained friendly, but changed. Instead of venturing to Toluca Lake, she had a ten-foot fence built around her house. Garbo no longer needed Brent's wall. She had her own. A few years later, Brent matter-of-factly shared his feelings about Garbo. "She has terrific intelligence, a great sense of humor," he told Gladys Hall. "We like a lot of the same things, dislike a lot of the same things—which makes for compatibility. At one time during our friendship, I was in love with her. Very much so. What of it? Nothing to whisper about, that I can see. Nothing strange or extraordinary about it."[320] Besides, with a bachelor like Garbo, no one need hit George over the head with a baseball bat.

1935 releases: (from top) Kay Francis
The Goose and the Gander (WB)
Bette Davis *Front Page Woman* (WB)
Ginger Rogers *In Person* (RKO)

6

Kay, Bette, Ginger, and The California Escadrille

George Brent's gift for buoying the performances of his female co-stars continued to keep his career afloat and in the spotlight. RKO, Paramount, and Columbia requested his services for their leading ladies. Though he frequently costarred with Bette Davis, his work with Kay Francis, the Queen of the Warner lot, proved the most popular. Brent continued to be offered fair roles, but not major ones. In *The Debonairs*, the authors put it thusly, "Through the inducement of periodic salary raises, George obediently acted the role of the well-dressed male prop for the 'sob sisters' of Warner Bros."[321]

The year 1935 began with a proverbial bang for George and Kay Francis. Taking a break from Garbo, Brent offered praises to Francis, and more. On January 4, they were guests on radio's *Hollywood Hotel* to promote the release of *Living On Velvet*. Brent had just flown in from Palm Springs during one of the worst storms of the season. Details of what happened immediately following the broadcast are hinted at in Kay's diaries now held at Wesleyan University. "He told me afterwards that I helped him tremendously," wrote Kay, "and that he appreciated that." Francis then noted there was "Big fucking! And he got the jitters."[322] Brent hopped on his plane and flew right back to Palm Springs. Apparently, there was no repeat performance. A year later, Los Angeles writer Harry Lang commented, "As far as George is concerned, Kay could be a man—because in their friendship there's exactly zero of sex."[323] Shortly after their one-night stand, Kay and George met up again near Lake Arrowhead to shoot *The Goose and the Gander*. Joining them in the cast was the other ex-husband of Ruth Chatterton, Ralph Forbes. Chatterton's exes were still pals and seen lunching together on the set.[324] Forbes, who also had a passion for aviation, had married actress Heather Angel. Occasionally, George would join the couple for one of his rare evenings on the town.

In *The Goose and the Gander* George and Kay meet officially over spilt cocktails at a resort bar. He suggests a peace offering for his clumsiness. "A war might be more exciting," she suggests flirtatiously. Recently divorced from Forbes, Kay has learned that his frivolous new wife (Genevieve Tobin) has planned a romantic fling with Brent. Charles Kenyon's screenplay is a tight bit of froth that has many a chuckle and good ensemble playing. Due to Kay's scheming, George and Genevieve retreat to Kay's cabin home pretending to be man and wife. A madcap plot ensues when two jewel robbers also show up. By the *finis*, George and Kay end up in jail for stealing *her* pearls. Alfred E. Green did a fine job directing the sparkling sixty-five-minute feature. "Gay as Champagne!" cried the ads. Los Angeles critic Jimmy Starr went a bit overboard claiming, "The screen hasn't enjoyed such a delightful farce and marital mix-up since *Private Lives*. What *It Happened One Night* did for Clark Gable ... so will this film bring new praise for George Brent."[325] *The New York Times* gave the marital scramble a thumbs-up saying, "The narrative is so deviously complex that if you stop to light a cigarette . . . it requires five minutes to reorient yourself in its labyrinthine ways."[326]

While filming his next Warner Bros. release, *Stranded*, Brent invited costar Francis and director Borzage to dine with him in Toluca Lake. "Frank Borzage and I went over to his house one night when we were working late," said Kay. "The place is charming; the dinner was delicious and beautifully served. If he were married I don't know how anything could have been improved upon."[327] Francis was adamant that Brent didn't need a woman's refining influence. She had given up on matrimony herself, saying she was a "lousy wife; happy lover."[328] During *Stranded*, Kay and scenarist Delmar Daves became constant companions. "He's a darling," she told her diary on March 16, and a week later, "Christ, he is a good lover. All hell broke loose. He came in his trousers."[329] Daves turned out to be a match "made in heaven" for Kay. He also provided a tight screenplay for *Stranded* with a neat feminist twist.

Stranded is easily the best Francis-Brent offering for 1935. The duo had worked together steadily since November. It allowed for familiarity, enabling them to delve deeper into their roles. Brent felt it helped them to be more relaxed, "just as you are with someone you know well," he explained. "It gives greater ease, and, after all, that is the aim in making pictures—to be at ease and be natural."[330] The result registered in their faces, in reaction shots, and was amplified in every word they had to say. It helped immeasurably that Brent and Francis were completely sold on director Borzage and scenarist Daves. Daves had the ability to develop an uncomplicated narrative and straightforward story around important social issues. *Stranded* takes place in San Francisco where Brent and Francis find themselves building bridges out of steel and human relationships. Francis is the guiding hand for the Traveler's Aid Society (America's oldest non-profit service organization), while Brent is foreman on the Golden Gate Bridge (which was currently under construction). The mutual attraction between the costars is inevitably challenged by their individual world views. Brent disapproves of Francis's social work. "Only weak people need help," he argues. She counters with "I see life in terms of human beings."

Francis embodies a strong-hearted woman directing lost souls. She also deals with gruff customers like Brent, who barges into Traveler's Aid demanding information on one of his missing steel workers. She's direct and blunt, tossing him a pencil to fill in the necessary form. He continues to gripe. She offers him a priceless glare. "Sorry to keep you *waiting*," she says, snatching the form back. When he complains about wasting his time, scenarist Daves provides a remedy to lighten things up. Francis looks at Brent and says, "Boo! I bet my father can lick your father." The romance is propelled forward. They have dinner and he takes her to his job site.

Actual footage of the Golden Gate Bridge was included—capturing the daring heights and dangers workers faced. One dizzy shot shows a crew member light his cigarette with a hot iron rivet. Brent went on location. "I had to fly up the coast for several of the bridge scenes at the Golden Gate," he said. "Being around those gigantic steel towers is exciting in itself. We had real steel workers in some scenes. Someone had to drop a rivet on me from above. They used a real, white hot rivet. I wore a helmet, but they tell me if it had hit flesh or bone that hot rivet would have gone right through."[331] *Stranded* captures the flavor of the times when a racketeer named Sharkey shows up demanding that Brent join The Builders Protection Organization. Brent calls him a professional agitator and asks him to leave. Before long, Sharkey is bribing crew members to pass around alcohol on the job. Brent dismisses those involved, but some workers call him unfair. "It's a hard business," Brent fires back. "If you guys don't like it you can find yourselves a construction job run by a committee of old ladies."

To underscore her sense of purpose, there are scenes showing Francis counseling an unwed mother, the elderly, and the homeless. When Brent asks her to give up the job and marry him, she's offended. "I like my job.

On the set of *Stranded* (WB1935) with scenarist Delmar Daves, Kay Francis, director Frank Borzage and Frankie Darro. (below) Engineer Brent sketches the Golden Gate Bridge while dining with Francis.

It's part of me," she explains. "I want you on a self-respecting fifty-fifty basis. One that's fair to both of us." Brent's male bravado turns ugly. He calls
the people she helps "muck." "You've wasted every hour you've given
them," he tells her. Francis's anger is piqued. She's hurt but hasn't given up
on him. After a tearful farewell she finds herself storming a union meeting
where Brent's crews are organizing a walkout. She's jostled around, forces
her way to the front, points out the agitators and shows that she knows
how to *deliver*. Brent begins to see Francis in a new light. He takes her
aside and opens up. "I told you once that you were wasting your time," he
says. "But tonight you cracked my heart and my eyes wide open."

The Golden Gate Bridge becomes a metaphor for Brent's change of
heart. He sees that their careers complement each other—especially after
Francis comes to his rescue. "You build with steel," she tells him, "and I
try to build with people." This was a reversal of *Living On Velvet*, where
Francis was given the hard-to-swallow line at the film's conclusion, "I'll
be what you want me to be … I'll do what you want me to do."

The Production Code prescribed that women were required to give
up careers for their men. In *Stranded*, Francis was able to continue her
work. Borzage's belief that love redeems those who find it remained intact.
Los Angeles critic Harrison Carroll thought the film "well worth seeing"
and noted the unusual female-male plot line, the "swift give-and-take repartee and the un-stereotyped love scenes." *The New York Times* thought
"The Francis-Brent team … a happy combination." Brent remarked that
he liked Francis playing across from him on screen, because of her fair-
ness and willingness. He believed those qualities gave their work together
a definite allure. "Perhaps you would like to call it alchemy of photography," said Brent. "I have done [four] pictures with Kay, and enjoyed
every one of them."[332] He liked doing *Stranded*—which was adapted from
a story written by fellow aviator Frank Wead. Wead helped promote U.S.
Naval aviation on screen. Brent would star in Wead's military recruitment

booster *Submarine D-1* two years later. In the meantime, Brent, with every good intention, volunteered to command a pseudo-patriotic aviation corps christened:

California Escadrille

Brent enjoyed flying to San Francisco during *Stranded*. "If you don't think that route isn't adventure," he said, "try it. For many miles, you'll see nothing but broken country or steep shoreline beneath you. The only thing you could do would be to bail out." After installing a powerful new motor in "Desert Breeze," he enthusiastically announced being designated as commanding officer for the newly organized California Escadrille/Esquadrille. Brent, who held his own transport pilot's license, negotiated with a local airport to use their facility as headquarters for his legion of young flyers. Escadrille's avowed purpose was to enable airminded males, sixteen and over, to study aeronautics, meteorology, navigation and radio communication for a fraction of the normal cost. Brent enjoyed taking his nephew Patrick up for plane rides in the summer of 1935. Louella Parsons reported that the youngster "loved it!"[333] "Flying is healthful and mentally stimulating," Brent told reporters. "It not only encourages but demands clean living, temperance and the cultivation of quick thinking and resourcefulness. Nothing is a finer influence on the character of growing boys."[334] Brent envisioned the outfit having sky meets around the country.[335]

Brent's position was advised by Captain Gene Tiger of the army reserve. Problems for the new organization immediately surfaced. Applications began pouring in from young women. Brent wanted Escadrille to be strictly for males. One report hinted that he was trying to get "a certain feminine star" known for her aviation skill to take over a woman's corps.[336] Of course, this was ex-wife Ruth Chatterton, who was already making aviation news. She was prepping to sponsor her own highly successful amateur air derby. Chatterton, known for her skill and courage as a pilot, was a good friend of Amelia Earhart. Chatterton had enough political savvy not to associate herself with something like California Escadrille. It soon gained a reputation as just another paramilitary group spouting the "ideals of true Americanism" while "basking in the friendly sunshine radiating from the [conservative] Hearst press."[337]

Escadrille appeared to be a logical undertaking for Brent. Kay Francis commented that he was always fraternizing at the airport whenever he went to Palm Springs. "All his time is spent talking to the pilots, mechanics and their wives," said Francis. "More than once I've caught him buying a baby carriage for some pilot's wife. Do you think when he goes down there between pictures that he rests like normal people do? Oh, no! He went out to the airport once and cleared a runway of about two thousand feet that was all grown up in weeds. When he can't find anything like that to do, he washes his plane. If his plane is clean, he washes someone else's."[338] After a few months, Brent would also wash his hands of California Escadrille.

In a March 1936 issue of *The Student Advocate*, Jeanne Adelman offered her views on organizations designed to promote Americanism, combat radicalism, and shape U.S. foreign policy. She pointed out three such

Pilot Brent in his plane (c. 1935) "Flying demands clean living!" he proclaimed

groups in Hollywood: California Light Horse Brigade led by Victor Mc-Laglen; Hollywood Hussars that Gary Cooper temporarily endorsed; and California Escadrille. Adelman emphasized that Brent's "aviation-minded group never achieved much prominence." An earlier article from the left-wing *Nation* magazine, "Hollywood Plays With Fascism," declared such "fascist units" were designed to counteract the film industry's more liberal groups such as the Writers Guild of America. McLaglen's Brigade warned of the coming Communist menace "and issued instructions on how to red-bait."[339] *Nation* described the Hussars as "armed foolishness." Recruitment focused on male Americans eighteen to forty-five of "excellent character and social and financial standing." Following the *Nation* exposé, Cooper demanded that his name be dropped from Hussars.[340] The American League Against War and Fascism had threatened to boycott his films. In reality, these groups were little more than male bravado drilling in uniform with veteran officers or, as in the case of Escadrille, receiving flying lessons. Brent certainly wasn't out to "save the country." It would be another two years before he became a U.S. citizen. As an active organizer for Escadrille, Brent's last activity (c. August 1935) for the group was "bailing out" of one of their planes onto the flat desert country beyond the San Bernardino Mountains.[341] Brent would wisely wait to implement his skills as an aviator and trainer when the United States entered World War II.

In the summer of 1936, Brent quite suddenly sold his plane. Initially, he said that he wasn't finding enough time to fly. In reality, his decision was based on intuition followed by tragedy. He was never able to shake it from his mind. "I gave up my airplane following a hunch," he later revealed.[342] "I had the hunch someone would get killed in it. There was no tangible reason for such a thought. The motors were perfect. It was a slick job throughout. I'd only flown it 200 miles. But it let me down a couple of times. And that did it. I sold my plane. Two weeks later the fellow I sold it to was killed in it, he and his little girl eight years old."[343]

∞

When Brent costarred again with Bette Davis, she had been elevated to star status. She was entitled to top billing for two consecutive films shot with Brent during May–July 1935. Producer Henry Blanke mentioned that Jack Warner called Brent into his office and gave him the news about Davis. "I'm putting you two in another picture together," said Warner. "Two in a row, in fact. The public likes to see you together. They sense the sexual tension." Brent backed off, replying, "Maybe from her. Not from me."[344] *Photoplay's* Ruth Waterbury recalled that Davis had the continuing hots for Brent. "The chemistry between them onscreen was always exciting," said Waterbury. "But for years it was more on Bette's side than George's. She finally got her reward—reciprocity—but it took her years!"[345]

Playing reporters for two rival newspapers in *Front Page Woman,* Davis sets the tone. "You make me so mad I could spit!" she snaps when Brent chides her for thinking a female had the grit to witness a death penalty electrocution. Brent's notions are confirmed; she collapses on the spot. "I knew that daisy would melt!" smirks another gentleman of the press. Wisecracks spout from all directions while Brent and Davis compete for the next "big scoop" involving a murder. They have an understanding that if she loses she'll marry him. "I'm going to teach the future Mrs. Devlin that a woman's place is in the home!" he puffs. Brent gives Davis bum tips, trying to steer her in the wrong direction. We are led to believe that at the finish Davis still maintains her respect for him. Michael Curtiz directed this far-fetched tale with his trademark craftsmanship. "Another score for the dynamic Miss Davis," observed one New York critic.[346] The *Chicago Daily Tribune* thought Brent to be "at his best." "It's plain to see that Mr. Brent liked both his role and his leading woman and he acts with vim most refreshing to behold."[347] Davis herself summed up the film and the following one with Brent, *Special Agent,* as "stinkers."[348] While her role in the latter is basically a supporting player, the film itself is notches above *Front Page Woman*.

Bette Davis's trademark fire is not evident in *Special Agent*, nor would it have been appropriate. She comes across as instinctive and unaffected. Davis merged with Brent's low-key, natural confidence and contributed to the ensemble spirit of the piece. Director William Keighley had previously filmed the fast-paced crime genre success *G Men* (1935) starring Jimmy Cagney. *Special Agent* easily comes across as the best work of the early Brent-Davis combo. Scenarists Abem Finkel (*Sergeant York*) and Laird Doyle, a former newsman, provide a bold, interesting narrative that never lets up.

Special Agent establishes that the federal government had only one weapon to fight profiteers milking millions from illegal enterprises: tax evasion laws. That's how Al Capone ended up behind bars in 1931. Agent Brent's assignment is to nab racketeer Al Carston (Ricardo Cortez). We witness several vignettes of Cortez's shifty enterprises before entering his domain at the 122 Club—an upscale casino. Steely-eyed Cortez offers

Special Agent (WB1935) Easily the best of
the early Brent-Davis WB films

a sinister portrayal. He knows how to get what he wants and bumps off anybody who gets in his way. Moonlighting as a reporter, Brent's tough nonchalance is perfect—he holds his own with the tough guys, including Cortez, who allows him leeway, to a point. We learn that Brent has also taken an interest in Cortez's blonde accountant and "adding machine" (Davis). Their flirtation is a perfect buffer amid all the tension. They bandy dialogue with natural ease. Another stand out is Jack LaRue as a casino henchman. His slick, dark looks add to the menacing allure of the racket. Near the finish, the District Attorney gives LaRue a thorough grilling, threatening the electric chair. LaRue's breakdown alone is worth the price of admission.

We then witness a young clerk at the D.A.'s office steal LaRue's signed confession and hand it over to Cortez, who offers him ten grand—underscoring America's worship of the almighty dollar. Cortez's blasé confidence is rooted in the shallow character of his countrymen. "You can buy ninety percent of the public at your own price," he says confidently. "The other ten you give the choice of either crawling on their bellies and being live cowards or taking it in the belly and being dead heroes." Cortez goes so far as to sugarcoat his public (like Capone did) by donating heavily to an orphanage—and not for a tax write off. He pays no taxes. The only reason Cortez hired Davis to keep records (in code) was to detect anyone cheating on him.

The climax occurs when Davis, the prime witness for the prosecution, is shoved into an elevator and kidnapped. Although we are obliged to see the fade-out Brent-Davis kiss, the real story is the action, the menace that surrounds them. Most reviews offered their raves to Cortez. Los Angeles critic Jimmy Starr nodded, "Ricardo Cortez is positively outstanding. . . . He gives the part a cool, menacing touch that is absolutely chilling."[349] The Brent-Davis combination continued to please. "George Brent and Bette Davis again call out the cheering section for their team-ship in *Spe-*

cial Agent," praised another review.[350] Harrison Carroll complimented the swift-moving "packs in the punch" film, noting, "Bette Davis contributes her usual sharp delineation. Brent has the right degree of nonchalance."[351] The only person who complained about the Brent-Davis simpatico was her husband, Harmon "Ham" Nelson. According to director Michael Curtiz, at the screening of *Front Page Woman* he had overheard Ham accuse Davis of being too convincing in her attraction to Brent. She argued that she was just doing her job. Ham stomped off hissing "Horseshit!"[352]

When Robert Donat dropped out of Warner Bros.' highly anticipated production of *Captain Blood*, George Brent was the top contender for the role. The tale of an Irish physician who transforms into a swashbuckling pirate would have provided Brent a change of pace. The film's technical advisor, Dwight Franklin, an authority on pirates, thought Brent perfect for the role. However, the makeup test was a fiasco. Makeup genius Perc Westmore was of no help. Frank Westmore recalled, "Every time Perc put a long-haired wig on Brent, the virile actor looked like a beautiful girl. Even a flowing Moses-like beard didn't help; Brent still came across like a woman in pants."[353] Errol Flynn was virtually handed his career when he took over the role. Aside from Cagney and Edward G. Robinson, Brent now had a new competitor on the Warner lot. Flynn leaped to stardom.

Brent's seventh and final release for 1935, a loan-out to RKO, was a screwball comedy with music starring Ginger Rogers. He was a replacement for (of all people) Fred Astaire.[354] *In Person* was based on a novel by Samuel Hopkins Adams, who penned the short story for *It Happened One Night* (1934). While no award winner, *In Person* allowed Rogers to display her gifts as a light comedienne. She played movie star Carol Corliss, who suffers a "Garbo complex"—a morbid fear of being mauled by her legion of fans. She goes so far as to wear buck teeth and a veil so she isn't recognized—a female version of The Elephant Man. Brent played a (non-dancing) professional bird-watcher with just enough sex appeal to provide a therapeutic touch for Corliss's phobias. Ginger and George were better than their heavy-handed material.

In Person opened at Radio City Music Hall in December. Andre Sennwald for The New York Times labeled the film a "Pre-Christmas Turkey." "Mr. Brent," wrote Sennwald, "is gracious and prodigal in contributing his personal magnetism to the photoplay, but his efforts get neither him nor In Person very far." Even so, Rogers's comedic sense along with her musical numbers make the film worth watching. Hermes Pan, who helped choreograph Astaire-Rogers, was on hand, along with some catchy tunes by Oscar Levant and Dorothy Fields. In her memoirs, Rogers wrote, "George Brent was a love and a great straight man, as well as a joy to work with."[355] Brent's praise for his costar was unending. "She has everything it takes to be a top star," said Brent. "Ginger's sense of humor is catching. It lends a whimsical quality to her work. And more than that it makes her a spellbinder with the film unit in which she is working. And she has vivaciousness—all kinds of it." Most importantly, Brent emphasized, "[Ginger's] ability to take care of herself is definitely a part of her attraction for men."[356]

After completing In Person, George flew to New York on a promotional tour for Special Agent. While there, he attended the Max Baer-Joe Louis fight at Yankee Stadium along with 90,000 fans and such notables as J. Edgar Hoover, Ernest Hemingway, George Raft, Ricardo Cortez, and fan dancer Sally Rand. In less than twelve minutes Baer was left a bloody senseless wreck. He retreated to his dressing room yelling for a cigarette. "I've gotta have one now!" he roared. "Bring me a bottle of beer, too!" Ernest Hemingway described the fight as "the most disgusting public spectacle outside of a public hanging" he had ever seen.[357] "Brown Bomber Knocks Out Baer in Fourth Round" read a headline the day Brent hopped to Cleveland for his next personal appearance.[358] It was later revealed that raging hormones had fueled Joe Louis's lethal punches. He was anxious to get home and consummate a relationship with the nineteen-year-old bride he married a couple of hours before the match.[359]

In October, Brent took a break from playing hide-and-seek with Garbo and mixed with other celebrities. He had good reason. His divorce from Ruth Chatterton became absolute and final on October 14.[360] He even managed to talk Chatterton's secretary, Rita Gray, who had served as witness on Miss Chatterton's behalf, to come work for him. Brent turned up at the Shrine Auditorium for Evelyn Laye's performance in Noel Coward's *Bitter Sweet*. A few days later he escorted film star (and Hearst paramour) Marion Davies to the premier of Warner Bros. *A Midsummer Night's Dream*. In November was Countess di Frasso's Thanksgiving buffet dinner party, which was also attended by Kay Francis and Delmar Daves, Claudette Colbert, Virginia Bruce, Merle Oberon, Clark Gable, Charlie Chaplin, and a host of other celebrities. In the long run, Brent still preferred isolation with Garbo. "Going to a show should be a relaxation," he insisted. "Instead, you find yourself besieged by autograph seekers. Often, they are rude. The discomfort of doing these things, publicly, isn't worth it anymore."[361] Later that fall, he purchased a thirteen-acre estate in the San Fernando Valley.[362] Publicity from Garbo's visits had turned his Toluca Lake house into a mandatory stop for sightseers.

On the Warner lot Brent found himself *Snowed Under*, the title of his next film. As author John H. Reid put it, "What a waste of time this tedious programmer turns out to be!"[363] Brent played a playwright who retreats to the mountains to finish a problematic third act. Reid felt the scenarists for *Snowed Under* ran into the same problem. A few nondiscriminating fans may have enjoyed the convoluted plot in which Brent's

Snowed Under (WB1936) with Genevieve Tobin

first ex-wife (Genevieve Tobin) arrives on the scene to help him out, followed by ex-wife number two (Glenda Farrell) who wants alimony. Add
to this mix a schoolgirl (Patricia Ellis) who wants Brent to give her a *real*
education. *The New York Times* reviewer said that only a "strong sense of
duty kept [him] chained to [his] seat." He felt the actors in the "loud, wit-
less and tiresome farce" came across as "so many empty bags belaboring
each other."[364] *Snowed Under* wasted the talents of everyone involved, including reliable trouper Frank McHugh who stole every scene he was in.

Brent didn't fare much better re-teaming with Bette Davis for *The
Golden Arrow*—a Kay Francis reject. Davis regarded the assignment as
an "insult."[365] Neither Davis nor Brent had the ability to pull off screwball
comedy. Biographer Ed Sikov noted that Davis was a very funny lady in
person, "but she never *got* comedy the way Hepburn or Jean Arthur or
Irene Dunne did. She found screwball comedy unbecoming . . . and it
hampered her ability to let loose."[366] A Canadian critic stated the obvious,
"Miss Davis is not as good a comedienne as a tragedienne."[367] Scene after
scene in *The Golden Arrow* is set up for laughs that never come. Cosmetic
heiress Daisy Appleby (Davis) tricks aspiring novelist Johnny Jones

Golden Arrow (WB1936) **Easily the worst of the
Brent-Davis outings**

(Brent) into a marriage in order to discourage fortune hunters. "They all want to marry my money," she explains. Johnny goes along with the idea. Employed as her husband, he'll be able to work on his book. The press has a field day at Johnny's expense. One headline announced: "Johnny to Organize Air Militia – Daisy's Millions to Back Patriotic Venture." This inside joke spoofed Brent's now-abandoned stint with California Escadrille. It was films like *The Golden Arrow* that garnered Brent a reputation for being stodgy and wooden. He walks through the film as if he is on sleeping pills. Even perennial lady extra Bess Flowers, sans dialogue, made a better impression. Aside from the reliable Eugene Pallette, supporting players fail to put any zip into what critics considered a weak script. The film was an embarrassment to both Brent and Davis. It's easily their worst film as a team. It would be two years before they worked together again.

Producer Walter Wanger tried to rescue Brent, costarring him with British actress Madeleine Carroll in her American film debut, *The Case*

Esther Dale and Madeleine Carroll assist a tipsy Brent in
The Case Against Mrs. Ames (Paramount 1936)

Against Mrs. Ames. James Robert Parish thought the Paramount release "one of the most listless productions of the year."[368] William Seiter, who had directed *In Person*, had a way with light romances, but serious screen fare was not his forte. The first half leads us to believe that we are witnessing intense drama revolving around Carroll's purported murder of her husband. Carroll offers her usual contained performance. Brent is less convincing, although the British *Film Weekly* praised, "George Brent is easily the best of the cast."[369] As the prosecutor, he comes across as a smart aleck with obvious disdain for the accused. He's a sore loser, difficult to like, and throws a tantrum following the verdict, which lands him in jail for contempt. Brent's most credible scenes are while he's on a rip-roaring drunk. The scenario inexplicably throws in hokum that falls flat, as when Brent apologizes by bending over to offer Carroll his rump for a good swift kick. Comic relief was a common ploy in films of the '30s. In many instances, as author James Robert Parish points out, it could prove an "obnoxious stumbling block."[370] Nonetheless, the placid beauty of Miss Carroll not only convinced the jury, but most critics of the day.

In retrospect, *The Case of Mrs. Ames* feels like a lost cause. One gets the impression that the film would have been more stimulating had it focused primarily on Carroll, her small boy (Scotty Beckett), and formidable mother-in-law (Beulah Bondi). Carroll found Brent to be "very, very Irish" offscreen. "He can be very gay one minute," she told a British publication, "but depressed the next. I am half-Irish, so I was able to understand him."[371] Brent's stay on the Paramount lot confused one tongue-tied errand boy, who mistakenly introduced Cary Grant to a visitor as George Brent. In true form, Grant apologized with a bashful grin, "I'm sorry to disappoint you. I'd like to be George Brent, but I'm only Cary Grant."[372]

Fortunately, Kay Francis teamed with Brent for the box office success, *Give Me Your Heart.* Based on a popular British play (*Sweet Aloes*), the story focused on an English woman (Francis) forced to give up her child out of wedlock. She is told by Lord Farrington, the blueblood father of her lover (Patrick Knowles), that she doesn't stand on "firm moral ground." Francis embarks on a new life in New York, where she marries an upstanding millionaire attorney (Brent). Unable to shake her past, she becomes mentally unstable—always on edge. Husband Brent remains perplexed. She refuses to talk about her demons and walks out on him emotionally. "Sometimes you wander off in your thoughts to heaven knows where," he tells her quietly. There follows a terrific climactic scene where Brent and Francis unexpectedly mingle with her ex-lover and his wife. As Francis downs double martinis at the bar, a deeply concerned Brent maneuvers behind her, leans in closely, to caution, "Better take it easy." "Why?" she answers defiantly. "You think I'll get drunk and shock the aristocracy?"

Frank Nugent for *The New York Times* thought the film "an affecting, mature and sophisticated drama of mother love and applied psychiatry." He especially liked the face-to-face confrontation between Francis and the woman raising her child. "It is a crackling scene they have contrived," wrote Nugent, commenting on the "pathos and reticence" Francis brought to the proceedings. Nugent added, "George Brent gives to the role of [the] baffled husband a blunt, masculine incomprehension of his wife's turmoil, which is precisely what the part required."[373] It's one of Brent's better performances. Never showy, he embodies the tension and frustration of the disheartened husband. *Variety* felt Brent "far superior" to Patrick Knowles but barbed that the film was chiefly for "women and their handkerchiefs." George and Kay were welcomed to enact scenes for Louella Parson's *Hollywood Hotel*. Francis was at her peak as queen of Warner Bros. and rewarded a new contract at $5,250 a week. Brent's salary and supporting player status remained at a standstill.

Brent told film critic Irene Thirer, "No good actor is an actor first and foremost. Unless a man can be more than that—an all rounded human being—he will not succeed."[374] He also felt the impact of his youthful adventures and having "a past" was beneficial. Brent's intention to be at ease and natural on screen underscored his success. Los Angeles critic W. E. Oliver made an uncanny observation about Brent that would hold true until he quit films altogether. "The unusual thing about this actor," said Oliver, "is that he has kept his place in Hollywood for half a decade without any radical change in his acting style, nor his screen personality, outside the natural improvement any conscientious player achieves through the years. Most other stars have had to change their styles or have slipped out of fame's focus."[375] Oliver failed to observe, however, that Brent had indeed made a radical change for his most recent picture—he had grown a moustache.

A new moustache and a box-office hit with
Kay Francis in *Give Me Your Heart* (WB1936)

Citizen Brent being fingerprinted by
FBI Director J. Edgar Hoover (c. 1937)

7

Citizen Brent

George requested naturalization papers from the Los Angeles Federal Court in August 1934.[376] The following year he declared his intention to become a U.S. Citizen.[377] He didn't relinquish The Irish Free State for another two years. On July 16, 1937, as George Nolan, he appeared at the Bureau of Naturalization to swear in the necessary documents.[378] His witnesses were friend and stand-in Carter Gibson, and secretary, Rita Gray Vallee. In November, Brent was one in a group of 500 who became American citizens. His papers indicated that he was born in Ballinasloe, Ireland, and that his last foreign residence before arriving in the United States in 1921 was Cherbourg—thus confirming that the tramp steamer on which he escaped from England had sojourned to France. His final citizenship papers were granted by Federal Judge William P. James on November 26, 1937.[379] "I never was so happy in my life," the actor was quoted as saying.[380] Earlier that year, Brent, now living at his new residence on Woodman Avenue in Van Nuys, put a hold on his lone-wolf lifestyle. He became a husband for the third time. The marriage didn't last long. Following a messy divorce, he contented himself with onscreen romance in the confinement of his home studio. A Columbia picture, *More Than a Secretary* (1936), had put a temporary damper on Brent's loan-outs.

∽

More Than a Secretary, released in December 1936, had teamed Brent with Jean Arthur, who Robert Osborne calls "the quintessential comedic leading lady."[381] *Variety* pointed out that Brent's comic notions occasionally aped the quirky style of Edward Everett Horton—particularly in reaction shots—with odd results. Granted, he played a "health nut," which was considered fodder for comedy. As the cantankerous editor of *Body and Brain* magazine, Brent's publishing house is a "shrine to health"—at the sound of a bell, staff members hunker down for exercise. Jean Arthur rises to the occasion to play a mousy secretarial school instructor who opts for romance. She leaves her job to take dictation for Brent. It isn't long before she's complaining, "He looks in your eyes to find out the condition of your liver." With Arthur on board, *Body and Brain* achieves nationwide success. Just as the two seem to connect, the script lets them down. Things rapidly lose steam when Brent is distracted by a blonde nitwit named Maisie (Dorothea Kent), who is more irritating than funny. The contrived scenario limps toward a predictable ending. *Film Daily* mentioned that with five scenarists the story "did not seem to jell effectively."[382] The review added, "George Brent acts as if he hadn't been sold on his part." Madcap comedy often fell flat in Brent's hands. "The Brent sparkle is sadly missing," noted a critic for the *Los Angeles Examiner.*

Brent's first release for 1937 was Warner Bros. first feature-length film in luscious Technicolor, *God's Country and the Woman* (filmed before *More Than a Secretary*). Location shooting was near Mt. Saint Helens and Spirit Lake in Washington. Brent flew to Longview in late June 1936 to film "ice jam" scenes with costar Bette Davis, who was a no-show. She protested playing a lady lumberjack. "The heroine," wrote Davis in her autobiography *The Lonely Life,* "was an insufferable bore who scowled while everyone kept yelling 'Timber!' If I never acted again in my life I

More Than a Secretary (Columbia 1936)
with Jean Arthur

was not going to play in *God's Country*."[383] Newcomer Beverly Roberts
was substituted, and Davis went on suspension and fled to England. The
gimmick of Technicolor made the "B" programmer seem better than it
was. Not that the reviews were ecstatic. Frank S. Nugent for *The New York
Times* called it "a hearty melodrama in which a punch on the jaw counts
more than three pages of small talk."[384] For Nugent, the real stars were the
lingering shots of crystal blue lakes, cloud formations, and the big trees
sliding down flumes to pile up in gigantic Technicolor jams. We witness
Brent's transformation from a cosmopolitan playboy to a guy who shows
he's made of sturdier, two-fisted stuff. Apparently, this is what happens in
God's country where, according to Brent's character, "Men are men and
so are the women." He tells this to Beverly Roberts, the spitfire boss of a
lumber camp. She's less than enthusiastic about him, especially after he
kisses her. "Listen," he says, "What kind of woman are you? Aren't you
even curious?"

God's Country and the Woman (1937) **with Beverly Roberts.**
WB first full-length Technicolor release

Brent's big brother (Robert Barrat) is trying to force Roberts to sell. She hires Brent not knowing he is the opposition. Eventually Brent opposes his brother's underhanded methods. Roberts performed just as Bette Davis described the heroine, "an insufferable bore who scowled." Brent's character, propelled by lust, isn't any easier to like. A feminist's nightmare, he is relentless in his pursuit of Roberts. "You're being wasted," he complains. "Look at yourself—a woman trying to be a man. Neither fish nor fowl. It's practically indecent." In the end, Brent takes charge like any good hero, risking his life to create a merger that pleases everyone. As expected, Roberts succumbs to lip rouge and dresses, allowing Brent to take charge of her life. It was straightforward melodrama, and faithful to the popular 1915 novel by James Oliver Curwood.

Warner Bros.' penchant for showing the seamier side of life found Brent cast in the real-life story (and murder trial) of Edith Maxwell, a young school teacher from the hills of Virginia. Maxwell was accused of killing her abusive father on a hot July night in 1935. Reportedly, he was angry and drunk. She arrived home late, and he threatened to whip her. The alleged murder weapon was Edith's high-heeled shoe, but it was more likely an axe. Hearst-controlled news preferred the high-heel angle. The media circus turned Maxwell into a national celebrity during her sensational trial—a champion for a woman's right to protect herself from familial abuse. Aspiring screenwriter Luci Ward began her scenario for *Mountain Justice* in early 1936. Author Sharon Hatfield's 2006 book on the Maxwell case stated that the screenplay was a "bitter denouncement of the 'Appalachian Culture' that Ward had come to view through the warped perspectives" of a yellow press—the unreliable Hearst newspapers.[385]

While filming this saga in September–October 1936, the fate of Edith Maxwell was still undecided. Sentenced to twenty-five years imprisonment she asked for an appeal. It didn't matter to Warner Bros. They already had their story, making sure that Ward's screenplay was altered to avoid lawsuits. Instead of a teacher, the lead would portray a nurse. Bette Davis, originally cast for the role, was still on suspension.[386] The lesser-known Josephine Hutchinson portrayed the abused daughter (renamed Ruth Harkins). Screen heavy Robert Barrat played her brutal father. "I never had a role as mean as this one," Barrat wryly admitted.

Director Michael Curtiz went to extra lengths to make the film look authentic—going so far as to duplicate the crudity of the Wise County, Virginia, courtroom. Elizabeth Hearst, an Appalachian school teacher who worked actively for the release of Edith Maxwell, was hired as technical advisor. Her job was to ensure the accuracy of mountain folk speech and customs—even how to properly chew and spit tobacco. Before the film's release, the studio took further precaution by paying Edith the sum of $1,000 to endorse *Mountain Justice*.[387] Was it worth all the fuss?

On screen, Ruth Harkins wants to sell her one-acre inheritance to

finance a clinic. Her father, who had recently shot a power company employee for "trespassing," forces her to read the Bible instead—a verse
about corrupted children who have forsaken the Lord. Although attorney
Paul Cameron (Brent) gets Ruth to testify against her father in the shooting case, "mountain justice" only serves Harkins a ninety-day sentence.
After his release, Harkins learns that Ruth had been out with Cameron—
the man who got him convicted. He gives his disobedient daughter a relentless thrashing. Things only get worse for Ruth and her pubescent sister (Marcia Mae Jones) until the accidental death of their sadistic father.
During a struggle, Ruth had repeatedly hit him on the head with the blunt
end of his whip. He staggers out onto the front porch and collapses. Local
headlines call her a "Father Slayer!" The film then mirrors the national
hysteria that fueled the case of Edith Maxwell. The media has a field day
during a rip-roaring trial (held outdoors) in which mountain prosecutor
(Robert McWade) declares that holy scripture condones a father's right
to discipline his child.

Brent, as defense attorney, ultimately saves Ruth from the travesty of
hillbilly justice. On the Warner back lot, his anger and resolution during
cross-examination were amplified by three bees that stung him on the
forehead. "The swelling was so pronounced," claimed one report, "that
the company had to lay off for 30 minutes while medication and conceal-
ing makeup were applied."[388] As in the case of Edith Maxwell, the jury
finds Ruth guilty and sentences her to twenty-five years in prison. On
screen, however, it becomes a question as to whether or not Ruth can escape a lynch mob. Townsfolk want to hang her. In real life, Eleanor Roosevelt came to the rescue of Edith Maxwell. After Maxwell served four
years of her sentence at Goochland Penitentiary, Mrs. Roosevelt wrote a
letter on her behalf.[389] Edith received a pardon. She requested to leave the
penitentiary with an assumed name and $10 pocket money.

When Los Angeles critic Harrison Carroll visited the set of *Mountain*

Brent battled bees and director Michael Curtiz on the set of
Mountain Justice (WB1937). Here with Josephine Hutchinson

Justice he remarked, "Brent seems what he is, man from another world."[390]
Film Daily's review agreed that Brent fit "nicely into the part," but that the
film, which could "easily have been a standout as a dramatic thunderbolt
bogs down into the routine Class B specimen."[391] *The New York Times*
agreed, saying, "the film gallops posthaste in all directions and never
really gets anywhere."[392] The script included irrelevant comic relief provided by bumpkin doctor (Guy Kibbee) and his fiancée of twenty years
(Margaret Hamilton). The scenario also opted for a romantic interlude
between Brent and Hutchinson, which felt out of sync with the rest of the
film. While the chemistry between Brent and Hutchinson is tepid, their
performances are commendable. If *Mountain Justice* has a legacy, it is the
riveting portrayal by Robert Barrat as the sanctimonious male, fueled by
precepts of the Old Testament. He embodies the fear, power, and control
of such men and the havoc they wreak in their families' lives.

Columnist Sheilah Graham witnessed a nervous Brent "blow up" his
lines during the shoot—ten times in a row. This was shortly after director

Curtiz screamed reprimands at the children in a carnival scene. Brent admitted to Graham that he disliked making pictures. "The work's too hard," he complained. "I've only had four days off this year. My only excuse is money. I'll have enough in two years to retire and live comfortably for the rest of my life. But I'll keep on working until 1943 when my contract expires."[393] Twelve-year-old Marcia Mae Jones adored Brent, claiming she fell in love with him while filming *Mountain Justice*. "He had that charm and was so real," Jones recalled years afterward. "What a wonderful sense of humor he had. We'd be in the middle of an emotional scene, and he would come up with some joke. Curtiz got so mad at him, he ordered him off the set, because everything to [Curtiz] was a big deal."[394]

Brent's attitude about marriage hadn't changed since he split with Ruth Chatterton. To him it was still a joke. When fellow Warner Bros. players Joan Blondell and Dick Powell walked down the aisle, Brent gifted the actress a copy of *Gone With the Wind*—all 1,037 pages, to take with her on a New York honeymoon. Blondell biographer Matthew Kennedy stated that when Powell ended up in bed "with an ardor-suppressing cold" Brent's little joke was the perfect companion for the lonesome bride.[395] Blondell finished the book before the newlyweds returned home. After completing his next film, *The Go-Getter*, Brent played a joke on himself— he signed along the dotted line for marriage number three.

The Go-Getter is a light comedy directed by Busby Berkeley. Brent played Bill Austin, a sailor who lost his leg during the crash of the U.S. Navy's Macon dirigible in 1935. His diligence and optimism propel him forward. His heart is set on selling lumber. When a lumber executive calls Bill a "cripple" he fires back, "I'm going to sell lumber with my brains not my feet!" His persistence pays off when he's hired by the tough-skinned, soft-hearted Cappy Ricks (Charles Winninger). Cappy sends Bill on a wild goose chase

The Go-Getter (WB1937) Charles Winninger, John Eldredge, and Anita Louise
offer splendid support for Brent in one of his stand-out roles

to sell an overstock of useless skunk spruce—figuring it will test his mettle.
Bill succeeds beyond everyone's wildest expectations. He exemplifies the
old brigade motto "It Shall Be Done." The character of Cappy Ricks was the
popular brainchild of San Francisco author Peter B. Kyne. Delmar Daves's
script updated the 1923 silent version of Kyne's story, with a social con-
science and heart. Daves details the attitude of business tycoons, the manipulation—"every man for himself." This is contrasted with the integrity of
our unlikely hero. Brent's straightforward, sensitive portrayal is especially
winning. He incorporates a limp in such a way that it gives his character
more integrity as a man. And while it adds a sympathetic touch to the proceedings, one never doubts who he is deep inside where it counts.

Before Bill, the "go-getter," marries the boss's daughter Margaret
(Anita Louise), he is ordered to find a specific antique blue cloisonné
vase. A big portion of the film is devoted to this convoluted task, and for
good reason. What seems to be a mean joke by Cappy Ricks only un-

derscores Bill's loyalty and resilience. When he learns the arduous endeavor was a hoax, his spirits sink. Brent melts your heart and provides *The Go-Getter's* most powerful scene. "So, it was a plan … just a joke," he remarks thoughtfully. "I've stood a lot of things in my life, but this tops everything. I guess I can't take it. You see, I was trained to obey orders, not question them. Even when it was impossible. And above all, I've been taught loyalty. I see that means nothing to you." Scenarist Daves maintains your interest just as the shenanigans reach their limits. After Bill marries Margaret and takes over father-in-law Cappy Ricks's company, the symbolic blue cloisonné vase is thrown out the window. "We won't have any more trouble with that thing!" he announces—along with everything it represents: dishonesty, conniving, and debilitation of the human spirit.

If any George Brent film falls into the undiscovered gem category, *The Go-Getter* would be it. The film has a wonderful sense of the fantastic, akin to the spirit of Tom Hanks's *Forrest Gump* (1994). The critic for the *Baltimore Sun* praised, "George Brent drew this Herculean assignment and discharged it with such tact and easy humor that its absurdities are not immediately apparent."[396] The soft, delicate presence of Anita Louise is a perfect match for Brent's character. Charles Winninger came awfully close to stealing every scene he was in and puts the film in his pocket with gusto. *The Go-Getter* manages to be something extra special.

In 1972, Brent commented, "Some [directors] like Busby Berkeley were just hard to get along with."[397] Bolstered by Daves's excellent script, Berkeley gave tempo and style to *The Go-Getter*. Brent's comment may have reflected the personal turmoil that Berkeley was up against. The director was involved in a manslaughter trial after he recklessly sped down Roosevelt Highway, crashing head-on into a car in which two women were killed (September 1935). Witnesses testified there had been liquor on his breath.[398] Berkeley wouldn't be acquitted until 1939. Film historian Michael Barson said "the damage to his psyche may have been irreparable."[399]

Working with Berkeley took its toll. Immediately after the film was completed Brent failed to report to Paramount for a costarring role with Claudette Colbert in *I Met Him in Paris*. The film was two days into production when Brent notified the studio that he preferred to rest in Palm Springs. "George Brent Jilts Paris for Desert" headlined *Variety*. He was quickly replaced by Melvyn Douglas. It further dampened the prospect of Brent's loan-outs. He had already been receiving negative press for his refusal to join Screen Actors Guild (SAG), a requirement for Actors' Equity members on the west coast. Being suspended from Equity was of no real concern to George—he had no plans to return to the stage. Even so, SAG's mission was to stand up for actors' rights, better working conditions, and the "economic fraternity of the star, the freelance player, and the extra." The average annual income for extras at the time was $446.[400] Brent wasn't alone in his lack of cooperation. Rosalind Russell, Lionel Barrymore, Ricardo Cortez, Jack Oakie and a number of other Hollywood players were against unionization. SAG's motto, "He best serves himself who serves others," apparently didn't resonate for some. Brent focused on taking care of himself. He enjoyed his womanless Eden in the San Fernando Valley and his desert oasis twenty miles outside Palm Springs. The only way he could be reached there was by leaving messages at Ralph Bellamy's Racquet Club.[401]

George Shaffer, long-time journalist for the *Chicago Tribune*, had approached Brent on the set of *The Go-Getter* and asked him about Garbo. Brent's tune had changed on the subject. He was, if not exactly forthcoming, more relaxed. He mentioned that they still dined together on occasion; she played a fast game of tennis and covered the court well; and, she liked driving at night with the top of her car down. "I consider her a very, very good friend," said Brent. "Is she in love with you?" braved Shaffer.

"Why don't you ask her that?" smiled Brent, knowing full well the impossibility of such a task.[402] Besides, Brent had new distractions. He had been seen out with costar Anita Louise, but his head was completely turned around the day he met the young Australian actress, Constance Worth.

In the spring of 1937, George and blonde, blue-eyed twenty-five-year-old Constance were seen dining at the Trocadero. "This duet's going strong," observed one savvy gossip. Like Garbo, Miss Worth enjoyed tennis, swimming, and had the added plus of being a good horsewoman. She was contracted to RKO and recently completed *China Passage*. Constance was new to the Los Angeles area. The boat she was on, headed for England, got waylaid due to a shipping strike. She took advantage of the situation for an extended holiday. One evening, she had the good fortune to be a dinner guest at the home of actor Paul Lukas when MGM casting director William Grady suggested she make a screen test. The end result led to an RKO contract, a new name and even longer stay in the U.S. "I had engaged an attorney to arrange an immigration quota-number for me," explained Constance in her faint British accent. "He was also George's attorney. I happened to be at his house one evening, when George, just back from his first vacation [Cuba] in three years, happened to drop in. We met. He saw me home. And—well, that was the beginning."[403] Less than two months later, Brent proposed. Their hasty whirlwind Tijuana marriage on May 10, 1937, was quickly followed by a whirlwind divorce. After five weeks of reported marital bliss at Brent's San Fernando Valley ranch, he sought an annulment.[404] He indicated that he was "tired of it" and had been "pressured."[405] This did not set well with the Australian press, or his new wife, who claimed that Brent "was no gentleman" for making such a statement.[406] Chief Secretary Chaffey, an Australian government official, felt Worth's name had been besmirched and requested that films made by that "despicable man" known as George Brent be banned in the land "down under."[407] Brent aptly summed up the situation as being "a real mess."

May 1937. Newlyweds Constance Worth and George
Brent. Their marriage went sour after ten days

In reality, the relationship of Mr. and Mrs. Brent had turned sour after only two weeks. It wasn't until May 19 that the bride's mother revealed to the press that the two were married. On May 26 Brent disappeared for five days. When Constance asked where he had been, Brent allegedly snapped, "It's none of your business."[408] He said that he wasn't happy and wanted to think things over. The confused bride blocked her groom's bid for an annulment. One report stated that she tore up his pilot's license to keep him from flying. Constance Worth's one-way passage to England and long stopover in Los Angeles was offering her more adventure than she had bargained for.

Constance Worth

Constance Worth was born Joy Howarth August 19, 1911, in Sydney, Australia.[409] She had two older sisters, Gwen and Nance. Her parents were married in 1907. Her father, Moffatt Howarth, became a wealthy banker and owner of a 75,000 acre Australian sheep station. Joy was athletic and had been captain of the tennis team at St. Gabriel's. Her school-ing was completed at Ascham, an exclusive girls' school in Sydney.[410] De-spite her parents' divorce in 1921, Constance was reared in luxury.[411] At sixteen, she attended Miss Dupont's Finishing School in Paris. She was officially introduced to Sydney society and led a typical society girl's exis-tence. Evenings were filled with parties. "I knew Errol Flynn rather well in those days," Constance said. "He was engaged to my best girlfriend." After seeing Constance in an amateur production of *Cynara*, an Australian film director arranged for her film debut in *Squatter's Daughter* (1933). Now billed as Jocelyn Howarth, she made *The Silence of Dean Maitland* (1934), a rather scandalous tale of a clergyman whose steamy affair produces a love child. Jocelyn then headed for Sydney's legitimate stage. "For two years without a holiday, I played leading lady to a succession of guest stars from England," said Constance in a 1937 interview. "I was thin and hag-gard and worn out. I decided I needed a long rest . . . a boat trip to England. I traveled with a friend of mother's, a Mrs. Mackay. We arrived at the Port of Los Angeles for a brief stop-over."[412] After their arrival on April 1, 1936, no ships were allowed to leave the harbor for several months.

Constance Worth was still getting used to her new name when she met Brent. "I had seen him on the screen, of course," she said, "and I liked him. I liked his sense of humor. But I never thought I'd be telling him so. And, after we did start going out, the last thing either of us thought of doing was eloping. The fact that I was going off on location to Cata-lina Island precipitated matters." The couple impulsively drove down to Mexico, got married, and then attempted to return in time for her 6 p.m. departure to Catalina. Joining them was Brent's valet, John Remkus, and his secretary, Rita Gray Vallee, who served as witnesses.[413] "We didn't arrive back in Hollywood until 8 o'clock," said Constance. "Everybody had been waiting for me for hours. I had to say 'Goodbye' to George and rush off." Shortly after her return from Catalina, Constance ended up unconscious in the hospital with an injured hip and paralyzed legs. She had tripped and fallen on a dark sound stage. It took twenty-six hours for the paralysis to subside. She was in the hospital for an extended stay. Back home with Brent, she spent her time in bed and was subject to daily electric lamp treatments. Meanwhile, Brent wanted to keep their married life a secret. Between a week's location shoot on Catalina, several days in the hospital, and Brent's mystery disappearance—exactly how many days did the newlyweds actually live together? At the very most, perhaps ten.

On August 15, Superior Court Judge Charles E. Haas listened to experts on Mexican law who claimed that unless one of the parties is a legal citizen of Mexico, marriages were null and void. While George nonchalantly whispered to his attorney, Constance broke into "hysterical weeping" in the quiet refuge of Judge Haas's chambers. "I asked him if he wanted a divorce," Constance stated upon her return to the witness stand, "and he told me that it was not necessary, as we were not legally married . . . that Tijuana weddings were not worth the paper they were written on."[414] The court disallowed Brent's claim for an annulment, declaring the marriage was performed "in good faith." Constance made several attempts for reconciliation before filing for a divorce. It was finally granted on December 6.[415] "I've had bad luck with marriages," Brent admitted afterward. "Maybe it was my fault. Maybe it was fifty-fifty. I don't know. All I know is that I'm in no hurry to try again."[416] Chastised, Brent retreated once more to his solitary lifestyle and his work.

One thing Constance Worth kept under cover was an unfortunate incident that took place on August 4, 1936, four months after her arrival in Hollywood. Tyrone Power rushed to her apartment after he received a message from the young actress, still known as Jocelyn Howarth, which aroused his suspicion. He found her on the floor of her gas-filled kitchen apartment. After notifying the police, an inhaler squad worked on Jocelyn for an hour before she regained consciousness.[417] It was reported that Jocelyn was despondent because Hollywood hadn't offered her stardom.[418] This obvious suicide attempt indicated there was more going on in her life than a surprise holiday resulting from a shipping strike. By the end of 1936, things turned around. Constance had her RKO contract. She encouraged her mother to visit. In March, Mary Howarth arrived from Australia to offer moral support while her daughter further established a career. How straightforward had Constance been with Brent regarding her emotional traumas? Had RKO changed her name intentionally in order to further distance her from the suicidal Jocelyn Howarth? Following her brief status as Mrs. George Brent (and being awarded $25,000 in a divorce settlement), Constance Worth was marooned for life in the Los Angeles area. At one point she had to get a job as a waitress to make ends meet.[419] Her film career would be limited to small roles and bit parts through the 1940s.

During his marital-divorce ruckus, Brent completed two Warner Bros. releases. And, his films were not banned. An Australian spokesman stated that if they started questioning the character of actors appearing in films "there would probably be no films admitted" into the country.[420] Despite

Submarine D-1 (WB 1937) Brent went on location
to San Diego to escape divorce woes

the emotional turmoil in his personal life, Brent continued to offer solid, professional performances on screen. During his court battles he filmed *Submarine D-1*, a Commander Frank Wead story that focused on modern technology and the marvels of undersea craft. Director Lloyd Bacon and crew filmed on location at a San Diego sub base. The actors seemed incidental—as the title implies, the real star was the submarine. Pat O'Brien was first-billed, but it's the steady guidance of Brent's Lt. Commander Matthews that pulls the submarine and crew toward a suspenseful finish. When the sub unexpectedly sinks, he spits out orders with authority during a big rescue operation. The real highlight was witnessing survival procedures, including the use of a decompression chamber. Added to the mix was an on-shore romance contest between the cocky O'Brien and sweet-faced Wayne Morris for the same girl. Morris takes the opportunity to shine as a rookie who makes the transition from a smart aleck to a responsible shipmate. He gets the girl and Brent gets a submarine competition trophy. "Might even get a few recruits if we are able to believe all we see in this picture," jested one critic.[421] The *San Francisco Chronicle* complained about Pat O'Brien talking out of the corner of his mouth, but complimented Brent, saying, "George Brent is becomingly earnest as the ambitious lieutenant commander."[422] Critics agreed that the romance nonsense weakened the narrative. Consequently, Warner Bros.' attempt to educate the public on submarines felt overlong.

Brent completed *Submarine D-1*, then immediately began wardrobe and makeup tests for *Gold Is Where You Find It*. Cast and crew traveled in streams of limousines to Weaverville in Northern California for location shooting near an old hydraulic mine. The film had historical significance as it documented the clash between unscrupulous, gold-hungry San Francisco financiers and Sacramento Valley pioneers who depended on wheat farms for sustenance. The mining of California gold 1880s-style was recreated by using giant pumps to blast river water onto hillsides and into sluice runs. This time-consuming undertaking tested the patience of director Michael Curtiz, who bellowed at carpenters through his bullhorn. Technicolor crews and their cumbersome equipment also proved problematic. Curtiz's young stepson, John Meredyth Lucas (script clerk), recalled the impatient director cursing, "Hey, Technicolor bums! When you write your memoirs, tell them how goddamn slow you work." Lucas befriended Brent during the shoot and remarked, "It is strange what a calm and easygoing guy [Brent] was considering he had been in a very rough section of the IRA as a teenager. He was also a licensed pilot at a time when such was rare. I was worshipfully impressed."[423]

Filming another Technicolor epic took its toll on George. Columnist Sidney Skolsky talked to Brent, who had to bathe his bright red eyes between scenes. George admitted to Skolsky that he preferred ordinary black and white films due to the intense Technicolor lighting. As a result, *Gold Is Where You Find It* offered Brent few close-ups. Playing an educated engineer of a controversial mine operation, Brent's eyes are easily opened by the lovely Olivia de Havilland. Her lifelong connection to the farmlands runs deep. The two fall in love while talking about apples and irrigation. Her father (Claude Rains) is the feudal leader of the ranchers and represents them before the State Supreme Court. He succeeds in getting an injunction on hydraulic mining. Inevitably, the injunction leads to a climactic battle between the miners and farmers. The tension is resolved by a spectacular dam burst instigated by Brent and a few sticks of dynamite. Unlike the film's contrived prologue, the epilogue, enhanced by Brent's mellifluous voice, has substance. He predicts a future filled with *real* gold: wheat, grain, apples, and grapes—rich harvests that reach the far corners of the earth, benefiting not just a select few, but everyone.

New York critic, Frank S. Nugent, balked at the misuse of Technicolor to detail the devastation created by hydraulic floods: spoiled crops and collapsing homes. Nugent described the melodrama as "a story of ugliness,

"She was a bit shy ... but she was beautiful to look at," said Brent of co-star
Olivia de Havilland—seen here in *Gold is Where You Find It* (WB1938)

greed and mud. Technicolor's roseate approach is as indecorous as a May-
pole dance at a funeral."[424] Black-and-white cinematography would have
better served the stark realities and environmental issues in *Gold Is Where
You Find It*—unusual cinematic fare for 1938. Unfortunately, the romance
between Brent and de Havilland falls short, failing to generate the intimacy
one would expect. It's partially the fault of the script and camerawork, which
do little to enhance the relationship. Reviews were generally favorable, such
as *Time* magazine's assessment: "Like most Warner pictures, *Gold Is Where
You Find It* contains capsules of information for the curious, sugarplums for
the romantics, action for the whistle-and-stomp addicts."[425] In 1969, film
historian William K. Everson called the film "off-beat and sluggish."[426]

Although *Gold is Where You Find It* made a $240,000 profit, it was missing something—a charismatic leading man with spark, like Errol Flynn. Brent's low-key charm and appeal generated less voltage. He had the look for the role, but as critic Harlan Fisk put it, "Mr. Brent is not outstanding, but his physique is appropriate."[427] Brent seemed to lack the larger-than-life ingredient to shoulder a Technicolor epic. Fisk felt the "strong personality" of Claude Rains kept the story (and the film) in check. *Photoplay* gave acting honors to Rains, de Havilland, and Tim Holt (who played Rains's wastrel son), but no mention of Brent. Studio chief Jack Warner was so impressed with Curtiz's direction and handling of Technicolor that he put him immediately to work directing Errol Flynn in *The Adventures of Robin Hood.* The chemistry between Flynn and his Maid Marian (Olivia de Havilland) was tangible. Flynn had the requisite magnetism. "I didn't want to be in *Robin Hood* very much," Olivia recalled years later. "They decided to test me with Errol Flynn and after that there was no question. I got the part and was simply thrilled when the news came on the lot while I was making, ironically, *Gold Is Where You Find It*."[428]

Minna Wallis, the older sister of Warner Bros. producer Hal B. Wallis, was Brent's long-time agent. She was devoted to her clients, known for her hustle, and had the legacy of establishing Clark Gable's career. She had also guided Myrna Loy toward stardom. Loy said that Gable, Brent, and Errol Flynn were known as "Minna's boys." Throughout his career Brent accompanied Minna, a single, middle-aged woman, to various social events. They could just as well be seen eating up sandwiches at the Racquet Club in Palm Springs as hobnobbing together at a swank party in Beverly Hills. Typically, there is as much talk of them being lovers as there is about Minna being a lesbian. More importantly, Minna Wallis was a significant anchor for Brent. Fortunately, 1938–'39 would find star, agent, and producer Hal B. Wallis basking in the success of what are now considered Brent's best screen roles.

December 31, 1944 – Brent seated next to his agent Minna Wallis at an air show. At his right are Jack Benny and wife Mary Livingston

Honor-bound gents Henry Fonda and George Brent assist Bette Davis in winning her second Academy Award in *Jezebel* (WB1938)

8

Hot-Headed Gentleman of Honor

Bette Davis's long suspension at Warner Bros. ultimately paid off. She returned from England, having lost the battle in a breach-of-contract suit, but landing a major success with her role in *Marked Woman* (1937). When *Jezebel* (1938) was released it solidified her new status as Queen of Warner Bros. and placed a second Oscar in her deserving hands. It was Brent's good fortune to be cast in the handsomely produced *Jezebel*. Playing a Southern hot-headed gentleman of honor he scored one of his best performances. Two more successes for the Davis-Brent team, *Dark Victory* and *The Old Maid*, soon followed. As the decade came to a close, Brent's career reached its peak.

Taking a sabbatical from matrimony, Brent continued to pal around with Garbo. He enjoyed an occasional flirtation, such as the one he shared with the lovely songbird Alice Faye. In the summer of 1937, Alice was also avoiding serious romance. While Brent battled Constance Worth, Alice cooled her relationship with singer Tony Martin. Martin seemed more concerned about his mother's feelings than Alice's. In his autobiography, Martin recalled, "I heard [Alice] was dating George Brent, who was pretty stiff competition. I got panicky. What if I lost her? I never met the man, but I sure was jealous of him."[429] Columnist Harry Lang confirmed that "Alice was not altogether cold to the charms of George Brent. Alice got a bit bothered about George. Tony sensed it."[430] To compound matters, Martin found himself doing Brent an unexpected favor. He was shopping at Oviatt's, a fine men's clothing store, when the proprietor asked Martin if he would assist Garbo in selecting a cashmere overcoat for Brent. "I didn't feel much like doing a favor for George Brent," said Martin, "but I wasn't about to turn down a chance to meet Garbo." Alice and Tony patched things up and wed over Labor Day weekend. Brent's next serious attachment would be in the arms of Bette Davis.

Brent recognized that he had responsibilities to himself as well as to other players. "My job is being an actor—a salesman of emotion," he stated. "I must put my last bit of energy and imagination into the part I am playing. An actor can't let down for a second in any scene.[431] Brent's role in *Jezebel* gave him ample opportunity to sell emotion. The craftsmanship of director William Wyler allowed the actor to dig deeper into his role than usual. Wyler cautioned Bette Davis against using her trademark mannerisms. Davis recalled Wyler screaming at her, "Do you want me to put a chain around your neck? Stop moving your head!"[432] The fact that Davis and Wyler were having an intense love affair during the filming of *Jezebel* no doubt encouraged her ability to pay attention. "He was the only man strong enough to control me," said Davis. "I adored him."[433] Not that there wasn't a battle of wills. Davis would initially ignore Wyler's exacting methods, but after dozens of takes she would finally relent, admitting he was right.

Jezebel took place in the antebellum South during the 1850s. Davis, as the strong-willed Miss Julie, challenges social conventions, wreaking havoc in the lives of those who surround her. She creates a scandal by wearing a red satin dress in lieu of the customary white to the Olympus Ball. In so doing, she loses the respect of Preston Dillard (Henry Fonda), the man she loves. He breaks their engagement and heads north. Brent was Miss Julie's spurned admirer Buck Cantrell. Even though he has lost at love, he arranges a duel upon overhearing her name slandered in a New Orleans barroom. He tells his challenger, "I somehow don't like your hat and your ears, or anything in-between them." Brent convinces us that this is the kind of thing that honor-bound gentlemen are prone to say.

When Preston returns from up north with his Yankee wife, Miss Julie is determined to get him back. She toys with Buck's affections to make Preston jealous. Her family is perpetually aghast at her behavior, particularly her Aunt Belle (Fay Bainter), who warns her with the intimation, "I'm thinking of a woman named Jezebel who did evil in the sight of God." Miss Julie's wily behavior provokes Buck into a second duel in which he is killed. Before his demise, Brent makes a lasting impression. His ability to sustain the confident, arrogant edge of Cantrell and his ilk is impeccable. The film ends with Fonda's character falling to the scourge of yellow fever. The repentant Miss Julie begs his wife to allow her to accompany him to a quarantined leper colony . . . and inevitable doom.

Davis exudes an exhausting amount of energy in making her conniving Jezebel come to life. By the time filming wrapped, her physician warned Jack Warner that she was in danger of collapse.[434] George Brent, using a soft Southern slur, makes his performance look effortless. His Buck Cantrell is chivalrous, loyal to custom, and clueless as to how he's being manipulated. As writer Fred Watkins later pointed out, "Some of Brent's best scenes had a mature naturalness beyond his previous work."[435] Miss Julie was perfect fodder for Davis. However, she plays her greedy, needy character with such conviction that it is difficult to believe that the "redeemed" woman she wants to become is nothing more than another manipulation of her inner Jezebel. Some felt Davis's unsparing portrayal to be overdrawn.

Originally a 1933 Broadway play, *Jezebel* lasted thirty-two performances in the hands of Miriam Hopkins. Ruth Chatterton had dickered with Warner Bros. to play Miss Julie in 1935. Fortunately, the studio waited for Wyler's version, which was nominated for five Academy Awards including Best Picture. Davis and Fay Bainter won for Best Actress and Best Supporting Actress, respectively. Los Angeles critic Jimmy Starr raved about Davis, saying that "There isn't a moment that she is on the screen that she isn't entirely histrionically fascinating."[436] Frank S. Nugent for *The New York Times* wasn't as impressed. He felt Miss Julie's attempt to redeem herself at the film's finish "fairly painful" to watch. "*Jezebel* would have been considerably more effective," said Nugent, "if its heroine had remained unregenerate to the end. Once you refuse to accept its heroine, you see the picture dangling."[437] *Nation* magazine praised, "George Brent as the hot-headed gentleman of honor cuts an excellent figure."[438] *Variety* said he offered "the most virile characterization in the picture."[439] The *Chicago Daily Tribune* thought Brent "excellent in a not very sympathetic role."[440] Overlooked was Eddie Anderson's capable, unstereotyped Uncle Cato, the slave who helps Miss Julie cross the quarantine line into plague-ridden New Orleans. With only a few lines he brings certain depth and dimension to Cato. Anderson also managed to keep his sense of humor on the antebellum set. When Davis balked at joining him inside a tiny boat surrounded by muddy swamp water, she asked, "You know anything about boats?" "Why Miss Davis," replied Anderson reassuringly, "I played Noah in *The Green Pastures*."[441]

Comparisons between *Jezebel* and the upcoming Selznick production of *Gone With the Wind* were inevitable. Critic Philip Scheuer's review exclaimed, "The real surprise is George Brent's Buck Cantrell—or should I have said Rhett Butler?"[442] According to Bette Davis, Jack Warner had an option on *Gone With the Wind* before she went on suspension. "I can't have too many regrets about Scarlett," said Davis, "because it was my own fault in the first place. When [Warner] begged me not to walk out because he'd optioned some Southern novel with a marvelous role for me, I wasn't impressed. I asked him what it was, and he said the book was called *Gone With the Wind*. I said, 'I'll bet that's a pip' and went straight to England."[443]

While *Jezebel* was in production Louella Parsons reported that Brent played Thanksgiving host to needy children. He had a standing invitation with the San Fernando Valley orphan home to entertain ten children at his home on both Thanksgiving and Christmas Day.[444] Brent also came to the rescue of Kay Francis. She had unsuccessfully battled Jack Warner after he refused to cast her in the sophisticated comedy *Tovarich*. Kay took legal action to dissolve her contract. To everyone's surprise she dropped the suit. Rumor had it that she was being blackmailed. In a 1937 popular-

Secrets of an Actress (WB 1938) with Kay Francis

ity poll, Kay and Errol Flynn were the only two Warner stars that made it into the top twenty. It didn't matter to Warner. He was out for blood. "They moved Kay Francis down to the 'B' lot," Brent commented years later. "That was the ploy they used when trying to get rid of someone."[445] As James Robert Parish put it, "The public [was] forced to sit on the sidelines as Francis's film career was fed down the proverbial drain."[446]

Brent joined Francis in the lackluster, if mildly diverting, *Lovely Lady*. Although completed in March 1938, it remained on the shelf until its September release as *Secrets of an Actress*. *Variety* observed, "It involved no secret other than why it was made." Elegantly gowned as usual, Francis managed to utilize her natural sophistication playing Fay Compton, an actress who wants a chance on Broadway. Brent and Ian Hunter play architects who vie for her affections while backing her play. The threadbare love triangle elicited comments from critics who called it "innocuous," "boresome," "old hat," "dull and uninspired." Glenn C. Pullen for *The Cleveland Plain Dealer* found Brent "listless," Francis "synthetic," and *Secrets of an Actress* one of "the season's ripest pieces of tripe."[447] Brent, while surefooted and competent, failed to give his character much spark. The script didn't help matters. Warner historian Clive Hirschhorn noted, "It took three writers to devise a screenplay that director William Keighley was unable to rescue."[448] The scenarists did manage to sneak in a reference to Brent's biggest stage hit. Francis tries to convince him that her play could be another *Abie's Irish Rose*. Brent argues, "An *Abie's Irish Rose* comes along once in how many years?" Despite his misgivings her play's a hit, but *Secrets of an Actress* fizzled. Some theater owners complained that they had more walkouts than usual. The Francis-Brent chemistry was still there. Too bad the film was a less-than-satisfying finish for the popular screen team.

∞

**Humphrey Bogart was top-billed
over Brent in *Racket Busters* (WB 1938)**

Humphrey Bogart took top billing in Brent's next assignment, *Racket Busters*. Brent had the lion's share of screen time and was the film's central character—a scrappy, hard-nosed trucker who, while on good terms with his local union, believed he could look out for himself. That is, until Bogart and his slick racketeers muscle in. If being billed below Bogart bothered him, Brent didn't mention it. *Racket Busters* was a fast-paced exposé based on recent racket trials in New York. District Attorney Thomas Dewey's successful fight had broken the gangster hold on truckers and labor unions. Dewey's onscreen look-alike, Walter Abel, played a similar character in *Racket Busters*. Scenarist Robert Rossen, who would later direct *All the King's Men* (1949), and Leonardo Bercovici created a treatment from trial transcripts, detailing the bribery, extortion, and murder exposed by Dewey's campaign. At the time, Rossen and Bercovici were members of the American Communist Party, anti-fascist, and dedicated to social causes. Consequently, *Racket Busters* leaned towards collective action and concerns of the proletariat rather than a fact-based crime drama.

"I got plans. Nothin's gonna to stop me!" Bogart snarls to his stooges as the story gets underway. Walter Abel is just as determined to force frightened witnesses to testify against the racket or be held in contempt. We also get up-close-and-personal with the truckers themselves. Brent and his partner (Allen Jenkins) are union members, but Brent doesn't expect much. "Oh, don't give me that stick together stuff," he tells his union buddies. "I've been around too long. It's every man for himself." He comes across as a regular guy who is more concerned about his pregnant wife. Even so, Brent seems lost in a role that Cagney would have reveled in. As the racket zeroes in on Brent we find him begging Jenkins for help. He gets his lines out, but there's no emotional force or pause for effect. It's an important scene. As a result, the viewer remains distant, less prone to empathize. When they come face-to-face, Bogart stares right through Brent and smirks, "I don't want to keep having to knock you guys off but you're forcing me to."

Brent was no hero. He gives in to the racket. Although he becomes pro-union and comes to the rescue by the finish—nearly choking Bogart to death in a climatic fistfight—his retaliation comes only after his pal Jenkins is shot. Brent is basically unworthy of trust. As "unofficial leader" of the truckers, his wavering character was not up to the task. Some critics insisted Brent, the actor, wasn't up to the task.

New York critic Bosley Crowther graded Brent's dramatic range in *Racket Busters* as "infinitesimal." Much as he may have tried, Brent's emotions remained on the surface. Crowther felt the ploy of shifting heroic emphasis upon Brent's "awkward shoulders" at the finish was "neither credible nor just." "With the exception of Mr. Brent," said Crowther, "the cast is excellent. Humphrey Bogart as the boss of the rackets is tops, as usual."[449] It was the character actors who came across as authentic: Allen Jenkins playing a real person for once instead of an attitude; Elliott Sullivan as a brain-battered trucker; Fay Helm as his concerned wife; Oscar O'Shea as "Pop," the old-timer who speaks up for the truckers until the racket snuffs him out. The critic for the *Syracuse Journal* complimented the melodramatic tinge of Lloyd Bacon's direction and found the film "timely, truthful and instructive." Brutality, riots, and reform were the main attraction in *Racket Busters*, while cast members dodged bullets, bombs, and subpoenas. Over the next few decades, independent truckers such as Brent's character became so over-regulated by corporate influences in Washington, D.C., that the trade was seldom cost effective. Along with fuel prices, "racketeering" had acquired a new face.

Shot on location in Florida, *Wings of the Navy* focused on turning raw recruits into flying cadets at Pensacola Naval Air Training station. The government provided planes, ground crews, and exhibitions showing the

Wings of the Navy (WB 1939) with Olivia de Havilland and John Payne

discipline of formation bombing and combat flying. *The New York Times* commented, "All in all, the educational part is so interesting that we return to the romantic part—in which Olivia de Havilland switches her affections from George Brent to John Payne with a feeling almost akin to pain."[450] The actors' love triangle seemed incidental to Elmer Dyer's aerial photography. The *National Aeronautics* magazine enthused, "By far the better of the aviation films to flash on the screens lately is *Wings of the Navy*—with just enough of the breathtaking stuff to make it enjoyable."[451] Brent wasn't allowed to do his own stunts. Stunt fliers Paul Mantz and Frank Clarke did the beautifully executed risky stuff. "When a producer really wants to put on a show, like *Wings of the* Navy," said Mantz, "and can show the authorities that he's not maligning the service or not preaching pacifism, he can get the use of Government equipment and cooperation."[452] Consequently, the film had considerable propaganda value.

Brent's matter-of-fact approach to his role is effective. Especially when he argues that his young brother Payne has no business performing a death-defying high-velocity power dive. The friendly onscreen rivalry between the two culminates with Payne, the shining hero, defying his brother's wishes. In turn, Brent sacrifices his love for Olivia de Havilland, who really loves Payne anyway. Brent does a believable, graceful job of telling de Havilland that she belongs with his younger brother. The offscreen competition between Brent and Payne was the reverse. Brent, an avid tennis player, defeated Payne in the *Wings of the Navy* tennis competition: 6-4, 4-6, 7-5.[453]

During production, Louella Parsons reported that Brent would join Errol Flynn in a new version of *The Dawn Patrol* to be directed by Edmund Goulding. As Brent was three weeks on location for *Wings of the Navy*, followed by another week at the San Diego air base, he was dropped from the cast. In October however, he had the good fortune to join Goulding and Bette Davis for the powerful drama *Dark Victory*. After reading the script, he waxed enthusiastic. Brent told Davis that he was less than happy about the three films that had followed *Jezebel*. "I believe in this one," he cheered.[454]

The Bette Davis-William Wyler affair had burned out by the time filming began on *Dark Victory*. Davis had recently separated from her husband. Brent was unattached. Her longtime crush on the actor was finally reciprocated. Davis was now roosting in the gorgeous Kay Francis bungalow on the Warner lot (Francis had taken her final bow at the studio). Bette often ate and slept there during the filming of *Dark Victory*, while concentrating on how she would feel if she had six months to live, which was exactly the challenge her onscreen character, Judith Traherne, faced. When reporter Gladys Hall asked Davis how she would react if such a fate was her own, Davis went into a rage. "I would resent it horribly," Davis answered. "I'd scream, 'Why should this happen to *me*?' I'd go crazy, wild, mad! I'd try to forget by any means I could lay my frantic hands to—drinking, love affairs . . . anything to dull the edges of the essential nightmare." Coupled with her offscreen love affair with Brent and his onscreen bedside manner as her doctor, Davis was fortunate to pitch her portrayal in a less fervid key. Davis biographer Ed Sikov noted that "the actress in her won out." "In *Dark Victory*," said Sikov, "she plays her character's impending death much more delicately. Many years later, with the critical distance afforded by age and experience, she called Judith Traherne 'my favorite—and the public's favorite—part I have ever played.' "[455]

Brent echoed Davis's sentiments. "You have to admit that was a damn good picture," he reflected years later. "It had a good script; something clicked. Bette was a professional. She always knew her lines, her blocking, and how to play a scene. It's a pleasure to work with someone like that."[456] As far as the Davis temperament, Brent declared, "I worked well with her and had no difficulties. I don't mind temperament if an actress has talent and can deliver."[457] *Dark Victory* had failed on Broadway with Tallulah Bankhead as the flighty, stricken heiress. It took the combination of Davis, producer David Lewis, and director Goulding to convince Jack Warner to buy the property. Warner balked at why anyone would want to watch "a picture about a girl who dies."[458] Goulding himself had great admiration for Casey Robinson's sensible script of an implausible story. "Miss Davis and George Brent … felt the same way about it," said Goulding. "And I needn't add that such unanimity of opinion is rather rare in Hollywood."[459] Goulding cued his actors with the idea that death in *Dark Victory* evolved into something beautiful and constructive. "It is as she faces death that Judith learns how to live," he emphasized.[460]

Brent's enthusiasm for the project was coupled with anxiety. Scenarist Robinson had pushed for Spencer Tracy to play Judith's physician, Dr. Steele, but Tracy was unavailable. Brent flubbed up more than once on the first day. Bette Davis and reporter Jack Wade sat on the sidelines while George Brent struggled through the opening-day jitters. Brent excused himself after several disheartening breaks before the camera. He walked off the set to his chair, and sat there, alone and mad at himself.[461] Davis went over to encourage Brent using his pet name. "I wanted to see you at the starting post of this one, Brentie," she told him. "Frederick Steele, M.D. is going to do great things for you."[462] Two days later, Davis returned to the studio for her first scenes with Brent. They were now doctor and patient—moods shifted subtly and often. Goulding told them to go easy and slow the tempo when Judith tries to convince the doctor and herself that nothing could touch her. "You can't make an invalid out of me. I won't let you!" she declares. "That's right," Steele replies, "run away. Run away because you're frightened." Goulding cautioned the costars that the scene was the keynote for everything that followed.

Initially, Brent's Dr. Steele scoffs at the idea of taking on the problems of the idle rich, especially a spoiled, out-of-control, high-strung social butterfly like Judith. Brent does a convincing job. He exhibits the appropriate analytical mind as he listens and observes. A perpetual bundle of nerves, Davis's character is not easy to like. Ultimately, it takes a tumor to put her out of her misery.

Davis was on edge herself during filming. She was preoccupied with divorce proceedings and wondered if she should quit and be replaced. Brent reassured her, "You won't crack. You have too much vitality. Too much pride."[463] When she complained that she was "sick" to Hal Wallis, the formidable producer had seen the rushes, and replied, "Stay sick."[464] The day her divorce was granted (November 22) Brent knew how shaken she was. They were shooting the scene where Judith tells Dr. Steele that she is giving up her undisciplined ways and . . . that she loves him. She wants to make the rest of her life count. "Where is peace?" she implores. The actor and friend answered with warmth and understanding, "Within yourself." When the script called for tears, Davis wept for herself. "Davis was ashamed and horrified," said writer Adele Whitely Fletcher. "She asked that the company be dismissed."[465] Lawrence J. Quirk's biography on Davis detailed,

> *George Brent did his bit offscreen as well as on. During the shooting of Dark Victory, Davis won a prize she had sought for six years—a reciprocation of Brent's feelings. The deep sympathy and concern that he came to feel for Davis as he watched her offscreen disasters accumulate broadened into a love for her that eventually became sexual as well. The two became lovers. The soothing romantic and physical addresses from a man she had always felt deeply for, acted out night after night … gave Davis an emotional release and sensual catharsis that added greatly to her portrayal of Judith.[466]*

The five-week shoot turned into ten before filming was completed. No one complained. Warner Bros. were confident they had something special. In author Bernard F. Dick's treatise on the film, he writes, "Apparently [Davis's] affair (or romance as she calls it in *The Lonely Life*) with George Brent, made her less despondent; it certainly made Brent less stolid."[467] In her 1987 reminiscences, *This 'N That*, Davis graciously acknowledged, "[Brent's] performance as the doctor in *Dark Victory* was superb. It made the film a far better one than it would have been without him."[468] Davis knew that Brent had helped her get through her own personal problems as well as *Dark Victory*—"One of the few men who gave me something besides himself," she admitted.[469] For over a year Brent became her shoulder to lean on, and she was forever grateful.

Brent gave what many consider to be the best performance of his career. Humphrey Bogart (billed third) was cast against type as a horse trainer who has an unrequited crush on Judith. Goulding, who had taken a shine to young Ronald Reagan, attempted to coach him to play a fey, alcoholic suitor of Judith. Reagan balked. The future president later commented, "I was playing, [Goulding] told me, the kind of young man who could dearly love Bette but at the same time the kind of fellow who could sit in the girls' dressing room dishing the dirt while they went on dressing in front of me. I had no trouble seeing him in that role, but for myself. . . ." Reagan was disappointed with an important scene in which he concedes that Brent is "the one *man*" in Judith's life. He wanted to play with sincerity, but Goulding rejected the idea, feeling that it would detract from the serious nature of Brent's character. "[Goulding] didn't get what he wanted," said Reagan. "Whatever the hell that was."[470]

Photoplay gave honors to Davis and Brent as "Best Performances of the Month." "Brent has never looked so well," said the review, "and he has the intelligence to underplay Davis." *The New York Times* praised, "George Brent is—dare we say?—self-contained and mature." In Los Angeles

Dark Victory (WB 1939) Off-screen, Brent gave Bette Davis another shoulder to cry on, along with a therapeutic love affair

Jimmy Starr opined, "George Brent turns in his finest performance; a bit of work that will lift him to new popularity and acclaim."[471] *Modern Screen* raved, "George Brent's sincere and appealing characterization is flawless." The profitable tearjerker was nominated for an Academy Award as Best Picture. Davis and Geraldine Fitzgerald received nominations for Best Actress and Supporting Actress. Brent was snubbed. When it came to the Academy Awards, Brent was plainspoken. He felt that actors should not take awards for themselves, because it belonged to the crew, the script-writer, and the director more than to the performer.[472] No doubt a significant part of Brent's own affection for *Dark Victory* is tied to the salary raise Warner Bros. gave him for his convincing portrayal: $3,000 a week. It was the most he was to earn while under contract.

Camaraderie between Brent and his director blossomed while filming *Dark Victory*. Brent liked to kid Goulding, calling him "Lucy"—a nickname the director had gained while showing a bit player how to do her scenes. After shooting each day, Goulding and Brent met in a dressing room called "The Club." "Ice, Lucy?" Brent would ask as the cast talked over scenes and enjoyed Scotch, soda, and cigarettes. "Be a good girl,

Lucy, old thing, and chuck me a cigarette."[473] Goulding sheepishly complied. The two talked about taking in the winter sports together in St. Moritz.[474] Surprisingly, after filming wrapped in December, during the heat of the Brent-Davis love-fest, Brent and Goulding eloped to bask on the sunny shores of Waikiki. "Poor Bette is sick with the flu!" explained Louella Parsons.

Sailing December 15, 1938, on the *S.S. Matsonia*, Brent and Goulding arrived in Honolulu on December 21. Tagging along was Brent's twenty-eight-year-old stand-in Don Turner. What's peculiar is that af-

1938. Arriving in Honolulu.
Photo taken by a receptionist
at the Royal Hawaiian

ter two days in Honolulu, Brent and Turner returned to Los Angeles.[475] They arrived home on December 28. On December 29, Brent boarded the *S.S. Matsonia*, alone, and headed back to Honolulu to join Goulding. He skipped Bette Davis's New Year's Eve party. Upon his return from Honolulu on January 13, columnist Jimmy Star reported, "George Brent seems to be creating considerable mystery about himself and his rather unusual behavior aboard a Matson steamship en route from Honolulu to San Francisco. Even Bette Davis, who is supposed to have received various endearing cables from George, hasn't any knowledge of what he's up to."[476] Goulding postponed his departure until January 20. Part of the "mystery" surrounding Brent's early return from Honolulu was his invitation to attend the President's Birthday Ball in Washington, D.C. Mrs. Roosevelt invited Brent, Errol Flynn, and other stars for a luncheon prior to the January 30 event.[477]

In March, Brent reunited with Goulding on the set of *The Old Maid*, the second of four films they would make together. "Ah, Goulding," Brent told writer Don E. Stanke in the early 1970s, "I enjoyed working with him the most; an extremely sensitive man."[478] Aside from his superb directing skills, the adventuresome Goulding was well-known for his bisexuality and throwing parties that celebrated the body erotic.[479] It is highly unlikely that the shy, retiring "Brentie" indulged in these affairs. Prolific film author Lawrence J. Quirk, who was friends with many Hollywood actors and politicians, wrote that Goulding "had long cherished a secret passion for George."[480]

Brent's role as Clem Spender in the Civil War drama, *The Old Maid*, was first assigned to Humphrey Bogart. Clem was the romantic interest who triggers rivalry between two cousins played by Bette Davis and Miriam Hopkins. In the original Pulitzer Prize-winning play by Zoe Akins, Clem was mentioned, but never seen. After two days shooting, producer Hal Wallis and Goulding agreed that Bogart lacked sex appeal. Goulding

The Old Maid (WB 1939) with Bette Davis and Miriam Hopkins

sent a letter reminding Wallis, "I do feel that the picture needs George. Unless the man has the requisite strength and personality to be remembered—and is a man whom the women in the audience will believe could have been this important to our *two* girls—the picture will lose something of what it requires."[481] Davis also urged Wallis to replace Bogart with Brent. Brent's presence would also help compensate for her having to put up with Hopkins. "Miriam used, and I must give her credit, knew every trick in the book," said Davis. "I became fascinated watching them appear one by one. . . . Keeping my temper took its toll. I went home at night and screamed at everybody."[482]

Brent had the task of establishing a pivotal character in four scenes—less than eight minutes of screen time—before he is killed off. As in *Jezebel*, he played another hot-headed, reckless gentleman. Clem Spender returns home after a two-year absence expecting his fiancée Delia (Hopkins) to be patiently waiting. Instead, he learns that she is to marry a wealthy banker—on the very day of his arrival. "I couldn't bear to be an old maid," Delia rationalizes to her cousin Charlotte (Davis), who hurries off to the train station to give Clem the bad news. Clem threatens to break Delia's neck, but he opts to give her a tongue-lashing prior to the ceremony. "I can imagine a person developing a consuming passion for the First National Bank," he chides her. Brent allows Clem to soak in his disappointment realistically. He's hurt and angry. The smitten Charlotte skips her sister's wedding and runs off with Clem for the evening. When he accompanies her home, she begins to weep. Clem seems a bit patronizing before he admits, "I'm not worth it, Charlotte." Instead of dwelling on the past, he joins the Union Army. Clem faces Charlotte and Delia for farewells at the train station. As Delia's new husband has made heavy investment in munitions, Clem reassures her, "I'll use all I can. And I'll remember that every shot will make you richer!" It's the last we see of him. Brent justifies all the fuss the two cousins make of him. His attractive, dark presence never quite fades from the audience's memory.

We learn that Clem and Charlotte had "done the deed." Essentially, Brent's role was a plot device to get the leading lady pregnant. We watch as Charlotte loses her only opportunity to marry, as well as true motherhood. She becomes only "Aunt Charlotte" to her illegitimate daughter. Davis offers a tear-inducing performance—especially as she ages. Her hidden anguish and bitter efficiency leave a touching legacy to the actress's résumé. And, Brent? He provided ample magnetism (never his strong point). His presence is felt throughout the ninety-five-minute feature. The *Los Angeles Times* gave praises to the supporting cast, "especially George Brent as the careless, debonair Clem Spender."[483] *Film Daily* critics placed *The Old Maid* and *Dark Victory* among the "10 Best of 1939" in their annual poll.[484]

When working, Brent usually retreated to a corner table in the more intimate section of the studio café Green Room. He never sat at the round table in the room's center with other top flight actors and directors. Considerable mirth filled their lunch conversations. Brent ate alone unless Bette Davis, Olivia de Havilland, or Frank McHugh joined him. McHugh commented on the wistful look Brent sported on these occasions. "Why don't you go and sit with the boys sometimes?" Frank asked. "Tell 'em some of those stories! Let 'em get acquainted with you! Do you good!" George explained that he simply did not have the courage. "It's no use," he told McHugh. "I just don't know how to handle or get along with people. Especially people in numbers. I can't take the initiative or make overtures. I don't know what to do about it. . . ."[485]

When not working, Brent shied away from "people in numbers"—enjoying respite at his desert retreat. "I spend as much time in the desert and mountains as I can," he said. "I enjoy my picture work but I feel like getting away from it as far as possible and as completely as I can during my weeks off. I have been called secretive, unsociable, a lone wolf. Even so, the lone wolf has some things in his favor. One of them is a peace of mind. In the desert one finds a lot of other lone wolves, fine fellows too, but men who don't ask too many questions and who don't talk much about themselves." Brent added the sage observation, "I would rather [friendship] be founded upon the present than upon the past or the future."[486]

Brent may have been a lone wolf, but he was seldom without the simpatico of male company. Brent's good friend and stand-in Don Turner became his steady male companion. Turner was a graduate of the University of Southern California. He was considered one of the best stuntmen in Hollywood. He would get $100 for one horse-fall. Similar in height and looks, he got the job as Brent's stand-in for *God's Country and the Woman*. "George Brent's closest friend and inseparable companion," said a 1937 report, "is not a fellow motion picture star, but an obscure stunt man Don

Turner."[487] After the completion of *Jezebel* in 1938, the duo vacationed together in Monterrey and Mexico City. Turner also performed risky stunts
for Errol Flynn. No stranger to danger, Turner modestly explained why
he never suffered a scratch. "It's all a matter of sheer mathematics," he
said. "You lay out a stunt just as an architect does a blueprint. Everything
is planned to the split second. You rehearse until it's down pat. After that,
it's easy."[488] Reporter W. Ward Marsh remarked that Don Turner easily
stood out among the extras at Warner Bros. During filming of *The Roaring
Twenties* with tough guy Jimmy Cagney, Marsh observed Turner's habit
of knitting between takes. No one dared open their mouth about it. "He'll
jump off a building, a cliff, drive a car into a brick wall, hop from a plane,"
said Marsh, "and no one feels any desire to speak slightingly of what he
wants to do on a set when he's not risking his neck!"[489]

Brent's remote hideaway was located halfway between Hollywood
and Palm Springs, deep in the Sonoran Desert. He cleared sagebrush on
his twelve-acre lot to create a landing field for a plane. The road to the
nearest town was described as "abominable." It was here that he enjoyed

Brent's Sonoran Desert retreat and his pal/stand-in—stuntman Don Menefee Turner

sunbaths and did exactly as he pleased—and, there was no telephone. "No woman has ever darkened the door of that shack," he told writer Franc Dillon, a female.[490] "You'd be surprised what that does for me." On hand was a seventy-year-old Mexican cook/caretaker named Pedro. Brent was convinced that it was the only place where he could get Hollywood "out of my hair." "But any day," he predicted, "it may be discovered and then Hollywood'll bother me there."[491] Brent refused studio permission to send a cameraman to his hideaway. When amateur photographer Ray Stricker showed the publicity department 160 photos of Brent's "private" oasis he admitted he had never met the actor. Stricker said, "I got all these shots when I climbed a tree and photographed Mr. Brent through a telescopic lens."[492] The studio gave Stricker a hefty check. Shots included Brent fixing a tire, boxing with Don Turner, and sleeping with his mouth open in a hammock. Brent was pretty miffed. By 1940, he would sell his hideaway and find peace of mind elsewhere.

At 440 feet above sea level, Brent's desert retreat was unusually dry. There had been 300 days of annual sunshine, temperatures reaching 106-112 F, and an average rainfall of 4.83 inches. In April 1939, while his hideaway basked in sunny skies, Brent was shivering, drenched, and nursing a large cup of scalding tea. "For 10 days we have been soaked in studio rain," he said on a set at Twentieth Century-Fox. The actor wasn't a bit sorry that he traded in the dry Sonoran Desert heat for the catastrophic monsoons of Ranchipur, India. He felt honored. The highly coveted role of Tom Ransome in Louis Bromfield's 1937 bestseller, *The Rains Came*, along with heavy rain, had fallen into his lap.

The Rains Came (20th Century-Fox 1939) Dissipated Englishman (Brent) meets his match in Lady Esketh (Myrna Loy)

9

The Rains Came

It had been three years since Brent filmed outside his home studio. On parole at Twentieth Century-Fox for *The Rains Came,* he was given the perfect opportunity to utilize his subdued style and talent. He was well-suited to portray Tom Ransome, the dissipated Englishman from the Bromfield novel. Brent had his own ideas about the role and objected when he was told that Ransome was to appear unkempt, even slovenly. He locked horns with producer Darryl F. Zanuck. Brent felt that Ransome's disintegration was less obvious, something one would only notice after knowing him awhile. Ransome had money. He would look well-heeled out of habit. "We will confine my badness to my state of mind only," Brent insisted.[493] "If you want a beachcomber for the part," he told Zanuck, "why don't you hire Charles Laughton? He already has the wardrobe."[494] Laughton's shiftless bum in *The Beachcomber* (1938) wasn't a look that Brent would *ever* consider on or off screen. He won the argument. Zanuck conceded that Brent's interpretation could not have been improved upon.

Brent showed the script of *The Rains Came* to Bette Davis, who was thrilled that he got the coveted role. She wasn't as pleased with reports that she and Brent were going to marry. "Nobody seems to pay any attention to the fact that I am still married," she said. "What do they want me to be? A bigamist?"[495] The Brent-Davis liaison was still going strong during the filming of *The Rains Came*. They would show up at night spots like Café LaMaze, sometimes accompanied by Davis's mother. In her memoir *This 'N That* Davis shared that she had often hoped that Brent would marry her. She related only one minor disappointment with the actor. "During our romance, he gave me a charm bracelet with the letters B-E-T-T-E in diamonds. I was a little less enchanted when he said, as I was oohing and aahing over it, 'I'm glad you have such a short name.'"[496] Davis confirmed years later that Brent's hair was snow white. "He used to stain my pillow cases with hair dye," she giggled.[497] Soon after *The Rains Came* was released, Davis met hotel manager Arthur Farnsworth in Vermont. It wasn't long before "Farney" was driving Davis cross-country back to Hollywood. On the last day of 1940 they wed.

June 5, 1939. Lovers Bette Davis and Brent take in a
performance at the Beverly Hills Hotel

Brent became preoccupied with a rising star who had talent *and* sex appeal. He first spotted Ann Sheridan in the studio's Green Room just as she settled down to ham steak, mashed potatoes, gravy, and two side orders followed by a chocolate sundae. "Don't tell me that's Ann Sheridan the Oomph Girl," he remarked rather loudly to his lunch companion. "Delicate little thing, isn't she ... especially her appetite."[498] He had seen none of her films. Sheridan ignored the remark, but not the man. Brent was always open for a new, comely diversion. After a so-called studio-engineered date, Brent and Sheridan continued seeing each other.[499] By January 1940, Jimmy Fidler posted, "Keep an eye on George Brent and Ann Sheridan—their romance is more than a rumor."[500]

The Rains Came was the costliest production in which Brent ever starred — budgeted at $2.5 million, according to the publicity. $500,000 was allotted for filming the earthquake, dam burst, and devastating flood, which, along with the rains, entailed the release of 33 million gallons of water. The special effects for the disaster scenes were nothing short of spectacular and won an Academy Award. Some of the same footage (intercut) was used in a 1955 remake, *The Rains of Ranchipur*—a film that was inferior in every respect. Cinematographer Arthur C. Miller also received an Oscar nomination for *The Rains Came*. He was obsessed with getting the rain to fall at its customary angle instead of straight down. "Oh my God," he recalled, "you never saw so much water in your life! Brent and the others took a hell of a beating on that picture."[501] Brent also took a beating financially. While he collected his $3,000 weekly salary, Warners raked in $150,000 for his services.[502]

Director Clarence Brown elicited from his cast characterizations that were sensitive and well-defined. Bromfield's novel was in good hands. The author sat on the sidelines during filming. He admitted that some of the characters he cherished were eliminated from the screenplay. "They had to go," said Bromfield. "The two [scenarists] selected brilliantly and kept in the script what was in the book—the feeling that no matter what happened to the characters, India was always there in the background, bigger than any individual or any government."[503] The earthquake and devastation reinforce this idea, foreshadowing the end of British Rule.

Bromfield was in Europe while casting of *The Rains Came* was completed. Marlene Dietrich, Kay Francis, Tallulah Bankhead, and Constance Bennett had been mentioned for the female lead of Lady Esketh. When Zanuck announced his choice as Myrna Loy, Bromfield balked. "I was flabbergasted," he said. "It did not seem possible that the wife of the *Thin Man* could also be Lady Esketh." He changed his mind rather quickly when he arrived on the Fox set. Bromfield observed a half dozen takes, noting the way Loy walked and spoke—thwarted and desperate. "But more than that," he said, "the personality of Miss Loy herself became revealed as of great importance. In the scenes where Lady Esketh was her most spiteful and hateful, a simplicity, a gentleness, came *through* the performance. One felt that in spite of everything Lady Esketh wasn't so bad. That element was of great importance to the latter half of the film. I think that as Lady Esketh Myrna Loy gives the best performance of her career."[504]

Ronald Colman, originally announced to play Ransome, was reported to have asked $250,000 and a percentage. Clive Brook also tested for the role. Colman later admitted that money had nothing to do with his failure to get the part. "I think it will be a great picture," he said. "I just didn't like the part for myself."[505] Ransome was a perfect match for Brent. His portrayal also pleased Bromfield. "George Brent was a 'natural,' " he said. "As Ransome he is charming, sadly gay, disillusioned, and courageous. He has achieved what is an immensely difficult thing for an actor to do. He has conveyed brilliantly the despair of the spirit that lies beneath any actor." Brent's well-delineated Tom Ransome sets the tone for

The Rains Came (20th Century-Fox 1939) Here with Marjorie Rambeau,
Harry Hayden and Brenda Joyce. Brenda disliked kissing George,
because of his moustache.

the film and what follows. The son of an earl, Ransome finds refuge from
the British class system while idling in Ranchipur (based on the province
of Baroda) for seven years, and avoiding his designated talent: painting
portraits. He's more prone to pick up a shot of brandy than a paintbrush.
Like most of the white characters in *The Rains Came*, Ransome is iso-
lated from native peoples. His friendship with the handsome, progressive Indian physician Major Safti (Tyrone Power) is the one exception.
When Safti comes to visit, Ransome complains about wars, bombs, and
dictators in a world—as he puts it, "Trying to commit suicide as fast as it
knows how." This all takes place in 1938.

When Ransome reluctantly accepts an invitation to tea at the home of

Mrs. Simon (Marjorie Rambeau), a social-climbing missionary's wife, it's understood why his presence is considered a coup. He has a title, exudes charm, has looks and personality—that is, until his biting humor rattles the guest of honor, Lily Hoggett-Egburry (Laura Hope Crews). Forecasting the upcoming monsoon season, Egbury titters, "No one stays in Ranchipur during the monsoons!" "No?" Ransome gibes. "Only about five million people." His pointed remark lays bare the dismissive attitude the British-American colony reserve for the natives. Before long, Ransome is fending off Simon's virginal daughter, Fern (Brenda Joyce). She wants him as an accomplice in her ruse to "escape" her stifling environs. He's amused, but noncommittal. A royal summons from the palace comes to his rescue—an invitation to welcome the visiting Lord and Lady Esketh.

Lady Esketh, a former lover of Ransome, is married to the boorish, much older Lord Albert (Nigel Bruce), who has money—lots of it. The film cagily points to the differences between the inherent dignity of the Maharajah and the exploitive nature of British nobility. Albert tries to outmaneuver the Maharajah for one of his prize horses. The English Lord is completely taken aback when offered an equally coveted stallion for free. Such generosity leaves Lord Albert speechless. Incredulity never had an uglier, greedier face. Touches like these reverberate directly from the Bromfield novel.

Los Angeles critic/reporter Harrison Carroll was on the set the day they shot Brent's love scene with Loy inside the exotic royal palace. Carroll sat on the sidelines with Brent, while cast members filmed an after dinner poker game: Tyrone Power with tinted makeup and a turban; Montague Shaw as a British general; and Maria Ouspenskaya, the wise old Maharani, who loves to gamble. Carroll asked Brent, "When do you come in." "Oh, not for a while," he answered. "At the moment I am supposed to be having a tête-à-tête with Lady Esketh in another part of the castle."[506] Harrison explained to his readers that if they had read the book "tête-à-tête" was a masterpiece of understatement. The scene in question is one of the film's best. In a secluded area of the palace, Edwina attempts to listen as Ransome rambles on about the elementals of Indian life. She yawns. "Tom, you've changed. You didn't used to be such a windbag." He gets the message. It's obvious she wants something more than just "talk." Upon returning from their tête-à-tête, Edwina spots the strik-

The Rains Came (20th Century-Fox 1939) with Maria Ouspenskaya. Brent enjoyed downing highballs with Madame Ouspenskaya. He affectionately called her "Mousie." She would admit, "I have quite a crush on him!"

ingly handsome Major Safti. "Who's the … pale copper Apollo?" she asks. Ransome detects the lust in her eyes. She's already seeking a new thrill. "Well, don't waste your time," he tells her. "He's a surgeon and a scientist. Any interest he might have in romance is purely biological." "You make him sound even *more* exciting," she purrs.

Ransome arrives home from the palace to discover young Fern Simon. She plans to stay the night reasoning that it would create such a scandal she'd *have* to leave Ranchipur. "Your reputation is already so . . . so, tarnished," she gushes. He responds with a hearty chuckle. She looks anxious and asks, "Don't you feel anything about me?" He softens. "I'd be a fool if I didn't." They kiss. He sends her home. Associate Producer Harry Joe Brown was set on having the delicate allure of eighteen-year-old Lana Turner for the role of Fern instead of newcomer Brenda Joyce.[507] Brent told columnist Sheilah Graham how pleased he was with *The Rains Came*. "But," he qualified, "I got awfully weary doing twenty-seven takes for each scene with Brenda Joyce."[508] This may explain why some of their scenes lack the necessary sensitivity. Another report stated that the twenty-two-year-old novice was "petrified" of Brent. Jimmy Fidler revealed that, prior to their first kiss, Brenda could not be found anywhere. Director Brown instituted a search. "She was in a far corner of the stage," said Fidler, "practicing the kissing scene with her best girl friend. She explained that she hadn't been able to sleep the night before, because she was so worried about … kissing Mr. Brent."[509] Apparently, Brenda's longtime boyfriend Owen Ward wasn't around to facilitate. Film historian Anthony Slide observed on the DVD commentary for *The Rains Came* that he found Brenda Joyce "not a great actress," but "very serviceable."

Inevitably, Edwina manages to delicately coo her way into having her "copper Apollo," Major Safti, as her escort—for sightseeing. Lal Chand Mehra, a native of India and popular lecturer on the "subconscious" and "superconscious," adapted and sang a Hindu song for the Loy-Power screen romance.[510] A beautifully lit, entrancing bit of cinema magic captures the dynamic of the ill-matched duo as they listen to the mystical melody. Safti thoughtfully translates the Hindu lyric: "In your heart my love has found a home and it can never die." Alfred E. Newman's Oscar-nominated original score wove this musical motif beneath the narrative with effective results.

Before the monsoons and earthquakes, it's a joy to watch Brent and Loy lock horns over their characters' respective budding romances. Ransome chastises Edwina's attentiveness to Major Safti and she, in turn, retaliates. "Listen to who's moralizing!" she snaps. "I suppose that comes from philandering around missions." Loy later revealed that Lady Esketh and Safti were modeled after Lady Edwina Mountbatten and Nehru—a central figure in Indian politics during that time, and later the country's first Prime Minister. He was considered the architect of the modern Indian nation-state. Loy, herself, while living in New York, met Nehru at the mayor's house. "He was very charming," she recalled, "a handsome and compelling man, who flirted with me throughout the reception. . . . I was not unreceptive. I could understand how Edwina Mountbatten might have been attracted to him."[511] Lady Mountbatten, much like Lady Esketh, sparked scandals and indulged in numerous love affairs during her life. Lord Mountbatten admitted, "Edwina and I spent all our married lives getting into other people's beds."[512] Mountbatten had a sexual preference for men.[513]

Mother Nature, abetted by a cholera epidemic, resolves the romantic dilemmas in *The Rains Came.* In the devastating aftermath, the widowed Maharani appoints Ransome to administer supplies for the ravaged nation. She's aware of his friendship with Major Safti, and feels Ransome is "one of us." Edwina volunteers at Safti's hospital to save the sick and dying. Safti begins to perceive her in a different light. When he asks why she hasn't left, the answer is in her eyes. "We mustn't let anything happen to you," he smiles warmly. "You're too valuable." As Edwina and Safti's relationship intensifies, Ransome is paged by the Maharani. She wants Lady Esketh to leave the country, tomorrow. Ransome agrees, offering the curious assessment, "Her kind of civilization is on its way out." Apparently, along with her voracious sexual appetite, Edwina is seen as the perpetrator of corruption and colonialism. *The Rains Came*, although a decisive break from films of the era that glorified British rule, promotes indirect rather than direct rule for the "new" India. Consequently, the British Board of Film Classification offered their seal of approval for the production.[514] However, by 1939, there was much opposition among Indian nationalists to the British alliance with these designated princely states.

While on ward duty at the hospital, Edwina mistakenly drinks from a contaminated glass. One of cinema's most unique love scenes follows when Safti confesses his feelings for her. As he pours out his heart, Loy's eyes show the full extent of her character's emotions—she's completely overcome. They embrace, but Edwina avoids Safti's kiss, suspecting the inevitable. On her deathbed, romantic love changes into something deeper—she sees beyond it, facing her inner truth. After graciously disposing of her precious worldly possessions, Edwina bids adieu. Loy appears to reside outside of life itself, duplicating the experience of her character. The actress performs completely, in the moment, without ego.

If anything, Edwina's death is a reminder of what human beings are capable of when they're not grasping. She gives the film soul. Edwina is bright enough to recognize the prejudice reserved for women like herself—a double standard with no redemption. She had crossed race and color barriers and knows exactly what she would be up against facing a world of ignorance and religiosity. Brent's Tom Ransome understands Edwina. In many ways they're the same. Both recognize that there is nothing to hang onto, only surrender to the next step. In Ransome's case it's a matter of aligning himself with the widowed Maharani and helping to ensure Major Safti's vision for India. On screen, Safti is flanked by British officials during his coronation. He appears to be an anachronism—as doomed as the Victorian Age. As Jeannine Woods points out in her 2011 study, *Visions of Empire and Other Imaginings*, Mahatma Ghandi and Indian nationalist leaders were protesting that princely India "had no place in the free India of the future."[515] This was not the message of the film, however.

Lady Esketh achieves transcendence—Safti, Ransome and the others, are left with only the promise of dreams. As Safti readies himself to be crowned prince, he "hears" the ancient love song he had shared with Lady Esketh. He seems lost for a moment; lost in something far greater than the pomp and circumstance of his new responsibility. Power had the grace and innate ability to convey such feeling. Loy never forgot this

Power, Loy, Brent - Photoplay awarded the star trio "Best
Performances of the Month" and singled Brent out for "giving the
finest performance of his career." (20th Century-Fox)

about him and years later stated, "Ty Power was one of the nicest human beings I've ever known, a really divine man, perceptive and thoughtful. He had a very strong sense of other people, heightened by a kind of mysticism, a spiritual quality. You saw it in his deep, warm eyes."[516]

Although there would be retakes, cast and crew for *The Rains Came* celebrated the picture's completion the weekend of June 17. Director Brown had a party for Brent, Loy, Power, and the others at his Calabasas ranch. Brent brought along Bette Davis. After previews, *Film Daily* predicted a "sure-fire box office smash."[517] *The Rains Came* received extended runs in ninety-seven percent of its bookings throughout the United

States.[518] It was among *Photoplay's* "Best Pictures of the Month"—along with "Best Performances" for Loy, Power, and Brent—"the latter," commented the editor, "giving the very finest performance of his career."[519] *Photoplay's* review elaborated, "It is as though you had never seen [Brent] before, so freshly touched is he with humor, charm and the tired cynicism of the eternal romantic." A critic in Sydney, Australia, gave high marks for Loy's discerning portrayal, saying, "Her impudent directness of thought, her feline grace, her crafty way of going after the men she wants—all these seem refreshing and stimulating, and strangely actual. Mr. Brent, as Ransome, provides a diverting companion picture of a drunkard with a strong streak of pessimism, who, in spite of everything, retains a definite twinkle in his eyes."[520]

Not everyone was pleased. Frank S. Nugent for *The New York Times* gave the film a scathing review, calling it "the merest skeleton of the Bromfield work." "All that emerges," he railed, "is an Indian romance of little significance."[521] Los Angeles critic Harrison Carroll countered, "The mysticism of India … has been fully captured by director Clarence Brown, who is entitled to draw a bow. The players selected by Zanuck bear him out by their performances. Myrna Loy shows unexpected resources in illuminating the spiritual rebirth of Lady Esketh. George Brent leaves you with no regret that Ronald Colman did not get the role of the world-weary Ransome."[522] More recently, film buffs have theorized that Lady Esketh fell victim to the Production Code. It's highly unlikely. She dies in Bromfield's book. After all, cholera epidemics take saints and sinners alike. Others point to the omission of *real* Indians in the film. Such a prospect would have been a *real* challenge for central casting. Besides, filmgoers in 1939 had great capacity for suspending disbelief. Aside from Merle Oberon (whose mother was Ceylonese) and the aforementioned Lal Chand Mehra (a native and personal friend of Nehru) casting options were, understandably, limited.

1939 was a banner year at the Academy Awards: *Gone With The Wind, Dark Victory, Goodbye Mr. Chips, The Wizard of Oz, Mr. Smith Goes to Washington, Stagecoach,* and *Wuthering Heights.* While *The Rains Came* garnered six nominations, the actors, director, and picture itself were overlooked. Two of Brent's most highly praised performances were released that year. The understated style of Brent and Loy was rarely recognized as being in the same league as the larger-than-life histrionics of stars who carried home the little gold statuette. In lieu of attending the Academy Awards (February 1940) Brent was basking on Waikiki with his buddy Ralph Forbes. In March, Chatterton's two exes packed up and took the next steamer back to Hollywood. Cecil B. DeMille had paged Brent to repeat his role as Ransome for *Lux Radio,* costarring Kay Francis as Lady Esketh. During the broadcast, DeMille inquired, "How did you leave Hawaii, George?" "Practically the way I found it C.B.," he replied, "except for a slight hollow on the beach where I had been lying for four weeks."[523]

After Brent and Ralph Forbes saw the sights at San Francisco's "Golden Gate International Exhibition," George contracted with Paramount for *Adventure in Diamonds.* It was a case of going from the sublime to the ridiculous. Although the film tried to have a sense of humor about itself, this diamond caper lacked sparkle. It was delayed several months before release. *The New York Times* felt the plot was "too delightfully complicated to be followed by anyone."[524] To start things off we see Brent, a British army pilot, aboard a steamer for South Africa. He and a buddy (Nigel Bruce) enjoy double-gin slings at the bar. They need a highball to get through this turkey. The old chums banter about polo ponies, diamond thieves, and, more seriously, Bruce's "emotionally undernourished" love life. Who should belly up to the bar but a ridiculously plumed and bejeweled glamour puss (Isa Miranda) who, by the end of the convoluted plot, Brent tricks out of some stolen African diamonds. The British Empire obviously has more right to these precious commodities. Miranda's Dietrich-like persona lacked chemistry with Brent. Her creature is unscrupulous and unlikable, and it is baffling why Brent is compelled to show any interest. Eleventh-billed in this little gem is Ralph Forbes, who pops in for a minute-and-a-half to announce, "The Negro was alive when we left him!" The scenarists managed to throw in an ostrich race to keep audiences from dozing off.

September 3, 1939: England declared war on Germany. Tom Ransome's remark about the world committing suicide "as fast as it can" had credibility. While the Lockheed plant in nearby Burbank began turning out a new bomber for Great Britain every seven hours, Warner Bros. felt a patriotic duty to call to arms—on their back lot. The studio's Irish lads were recruited for *The Fighting 69th*. James Cagney, Pat O'Brien, George Brent, and Frank McHugh put on uniforms for the World War I saga, which Warner archivist Clive Hirschhorn describes as "not to be taken seriously for a moment."[525] Brent (third-billed) played the decorated war hero Colonel "Wild Bill" Donovan. As he had in *Submarine D-1*, Brent both looked and played the part of an officer in command. Orders rolled off his tongue convincingly as he pulled together his combat unit. One outtake shows Brent in the trenches as a large clump of debris from an explosion lands on his back. "Son-of-a-bitch!" he yelled. "Who in the hell threw that?" It was used in *Breakdowns of 1940*, an annual blooper reel with stars' flub-ups and expletives. The fact was, Brent wasn't feeling well—he had contacted influenza. He recalled years later, "I got real sick. Spots came out all over me; fingernails fell out with the fever—toenails came off. You'd just choke to death. But I got through the picture alright. This was my only picture with my good pal James Cagney."[526] Despite Brent's valiant efforts, the script for *The Fighting 69th* afforded little opportunity to get to know Donovan, the man. Donovan's biographer noted that

"Donovan loved Irish star George Brent" and happily promoted the film on New York radio.[527]

Pat O'Brien played the regiment chaplain, Father Duffy, a walking-talking Lord's Prayer. Tales about his flock of soldiers were purported to be the basis for the film. Cagney was the 69th's fictional, cocky thorn-in-the-flesh who, at any moment, was apt to snarl, "Take your hands off me you son-of-a-Banshee or I'll knock

The Fighting 69th (WB 1940) Brent and James Cagney would remain life-long friends

your teeth down your throat." Unfortunately, his prolonged onscreen cowardice, resulting in the demise of several comrades, becomes tiresome. Predictably, Cagney finds religion and dies a hero. It was obvious that the scenarists had a good time. So did audiences. Cagney himself observed that Warner Brothers knew what the public wanted "no matter how derelict they were in helping the material get fashioned."[528] A huge moneymaker for 1940, *The Fighting 69th* was reissued nationwide in 1948. Contract player Dennis Morgan (previously seventh billed) was promoted above the title with Cagney and O'Brien. Brent was demoted to a supporting player.

Although Brent and Cagney had met early in 1932, they hadn't interacted much. They took an instant shine to each other during filming. Cagney called Brent "Puss" as they swapped yarns and played pranks. After Brent contacted influenza, the studio considered replacing him with William Gargan. Cagney was adamant that Brent's participation was a key to the film's success. "George Brent was an essential ingredient of *The Fighting 69th*," Cagney recalled in his memoirs. "George was and is a solid actor and fine gentleman."[529] While filming, Cagney invited Brent to be guest at the "Boy's Club"—a group of Irish actors that regularly got together for dinner, conversation, and laughs: Cagney, Pat O'Brien, Frank McHugh, Spencer Tracy, and Frank Morgan. George happily showed up. Cagney elaborated that while they were eating he got going on Hollywood's reputation of being the divorce capital of the world. He was indignant and felt such notoriety was undeserved. He looked over at O'Brien. "Pat," he said, "look how long you've been married, and to the same woman. Frank, you too. Spence, you. Me." After a pregnant pause, Cagney gulped. Sitting right in front of him was George with his track record of three divorces. "George," he apologized, "me and my goddamned big mouth. I'm sorry."[530] Brent said, "Forget it. It's very unimportant." He grew a little pensive, then remarked, "You know, boys, I married four (sic) of them. And I didn't like a damned one of them." "Well," said Cagney. "We all fell to pieces after that."

In 1932, Brent was considered for the male lead in *One Way Passage*—a shipboard romance of a condemned man and his terminally ill sweetheart. The William Powell-Kay Francis film was hugely popular. It won an Academy Award for Best Original Story and was on most "Top Ten Lists." In the fall of 1939, it was announced that Bette Davis and Brent would be in the remake, *'Til We Meet Again*.[531] Jack Warner was hoping for another *Dark Victory*, but Davis refused. She was hastily replaced with Merle Oberon. Although Brent lacked the innate charm and irony William Powell brought to the original, he provided his own solid sensitivity, especially when he discovers the truth of lady love Oberon's fatal condi-

Brent considered *'Til We Meet Again* (WB 1940) one of his best films. Seen here with George Reeves, Geraldine Fitzgerald, Pat O'Brien and Merle Oberon

tion. One senses their doom as they philosophize over "Paradise Cocktails." "Anyone who knows that every second of life is important should have one of these," Brent advises Oberon, who, against doctor's orders, willingly complies.

Oberon, in her first important role since *Wuthering Heights,* is heartbreaking. The script offers a number of emotional opportunities that she handles delicately, never overplaying—a porcelain-like figure who wants to live life to its fullest. Her most poignant moment is buoyed by Hawaiian slack-key guitars throbbing strains of "Where Was I?" Overcome with angina pain she pleads to the heavens, "Not yet please! Not now!" She is touchingly human—never just an actress savoring a dramatic moment. To her credit, Oberon was in poor shape during the shoot, battling influenza. Edmund Goulding was in the director's chair (when he wasn't battling his own bout with the virus). Anatole Litvak ended up shooting about one-fourth of the footage. Goulding's skill with melodrama was otherwise in full force. Years afterward, Brent fondly recalled it as "a lovely, romantic story."[532] He considered it one of his best films.

One Way Passage had a whimsical edge that left audiences with both a tear and a smile. *'Til We Meet Again* was keyed more tragically, slicker— and over thirty minutes longer. Audiences and most critics were still pleased with the end result. New York critic Herbert Cohn thought that although the story (dragging in spots) had lost some of its suspense, it had "lost little of its warmth." Cohn felt that Brent was offering "superb work at the peak of his career."[533] W. Ward Marsh, in Cleveland, thought *'Til We Meet Again* no better than the original, but raved, "They have given us one of the best film remakes I have ever seen. Mr. Brent has never done better work. His voice, his timing, and his manner are all this hero ever needs."[534]

The Man Who Talked Too Much was a remake of *The Mouthpiece* (1932). The story was based on New York's flamboyant criminal law-yer Bill Fallon. Brent let it be known that he hated the leading role but admired director Vincent Sherman. It was rumored that Ann Sheridan

The Man Who Talked Too Much (WB 1940) with Virginia Bruce

was upset about not being selected to play opposite Brent. That task was placed in the capable hands of Virginia Bruce. Despite a riveting start in which a respected attorney (Brent) unwittingly sends an innocent man to the electric chair, the film lacked the ruthless, risqué intensity of the original. Under Sherman's direction Brent is more animated than usual as he transforms into a trickster lawyer intoxicated with power. While perverting justice, he saves thugs and murderers from the "hot seat" as a steady cash flow is supplied by an underworld kingpin (Richard Barthelmess). Virginia Bruce is both smooth and appealing as the secretary who sticks by Brent despite his underhanded courtroom tricks. For the climactic frame-up, Barthelmess gets Brent's idealistic kid brother (William Lundigan) onto death row. Unfortunately, an abrupt, tagged-on happy ending took the film out of the dark clutches of *film noir* where it would have fared better.

Director Sherman was baffled by Jack Warner's logic after the film wrapped. "You didn't want to make that picture," Warner grinned, "but we're going to net over a hundred grand on it."[535] "Neither George Brent or I liked the script," recalled Sherman, "but to refuse it meant a suspension—being taken off salary." *Film Daily* felt the remake was "prone to drag." *The New York Times* found Brent "perpetually sullen" and agreed that he "talked too much." *Time* magazine concluded that *The Man Who Talked Too Much* was merely an "echo" of the original and balked at Brent's "willingness to appear in almost any kind of picture," adding smugly, "Warner is happily paying him $3,000 a week, and his popularity was never greater."[536]

"Any kind of picture" best describes Brent's next film, *South of Suez*—a George Raft reject. Raft preferred four months suspension. *Photoplay* gave it a resounding "Phooey!" upon release. "Help!" cried the review. "Come to the rescue of George Brent who gets so bewilderingly lost in these complicated little Bs and can't seem to do anything about it."[537] In

Lee Patrick spells "trouble" for Brent in *South of Suez* (WB 1940)

this serial-like saga, Brent's wanderlust from the diamond mines of Tang-anyika into pea-soup London fog is triggered after his unscrupulous boss (George Tobias) frames him for murder. Also willing to implicate Brent is Tobias's vengeful, flirtatious wife (Lee Patrick) who Brent had rebuffed once too often. "You little tramp!" he snarls, before his miraculous escape from a posse of vigilantes. Fast forward five years later. Graying around the edges, Brent has a new name and new *raison d'être*—wooing the dead man's daughter (Brenda Marshall). The implausible plot is somewhat compensated by Brent's good looks and resolute masculine integrity. The *New York Sun* reported, "*South of Suez* goes in heavily for coincidences … and rather clumsy plot."[538] "Falls rather flat despite a surprise ending," warned *The New York Times*.[539]

While wrapping up *South of Suez*, Brent hosted one "helluva" Hawai-ian luau at House of Murphy's Fight Room. Potted palms surrounded a pig and poi feast served in cocoanut shells. Brent's gesture was on behalf of his guests: Honolulu singer Clara "Hilo Hattie" Inter and the Royal

Hawaiian Surf Riders. They gave George the royal treatment during his past sojourns to Oahu. Dessert was a huge cake topped with a tropical beach scene. The icing . . . was Ann Sheridan in a South Seas frock garnished with a lei of seashells.[540] For fun, she called George by his Hawaiian name, Keoki.

Brent felt a special connection to the islands. He was asked who his best friends were and replied matter-of-factly, "Some Hawaiians. In the Islands." He commented on their ability to make him feel welcome and the touching letters they had written.[541] On his visit to Oahu with Ralph Forbes, Brent did more than just lie on the beach. He closed the deal on a seventy-five-acre pineapple plantation just outside of Honolulu.[542] He had placed three previous bids on the property. During the process, he sold his desert hideaway and his larger residence in the San Fernando Valley—calling it a "big oversized elephant-of-a-house." He returned to the simplicity of his home in Toluca Lake. Brent didn't stop there. He put a produce grocery store and two gas stations he owned in Los Angeles on the market.

It became obvious that Brent had definite plans for Hawaii. "I want to buy a home in Hawaii," he explained to writer Irving Wallace. "And I want to stay there six months out of the year." He would focus on making two films a year. "As a result," he emphasized, "in the future I think I'll do better work. I'll have the time to select important well-constructed stories. No more fantasies hacked out in limited time!"[543] In the meantime, Brent kept venting, "I've got to get somewhere where I can clear out my emotions and my thoughts, readjust a perspective that's been thrown out of gear by being too close to Hollywood for too long—and get myself either a new sense of values, or the old sense of values back again."[544] The showpiece for his tropical dream was the purchase of the eighty-six-foot yawl *Southwind* from Western star Buck Jones. Jones had sailed the yawl in the 1936 Honolulu race. Brent intended to enter in the next Honolulu competition and seriously began taking navigation lessons.

In early 1941, Brent announced *Southwind's* entry for the 2,200 nautical mile race from San Francisco to Oahu in July. The event was backed by Commodore Morgan Adams of the Transpacific Yacht Club. Ann Sheridan planned to take a steamer to Oahu and greet Brent with a traditional Hawaiian lei. Fate and a serious back injury intervened. In the months that preceded World War II, *Southwind* was inducted into the coast guard as an auxiliary fighting craft.[545] The Honolulu race was cancelled. During his recovery, Brent purchased *Santana*, which became the belle of the Hollywood fleet. He moved the main mast forward converting it into a yawl. The addition of a small mizzenmast was intended to give *Santana* an advantage on long ocean races. In 1944, *Santana* would transfer from Brent to Ray Milland to Dick Powell. In 1945 Humphrey Bogart bought the fifty-five-foot yacht. *Santana* forever became known as "Bogie's boat." For Bogart, sailing was usually a stag affair. He took it seriously—thirty-five to forty-five weekends a year. "The trouble with having dames aboard," he explained, "is that you can't pee over the side." Brent also gained a reputation as a fine sailor and navigator. After the war, he repurchased *Southwind* and completed a San Pedro-to-Honolulu race in 1947.[546]

Brent acquiesced to Warner Bros., not caring whether they put him in "B's" or the more prestigious films under the helm of Hal B. Wallis. Did the almighty paycheck pacify his ambition for greater things? "I'm extravagant, God knows," he said at the time. "I don't know what I want. It's nothing material, I do know that. Once I've got a thing, *I don't want it.*"[547] Brent reminded everyone that he was happily unmarried. His steady relationship with Ann Sheridan was rooted in what Brent called "her earthy simplicity." "Ann works hard and enjoys life; she's more fun to be with than any woman I have ever known," he admitted."[548] When *Photoplay's*

Howard Sharpe asked Sheridan to describe Brent, she answered with a musical metaphor:

> *First you imagine a Dublin pub, with a lot of good fellows singing lusty barrack ditties. Suddenly, someone turns on the radio—Toscanini is conducting a Tchaikovsky concert. The men in the pub sing louder, banging their glasses on the bar, and whoever turned on the radio kicks the volume higher, and so on, until the voices of the men give out and Arturo triumphantly presides, the winnah.*[549]

Obviously, it was Brent's way or the highway. Fans held a collective breath waiting for an announcement of the Brent-Sheridan nuptials. The studio took advantage of the situation and finally paired the duo in screwball comedy—not exactly Brent's forte. *Honeymoon For Three* (filmed before *South of Suez*) stayed on the shelf for five months before release. It managed to turn a quick profit due to a publicity gimmick that touted Brent and Sheridan's record-breaking 56.2-second screen kiss. "I'll put up $10,000 cash, at odds of 10 to 1," said Brent, "that I don't step to the altar for three years. And that's no reflection against Ann. She's a swell girl."[550] That was in May 1940. Three years later, Ann had succeeded in helping Brent chalk up his fourth divorce.

Honeymoon for Three (WB 1941) with Ann Sheridan and Johnny Downs. (below) For his birthday in 1941, Sheridan gave Brent a working model of his yacht *Southwind*. (The miniature was made at Reginald Denny's toy factory)

10

A Little More Oomph

In *The Debonairs*, authors James Robert Parish and Don E. Stanke comment that Brent's "quiet, gentlemanly charms were qualities to envy, not dismiss." They also say that Brent "would have done even better professionally had he had a little more oomph."[551] Brent must have felt the same way while he pursued "Oomph Girl" Ann Sheridan. Her earthy reputation, use of salty language, and reveling in off-color jokes made her a congenial favorite of cast and crew on the Warner lot.[552] By the time Sheridan and Brent began filming *Honeymoon for Three* in July 1940, they were seeing each other exclusively. In December, matrimony was predicted to be just around the corner. "I read that we will be husband and wife before 1941," remarked Sheridan. "We keep telling each other, 'It's getting mighty close now.' "[553]

If the Brent-Sheridan celluloid combination was any measure of offscreen marital success, it was best that the duo hold off . . . permanently. A Los Angeles critic after witnessing *Honeymoon For Three* thought that Sheridan's "oomph" was "held in suspension" and lamented Brent's "heavy-handed buffoonery."[554] New York's Herbert Cohn groaned, "Ann Sheridan and George Brent strain their broadest comic styles and fall rather flat."[555] Playing an author of romance novels, Brent is bombarded with female fans during a book tour. Sheridan, his wisecracking secretary, keeps her cool amid the chaos. By the time he bumps into an old college flame (Osa Massen), Brent's bug-eyed "buffoonery" becomes tiresome. He tries too hard. What the film needed was a better script and Jimmy Stewart (originally cast for the lead). Sheridan's silky presence, disarming good looks, and chic Orry-Kelly wardrobe are the film's only assets. She's a knockout. Why would Brent look at anyone else? Osa Massen aptly summed the film up with her line: "This started out to be so empty of somethingness, and now it's so something of nothingness." Patrons who remained in their seats weren't even privy to the heavily advertised 56.2-second screen kiss. Censors had it snipped down to thirty. This record-breaking smooch was director Lloyd Bacon's idea. "George may be a little self-conscious," Ann told Bacon beforehand, "but I'll just hold on if he tries to break."[556] Although the prolonged pucker wasn't long enough to boil an egg, it was reported that George was visibly shaken afterwards.

"Ann Sheridan never looked lovelier or had less to do," complained another critic after seeing *Honeymoon For Three*.[557] Sheridan, understandably, felt the same way. She was fed up with Warner Bros. She was tired of "Oomph" and glamour. "It's so limiting to any actress who really yearns to do something," she complained to Louella Parsons. Sheridan decided to go on suspension. George, who took whatever came along, completed the lackluster *South of Suez* before being rewarded an "A" production co-starring Bette Davis and Mary Astor. Before filming began in October 1940, he offered consolation to the unemployed Ann aboard *Southwind*. They cruised lazily along the Mexican Coast.[558] Brent was in his element. "Believe me," he said, "There's nothing like it—the blue sea, the bluer sky, the sparkling sunshine, the salty air—it puts new life in you." He called Sheridan a "comfortable companion."[559]

Variety had reported the re-teaming of Brent and Bette Davis for two of her popular 1940 successes: *All This and Heaven, Too* and *The Letter*.

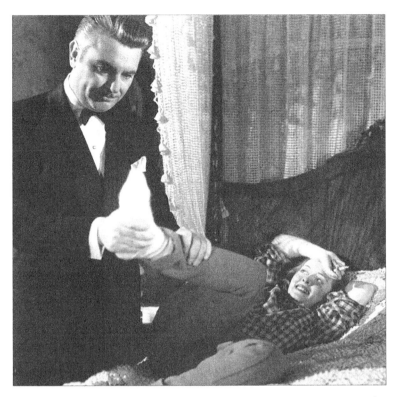

Bette Davis blamed Brent for her constant giggles on the set of *The Great Lie* (WB 1941). (below) with Davis and Mary Astor. "A three-way triumph!" cried Photoplay.

Herbert Marshall replaced Brent in the latter. It was a missed opportunity. *The Letter* went on to receive seven Academy Award nominations including Best Picture. Brent's reunion with former sweetheart Davis on the set of *The Great Lie* was copasetic. She had returned from her ranch in New Hampshire and the arms of her almost-husband Arthur Farnsworth. Eddie Goulding directed his star duo for the third and last time. *The Great Lie* cast Brent as a playboy aviator who is prone to binge. After one bender, he finds himself married to a temperamental concert pianist (Mary Astor). He learns she hasn't received the final decree from a previous marriage. This affords Brent the opportunity to marry the gal he really loves (Davis). He flies off to Baltimore but lacks the nerve to tell her the good news. It was a thrill for Brent's fans to see him in the cockpit landing the plane. He did all his own flying in *The Great Lie*.

Astor steals every scene from her costars. "If I didn't think you meant so well I'd feel like slapping your face!" she snaps, when Davis arranges a position for Brent as an aerial navigator for Uncle Sam. After Brent and Davis finally tie the marital knot, the government calls him away to the jungles of Brazil. His plane goes down, and everyone assumes the worst. Before this bad news, Astor informs Davis that she is pregnant and determined to get Brent back. A distraught Davis decides that the two "wives" should retreat to a remote shack in Arizona until baby is born. For a cash settlement, Astor happily agrees to turn the bouncing bundle over to Davis. She would rather play the piano than change diapers. The "great lie" is born when Brent unexpectedly returns home to discover his baby boy. It's all very contrived, but danged if it doesn't manage to pull you into its sentimental pocket, along with a tear-stained hankie.

On the Warner set, freelance writer Jack Holland observed Goulding referee. In the middle of filming a quarrel Davis got the giggles. "I'm sorry Eddie," she apologized, "but it's George's fault. Drat him anyway. He gets a certain look in his eyes, and I can't go on." "I don't do a thing," Brent smiled. Holland enjoyed watching the compatible trio.[560] When Brent complained about playing worse than third fiddle in the movie, Goulding hugged him and purred, "Well, *I* still love you, George!" Brent disengaged himself from Goulding's embrace, lit up a cigarette, and laughed, "That's what I'm afraid of, Eddie."[561]

At first, Davis wasn't thrilled with the script. She sat in her canvas chair, smoking furiously. She finally told Astor, "All I do is mewl to George about 'that woman you married when you were drunk,' and to 'please come back to me' and all that crap."[562] The two actresses joined forces. Astor's role was built up and together they reworked the implausible script. It got to the point where Goulding would clap his head and say, "Well, ladies—if you're *ready*—would you kindly inform me as to what you are going to do?" What they did, enhanced by Goulding's patina of sophistication, worked. After Brent's surprise return, Astor uses the baby as leverage to get Brent back. Davis, reluctantly, tells him the truth. He solves the riddle with one of the film's memorable lines, "He's a fine little chap," he tells Astor, "and we'll miss him." Astor is the loser, or was she? In writing her memoirs, she called her character "a real bitch. I was delighted to test for it."[563] Astor runs away with the film. Such a departure afforded her an Academy Award for Best Supporting Actress.

Photoplay called *The Great Lie* a "three-way triumph." The review thought Brent "terrific." *Film Daily* recognized the marquee value of Davis-Brent-Astor and emphasized, "Brent capably carries the burden of the principal male role on his shoulders, registering strongly."[564] The film was solid box office and held over at theaters across the country. Brent's onscreen character was no hero, but the stimulus of Davis, Astor, and Goulding triggered something special in the actor. He manages a credible, impressive performance. Davis herself was puzzled at times by Brent's screen persona, describing him as "an enchanting man with wit and beauty, and an excitement he rarely was in the mood to transfer to the screen."[565] Of course, he had to compete with the camera's love affair with his leading ladies. George once remarked, "All a leading man needed was a good haircut, as the back of his head was the only part of him that an audience was ever likely to see."[566]

Ann Sheridan managed to coax Brent into the Hollywood nightlife. Wearing a black satin gown, she celebrated the holidays dancing with him under palm trees at the Cocoanut Grove. She praised that he was generous and always picked up every check in sight when they were out with other couples. "Money doesn't mean that much to me," Brent would say. "I like to be a giver."[567] His salary was modest compared to top tier players. Brent's annual earnings for 1939 totaled $99,208 vs. James Cagney's $243,000.[568] Brent's romancing Sheridan paid off the following year when *Film Daily* reported that his salary had oomphed to $110,833.33. In 1941, Sheridan had extra reason to celebrate. She got a hefty raise, retroactive pay, and a plum role in *Kings Row*. She had become the studio's top female draw after Bette Davis.

Upon completing *The Great Lie*, Brent was loaned to Columbia. The studio continued to farm Brent out for most of 1941, in roles that did nothing to further his career. *They Dare Not Love* was the last film directed by James Whale. Whale's legacy

A princely Brent and Bodil Rosing in James Whale's *They Dare Not Love* (Columbia 1941)

included such horror classics as *Frankenstein* (1931), *The Invisible Man* (1933), and what many consider his masterpiece, *The Bride of Franken-stein* (1935). The horror of Nazi persecution fueled Whale's swan song. According to the *Hollywood Reporter* Whale fell ill after filming began and was replaced. It was a cover-up. Some theorized that it was a personal thing between Whale and studio head Harry Cohn. Film historian Ken Hanke points to a few misguided authors who gave Brent the "unjusti-fied rap" of being homophobic toward Whale—and partially responsible for getting him fired. A highly unlikely claim, considering Brent's close friendship with Goulding. Cast member Kay Linaker also refuted the idea. She was an eyewitness to what really happened.

In a 2004 interview, Linaker stated that Whale was in a desperate emotional state and "had nasty things to say about *every*body."[569] During a profane screaming fit targeting Linaker and leading lady Martha Scott, Whale ranted, "Not only do I have the two ugliest broads in town, I've got the two lousiest fucking actresses!"[570] Finally, Scott's husband, who was visiting the set, put a stop to it. He told Whale to shut his mouth and "keep it shut … until I come back from talking to Harry Cohn." Cast and crew sat in a daze until Cohn arrived on the scene and very quietly informed the director, "You're through." Linaker, who later penned the 1958 horror classic *The Blob*, said that none of the cast members had any animosity toward Whale. They felt sorry for him. In the aftermath, Cohn brought in Charles Vidor to complete what was intended to be the most important picture Columbia had made up to that point. The dramatics on the set fueled by Whale's erratic behavior might have made a better film than what was released.

They Dare Not Love cast Brent as Kurt von Rotenburg, an Austrian Prince who flees from Vienna to America after Germany invades his homeland. Opening scenes establish the requisite suspense and glamour. While being tailed by the Gestapo, Brent finds time for a shipboard romance with an Austrian refugee (Martha Scott). They have a few laughs over champagne cocktails after a bartender describes Prince von Rotenburg's flamboyant attire. "Do I really look that gay?" Brent asks. In America, Brent finds not only refuge, but more distraction in the company of wealthy socialite Barbara Murdock (Kay Linekar). Feeling a bit guilt-ridden for abandoning his homeland, he finally bargains with Gestapo officer von Helsing (Paul Lukas) for the release of friends being held in concentration camps—offering himself as the bargain in the deal. Von Helsing agrees, but the Prince soon finds out that he has been double-crossed.

A Cleveland critic found the film "satisfying drama. Brent is at his best in a serious role."[571] Some thought Brent "woefully miscast." To be fair, although he may sound American, Brent offered enough continental charm and dash to be convincing. He also looked the part. *Photoplay* thought the slow tempo and weak direction had left Brent and Scott "more or less at sea." With a defter touch, claimed the review, "this would have, undoubtedly, resulted in a gem of a little picture."[572] The only comment Brent made about the film was in regard to his leading lady: "She'll crack up in ten years—throws herself too intensely into every part."[573] Surprisingly, *Photoplay* editor Ruth Waterbury warned readers not to go see *They Dare Not Love.* "George Brent is in this," she said, "but Brent has already survived so many horrors as to be absolutely turkey-proof."[574] Despite its reputation, the film is surprisingly watchable. Not long after the film wrapped, Minna Wallis threw a joint birthday bash for George and Eddie Goulding at the Mocambo. Ann Sheridan, Merle Oberon, Alexander Korda, and Charlie Chaplin were among the revelers. Harrison Carroll reported that the celebration was "really something."[575]

Brent braved similar, if less promising, fare in *International Lady.* Despite its comic book plotting, the United Artists release still had its moments. From London to Lisbon to Long Island, glamorous concert singer Ilona Massey, a Nazi agent, is being tailed and wooed by FBI man Brent.

Massey's low-key style meshes nicely with Brent, and her warm contralto is easy on the ear. Brent eventually nabs her for transmitting confidential information to saboteurs. She does this by singing over the airwaves … in code. Basil Rathbone, from Scotland Yard, joins in the fanciful plot while attempting to decipher Brent's use of American slang. When Rathbone begins deprecating Americans, he snidely asks Brent, "You're always in a rush and you haven't got any time. What have you got?" Brent paused a moment and ad-libbed, "We've got oomph." Director Tim Whelan left it in the script. Unfortunately, at 102 minutes, the story is so drawn out that all the flippancy becomes tiresome and the suspense loses its edge. Bosley Crowther thought Massey had all the acting ability of a manne-quin. "And Mr. Brent," he added, "seldom encourages her by so much as a change of expression."[576]

After *International Lady*, Brent was rushed to Queen of Angels Hos-pital. He sustained a serious spine injury while on Catalina Island. Brent was scheduled to join James Cagney in Canada to film the Royal Canadian Air Force saga *Captains of the Clouds*. Following surgery he was bedridden for a month. Grace Morphy-Hulst, a nurse at Queen of Angels, was com-

International Lady (UA 1941) with Basil Rathbone and Ilona Massey

pelled to write about what she witnessed during Brent's stay. She mentioned a daily visitor in Room 226—a beautiful redhead, who spent all her spare time with George. When Sheridan wasn't working on *Kings Row*, she would wheel Brent out onto the sun porch. They were usually joined by a small boy of African descent wearing a full-body cast. Brent asked the youngster if he enjoyed reading. "Yes!" he replied enthusiastically. George insisted that Ann purchase a handsomely bound illustrated volume of Aesop's Fables. The boy was thrilled, read it daily, and kept it under his pillow at night. The gesture spoke well for one of Hollywood's reliable leading men, and the daily vigil spoke volumes about Ann Sheridan.[577]

The *New York Times* decided that Brent's next outing for United Artists was "as musty as an abandoned attic" and just as unfunny. *Twin Beds* kept newlywed (Brent) from having a quiet, romantic honeymoon with his bride (Joan Bennett). She's too busy at the USO giving her kisses to soldiers. Being a good patriot, Brent doesn't mind—until a celebrated baritone (Misha Auer) is in hot pursuit of his wife. Brent's funniest moment is when Bennett insists he greet a multitude of unexpected party guests one evening. He stomps through the crowd snarling "hello, hello, HELLO!" before retreating to his library. The film's last half-hour is filled with Auer's relentless mugging as he tries to escape from the happy couple's boudoir. *Twin Beds* had been made twice before in the 1920s when such hokum was considered risqué. *Photoplay* felt that Brent appeared "ill at ease." To his credit, Brent is no worse than anyone else in this fiasco, including troupers like Una Merkel, Glenda Farrell, and Margaret Hamilton.

Two years had passed since Brent's praiseworthy performances in *Dark Victory* and *The Rains Came*. The ten films that followed, with a couple of exceptions, had wasted his talent. He would have fared better by joining Sheridan on suspension. Cecil B. DeMille wanted Brent for the

Twin Beds (UA 1942) with Joan Bennett

lead in his blockbuster *Reap the Wild Wind*, but a Paramount executive persuaded De Mille to use Ray Milland, by then considered a better box office draw.[578] Before Brent reported back to Warners for *In This Our Life*, he returned to Queen of Angels Hospital for a second spinal operation. It wasn't as serious but held up production. Afterward, he and Sheridan were spotted on the dance floor of the Miramar Hotel celebrating his recovery.

In This Our Life told the story of the Timberlakes, a dysfunctional family living in Virginia. In the center of the storm is their spoiled, selfish daughter Stanley (Bette Davis) who dumps her lawyer fiancé (Brent) and runs off with the husband (Dennis Morgan) of her sister Roy (Olivia de Havilland). It isn't long before Stanley's histrionics drive the guilt-ridden Morgan to suicide. Stanley's recklessness at the wheel leaves behind a hit-and-run victim—a child. She blames the accident on Brent's young legal assistant, Perry, an African-American, who also does odd jobs for the Timberlakes. When Stanley isn't creating havoc, she toys with the affections of her doting uncle (Charles Coburn) whose incestuous inclinations aren't exactly subtle. He tries to spoil her rotten, but she is already rotten. While Davis chews up the scenery, Brent and de Havilland carry on a slow burning romance. If the camera tended to favor de Havilland, it was with good reason. She and director John Huston began a love affair. After seeing some of the early rushes, Jack Warner took Huston aside, reminding him that Davis was the star and to direct accordingly. Huston had recently made his directorial debut with *The Maltese Falcon.* Still considered a novice, he had no choice but to allow Davis to run the gamut. "There is something elemental about Bette," said Huston in his memoirs, "a demon within her which threatens to break out and eat everybody, beginning with their ears."[579] Davis's reaction to the Huston-de Havilland romantics? "He fawned on her like a lapdog," she said years later.[580]

De Havilland's controlled performance and Brent's gentle intelligence offer the film some semblance of reality. Brent's character loses self-respect after Davis leaves, but he does an about turn. His appeal is underscored by his concern for civil liberties. He refuses big bucks to represent the rich uncle's lawsuit involving a dilapidated low-income housing project. Brent and de Havilland are determined to protect young Perry (Ernest Anderson) from Davis's accusations. When they confront Davis, she wails, "They always lie for each other!" Ironically, it was Davis who noticed Anderson working as a waiter in Warner's Green Room. She pointed him out to Huston, who hired him on the spot.

The most modern elements in the film are the poignant portrayals of Perry and his mother (Hattie McDaniel). Her quiet underplaying is of special significance after Perry is arrested. She speaks plainly, "He tried to tell them, but they don't listen to no colored boy." It was a landmark film speaking to the injustice toward African-Americans. In 1943, the U.S. Office of Censorship refused to pass the film for export, because it confirmed that a black individual's testimony in Virginia would be disregarded if it conflicted with the testimony of a white person. Government hadn't caught up with Hollywood when it came to social injustice. James Baldwin said that Davis's "ruthlessly accurate" portrayal made her the

In This Our Life (WB 1942) Brent, Olivia de Havilland, Billie Burke
and Frank Craven face demon Bette Davis

"toast of Harlem"—that she completely grasped the evils of white privilege and understood the machinations of a racist southern belle.[581]

New York Times's Bosley Crowther praised the "frank allusion to racial discrimination" and the "realistic manner uncommon to Hollywood" of Ernest Anderson's "educated and comprehending character." "Otherwise," said the review, "the story is pretty much of a downhill run with Miss Davis going from bad to worse."[582] Crowther thought de Havilland "warm and easy" and Brent "presentable." *Photoplay* found *In This Our Life* "abnormally unpleasant" and Davis's character "mentally ill." Critics were so overwhelmed by Davis's antics that any mention of Huston's atmospheric touches, or the commendable performances of Brent, de Havilland, Dennis Morgan, Charles Coburn, and Billie Burke, seemed negligible.

Davis's overblown portrayal is a favorite among her many gay fans including author Mathew Kennedy, who finds her Stanley Timberlake to be "wildly entertaining." The Mike Black/Carole Summers documentary *Queer Icon: The Cult of Bette Davis* (2009) pays homage to Davis as the ultimate screen bitch. They zero in on the excessive quality of Davis's acting, saying, "You can never know what's enough, until you know what's too much. Bette Davis wasn't afraid to take us there." In *Queer Icon* Kennedy describes Davis's willingness to go over the edge throughout *In This Our Life* with Byzantine gestures, bulging eyes, clipped speech, and unexpected pauses. "She's becoming the Bette Davis who provides the red meat for drag," he explains. *In This Our Life* was based on the 1942 Pulitzer prize-winning novel by Ellen Glasgow. The author was outraged after seeing Davis's portrayal. When the two met face-to-face, Glasgow minced no words in telling Davis what she thought. Davis spoke apprehensively, "You should have been an actress, Miss Glasgow. You're so volatile!" Glasgow fired back, "If I had chosen acting over writing, I wouldn't be the overacting ham you are!"[583]

In the summer of 1941, Brent chatted with the veteran magazine writer Maude Cheatham about why he wouldn't marry Ann Sheridan. He insisted that they were happy as they were. Why complicate their relationship with the "musts" and "don'ts" of marriage? He recognized that Ann was ambitious and had a brilliant career ahead of her. A monotonous round of domestic duties would spoil the tempo. Cheatham felt that the Brent-Sheridan combo had benefited them both. Ann had gained poise and assurance from Brent. "George is more approachable," said Cheatham, "laughs easily and often."[584] "Thank heavens," he cheered, "Ann's not one of these restless, chattering women who must be up and doing every minute."

Many were not convinced that George was a positive influence. Grips and prop men were used to calling out, "Hi ya, Annie!" when she walked onto the set. George, if present, would wince. It just wasn't his style. Ann made herself accessible. She enjoyed the company of her hairdresser and wardrobe girls. In the commissary she was besieged with smiling faces. Messenger boys shared their latest joke. "Brother that's a honey," she'd laugh. Ann's studio friends weren't too happy when Brent entered the picture. He preferred that he and Ann eat their well-prepared meals elsewhere and attempted to mold her to his secluded approach to life. It had stifling effect. Ann loved George, but her nature craved the fun, the laughter, the music of a social life.

Fall 1940. Ann Sheridan and George in the throes of romance.
James Cagney looks on.

On December 7, 1941, Ann and George were having lunch by the poolside at the home of screenwriter Bess Meredith. Meredith's son, John Lucas, brought out a portable radio and they listened to news reports detailing the attack on Pearl Harbor. "It was a very quiet lunch," recalled Lucas years later.[585] Everyone had been aware of the possibility of war. "What incentive is there to plan for a future with the world in this state of chaos?" Brent asked, shortly before the attack. "We don't know what will happen next week, let alone next year!" His declaration was confirmed when he and Ann reneged on their anti-marriage vows. For Christmas he gave her a luxury car; then came the engagement ring. After New Year's, they tied the proverbial knot in Palm Beach. They arrived in Florida, unheralded, on January 5, 1942. During a downpour of rain, they headed for the residence of Brent's sister Kathleen. The ceremony took place at her home that evening. Brent's nephew, Patrick Watson, served as Best Man. Attorney William Cain gave the bride away, while Judge Richard Robbins presided. Ann took her vows wearing a white mantilla, a gift from George. The only other attendees were Mrs. Cain and Kathleen's close friend, former film actress Constance Talmadge.[586]

Kathleen's luck with marriage ran into dead ends, literally. Several years after she divorced Marcel De Sano, he committed suicide in Paris. Shortly following her 1938 divorce from Victor Watson, the Hearst editor jumped to his death from the eleventh floor of the Hotel Abbey in New York. He reportedly suffered from "melancholia."[587] The following year, she married Broadway producer Sam H. Harris (*Dinner at Eight*), thirty years her senior. He died two years later, leaving Kathleen (now going by the name China Harris) a wealthy woman.

George and his new bride planned to honeymoon on *Santana*. He had the old motor removed for the occasion, but war regulations blocked the purchase of a new one. When he tried to retrieve the old motor, it had been junked. Instead of an extended honeymoon, they reported to work.

Kathleen "China" Harris — One of the few shining lights
in the life of George Brent. Here with her son Patrick
Watson, 1941 (Courtesy of Ian Watson)

Ann was assigned *Wings for the Eagle*—a love triangle with the backdrop of America's fighting aircraft industry. George reunited with Barbara Stanwyck for *The Gay Sisters*. In March, headlines read, "Ann Takes Oomph to the Army." In twenty streamlined dresses, she entertained draftees making it clear that she wanted to circulate among the soldiers, not just officers and their wives.[588] Before long, Sheridan was the selected screen favorite at Fort Devins, Fort Jackson, and Fort Davis in the Canal Zone.[589] While she was away, Brent offered his own brand of oomph to the War Bond drive. A Detroit nightclub, The Bowery, offered direct phone calls to Hollywood stars for the purchase of $100 defense bonds. First to sign up was a woman who nabbed the opportunity to gab with Brent for three minutes. After she hung up, she said, "I'd like to increase my purchase by $500 more!" She refused to divulge what Brent had said to her.[590]

Upon Ann's return, George insisted that she have ten days rest before reporting back to the studio.[591] He was finishing *You Can't Escape*

Forever—which came close to completing his contract. The pressure of touring and work didn't leave much time for domesticity. They each continued to live in their own separate residences—George in Toluca Lake, and Ann on her ranch in Encino. Their plans to build a new home were hampered by wartime restrictions.

Ann Sheridan had an uncommonly high rating for honesty in Hollywood. In a conversation with Gladys Hall, shortly before the wedding, Ann claimed that she and George were never serious about marriage. She was tired of him reneging on going out and seeing people. So, she renewed her friendship with Cesar Romero for evenings of dancing and fraternizing with friends. The summer after their marriage, Ann and George were seen quarreling while out for dinner. In July, Ann and an ex-school chum from Texas took a bachelor-girls vacation to New York. Then George flew to Washington, D.C., without Ann, to volunteer for the Civilian Air Corps. For Sheridan, the challenge of marriage was familiar territory along her bumpy road to stardom.

Clara Lou Sheridan

Born Clara Lou Sheridan on February 21, 1915, the future "Oomph Girl" grew up in Denton, Texas. She had Scotch-Irish ancestry. Her father, George W. Sheridan, was a garage mechanic and rancher. Clara, a tomboy, loved to ride horses and play tackle football. "If she punched you," recalled one neighbor playmate, "she'd break your damn arm."[592] Her family called her "Ludie" and Dad was "The Boss Man"—she adored him. He instilled in her the idea, "You have to do what you have to do."[593] Clara's creative side leaned towards art, drama, and music. Following high school she attended North Texas State Teachers College. "I'm afraid teaching school was only a rare possibility," Ann laughed, later. She was more interested in having fun.[594] Clara's smoky contralto got her a regular gig as blues vocalist for the school's band, as well as a guest spot at the annual Dallas Country Club Stag Night in 1933.

Clara's formal education came to a halt when her sister Kitty entered her in Paramount's "Search for Beauty Contest." Sheridan admitted, "I was very young with pudgy fat and kinky hair and a space between my teeth—oh God." Regardless, on October 11, 1933, the eighteen-year-old found herself headed for Hollywood. Clara was rewarded a ten-second bit part in the Buster Crabbe film *Search For Beauty* (1934) and a six-month contract. After all, she could ride a horse—they

January 11, 1942 Newlyweds Sheridan and Brent arrive in San Bernardino. A rumor surfaced years later that Brent and Errol Flynn had an altercation over Sheridan, while she and Flynn filmed *Edge of Darkness* in Monterey, California (August-September 1942)

could use her in Westerns (and they did). It wasn't long before Clara, now being billed as "Lou Sheridan," was missing her family. She found Hollywood a cold town. "I'm going back. Can't stand it. Nothing happens here," she'd cry.[595] Her sister Kitty was the only one who knew and sent Clara money when she was strapped. "Dad believed in me," recalled Sheridan. "He'd take his cronies to see his little Ludie on the screen. I just couldn't let him down."[596] Rechristened Ann Sheridan in October 1934, director Mitchell Leisen offered her encouragement and a small role in

Behold My Wife, in which she commits suicide. "Committing suicide was the great thing, you know," Ann told writer Ray Hagen in 1965.[597] Her minor success spared her the drudge of doing work as an extra. *Dallas Morning News* predicted that "in a few months she will be among the Shearers and Garbos."[598] When Paramount finally dropped Ann's option she found a new agent. She signed with Warner Bros. and began taking her career, and acting, more seriously.

Ann married another struggling young actor, Edward Norris, in Mexico (August 1936). "It was a case of love at first sight," Ann happily told reporters. It was Norris's third marriage. Ann's career picked up (as did her cigarette habit). Norris, a Robert Taylor look alike, indulged in self-pity after MGM cancelled his contract.[599] He told Ann that their marriage was a mistake. She filed for divorce in the fall of 1938. Prior to the divorce, columnist Walter Winchell suggested that Ann be given roles with more "umph" to display her "eye-filling chassis" preferably in Technicolor.[600] Winchell got his wish when Sheridan was cast in Errol Flynn's *Dodge City* (1939) as a rowdy saloon singer. "Almost made me blind," recalled Sheridan, "that incredible color lighting."[601]

Warner publicity translated "umph" to "oomph" and promoted Ann's assets: red hair, hazel eyes, full lips, and irresistible smile. Her "Oomph Coronation" was made official on March 16, 1939, in Los Angeles. The "in the bag" publicity stunt was theoretically made by a jury consisting of twenty-five men in the arts and sciences. The campaign, coupled with stunning portraits of Sheridan done by ace photographer George Hurrell, gave her enormous visibility. She made the coveted cover of *Life* in July.

When asked about her new moniker, Sheridan was purported to have replied, "Oomph is what a fat man says when he leans down to tie his shoelace in a telephone booth."[602] She admitted that the remark was a press agent's invention. "I adopted it wholeheartedly," she said.[603] Sheridan's tart onscreen delivery had turned heads when she was paired with

Cagney and Bogart in *Angels With Dirty Faces* (1938). Her work was skillful and conscientious. By the time Cagney's *Torrid Zone* (1940) was released, Ann's stellar status at Warners was assured. Bette Davis was asked to name the most promising new personality on the lot. Davis answered without pause, "Ann Sheridan."[604] Ann was thrilled to death with this bit of news. When the two actresses costarred in *The Man Who Came to Dinner*, Sheridan asked Davis for advice on the timing of her lines. "Davis ate it up," recalled director William Keighley. "She loved playing God."[605]

When Sheridan went on suspension, she explained, "I knew I was getting nowhere fast. The studio had given me terrific publicity, but no chance to live up to that publicity. I got sick of that." There were also salary issues. She was only making $600 a week and her pictures did well at the box office. She asked for $2,000 a week and was refused. She was instructed to report for work on *The Strawberry Blonde* but didn't show up. "Maybe it was just plain old Texas stubbornness, but—well I had to do what I had to do." Since her dad had passed away, his words echoed in her ears. Some gave Ann the cold shoulder during her battle. Some blamed Brent for encouraging her.[606] A few were supportive: Cagney, Bogart, and the gas station attendant who filled up Ann's tank and refused to take her money. She was moved by such gestures. When Ann returned to film *Kings Row* she felt secure. It became her favorite role. "It's fun to be an actress at last," she said. "I've never been anything more than an ornament."[607] Her salary was raised to $1,000 a week. Ann didn't feel up to combining marriage and career. "I'm saving me for myself," she insisted.[608] Ironically, Brent had paraphrased the same idea to producer Hal Wallis, "No woman will ever own me; I own myself!"[609]

Brent and Sheridan surprised everyone by tying the marital knot, but skeptics wagged that the couple must have wanted to marry while they were still in love. It turned out to be true. Several months later they were bent on being ex-mates. They weren't speaking or acknowledging each other. "George and I didn't part the best of friends," Ann remarked after divorcing ex-husband number two.[610]

It was assumed that all was well with George and Ann when they showed up at a USO opening in early '42. By the end of August, Ann announced they had separated. She was on location filming *Edge of Darkness.* George was busy putting in a solid fifty hours flying government planes in Oxnard. His position in the Civilian Air Corps necessitated his replacement as the male lead in *Old Acquaintance* with Bette Davis and Miriam Hopkins.[611] He was absorbed in this new endeavor. Checking in on Ann wasn't a priority. "George hadn't spoken much for a month," Ann candidly told a writer for *Screenland.* "He drove down from Oxnard and arrived at my ranch in the Valley. From four o'clock until late that night we talked things over. George very frankly told me what was wrong with me, and that took some time." Among Brent's revelations was that Ann was too focused on her career. When he was finally finished, she agreed to call the head of Warners publicity, Alex Evelove, and give a statement for the press. Early the next morning, September 28, Brent jumped the gun. He informed Louella Parsons in a broken voice that "Ann wants her freedom." "It's the last thing in the world that I wanted," he whimpered, "but I don't see what I can do about it."[612] Parsons, naturally, followed up with a phone call to Sheridan, who countered, "George said he wanted his freedom and so I'm going to give it to him." Was Brent's ungallant approach a push for sympathy? A few days earlier, news of his position with the Air Corps had hit the newsstands. Brent told Parsons that he was so distraught that officials gave him a day off to talk it over with Ann. "I just couldn't work. I was too upset," he said, adding that he wanted to protect Ann, because he was still in love with her.

"I'm sure the fact that we had two homes had much to do with failure of our marriage," Ann later explained. "I tried to live at George's little house … and when I suggested that we live at my ranch house George would complain. The war is blamed for everything these days. It might as well be blamed for the failure of the Sheridan-Brent marriage."[613] Ann talked about George's dark moods, their differing likes and dislikes— things that she was very familiar with before they married. She thought the rough spots would smooth themselves out but claimed that George was determined to change her. "A marriage cannot last if one tries to dominate the other's life," she said pointedly. Ann also zeroed in on George's shyness—his phobia about mingling with people.

> I like to go out and mingle with other people and have fun now and then. What girl doesn't? We simply had too many odds against us. At George's … there wasn't even a place for me to hang my clothes. And since my home had also been designed for a state of single blessedness, George had his problems when he came to live with me. Our greatest mistake was not having a common home we could call our own.[614] But the real break came after I had been on location with Edge of Darkness. George had not communicated with me in any way during this time, and I was naturally angry. It turned out that we didn't see or speak to each other, even by phone, during the entire month I was away. And I was not exactly in the most pleasant frame of mind … when I did return to Hollywood."[615]

Columnist Jimmy Fidler insisted that the bust-up was due to Brent's "dictatorial attitude vs. her refusal to take orders."[616] Overall, their individual views and approach to life had to change radically for a happy marriage. Ann set up no barriers between herself and others. George felt barriers were a necessity. On the plus side, it was reported that, for Ann's sake, he learned to rumba.

In October 1942, Ann retained an attorney in Las Vegas to schedule divorce proceedings. In December, she opted for Mexico instead, where she established residence. Ann was frequently seen with Errol Flynn around Mexico City. Flynn was making headlines for an upcoming trial involving two underage girls who accused him of statutory rape. "Sure I saw Ann," admitted Flynn when he returned home at the end of the month. "We are pals. We have laughs together. We laughed about everything. We'd probably laugh right in the middle of a kiss. That's why we couldn't get serious about each other."[617] Ann finalized her divorce on January 5, the exact date of her and George's wedding anniversary. Civil Judge Acuna Pardo in Cuernavaca granted the decree.[618] Sheridan returned to the U.S., her two-bedroom ranch house, four fertile acres, and rumba records. The walnut crop paid her taxes, and a Victory Garden curtailed the need for ration points. The only gift that Ann kept from George was a burro named "Oscar" . . . a memento to remember him by.[619]

Writer Stuart Jerome, who worked in the Warner mailroom from 1938–'42, commented on Sheridan's lack of pretense. He recalled Louella Parsons asking Sheridan the reason for her short-lived marriage. Ann's answer was flippant but unprintable. "Brent bent," she replied.[620] When author Don E. Stanke interviewed Brent for a career article in the early 1970s, he asked about Sheridan. Brent sadly shook his head and murmured, "What a waste of what could have been a good life."[621]

Brent announced he was giving up his career for the duration of the war.[622] It became obvious that he was content to be on his own again. His duty as a flying instructor entailed acquiring expertise in every type of airplane. Brent had a new purpose: to instill knowledge and survival skills in the hearts and minds of young air cadets. His sister China came out to visit and made a point of saying that George had a difficult job teaching inexperienced boys to fly. According to her, George never complained but recognized that until the youngsters got broken in there was always an impending element of danger.[623]

1943 Sailing single along the California coast on *Santana*

11

Hates War—Joins Air Corps

In 1939, Brent made a point of expressing gratitude for his newly adopted country. "I'm happy here, intend to stay here and hope to be a good American. Good enough to stick by America no matter what happens and no matter what I'm asked to do."[624] In December of that year, Brent was among the many signers who petitioned President Roosevelt requesting that the government bring economic pressure against Germany. The idea to curtail aggression was sponsored by The Anti-Nazi League. Two years later, in the aftermath of Pearl Harbor, Brent offered his acreage on Oahu as an evacuation center for Hawaiian children. At his expense, the new facility provided surgical equipment, emergency rations, and a bomb shelter.[625]

"Just when things begin to sing . . . along comes the war," George Brent lamented in the summer of 1942. "But then . . . what can you do? There's a job to be done and we fellows have got to do it. It's mine for the air corps as soon as I finish this picture."[626] Brent was on the set of *You Can't Escape Forever*, talking with veteran Ogden, Utah, reporter Alice Pardoe West. He had been rejected for the Armed Services. His post as an instructor for the Civil Aeronautics Institute in Oxnard was a position he eagerly accepted.[627] West listened as Brent philosophized.

War is ghastly! Why do civilized people have to have such things? Look at all these young fellows out here… they struggle for years to get any place in their career, and just as they get a break … they have to give it all up and go to war. Oh, don't get me wrong. The fellows want to go … in fact, you couldn't keep most of them back … but the point is, they may never be able to come back to the place they have left.[628]

World War II was the deadliest military conflict in history; 60 million people were killed. Over 418,000 Americans, as Brent put it, never "came back to the place they [had] left." Many veterans who did return found the ghosts of war had followed them home.

Brent made five films during wartime. He was also reunited with some of his former leading ladies on radio. In 1943, he teamed with Kay Francis for Lux Radio's *The Lady is Willing*. Francis had recently toured combat zones in North Africa where she entertained for the USO. Brent paid compliments to Francis and her commitment to entertain overseas. Host Cecil B. DeMille pointed to her work at the Naval Aid Auxiliary where Francis held the hand of more than one dying soldier—staying with him until his last breath. DeMille introduced Brent as "one of our longtime favorites. We borrowed George from the Coast Guard." Brent transferred from aeronautics into the Coast Guard because of his skill in both navigation and flying. The vulnerability of the California coast made it imperative that the Coast Guard be on alert for Japanese submarines. Hedda Hopper's column raved how distinguished Brent looked in his Coast Guard uniform, while sporting a new silver mane. Several columnists made a point of Brent letting his hair go gray. He had been dying his hair black for years.

Despite his patriotic inclinations, Brent's participation in the armed services was limited due to his spine injury in 1941. After the draft call of 1940, Brent's African-American valet/chauffeur, Henry Johnson, registered. In November 1942, Johnson, who was a few years younger than Brent, was finally mustered into the Army. Brent, who was thirty-eight, felt remorseful upon being designated physically unfit for combat duty by both the Navy and the Air Force. When Johnson and other friends enlisted, Brent was fit to be tied. Relief came when he began his assignment as a civilian flight instructor. However, he found that he couldn't sit for long periods of time without excruciating pain. George had to give up his instructorship and his uniform. It was several months before he was paged to be a pilot for the Coast Guard.[629] In between assignments, he felt conspicuous wearing civilian clothes. He was glad to be back in uniform by February 1943. This new assignment didn't last long, either. On May 19, *Variety* reported that Brent had received a medical discharge from the Coast Guard.

Brent's first film after war was declared, *The Gay Sisters* (1942), was scheduled to star Bette Davis. She wasn't interested. Instead, Barbara Stanwyck jumped at the opportunity to play the bad apple of a prominent New York family. The moody story was touted to parallel the lives of wealthy New Yorkers like the Vanderbilts. The Gaylord sisters, an unhappy trio of prospective millionaire heiresses, were played by Stanwyck, Geraldine Fitzgerald, and Nancy Coleman. The film chronicles their long courtroom battle for papa's half-billion dollar estate. The fly in the probate ointment is George Brent, a wealthy construction engineer, who was once secretly wed to Stanwyck. Theirs was a marriage of convenience—a hundred-thousand dollars worth for her. The union also produced a baby boy. The film had echoes of the 1933 Stanwyck-Brent film *Baby Face* in which she played a money-hungry, hard-hearted woman, who inexplicably relents to love in the final reel. It was reported that when Stanwyck

The Gay Sisters (WB 1942) with Barbara Stanwyck and
(below) the duo with director Irving Rapper

met face-to-face with Brent on the first day of shooting, she said, "Well, here we go again!"[630]

As Fiona Gaylord, Stanwyck is coolly self-assured in a tailor-made part. She makes a meal of her role and personifies star-power acting. Brent, most admirably, provides the requisite contrast allowing Stanwyck to shine. One highlight, a flashback, has Stanwyck offering her sisters a sarcastic account of how she nabbed Brent for a groom. We see him in charge of a road crew paving a bridge. Along comes Stanwyck driving recklessly through a designated road block. Brent falls off the truck, lands flat on his rear end, and yells at her, "Now look what you've done to my asphalt!" The sisters scream with mirth at her ability, completely out of character, to maneuver Brent with coy tricks in order to claim an inheritance from her aunt.

Brent's chronic back problems may explain a ruckus that occurred during filming. He was required to carry Barbara Stanwyck across a stream. Director Irving Rapper chastised him during the shoot. "George," he pleaded, "try not to look so grim and strained. Barbara isn't that heavy." George tried to joke about it. "It's a strain just the same," he fired back. "I got to thinking about stumbling and dropping her—the picture would be held up. How'd you feel if you had to carry a million dollars worth of actress over slippery rocks?"[631] For Brent to complain about a back condition—that he wasn't up to snuff—placed his manhood, and perhaps his career, in jeopardy.

The Gay Sisters needed a lot of trimming. Critics targeted the film's length. Some felt the subplots involving the younger two sisters unnecessary. Others found the characters unappealing. The *New York Times* complained, "Simply to prove that life produces a singularly large crop of disagreeable people is hardly enough." The review could not understand why Brent loved Fiona "with all the ardor of a spring buck" after the way she treated him. Stanwyck brought a certain "bite" to her role, but the rest of the cast, said the review, "seem to be feeling their way around the gloom."[632] *Film Daily* found the film to be a "splendidly produced drama … richly lavish and atmospherically impressive … that will appeal chiefly to the ladies."[633] In 1978, the film's director, Irving Rapper, would drag Brent out of retirement for a cameo role in *Born Again*.

Geraldine Fitzgerald, who played the sex-hungry Gaylord sister, co-starred with Brent for the third and last time in *The Gay Sisters*. Not long after the film's release, she was traveling cross-country on the same train as Bette Davis. During a stopover in Kansas City the two decided to take a stroll around the station, despite the retinue of fans following close behind. "Bette had one favorite subject over all others," recalled Fitzgerald many years later. "Sex."

> 'Now Fritzy,' she asked me. 'What do you think of George Brent?'
>
> I said, 'I think he's a very talented actor.'
>
> 'No, I don't mean on the screen … I mean in bed.'
>
> The crowd following us looked at the ground, pretending they hadn't heard, which meant they had. 'But I've never been to bed with him,' I said. Bette looked at me, amazed, and said for the benefit of everyone else, 'Then you must be the only one on the Warner lot who hasn't.'[634]

Brent's next release was a loan-out to United Artists called *Silver Queen*— an 1870s Western saga in which he and Priscilla Lane play professional gamblers. Looking dashing and slim, Brent made a presentable vis-à-vis for Miss Lane despite her being eleven years his junior. Although their eye contact had punch, Lane's soft, lovely screen presence lacked the emotional fire required for her role. The *New York Times* felt her talent tended "to resemble an over-eager school girl."[635] *Film Daily* decided that Lloyd

A dashing Brent holds Priscilla Lane in *Silver Queen* (UA 1942)

Bacon's direction "brought little inspiration" and agreed that both Brent and Lane played their roles "without too much conviction."[636] A review from the *Boston Herald* emphasized *Silver Queen's* "remarkable sedative qualities." The production values, however, were handsome. *Silver Queen* was Oscar-nominated not only for Art Direction but for Victor Young's music score. It was reported that Brent suffered internal injuries during his big saloon fight with shifty bad guy Bruce Cabot. As further punishment, Brent was rushed into his second-to-last release under contract.

You Can't Escape Forever, shot between May–July 1942, cast Brent in the familiar role of a newsman who teams with a female reporter (Brenda Marshall). Together, they investigate the dealings of a gangster (Eduardo Cianelli) who runs a black market on rationed wartime goods. The film was an ineffective mix of fainting spells (Marshall) and ear-tugging

(Brent, whenever he had a hunch). Surprisingly, the two leads had little chemistry. They fail to capture the simpatico they displayed in *South of Suez*. The comic relief of Roscoe Karns, who tries awfully hard, didn't help. *You Can't Escape Forever* was little more than a perpetual cat-and-mouse chase in off-beat locations. Monotony instead of suspense led audiences to the inevitable Brent-Marshall fade-out kiss. *Variety* thought Brent "most successful in making both the comedy and the melodramatic phases of his role jibe."[637] Bosley Crowther's review's deduced that the film should have been avoided altogether.

Brent's stints with the Air Corps and Coast Guard delayed filming his final release for Warner Bros. Following his medical discharge he and the studio, by mutual agreement, postponed things indefinitely. Brent may have wanted to avoid another run-in with Ann Sheridan. In August 1943, the two stood face-to-face when Sheridan unexpectedly opened the door to the studio's Green Room. George gave her a curt nod, and Ann "countered with one even more frigid." Nary a word was spoken between them. Jimmy Fidler enthused, "I find such open hostility refreshing."[638] The columnist was tired of Hollywoodites proclaiming they had remained "good friends."

During his screen sabbatical, Brent made an unusual mix of news headlines. A few days after his divorce from Sheridan, he found himself in hot water with actor Alan Curtis. Brent had told Louella Parsons that he found Ilona Massey the most attractive woman he ever hoped to meet and that as soon as he was free he hoped her answer would be "yes."[639] Curtis was outraged. Though he and Massey had divorced a couple of days prior to Brent's confession, Mr. Curtis told Sheilah Graham, "I think that it's bad taste for Brent to say all that. Why she's hardly divorced from me yet. That guy was always calling her up. I dislike him very much."[640] George made Parsons retract every word she had written. "Your story intimated we were having a secret romance while each was married," he fumed.[641] Wisely, Brent backed off from Ilona, who had advised Curtis to make several poor career choices. Not that Brent would have ever listened to her. Instead, he flew to Acapulco to hobnob with socialite Dorothy Di Frasso. Not long afterward, Brent made more headlines for gambling in a whiskey fraud. U.S. Attorney J. Albert Woll revealed that the actor had lost $5,000. The Chicago-based operation had promised to pay profits from a label called "Old Switch." They filed for bankruptcy instead, and investors were left hanging[642]

It became obvious that Brent was not eager to return to picture work. Aside from his final obligation with the studio, he had considered filming *The Raft* based on the true experiences of three U.S. Navy Fliers who survived thirty-four days in the Pacific Ocean without food or water until they hit the Puka Puka atoll. Being reduced to skin-and-bones may have proven too much for Brent. The film never got underway until 2013 as *Ghosts of the Pacific* (scheduled for a 2014 release). During 1943, Brent's acting was limited to radio. Aside from Kay Francis, he was paired with Alice Faye in *This Thing Called Love* for Lux. Cleveland critic Robert Stephen found the bedroom farce amusing and Brent "very good in the light male lead." Stephen was unimpressed with Faye, saying she was "amateurish." What few knew, until Hedda Hopper told them, was that Faye was so emotionally tied up in knots that she collapsed into Brent's arms while uttering her last line. "The audience thought it was part of the show," reported Hopper, "but it wasn't."[643] Did Alice still harbor feelings for her old beau? Next up, Brent played Roddy McDowell's father on a Lux version of *My Friend Flicka*. This was followed by Brent's Lux teaming with Rosalind Russell in the flag-waving *Flight for Freedom*—RKO's thinly disguised biopic about Amelia Earhart's last solo flight. Playing an ace pilot, Brent was a natural choice to accompany Russell on a doomed mission tinged with espionage. Host Cecil B. DeMille proclaimed, in politically incorrect terms, that the story "delivers a screaming message of death to the Japs." Brent appeared in a total of twenty Lux productions from 1938–'47.

In December 1943, seventeen months after completing *You Can't Escape Forever*, Brent checked into Warner Bros. studio for the last time. *My Reputation* offered a bold treatment of wartime morality. As a war widow with two sons, Barbara Stanwyck becomes the target of gossip when she sheds her widow's weeds to romance George Brent, a major. Brent personifies the noncommittal guy—a ladies man, yet one who is sensitive and knows how to listen. He is comfortable in his own skin and up front about his aversion to marriage. As author Jeanine Basinger puts it, "He is not really interested in marriage, but would enjoy having a mutually satisfying sex relationship . . . and he makes his intentions clear."[644] Stanwyck's adjustment to widowhood coupled with her attraction to a man of Brent's character strikes an honest chord. Her mother (Lucile Watson) offers Stanwyck only a baggage of guilt for not wanting to wear black and adhere to the dictates of convention. A chum of her late husband (Jerome Cowan) makes unwanted sexual advances. Only one individual (Eve Arden) encourages Stanwyck to stop allowing others to manage her life. Thirty minutes into the film Brent arrives to offer the same message. He has a direct, masculine charm that both attracts and frightens Stanwyck.

After a year-and-a-half off screen, Brent brought a new maturity to his acting. He looked more distinguished than ever. He also had some of the best lines in *My Reputation*. When Stanwyck talks about her travels to Europe, Brent deduces that her itinerary was "by the book." He muses, "I've seen hundreds of people like you all over the world, guidebook in hand, walking ruthlessly from cathedral to cathedral." When he makes the logical move to kiss her, she panics. He assumes that she is a grown-up. "Or,

My Reputation (WB 1946) Brent, Eve Arden and John Ridgely watch
war widow Barbara Stanwyck "hatch"

aren't you?" he asks. There is no question as to what he's after, but he has
the intelligence to recognize that she simply isn't ready for someone like
him. They meet up again a few months later. Stanwyck has shed a few lay-
ers of insecurity. "If you hadn't been poured into the icy mold of conven-
tionality," Brent tells her, "you'd be a good egg. You're going to hatch one
of these days." And, in the process of watching Stanwyck "hatch," Brent's
pleasure-seeking lone wolf has his own metamorphosis.

It was reported that the film's director, Kurt Bernhardt, a German
émigré, was out of touch with Americans. Stanwyck found him difficult.[645] Behind the camera, however, was the guiding light of photographer James Wong Howe. Howe enhanced Stanwyck's every move and
mood. High-angle shots, for example, emphasized her character's emotional loneliness in the first half. Completed in January 1944, the film
was viewed by servicemen overseas in 1945. It wasn't until 1946 that U.S.
audiences saw *My Reputation*. Brent's farewell to Warner Bros. was a mas-

sive box office hit. Bay Area critic Wood Soanes praised the intelligent script for being "peopled with real individuals" and found the acting first rate. Soanes called Stanwyck's portrayal a "triumph" and thought Brent "forthright and compelling."[646] *Variety* cheered, "Brent turns in an outstanding performance, endowing his role with rich humor."[647] *My Reputation* would remain one of Stanwyck's personal favorites. Accolades were also offered to Brent by the Thomas A. Edison Society. The group announced in May 1946 that they were honoring Brent for the "most consistent record for sanity in acting."[648] While some preferred the acting chops of Claude Rains, Paul Henreid, or James Cagney, others found relief in Brent's rational approach.

In 1941, Harvard University's *Lampoon* magazine put a hex on George Brent and Joan Crawford, saying the star duo were the "most qualified for a pension." Brent's retort to *Lampoon* was fueled by frustration. "Tell those babies any of them can have my contract," he argued. "I'd even retire without a pension, if they could fix it up with Warner Brothers."[649] *Variety* elaborated that it took George twelve years to wind up a seven year contract for various reasons, including suspensions.[650] Before leaving the Warner lot for good, Brent did a couple of good deeds. On February 10, 1944, he and Stanwyck tossed a party for still photographer Jack Woods, who had been inducted into the army. Brent also made arrangements for young Al LaRue, a Bogart look-alike, to make a screen test. It wasn't a go, but Brent's encouragement whetted LaRue's ambition. Within a couple of years and an acquired skill with a bullwhip, Al became known as Western star, Lash LaRue.

Prior to starting *My Reputation*, Brent had signed with International Pictures. His first assignment, *Tomorrow Is Forever*, didn't begin shooting until March 1945. In the meantime, he completed two popular releases with leading ladies Hedy Lamarr and Joan Fontaine. For the Lamarr picture, *Experiment Perilous*, Brent replaced the previously announced Gregory Peck. The psychological mystery was based on Margaret Carpenter's 1943 novel. Scenarist Warren Duff changed Carpenter's contemporary setting to the Victorian, tapping into the Freudian motifs of that era. The story begins in 1903, with Dr. Huntington Bailey (Brent), a psychiatrist, investigating the death of an elderly woman he had briefly encountered on a train bound for New York. He pays a call to the home of her brother Nick Bederaux (Paul Lukas) and his disturbingly beautiful wife, Allida (Lamarr). It becomes obvious to Dr. Bailey that Allida is riddled with fear. The domineering Bederaux has cut her off from the outside world. Bailey's sleuthing uncovers Allida's close friendship with a young poet who had died unexpectedly. His suspicions are further confirmed by the dead sister's diaries.

Mentally unhinged, Bederaux eventually confesses to murder and attempts to blow up his home by gas combustion. Bailey, who by now has fallen in love with Allida, rescues her and her young son in the nick of time.

Brent found beautiful Hedy LaMarr "exasperating" in *Experiment Perilous* (RKO 1944)

The great beauty Lamarr, according to Brent, was inept. "Hedy was a lovely woman," he admitted, "but her memory for remembering lines or set-ups was god-awful. The delays, cuts and re-takes caused by this woman were unbearably exasperating."[651] Lamarr's inquisitive, scientific mind was less inclined for memorization. Two years earlier, she acquired a U.S. Patent for the invention of frequency hopping. Even so, Lamarr's performance in *Experiment Perilous* is perhaps her best. The haunting look in her eyes, filled with presentiments, captured the essence of the character she was asked to portray. Brent's frustration with Lamarr translated into a lack of sexual chemistry between them. He offers Allida reassuring looks, but deep love? They make a peculiar screen team. Similar themes were explored in the previously released *Gaslight* (1944), which Lamarr had turned down.

Variety complimented the "good pace of suspense" in *Experiment Perilous*. Director Jacques Tourneur (*Cat People*) created the requisite tension and sense of peril, along with Tony Gaudio's exquisite, moody photography. The *New York Times* called *Experiment Perilous* "one of the better psychological dramas." It praised the skill of Paul Lukas, the fascinating Lamarr, and remarked that Brent's straightforward portrayal was a "good, solid performance."[652] Cleveland's W. Ward Marsh declared, "George Brent plays the doctor a little stiffly in the melodramatic scenes and a little doubtfully in the love scenes." Marsh thought Lamarr gave the prize performance, saying "never has she given such an exacting interpretation of a character … her heroine is far above everything else she has ever done."[653] So much for Brent's less than enthusiastic assessment of his lovely costar.

For his next assignment, Brent went directly to Paramount. *The Affairs of Susan* was Joan Fontaine's first comedy lead. "After all the tears I shed in other roles," recalled Fontaine, "I adored this!" She said that director William Seiter had a rare ability to boost an actor's confidence.[654] She and Brent were also boosted by a screenplay nominated for an Academy Award. Fontaine appeared to enjoy herself as Susan Darell, a sheltered Broadway star adjusting to the "real world" and the complexities of romance.

Through a series of flashbacks we discover that Susan's ex-husband, Roger Berton (Brent), a smooth Broadway producer, discovered her

Joan Fontaine displays her résumé in
The Affairs of Susan (Paramount 1945)

when she was still a young "innocent." Raised in a remote location near
Rhode Island, Susan had never read a newspaper and had no interest in
theater. She was honest to a fault. Berton falls for her completely, especially after a moonlit walk where Susan breathes in her natural surroundings—the stars, trees, and ocean. "They're telling us to be brave, and to
be strong, to be truthful, to be kind and to be happy!" she says brightly.
Berton has found his Joan of Arc, the play he is currently casting. He confesses that he loves her and asks if she's ever been kissed. A young mailman had once offered, but Susan declined. Berton takes her in his arms
and plants an enthusiastic smooch. Susan discovers that she likes kissing.
"In fact," she sighs, "I'm sorry about the mailman."

After their marriage and Susan's successful stage debut, Berton discovers that her candor isn't exactly *de rigueur* in the theatrical world. They divorce. *The Affairs of Susan* continues with flashbacks of her subsequent romances with almost-husbands (Dennis O'Keefe, Don DeFore, Walter Abel) from which she learns to "play the game" of clever half-truths and outright lies. Twenty-one-year-old Ruth Roman had a bit that required her to approach Brent at bar, greet him with "Hello, Angel Face," and give him a peck on the cheek. Roman later recalled, "I walked up, spoke my line and then froze. It was the closest I had been to a star and I just couldn't take it."[655] Director Seiter barked, "Well, do you want him to beg for it?" "Do I really kiss him?" whispered Roman. The whole company howled. "I would have run away never to come back," admitted Roman, "if George hadn't caught me and talked me back into some command of myself again."

Overlong in the telling (110 minutes), *The Affairs of Susan* still has its moments and Brent's role is sizeable. "Producer Hal Wallis should have condensed the whole romp into an hour or so," suggested Bosley Crowther. Another critic enthused, "A new, versatile Joan Fontaine kicks up her heels and sets a whirlwind pace for Brent, who comes through with his most lively performance in years."[656] Fontaine and Brent reprised their roles for *Lux Radio Theatre*.

Brent's feature for RKO-International, *Tomorrow Is Forever*, cast him as Claudette Colbert's second husband, the first being Orson Welles. The story dealt with a World War I widow (Colbert) who marries a wealthy chemical industrialist (Brent) in order to give her son a father figure, and to assuage her own loneliness. Who should pop up twenty years later but her disfigured "dead" husband (Welles) accompanied by a little war orphan (Natalie Wood). Welles, who has recreated himself as a crippled German scientist, does not reveal his true identity and Colbert isn't a hundred percent sure about him. Not at first, anyway. She's appalled when he brings morbid details about the war into her peaceful home and encourages her now teenage son (Richard Long) to enlist. Through the miracle of Hollywood Zen, the perennially youthful Colbert realizes that her happiness is in the present and all its tomorrows, and that it's perfectly alright to allow Long to sign up with the Royal Canadian Air Force and fight the Nazis.

Tomorrow Is Forever, a variation on Tennyson's narrative poem *Enoch Arden*, was based on a novelette by Gwen Bristow. With penetrating insight, Bistrow conveys the odd mix of propaganda and internal conflict that war perpetrates. Director Irving Pichel elevated an age-old theme with restraint. Scenarist Lenore Coffee said, "I really tried to inject some freshness, some maturity into an essentially soapy situation."[657] What could have easily been reduced to far-fetched soap opera becomes bold subject matter in the hands of Colbert, Welles, Brent, and young Natalie Wood—convincing as the traumatized child who saw her parents killed by the Germans. Wood's biographer stated that her mother would pull wings off of live butterflies until Natalie's real tears were "camera ready."[658]

Brent stabilized the dramatic proceedings with his common sense approach to character and low-key playing. Welles claimed that his acting assignment was strictly for the paycheck. He was more focused on the political column he was writing for *The New York Post*. A critic for *The Miami News* felt that Colbert "handled her sensitive role expertly," praised the "scene-stealing" Natalie Wood, but gave highest praise to "the quiet masterpiece of acting by George Brent as the second husband."[659] On the west coast, the *Seattle Times Daily* deduced that "Miss Colbert gives one of her finest performances and George Brent's polished acting is of matching excellence."[660] A few critics found fault, saying *Tomorrow is Forever* was tedious and old-fashioned. Bosley Crowther thought Welles came across as "a studied display of overacting" looking like Ulysses S. Grant. "As for Brent," said Crowther (who never cared much for him), "he stands by, changing neither his expression nor his mood. Anything the others want to do … appears perfectly okay by him."[661]

Brent was especially impressed with Natalie Wood, whose real name was Natasha Gurdin. Director Irving Pichel had discovered Natasha while on location in Santa Rosa, California, using her for a small bit in the film *Happy Land.* Two years later, he tested her for *Tomorrow Is Forever.* Brent was surprised to learn that little Natalie had no agent. He advised her mother, Maria, that representation was a logical and essential step. Brent would go so far as to take mother and daughter by the hand to Famous Artists Group where Natalie Wood was signed to a three-year contract on May 8, 1946.[662]

In the fall of 1943, Brent was seen out frequently with different women. In September, Louella Parsons reported that the "newest romance in town is George Brent and Janet Michael and it's plenty hot."[663] Michael was a young socialite from San Francisco. By December, gossips were predicting the two were altar bound. *Photoplay* pictured George and Janet dining at Café Lamaze. That same month, Brent was seen dining at the Clover Club with honey-blonde June Millarde, daughter of silent star June Caprice. Come spring, Parsons referred to Millarde as Brent's "new girlfriend." June soon changed her name to "Toni Seven" to become a popular pin-up girl (and sweetheart of Senator Warren Magnuson.) Brent was then seen at Mike Lyman's restaurant, wooing Dolores, the girl orchestra leader—and being tagged as "still devoted" to Janet Michael. After four marriages, "playing the field" suited Brent just fine.

When it came to politics, Brent campaigned along with Barbara Stanwyck on behalf of the Republican National Committee effort to push Thomas E. Dewey for President in 1944. Dewey, governor of New York, led the liberal/moderate faction of the Republican Party and was in favor of the United Nations as well as the "Cold War" fight against Communism. On November 2, Brent rallied for Dewey during a broadcast of

Tomorrow is Forever (RKO-International 1946) with
Natalie Wood and Claudette Colbert. A "masterpiece of
acting by George Brent" raved one critic.

Abbott and Costello over NBC.[664] After Dewey lost, Brent concentrated on his assignments at Paramount and RKO. His salary was impressive. Brent's RKO contract registered at $17,500 a week and offered him what some consider his best performance in *The Spiral Staircase*. Audiences and critics were impressed, but Brent wasn't. "I was not very convincing," he later told writer Don E. Stanke. "I don't think I'm very good at being the heavy. Actually, the film should have been a hell of a lot better, too."[665] Regardless of Brent's skepticism, *The Spiral Staircase* was one of the heftiest moneymakers for 1946, as well as one of the most critically acclaimed.

Brent's twisted psyche in *The Spiral Staircase* (RKO 1946)
came as a surprise to audiences. Seen here with James Bell
(Photo courtesy of Jenny Paxson and Larry Smith)

12

Freelancing:
$100,000 a Picture

After freelancing with Universal-International in 1946, Brent's career slipped into "B" productions at Columbia and Eagle Lion. He managed to get $10,000 a week—up to $100,000 a picture, which appeared to be what mattered most.[666] The only film that seemed to impress him during this period was *Luxury Liner* (1948), a lavish, Technicolor MGM musical. "That film was gorgeous," he said. "It took three months to make and the whole thing was a lot of fun."[667] The studio's glamour and prestige still meant something to Brent—especially after his career nosedive in 1947's *Slave Girl*. As Virginia MacPherson for the United Press put it, "Not even a talking camel could save this prize flopperoo."[668]

Horse racing—Brent's new passion—was taking precedence over challenging acting opportunities. He also continued his interest in yachting and made extensive plans to sail *Southwind* on the ultimate adventure: Tahiti. And, after five years of bachelorhood, Brent was ready to attempt a fifth marriage. This time, he was lucky.

The Spiral Staircase

During preproduction for *The Spiral Staircase*, World War II came to a close. The U. S. dropped atomic bombs on Hiroshima and Nagasaki. Japan surrendered on August 15, 1945. Cameras for *The Spiral Staircase* rolled on August 16.[669] Postwar audiences were ready for a different kind of peril, one that would send chills up their spines and entertain. Director Robert Siodmak, who was familiar with the thriller genre, along with photographer Nicholas Musuraka, teamed for a million dollar winner at the box office. Critics began comparing Siodmak to Hitchcock. Inspired by the 1933 novel *Some Must Watch* by Ethel Lina White, scenarist Mel Dinelli concocted a grim gothic tale involving a mute woman named Helen Capel (Dorothy McGuire). Lurking in the shadows is a biology professor (Brent), who is determined to snuff out her life, just as he had other females he deemed "imperfect." Flickering candles, rattled by thunderstorms, add to the eerie menace that occupies a New England mansion where Helen is employed. Upstairs, a bedridden dowager (Ethel Barrymore) is filled with premonitions—murder in particular. "I always know *everything*!" she proclaims. She orders Helen, her young attendant, "Pack your things and leave this house tonight!" Everyone is suspect: Barrymore's son (Gordon Oliver) and professor stepson (Brent), the cranky nurse, the tipsy cook and her handyman husband—perhaps even the dowager herself. When Helen discovers the body of the professor's secretary (Rhonda Fleming) in the basement, she realizes she could be next.

Barrymore has a revolver carefully situated on her nightstand and keeps reminding everyone what a good shot she is, even the film's director. At the film's climax, Siodmak advised Ethel to hold the gun with both hands. She refused. "Have you forgotten? I'm supposed to be a great hunter!"[670] He sheepishly acquiesced. Still, it comes as a surprise when Barrymore gets around to proving her point by pulling the trigger and hitting the bull's-eye—stepson Brent—no less than five times. From the foot of the stairs, Brent glances up at her with incredulity, as if he were asking, "Are you *crazy*?" After all, he was doing the world a favor by eliminating the misfits that his father, her late husband, detested. The look on Brent's face is priceless.

The Spiral Staircase was originally a David O. Selznick project to star Ingrid Bergman. As Selznick needed funds to complete major films such as *Duel in the Sun*, the project was transferred to producer Dore Schary. Schary's skill, along with director Siodmak and Musuraka's prowling camerawork, allowed *The Spiral Staircase* to rely on suspense rather than blood and gore. The radiant performance of Dorothy McGuire is the film's standout. Many consider it the best work of her career. The prestige of having Ethel Barrymore in the cast was a given. She and McGuire create the mounting terror that breathlessly carries the film toward a memorable finish.

The close-ups of the killer's frantic eye that stalks these proceedings belonged not to Brent but to director Siodmak. This was done intentionally (according to a 1992 McGuire interview) to conceal the true identity of the deranged killer.[671] Brent was faced with the task of not being too obvious. How does a killer and a liar act without giving himself away? Brent's solemn, preoccupied scholar of biology wasn't scary, or conspicuous. It wasn't written as such. When he isn't onscreen one feels his presence, regardless. Brent took his cue from the character's dastardly deeds, which appear to be as taxing as they are exhilarating—wearing him down. He comes across as a tad weary and sanctimonious. Brent's delusional world is revealed when he corners McGuire at the climax. With disdain in his voice he forces her to face the mirror. "Look at yourself. Look!" he demands. "There is no room in the whole world for imperfection." He continues to rail, "What a pity my father didn't live to see me become strong—to see me dispose of the weak and imperfect in the world!"

The formidable Barrymore indicates that Brent and his womanizing

The Spiral Staircase (RKO 1946) (above) with Dorothy McGuire.
(below) with Rhonda Fleming and Gordon Oliver

stepbrother are weaklings—afraid of guns and hunting. In her opinion she was more of a man than they were. After all, she had shot a tiger. "I got him, before he got me!" she crows. "I was as good as any man." When the brothers share their mutual dislike for one another, it is revealed that their God-fearing, gun-toting, hard-drinking father was equally disappointed in them. He left them alone to indulge in their own vices.

It must have pleased Brent to work with Barrymore, whom he fondly recalled staring at him from her seat in the audience at Elitch Gardens back in 1929. Barrymore had singled him out as a promising talent. In *The Spiral Staircase* critics agreed that Brent's twist on the human psyche was commendable. "George Brent is in top form," observed New York critic Herbert Cohn. *Variety* noted the excellence of Brent's "out of the ordinary portrayal."[672] Bosley Crowther praised Siodmak's ability to sustain suspense and the film's brooding photography. He gave plaudits to McGuire for "the high degree of resourcefulness with which she … tackled the demanding and little-used art of pantomime."[673] New York audiences, according to Crowther, watched as if they were under a spell. Contemporary critics, such as Anthony Slide, note the staying power of McGuire's "wistful, ingratiating charm." "There is high praise," insists Slide, "to be heaped upon the rich talents of Ethel Barrymore and George Brent in other leading roles."[674] While McGuire was overlooked when Academy Award nominations were announced, Barrymore was selected for her performance in the Best Supporting Actress category. *The Spiral Staircase* registers in *The New York Times Guide to the Best 1,000 Movies Ever Made*. It is generally agreed that the 1975 remake with Jacqueline Bissett, Mildred Dunnock, and Christopher Plummer (in the George Brent role) came across as listless in comparison and wasted the talents of a fine cast.

Psychoanalysis of the gothic/horror genre can be rife with speculation. Some felt Brent's quest for human perfection was fueled by a repressed libido—that he was, as author David Brode suggests, "living in a

Freudian nightmare of denied sexuality." "In *The Spiral Staircase*," writes Brode, "the killer turns out to be a single male inflicted with sexual impotence."[675] In Amy Lawrence's *Echo and Narcissus: Women's Voices in Classical Hollywood Cinema* (1991), she goes out on a limb suggesting that Brent's murderous professor is anxious about his sexuality. "His 'latent' homosexuality marks him as an emasculated, castrated man," suggests Lawrence, "he must kill in order to preserve his precarious grip on his masculine identity."[676] Then there was British critic Leslie Halliwell's crass 1986 reassessment of professor Brent "hovering about like a man in search of the bathroom."[677] One can only imagine Brent's grappling these outré analyses of his performance.

Lucille Ball paid homage to George Brent for helping her through a rough period of marital woes with husband Desi Arnaz during the filming of *Lover Come Back*. "George Brent was a wonderfully supportive costar," said Ball, who, following a nervous breakdown, was also dealing with a stuttering problem.[678] Director William Seiter took Ball under his wing. "He told me just to talk to him," recalled Ball, "to talk and talk. He saved me and so did George Brent." A number of years later Ball found herself dancing with Brent at a party given by producer Bill Goetz. Ball recalled, "I said, 'George, I don't know if you realize how kind you were when I was broken down!' And he said, 'What are you talking about?' So I said, '*Lover Come Back*.' And he said, 'Oh yeah, I remember. You were beautiful … I just wanted to help out.' We never talked about it again."[679]

Released in the summer of 1946, *Lover Come Back* was an adult farce dealing with the double standard. *Film Daily* opined, "The combination of Lucille Ball and George Brent is well chosen to present the arguments for both sides."[680] The film, flavored with mix-ups, was diverting, and the duo had simpatico. Ball, a dress designer, suspects that husband Brent,

Lucille Ball had nothing but praises for co-star Brent in
Lover Come Back (Universal1946)

a returning war correspondent, may have been unfaithful. There's over-whelming evidence he had plenty of action during his absence. "A fellow can get lonesome," he tells Ball. "With you it's different. You're a woman." The battle is on. She strategically plants a few clues to make him think she has her own fleet of admirers.

Designed for chuckles, *Lover Come Back* had a good cast, elaborate penthouse sets and elegant gowns for Miss Ball by Travis Banton. As usual, *New York Times* critic Bosley Crowther complained about Brent, saying, "The spectacle of Vera Zorina and Lucille Ball mooning and swooning about him is the straw to break the critic's back."[681] Despite his reputation offscreen, Brent's lady-killer comes off as a trifle flat, but his onscreen shenanigans imply a knowing wink to the camera. A Milwau-kee critic commented on Brent's "customary assured performance" but credited Ball for keeping things moving with her "wide-eyed humor." To be fair, both lack the special zip to enhance this marital muddle. Ball definitely wasn't the madcap "Lucy" of 1950s TV. Still, it entertains. Leonard Maltin calls it "a bright little comedy."[682] In 1953, the film was reissued to theaters as *Lucy Goes Wild* to capitalize on the *I Love Lucy* craze.

For his next meal ticket at International Pictures, Brent was spoon-fed poison by his "loving" wife (Merle Oberon) in *Temptation*. On his deathbed he was able to gasp out a couple hundred words of dialogue in a single take. Director Irving Pichel was impressed. The real acting honors, however, went to Miss Oberon, who manages to make her vain, manipulative femme fatale believable. *Temptation* was a remake of Pola Negri's 1923 silent success *Bella Donna*, which was based on a 1909 novel by Robert Hichens. The mothball-ridden tale of sin in exotic settings had Brent as Nigel, an Egyptian archeologist who discovers the tomb of Rameses V. His wife Ruby (Oberon) doesn't share his passion for mummies and, out of boredom, wraps herself around a handsome gigolo named Baroudi (Charles Korvin). Their mutual passion for lying turns to lust. Baroudi encourages Ruby to administer doses of poison to Nigel, which she does. Brent's big moment comes while giving a speech at a banquet in his honor. His portrait of unblemished gentleness and nobility avoided any heavy dramatics—even while enduring the grip of deadly bella donna. He acts as if he's simply dozing off. It was a missed opportunity.

Ruby's main dilemma was deciding who she wanted to poison next. She stops trying to murder her husband, because she suddenly realizes that she loves him. Instead, she offers a double dose of bella donna to Baroudi, who was double-crossing her. Oberon's conniving creature is fascinating to watch, but it isn't enough to save the creaky plot. While sitting amidst ancient ruins in the moonlight, Ruby is crushed to death by a rockslide. We learn afterward, from a friend and physician (Paul Lukas), that her death was "an act of God."

Audiences were tempted to leave the theater while watching *Temptation.* One theater owner grumbled, "I have had plenty of walk-outs in the past 30 years, but this was my first experience with a stampede."[683] Evelyn Schloss's review of *Temptation* offered Brent a back-handed compliment. "Range and variety distinguish Miss

Temptation (Universal-International 1946)
with Merle Oberon

Oberon's playing," said Schloss. "Brent is well cast as Nigel, her color-less, devoted husband."[684] Bosley Crowther ranted, "The whole thing is as claptrap in its nature as when Pola Negri played it back in 1923. George Brent is sufficiently unimpressive."[685] The *Baltimore Sun* agreed, "George Brent's job is to be good and tiresome as the husband, and he is."[686] Pittsburgh critic Kaspar Monahan commented on the "wan and wooden indifference" with which Brent played his role. "George Brent acts like an actor who wishes this nonsense was finished so he could get away to the golf links."[687] Monahan's assessment was incorrect. It was yachting, not golf, that lured Brent from concentrating on the task at hand.

In the summer of 1946, Brent announced that he would sail his favorite schooner *Southwind* in the San Pedro-Honolulu race beginning July 4, 1947. It would be the first scheduled race since before the war. "I've always wanted to participate in that race," he told reporters. "In past years, circumstances have arisen to prevent it, but next year I'll be in there for sure."[688] Frank "Wizard of Oz" Morgan also planned to join the race with his seventy-one-foot schooner *Dolphin II.* "I'm a good sailor," bragged Morgan. "I come from a long line of seafaring men on my mother's side."[689] For months on end, Brent spent his spare time prepping his yacht. Brent, his nephew Pat Watson, and a crew of seven were on board for the event. At high noon on July 4, moderate winds greeted a record fleet of thirty-four yachts in the 2,225 mile race. A double shot blast signaled the getaway as yachts knifed through the blue Pacific waters. Within three seconds eighteen boats swept past buoy 2-A, the official starting point. Morgan was among the early leaders. It was first reported that Brent wasn't aboard *Southwind.*[690] He probably wished he hadn't been. Columnist Erskine Johnson later recalled, "I'll never forget the time George Brent's schooner crossed the starting line for Honolulu. It was a lovely sight except for one thing—George's boat was going in the wrong direction."[691] Eighteen minutes into the race, Brent was at the helm of *Southwind* when it passed buoy 2-A—the last yacht in the fleet of competitors.[692] Eleven to twenty-five days of sailing lay ahead before reaching Diamond Head.

Brent's grandnephew Ian Watson (Pat's son) forwarded me the log book from this fiasco, which he and Brent referred to as "Operation Miserable." Tom Fleming, *Southwind*'s bullheaded skipper, had insisted that the starting line was outside the breakwater. He was wrong. No one aboard heard the starting gun. "The tension on deck was becoming impossible," noted crew member Carl Cook. Brent was speechless and went under deck. Cook, a Pacific veteran, wrote that skipper Fleming was a "hopeless, nasty sourpuss" and "absolutely no sailor."[693] By the close of day they had made no headway and ended up east of San Clemente . . . in calm waters. They realized they had lost the race.

The fifth day out, Cook wrote, "Mr. Brent takes his first sunbath. His dislike for the skipper is intensifying." Brent remarked, "Since this appears to be a Malibu Charter Cruise, I might as well get a tan." Tension was also released when someone placed a "raspberry bladder" under Cook's din-

July 18, 1947 "Operation Miserable" — Brent and nephew Patrick Watson soak in the news that most competitors had crossed the finish line. (below) Uncle George "flaked out" sporting a cigarette holder. (Courtesy of Ian Watson)

ing chair cushion. "It sounded horrible," he admitted. "We had had beans the day before. Pat Watson almost died laughing."

Seventeen days out, with most contestants docked in Honolulu and celebrating, Pat Watson entered a popular military acronym into *Southwind*'s log book. Under latitude and longitude, he jotted "snafu" ("situation normal, all fucked up"). The consolation prize on this voyage was Bob Singleton, the crew's extraordinary cook. The men feasted on freshly baked bread, wonderful salads, and a varied menu that included a turkey dinner. Single-ton had previously sailed the *Zaca* with Errol Flynn on numerous occasions.

Upon arriving in Honolulu (July 22, 8:30 p.m.), Brent allowed Carl Cook to sail *Southwind* across the finish line. Perhaps Brent was too em-barrassed to be seen at the helm himself. The log book noted, "Under the lights on shore, a solid black wall of people, easily a couple of thousand. No chance to get on shore unnoticed." They were greeted by a Hawai-ian orchestra, and within five minutes after docking, a hundred visitors climbed on board. "Mr. Brent managed to get off," wrote Cook, "but not without losing his tie and most of the buttons off his coat. They are just as bad in the islands as they are [in the states]."[694]

The shiny trophy from the Transpacific Yacht Club went to none other than Frank Morgan, who crossed the finish line at 12:12 p.m., the afternoon of July 17. Morgan also received the Governor of Hawaii Cup, a hand-carved Koa wood model-trophy of a Polynesian outrigger canoe. "I never won a Hollywood 'Oscar' for acting," said Morgan, "but as far as the two go, I'd rather have this one."[695] Four yachts that had finished ahead of him had shorter handicaps, thus Morgan was "in" with a safe margin of two hours.[696] Needless to say, Brent's experience in the com-petition was not a happy one. In early August, reporter Bob Thomas said the actor was worn out from the trip and going to sell his yacht. Brent told Thomas that operating a big boat was like "running a factory."[697] While in Hawaii, Brent was cabled by MGM for the film musical *Luxury Liner.* He returned home August 1, on the luxurious *S.S. Matsonia*—which was now his preferred mode of sea travel.

Brent had four releases in 1947, each from a different studio. *The Corpse Came C.O.D.* was written by columnist Jimmy Starr. Brent costarred with Joan Blondell as rival reporters on the Hollywood beat trying to solve a studio murder. Blondell gets in the way of Brent, and together they badger the police during the investigation. The only funny moment in this tedious

One of two 1947 releases that teamed Brent with Joan Blondell was *Christmas Eve* (UA), with costars Dolores Moran, Randolph Scott, Ann Harding and George Raft

whodunit has Brent waking up in the hospital after getting knocked out. The first thing he sees is Blondell. "This can't be heaven," he mutters, "*you're* here." As Brent and Blondell go through the motions, their humor feels forced. The *New York Times* surmised, "George Brent and Joan Blondell have seldom appeared to less advantage." The review stated they were up against a ludicrous script and "the poorest direction imaginable."[698]

The duo teamed once again for the celluloid misfire *Christmas Eve*. Producer Benedict Bogeaus had a penchant for casting his films with aging stars the studio system ignored. On hand were George Raft, Randolph Scott, and Brent—who come to the rescue of elderly Matilda Reid (Ann Harding), their wealthy adoptive mother. She is about to be hauled away to the insane asylum by her nefarious nephew (Reginald Denny). Designed mostly for laughs, the three male leads parody their screen personas. Raft's more serious gambler role was amply beefed up by producer Bogeaus and clashes with the film's spirit. It's as if a mini-noir Raft film was inserted midway into the tale. Brent's smaller vignette had him passing bad checks to sustain his playboy lifestyle. Blondell plays an old girlfriend he tries to dump for the richer variety, but her sizzling kisses keep getting in the way. As a team, they entertain and add a welcome dash of humor. Blondell told *Saturday Evening Post* that she was fully aware that her services were often used to, as she put it, "instill life into dead-duck pictures." The *New York Times*, however, felt the episodic potpourri only succeeded in being "plodding, transparent, and occasionally confusing."[699] Bay Area critic Wood Soanes found *Christmas Eve* "pretty awful" saying, "As Miss Harding played the role, the booby hatch was the only place for her." Soanes agreed that the way Raft, Brent, and Scott handled their assignments "they should have joined her."[700]

While Brent was wrapping up *Christmas Eve*, Rosalind Russell pegged him for one of the male leads in her upcoming film drama *Mourning Becomes Electra* by Eugene O'Neill. Brent thought it might interfere with the Honolulu race. "I'd like to do it," he told Sheilah Graham, "but the picture has a fifteen-week shooting schedule, and you know what that can mean."[701] *Mourning Becomes Electra* wrapped on June 23, two weeks prior to the Honolulu race. In the meantime, Brent completed an amusing romp for Eagle Lion, his third comedy in a row.

Vera Caspary, who penned the noir classic *Laura* (1944), turned her hand to write a zany farce set in New York's Greenwich Village. In *Out of the Blue*, a good cast was thrown into multiple mix-ups filled with breezy banter. It scored with audiences and critics. As a milquetoast husband ready to break out of his henpecked shell, Brent lets loose once his wife (Carole Landis) leaves town. He hooks up with a brandy-guzzling interior designer (Ann Dvorak) and takes her to his penthouse, where she proceeds to pass out, dead drunk. He believes she's really dead. She kept

Out of the Blue (Eagle Lion 1947) Brent finally scored in a comedy, with Carole Landis. (below) *Slave Girl* (Universal-International 1947) with Yvonne DeCarlo "signaled that the best part of Brent's career was over."

insisting the brandy was for her weak heart. Panic-stricken, Brent places her body on the terrace belonging to his next-door neighbor (Turhan Bey), a Bohemian artist, and the fun begins.

Bryan Foy, formerly in charge of Warner Bros. B-unit, was production supervisor. He specifically selected Brent and Dvorak to play against type. In spite of its limited budget, *Variety* thought *Out of the Blue* "smartly produced and directed. Brent, enacting a naïve character never too sure what it's all about, scores in his comedy. Miss Landis fetchingly follows in line."[702] Another critic praised, "Miss Dvorak reveals an entirely new talent and livens up every scene. Brent, too squeezes every line of its laughs. [He] does a surprisingly smooth comedy job."[703] Dallas critic John Rosenfield raved, "With priceless performances by George Brent and Ann Dvorak … the picture adds up to the most valid fun of the last several months." Rosenfield assessed Brent's role as "one of the best light comedy jobs you ever saw."[704] *Out of the Blue* is easily Brent's best comedy. Director Leigh Jason managed to create what cinema historian David Bleiler calls "an enjoyable screwball comedy."[705]

One is prone to overlook *Slave Girl*, an Arabian action picture that Brent had filmed in the summer of 1946. It was an embarrassment for all concerned. In May of that year, Hedda Hopper announced Brent had been cast as a dashing hero who saves Yvonne De Carlo in *Tripoli*. By August, the newly titled *Flame of Tripoli* was rechristened *Slave Girl*. Cast and crew were surrounded by pink sand dunes in Kane County, Utah, for location shooting. Following a couple of test screenings, executives at Universal realized they had a "$1,600,000 'turkey' on their hands."[706] It was shelved. In February 1947, additional scenes were added to poke fun at the Technicolor mess they had created. Some scenes required the services of Humpy, a talking camel. Humpy, as the film's narrator, reminded everyone to laugh. The ploy didn't help. The film is easily Brent's worst.

Sheilah Graham thought Brent looked dashing wearing what she called "impossibly tight pants" while shooting the opening scenes of

Slave Girl. They were so tight, according to Graham, that he was unable to sit down. "What do you do at lunchtime?" she asked Brent, who was using Lou Costello's dressing room on the Universal lot. "I take them off," he smiled. Brent mentioned that he didn't eat lunch. He simply gave his pants a rest and relaxed.[707] As a spoiled, nineteenth-century American playboy who comes to his rich uncle for more cash, Brent's role seemed perfect typecasting. As punishment, the uncle sends Brent on a government mission to Tripoli where he is to deliver a case of gold for the release of American hostages. Once he arrives there, the inevitable villains, intrigue, and dancing girls show up. Brent's impetuous smooching of slave girl Yvonne De Carlo was to be expected as was her conniving to steal his gold. He is jailed along with the prisoners he is there to save. (Among them, former pal and stand-in Don Turner.)

Dialogue and acting make it clear that *Slave Girl* was not to be taken seriously. With or without Humpy the Camel's lame wisecracks, the humor falls flat. The only good laugh arrives seven minutes to the finish, when Brent and De Carlo are about to be shot by a firing squad. Brent protests, "Isn't it customary to allow the condemned man the last word?" "You have something to say?" demands the Arabian commander. "Go ahead and say it!" Brent fills up his lungs and bellows, "HELP!" His cry reverberates throughout the coral pink formations of Utah's Parria Canyon. Brent's lung power saves the day, but nothing could save *Slave Girl.*

The critics blasted *Slave Girl* to smithereens. Brent wasn't spared. "George Brent's attempts at slapstick," said one review, "are only as funny as a wooden Indian falling down a flight of stairs."[708] Bosley Crowther moaned, "The corn in this concoction is tasteless." "Year's worst film," complained the *New York Post.* Director Charles Lamont needn't have worried. He continued to churn out box office gold with Abbott and Costello and five entries in the Ma and Pa Kettle series.

While filming *Slave Girl,* Brent had sat in his trailer dressing room, banging away at a typewriter in self-defense. In an article titled "This Is My Side of It," he addressed rumors that pigeon-holed him as an anti-social money-grabber who was ready to thumb his nose at the world. Brent felt he got along well with coworkers and crew. "Otherwise," he said, "you'd slit your own throat professionally." As for the money, Brent claimed he couldn't afford to retire. "By the time I get through paying all my taxes," he grumbled, "seven cents out of a dollar stays with me, so figure that one out for yourself." In the same breath, he mentioned his stable of thoroughbreds and financial interest in the California Cabana Club, "a number of gas stations, markets and so on." He rhapsodized about his travel plans for Tahiti and Bora-Bora—possibly the Philippines. "After two years," he predicted, "I'll be ready to return."[709] Writer Brian Doyle surmised that films like *Slave Girl* "signaled that the best part of Brent's career was over."[710]

While filmgoers were avoiding *Slave Girl*, Brent continued to make it quite clear that he was headed for the balmy breezes of Tahiti for a permanent stay. "I have never been to Tahiti," he admitted, "but I have heard enough about it from Errol Flynn and other friends to know that life there will suit me perfectly."[711] According to Brent, the world had gone mad, and the tropics were his only escape from the insanity. Brent put off his intended loll in Tahiti following the Honolulu race, but after completing *Luxury Liner* he was more determined than ever to get there. His personal possessions and wardrobe were already packed and stowed on *Southwind*, still docked in Hawaii. Two members of his crew were living aboard and waiting for him. He explained to International News correspondent John Todd,

I may come back in five years. I may never come back. If I like it in Tahiti as well as I think I'm going to I can arrange to get out of commitments. Conditions in the world today … have never been worse and Tahiti seems to me about as pleasant a place to go as any. I wouldn't be surprised if war broke out within a year. You know where they'll drop the first atom bombs don't you? Right on Los Angeles.[712]

As to his career, Brent informed Todd, "I have never regarded this as anything more than a business. When I first came to Hollywood I thought that I might look on it as an art, but I soon got over that." On October 23, Brent flew from San Francisco to Honolulu en route to Tahiti. His stay there, according to Sheilah Graham, lasted about six weeks.[713] *Variety* columnist Florabel Muir revealed that once Brent arrived in Papeete, he saw what "cured" him from staying on: "French émigrés running the show."[714] He returned to Honolulu and reunited with his sweetheart, Janet Michael. Meanwhile, Dana Andrews and Clark Gable began talking about taking time off for indefinite stays in Tahiti. When Gable heard the news about George's change of heart, he told Bob Thomas, "I see Brent came back—and what's more, he got married. Haw!" Gable let it be known that he, personally, would never marry again.[715]

Columnists had been forecasting the George Brent-Janet Michael marriage since the fall of 1943. Their names were tied together frequently by Louella Parsons, Hedda Hopper, and Sheilah Graham, who reported in the summer of 1946, "George Brent says he is more interested in his horses than marrying San Francisco socialite Janet Michael. But that was the sort of talk I received from George the week before he married Ann Sheridan."[716] In April 1947, Janet accompanied Brent in his yacht along the coastline to San Francisco. *Variety* reported that Janet had George "in the palm of her little hand."[717] Parsons was surprised when Brent announced plans for Tahiti, and asked, "I wonder if he's going to take Janet Michael with him, when he goes native on us?"[718] Janet didn't tag along, but upon his return from Tahiti she flew to Honolulu and into Brent's eager arms. He was ready to settle down, permanently. After a week-long reunion, Janet returned to Los Angeles, while Brent stayed with the intention to sell *Southwind*. On December 17, George and Janet faced Superior Court Judge Henry C. Kelly in Yuma, Arizona. The crime: matrimony.[719]

The newlyweds headed back to Los Angeles for a honeymoon in their new home at 725 North Camden Drive, Beverly Hills, which Brent had been working on for over a year. He also took a four-month long honeymoon from filmmaking. In February, they entertained a large party of mostly what is termed "turf folk"—horse racing enthusiasts, such as Georgian Prince Djordjadze, Grand Prix winner and owner of Santa Anita thoroughbred winners. Also on the guest list were former cowboy star Rex Bell, Lee "Doctor to the Stars" Siegel, Robert Sterling, Arlene Dahl and Sir Charles Mendl, oilman Bob Neal and Diana Lynn, Jon Hall and Frances Langford, and Brent's former flame June Millarde.[720] Mrs. Brent was in her element mixing with stars, racing enthusiasts, and the society set. Her upbringing had prepared her to mix with the elite and be self-reliant.

Janet Michael

Daughter of attorney-at-law/investor M. F. Michael and Marie Monteith Michael, Janet was born in San Francisco on December 15, 1920.[721] An older brother, James, was born the previous year. The family resided on Larkin Street. Attorney Michael, an imposing six-feet three-inches tall, San Francisco native, and member of the University Club, was fifty-three when he married twenty-three-year-old Marie Monteith. Marie's father was also a prominent attorney. Michael made his fortune by represent-

George and Janet Michaels around
the time of their 1947 marriage

ing the secretly created, amply bankrolled Employer's Association of San
Francisco in their fight against local unions. In May of 1901 when metal
workers were striking for an eight-hour day, supplies were cut off to any
employer who acquiesced. Michael informed organized labor that the
Employer's Association, for which he was sole advisor and spokesperson,
had nothing to arbitrate.[722] By late summer, the Employer's Association
had acquired a small fortune "to support anti-union activity."[723] Michael
had a secure, stable connection to California's most powerful and wealthy
men. In 1927, he was designated as an honorary pallbearer for political
boss William F. Herrin, the vice-president and chief counsel for the controversial Southern Pacific Railroad.

Janet's mother, Marie, was a practicing professional artist.[724] In 1931, Janet's father passed away of chronic heart disease. Marie found solace by marrying portrait/landscape painter Albert Mundhenk. A member of the Bohemian Club, Mundhenk lent his talent as political cartoonist for the *San Francisco Chronicle*. Following their marriage, the family moved to Vallejo Street. Janet attended Miss Hamilin's School for girls. At sixteen, her photo was prominently featured in the society section of the *Chronicle* for hosting a dinner party.[725] Other news items included a dinner-dance she gave for her young friends at the Hotel Mark Hopkins. There were bridge luncheons, a Mothers and Daughters Tea, and farewells for classmates leaving on European tours. In the summer of 1937, Janet and her mother sailed on the *Santa Paula* to New York for a stay in Manhattan. Janet's smiling portrait made the *Chronicle* under the heading "Ride Neptune's Chariot."[726] While on Long Island, they joined spectators for the Star Boat Races, in which Janet's brother James had entered his yacht, *Roulette*. Mother and daughter returned by motor via Quebec. The following summer Janet's mother died unexpectedly. She was only forty-two. Janet and James stayed on at their home on Vallejo Street, along with the family's Chinese cook and a maid.

Janet's turn as a fashion model gave her the moniker "Glass Hat" when she wore a wide-brim cellophane creation to a function at the St. Francis Hotel. She explained that her expansive chapeaux made umbrellas unnecessary.[727] *Chronicle* gabber Herb Caen frequently reported on Janet's whereabouts and romances with rich yachtsmen like Kenny Lynch. For New Year's 1941, Caen tattled that the glamorous twenty-year-old celebrated by wearing a strapless gown, then wound up at a waterfront saloon at 8 a.m.—escorted by fight promoter Charlie Marsalli.[728] Janet then set her eyes on Hollywood. The *Los Angeles Times* warned young ladies, "Janet Michael, one of San Francisco's crème de la crème, has moved into the local camp."

By the time George and Janet married, she was designated as an "ex-model." The International Artists committee included Janet among the "10 Most Glamorous Women of 1946."[729] Like her mother, Janet developed skill as an artist. A gallery owner in Rancho Santa Fe observed, "[Janet] had a rare talent for painting on canvas and making it appear to be silk."[730] Although her art may have been abstract, Janet Brent provided a nurturing presence that afforded her husband a solid and lasting marriage.

Fans had to wait until September 1948 for Brent's next film release. MGM's *Luxury Liner* was his only musical other than *42nd Street*. Brent got first billing, but the real attraction was teen soprano Jane Powell. The plot was simple: stowaway Polly Bradford (Powell) plays cupid to her widower father (Brent), who happens to be captain of a luxury ocean liner. Brent and Powell team nicely, and their mutual affection is disarming. Aside from Powell's lighter repertoire, tenor Lauritz Melchior offered arias from *Die Walkure* and *Aida*. The film gave a musical nod to the Latin rhythms of Xavier Cugat—a typical MGM ploy at the time. All Brent had to do was look suave and amused. He succeeded. As one critic put it, "Brent has the easiest job aboard ship."[731] His young costar developed a huge crush on him. "I wasn't infatuated with Cugat," recalled Powell, "but I was with George Brent. I had such a crush on him I couldn't stand it. We never even had lunch together, but I thought about him all the time. He was so good-looking, and fun, and had a wonderful sense of humor. I never saw him after the movie ... schoolgirl crushes have a way of evaporating."[732] What Jane did not know was that Brent harbored a deep-seated crush on her. They 'fessed up to their romantic inclinations thirty years later . . . with interesting results.

Designed for relaxed, escapist fare, musicals like *Luxury Liner* had great appeal and did well at the box office. Luscious MGM concoctions

**Teen songbird Jane Powell had a crush on
co-star Brent in *Luxury Liner* (1948)**

were easy prey for the barbs of metropolitan critics, which moviegoers usually ignored. Bosley Crowther sniffed that Powell had no "noticeable charm or wit;" Brent, as her father, was "a definite liability;" and color made the film "brighter than it is."[733] Crowther missed the whole point. A drama critic in Florida put it best, saying, "*Luxury Liner* ... makes no effort to be serious about anything, but it is good screen entertainment. That is all it was meant to be."[734]

By the end of 1948, the writing on the proverbial wall for Brent's career was there for all to read. Bryan Foy, who had been executive producer for *Out of the Blue*, had the audacity to single out George Brent for "what was wrong" with the picture business. "Movies cost too much," complained

Foy, "and none of the millions that go into them get value back. My first rule now when producing a picture is not to hire George Brent."[735] Brent, according to Foy, cost more than he was worth at the box office. After the damage was done, Foy tried to lessen the blow by pointing fingers at Bette Davis, Fred MacMurray, and Hedy Lamarr. His remarks prompted Jimmy Fidler to come to Brent's defense. "I think that Mr. Foy is … off his nut for adopting such a line of reasoning. Any producer who tries to pass the buck to the stars, as Bryan Foy is now doing, is overlooking one of the most plainly written facts in show business—no star can be better than the role given him to play."[736] Of course, Brent wasn't too choosy with his assignments as long as the money was good. It had to be. He was now investing heavily in his new passion: horse breeding.

13

Home Turf

"My movie work is a hobby"
(**George Brent** – *July 1949*)

In the fall of 1946, Brent had a dozen broodmares stabled at the former Barbara Stanwyck-Robert Taylor ranch at Northridge. He also had seven runners touring the California tracks. During the racing season, Brent divided his time between turf and stables, conferring with trainers and observing workouts. He had on board Paul Lycan, one of the leading trainers on the circuit. While he wasn't prone to betting on the races, Brent focused on winning purses.[737] Big money was involved whether he was winning or losing. Brent paid $14,000 for the bay filly Zee to Bee and another $25,000 for the French stallion Le Roitele.[738] He also collected stud fees from the aptly named Bullroot. It was obvious that Brent had found new fulfillment outside of the acting profession. Among George and Janet's winners were Bangalore, Mild Stimulant, and Bomb Special. Over the next twenty years the couple invested heavily to reap financial reward at popular race courses at Hollywood Park, Del Mar, and the Bay Area's Tanforan. Horse racing lured many film luminaries. Hollywood Park, headed by Mervyn Le Roy, initially had as its board of directors Harry Warner, Al Jolson, and Raoul Walsh.

Brent's passion for yachting subsided. *Yachting Magazine* reported that he sailed *Southwind* in a "'Round-the-Island Oahu Race" during 1948's Aloha Week. He finally sold the yacht in the early '50s. In 1962, *Southwind* fell into the hands of Texas multi-millionaire Doyle Downey for the pricey sum of $400,000.[739]

Most importantly, Brent had found a companionable mate in Janet. Her passion for art wasn't career driven. She allowed Brent to be who he was. He was financially well-off and could afford the luxuries that she was used to. Their bank account easily accommodated pesky dilemmas such as the time Janet had $8,000 worth of jewelry stolen from her parked car while she and her attorney brother were dining in San Francisco.[740] Mr. and Mrs. Brent were compensated two years later with the arrival of a *real* treasure, their daughter, Suzanne. By then, they were living in relative seclusion on their fifty-acre Royal Oaks Ranch in Hidden Valley, forty miles north of Hollywood. "We've put a lot of money into the place," Brent would admit. "But the ranch more than pays its way."[741] Before long, Brent was receiving offers of triple the original price.

If anything should have cured Brent of making more movies it was an oddity called *Angel on the Amazon* (1948). George had been away from the cameras for seven months when he reported to Republic, a studio known primarily for B-films with second-string talent. The cast headlined other fast-fading stars from the 1930s: Brian Aherne and Constance Bennett. James Robert Parish thought the "celluloid embarrassment" a "downhill swing" for everyone involved.[742] The bizarre story line had Brent, a playboy-aviator, crash land in the Amazon jungle. He and his party are rescued from headhunters by a mysterious white huntress (Vera Ralston) whose biggest thrill is killing jungle cats. She also never ages. Brent is in hot pursuit. A physician on board (Bennett) attempts to distract Brent by making wisecracks and lounging around the jungle in designer slacks. Brent, Bennett, and Ralston meet up again in Rio de Ja-

Vera Ralston, Brent, Gus Schilling, Ross Elliott, Constance Bennett and
Walter Reed avoid headhunters in *Angel on the Amazon* (Republic 1948)
(Courtesy of Jenny Paxson and Larry Smith)

neiro—at the horse races. Brent (finally) seems in his element at the race-track—but not for long. He is rebuffed by Ralston, who warns, "I can't ever love you or anyone." "But … you're so young!" he pleads. "Don't ever use that word again," she snaps. "I hate it!" We are led to believe that a traumatic scare during a panther attack had affected Ralston's glands, leaving her hopelessly young. She is really fifty-something. Dr. Bennett sends her to a sanatorium where the aging process is miraculously reversed. Brent seeks refuge in the eager arms of Miss Bennett, and everyone is happy. When asked about *Angel on the Amazon* years later, Bennett stated that she didn't know what possessed her to become involved with such a "rancid turkey."[743]

The film was released during the Christmas season. One critic's assessment put it bluntly: "*Angel on the Amazon* can be nominated as one of the ten worst pictures of the year."[744] "We might as well not opened the doors," complained one theater owner.[745] The *New York Times* commented on Brent's "flabbily-boyish pursuit" of Ralston who, the review noted, was "a painfully incompetent performer."[746] A Los Angeles critic referred to her "emotionless acting."[747] Critics were usually harsh on Ralston, but occasionally her soft-spoken style proved affecting. Brent and Bennett managed to elicit a few chuckles with their repartee, but Mexican actor Alfonso Bedoya stole scenes at will from the entire cast. Despite its attention to detail, suspense, and convincing special effects, *Angel on the Amazon* is, at best, a curio for die-hard film buffs. Regardless, Brent walked away with $100,000.[748]

While at Republic, Brent signed on for several months as radio moderator for *Leave It To the Girls*. Guest stars such as Sylvia Sidney and Constance Bennett gave George a rough time while he spouted the male point of view during roundtable discussions on romance and marriage. Brent balked before doing his next assignment at Universal-International. "It's a small part," he told Sheilah Graham, "and I think they expected me to refuse and take a suspension, but rather than do that I'll play a bellhop with a beard!"[749] He owed the studio a picture within a given time frame, or they had to ante up $75,000. When they offered an extension, Brent refused, saying, "I'd rather be paid now." As a result, he was rushed into *Red Canyon*. While filming, Brent spent as little time as possible on the set. He took every opportunity to dash to his car and head for Hollywood Park, where he had four hearty steeds competing that season. Along with Bing Crosby, Brent augmented his income by wearing Stetson "Turf Club" felt hats for a national campaign targeting the equestrian set.

In the Technicolor *Red Canyon*, Brent played Mat Bostel, a gentlemanly horse breeder, widower, and ironhanded father of a headstrong teen tomboy, Lucy (Ann Blyth). More attuned to horseflesh than his own daughter, Bostel mistakenly buys Lucy a frilly frock for her eighteenth birthday. He may as well have given her a cow pie. She's more interested in taming horses. The plot thickens when wandering cowpoke Lin Sloane (Howard Duff) comes along. He and Lucy tame the "untamable" wild stallion Black

Red Canyon (Universal 1949) (above) with Jane Darwell
and Ann Blyth. (below) *Montana Belle* (RKO) filmed in
1948, was shelved until 1952. "The less said [about it] the
better," snipped co-star Jane Russell

Velvet, who they put up against Bostel's prized thoroughbred in the annual
horse race. Gunfire starts blazing when it is revealed that Lin's pa had killed
Lucy's ma during a raid way back when. The Zane Grey B-Western provided Brent with what amounted to a nothing role. He begrudgingly went
on location to Kanab, Utah, which kept him away from his stables. An im-
pacted wisdom tooth added to George's misery. Supporting actor Edgar
Buchanan, who formerly had a dental practice in Oregon, recalled, "On
location there was no dentist available for miles and miles. I fixed George

Brent's abscessed tooth. I had to bend back three tines of fork, sterilize it in alcohol ... but we fixed him up."[750] Brent did not join Blyth, Duff, and Buchanan for the film's world premiere in Salt Lake City.

The four-hoofed Black Velvet was more than a match for his two-legged costars. The *New York Times* surmised, "Here is a beautifully Technicolored movie set in the picturesque red canyon, sagebrush country of Utah that is full of visual wonders and little else. People who work as actors move about to relate a furiously hackneyed story."[751] Maurice Geraghty's script was chock-full of ludicrous cowpoke similes. "Gosh Miss Lucy you're prettier than a string of blue-nose trout," was typical of the gush Geraghty fed the cast. Despite the brevity of his role (nine minutes total) a Los Angeles critic thought Brent looked "mighty fine in the unfamiliar territory of the Western. He should do more of them."[752] So, he did. On November 3, 1948, he reported to Republic to play opposite Jane Russell in *Montana Belle*. Fans would have to wait four years to see it.

Howard Hughes loaned Jane Russell for Fidelity Pictures' *Montana Belle*, a highly fictionalized account of outlaw Belle Starr. Fidelity intended to release it through Republic. After viewing the completed film, Hughes instructed RKO to buy the film outright ($875,000—the budget was estimated at $650,000).[753] He thought it would do less damage to protégée Russell's career after she had a few more successes. The authors of *The RKO Story* later commented, "Very few people would have been disappointed if the film had remained permanently under lock and key."[754] The scenario had bandit queen Starr (Russell) tantalize outlaw Bob Dalton (Scott Brady) until a smooth-talking gambler named Tom Bradfield (Brent) shows up. Bradfield has lots of money. He owns the Bird Cage Saloon. Wearing a blonde wig and going by "Montana," Belle discovers that she prefers singing at the saloon rather than robbing banks disguised as a man.

Allan Dwan's biographer noted that the veteran director "clearly had fun reconciling the twin personae of Montana and Belle."[755] Earlier on, we see rebel Belle trying to wash dishes while the eagerly attentive Dalton boys contemplate her assets. "I can't stand much more of this!" she groans, before retiring to the hayloft. Dwan teases humor out of what is basically a conventional potboiler. At the finish, Bradfield promises to reign in his libido until Montana Belle fulfills a well-deserved prison sentence. If anything, the chemistry between a rather sedate Brent and emotionless Russell registered consistently . . . at zero.

Jane Russell's memories of *Montana Belle* were shaky when she got around to writing her 1985 autobiography. "I was put into a film about which the less said the better," she duly admitted. "For *Montana Belle* … I played Calamity Jane. I ran a dance hall and George Brent was my lover. I barely remember making it, which is just as well."[756] The fact that she had actually played Belle Starr eluded her. Upon the film's November 1952 release, the *Syracuse Herald Journal* surmised that the money RKO spent was "cast down the drain for this one." "The Daltons," said the critic, "act as if making a living as outlaws is both irritating and a bore."[757] The *New York Times* blasted that Russell was "exhausting her singular histrionic gamut." Critics generally ignored the heavily pomaded Brent, who lacked the necessary spark to spur a gal like Belle Starr. He comes across more like a father figure.

Back at Universal, Brent was cast in *Illegal Entry*, which concerned the smuggling of illegal aliens into the U.S. from Mexico. The public had been primed by news headlines involving human trafficking from war-torn Europe, as well as undocumented Mexican workers. Brent was third-billed, appearing intermittently as a Los Angeles immigration inspector who directs the case. The focus was on gruff Howard Duff's lead role as an ex-Army pilot who infiltrates a dangerous smuggling operation. (Brent's film work was interrupted after he was thrown from a horse at his ranch. He chipped a vertebra and returned to work in bandages.[758])

Filmed by master cinematographer William Daniels in semi-documentary style, *Illegal Entry* was reputedly based on an actual incident. The brisk, no-nonsense yarn pleased most critics. "Gruesome" best describes a load of human cargo (elderly Jewish refugees) being dumped into the blue Pacific before the suspected air freight company is intercepted by the feds. The hollow look on undercover pilot Duff's face after this tragedy isn't easily forgotten. For the climax, agent Duff, with a gun nuzzled in his neck, disobeys orders to turn back to Mexico. He crash lands the plane in order to deliver "hot" cargo to the law. There is the obligatory interlude between Duff and Swedish import Marta Toren, who was coerced into the smuggling racket. Romance doesn't bog down an otherwise surefire situation. Interestingly, love is mostly a fantasy of Duff's overactive imagination. Bosley Crowther thought Duff's "rough and ready style acceptable."[759] He left Brent out of his review. To his credit, Brent's matter-of-fact attitude was definitely more animated than the real-life U.S. Immigration officers who introduce the film. *Seattle Daily Times* commented, "Brent is entirely convincing as the immigration inspector."[760] Los Angeles critic W. E. Oliver praised director Frederick DeCordova (future producer for *The Tonight Show*) for a film that was "neatly packed with excitement, suspense, shocks and several fine performances."[761]

MGM's *Border Incident*, released shortly afterward, was far superior and dealt more specifically with Mexican workers. Directed by Anthony Mann, and starring Ricardo Montalban, the film avoided stereotyping common to Hollywood, while detailing the brutal abuse of undocumented workers in California's Imperial Valley. In the 1998 study, *Culture Across Borders*, the authors compliment the sensitivity of *Border Incident*, classifying it as one of the "very best social problem films of the decade." They point out that in *Illegal Entry* the plight of illegal Mexican workers is "alluded to only marginally and they remain as invisible subject matters."[762]

Upon completing *Illegal Entry* in January 1949, Brent flew to Chile to look over some stallions and fortify his racing stable.[763] He advocated travel for putting things in perspective. "First you learn to appreciate and understand the way other people live and think," he theorized. "Too many of us are bound up in our own group of friends and in certain prescribed boundaries of relaxation [and] work. It's shocking and it's good to discover that your way is not the only way. With so many governments and private organizations spending millions of dollars for this and billions for that, all of which are supposed to cure world ills, I wish someone would devise a plan so that all people could take a three-week travel trip every year."[764]

Brent was plainspoken about acting becoming his "hobby." "My movie work is a hobby," he stated emphatically, "and my horses make up my real occupation right now. Soon I'll have to give up the hobby."[765] It was reported that the actor had invested a half-million dollars into his horse-breeding farm.[766] However, he did not continue to stretch as an actor. William D. Russell, who directed Brent's next effort, *Bride for Sale*, a comedy that also starred Claudette Colbert and Robert Young, was blunt in his assessment of Brent at this juncture:

> *Claudette and Bob Young came up with some fresh ideas. They were both wonderful self-starters. George Brent, let's face it, wasn't the greatest in comedy. He tended to be heavy-handed, and by 1949 he was forty-five and looked tired and worn. I remember the cameraman had a hell of a time disguising his lines and wrinkles.[767]*

A Dallas review praised Colbert and Young as well as the clear comedy line of director Russell. When it came to Brent, the critic didn't hesitate, "As for George Brent, the producer should have heeded Rule No.

Bride For Sale (RKO 1949) with Claudette Colbert

1 promulgated by a rival filmmaker. It is 'never hire George Brent.' "[768] *Bride for Sale* pigeonholed Brent as an agitated, stern-faced owner of an income tax firm. His perpetual scowl subsides after hiring Colbert as his new office manager. The triangular plot has Colbert combing tax files for a rich husband. When boss Brent gets wind of her scheme he conspires with his wealthy pal (Young) to teach her a lesson. Halfway through their shenanigans things backfire. They both fall for her. With her customary élan, Colbert's warm chuckle and spontaneity keep things interesting. She gets her money's worth before resigning from the tax firm—toying with the affections of her two scheming suitors who end up in a slugfest.

Some felt that time was running out for the kind of screwball comedy that was Colbert's forte. One critic observed, "Miss Colbert does her level best to inject some spontaneity and verve into an extremely tired plot line. Mr. Young gives it his best try … but George Brent looks apathetic, tired, and frankly old, and seems to be along just for the ride."[769] Brent's self-satisfied take on his role lacked the easygoing sparkle and wit that made Colbert and Young so enjoyable. When Brent is finally hauled away by police, the paddy wagon seems the best place for him. To Brent's credit, he makes Colbert's final choice in this love triangle understandable. When

Lawrence J. Quirk asked Brent about Colbert, he responded with admiration, saying, "She was not a temperamental or demanding person. I always felt she was emotionally quite mature. And she held up her end. She didn't leave me holding the bag like some of my less talented costars did."[770]

Brent lent a great deal of sincerity to his next assignment, *The Kid from Cleveland*. As a sports broadcaster (and film's narrator), Brent meets a baseball crazy youth named Johnny (Russ Tamblyn). The film details their father-son-like bond with a good mix of actual footage from the 1948 World Series and its champions, the Cleveland Indians. Brent sounds like a pro when he's at the mike detailing play-by-play. Tamblyn impresses in the juvenile lead. He moves like a dancer—with the same catlike grace that he would display in such classics as *Seven Brides for Seven Brothers* and *West Side Story*. Art reflects life in a delicate scene where Tamblyn claims to be an orphan. Brent brings an unusual degree of tenderness when he puts his arm around the boy and shares that he had once been in the same spot. "I … never had any father or mother, either," Brent tells Johnny. "At least … not that I can remember." Knowing Brent's backstory makes the scene all the more compelling. When Brent learns that the boy steals and lies—that he's not an orphan, he carefully explains to Johnny that he's only double-crossed himself. Brent's steady presence provides an anchor for change. Despite a choppy attempt at psychology, the film entertains and is sensitively played by the cast.

Players from the Cleveland Indians pitch in to help Johnny. He receives advice from team owner Bill Veeck, who details how outfielder Larry Doby struck out his first time at bat in the big league. "He was batting for 15,000,000 people who really believed in him," explains Veeck. Doby was the first African-American in the American League after Jackie Robinson broke the color line in the National. In flashback, we see a white player, power hitter Joe Gordon, deliberately strike out so Doby doesn't feel so bad. The idea that team players take care of each other registers in the boy. It must be noted that upon being introduced to his teammates in 1947, some players refused to shake Doby's hand. In Doby's biography, *Pride Against Prejudice*, it is suggested that one reason *The Kid from Cleveland* was a "box office bust" was that it dared to be inclusive. Besides Doby, the film spotlighted Cleveland player Satchel Paige, the first African-American major league pitcher. "Most Americans did not like to see black performers in other than servile positions in the movies," wrote author Joseph Thomas Moore.[771] Visibility of African-American players in *The Kid from Cleveland* challenged die-hard prejudices. Also on hand was pitcher Bob Feller, whose barnstorming tours with Satchel Paige had set the stage for the eventual integration of the game. In his autobiography, Feller dismissed *The Kid from Cleveland* as "entirely forgettable." Player/manager Lou Boudrea later said of the film, "I would like to buy every print of it and burn it."[772]

Why the animosity? Was it the rather self-conscious mugging of the ballplayers in front of the camera? No one was expecting them to act. Aside from newsreel flashes and live footage of spring training, there wasn't much ball playing. This may have disappointed the team, as well as the fans. The focus was on a small but important story. It came as no surprise that the film was held over three weeks in Cleveland. W. Ward Marsh for the city's *Plain Dealer* wrote, "*The Kid from Cleveland* will win no Academy Awards, but it does tell a good, simple, honest story. Herbert Kline has done a first-rate job of directing. Certainly there is little in this film to tax the talents of either Brent as the radio announcer or [Lynn] Bari as his wife. The major dramatic work falls to Rusty Tamblyn."[773] As the *New York Times* put it, "the only mild salvation of this sentimental fable … is a reasonably decent conclusion and a general intention to do some good."[774] It would be two years before Brent filmed again.

∞

"I never had any father or mother, either. At least, not that I remember"—
Brent's line from *The Kid from Cleveland*—held true on a personal level
up until the time of his mother's death on Long Island in 1950.[775] A legal notice in the *Suffolk County News* (Long Island) on December 18,
1952, cited the next of kin of Mary Nolan to respond to issues concerning
her estate. Among the names listed were China Marin and Lucy C. Edwards (Brent's sisters), John J. Nolan (Brent's brother), Patrick Watson
and Robert Fletcher (Brent's nephews), and George Nolan, "sometimes
known as George Brent."[776]

The Nolan cottage in the hamlet of Mastic, Long Island, had been a
frequent gathering place for Brent's siblings during the 1940s. In 1942, his
mother became an active member of the Mastic Civic Association.[777] She
would spend summer and fall at the cottage socializing and playing bingo,
before closing up to spend the winter in Manhattan. Brent's nephew, Robert Fletcher, who had married, was a frequent visitor. During the fall of
1943, Mrs. Nolan resided at Sheepshead Bay on west Long Island where
Brent's oldest sister, Mary Fletcher (Robert's mother), was dying of cancer. Soon afterwards, Robert enlisted in the army. For Christmas 1944,
Ensign Fletcher, his wife (Susan) and their two children, celebrated the
holiday with Mrs. Nolan at the home of Brent's brother John J. Nolan in
Manhattan.[778] Brent's sister Lucy and her husband Gordon C. Edwards, a
Toronto inventor/financial agent, were also present.

In February 2014, when I talked with Brent's grandnephew Robert E.
Fletcher, he fondly recalled his great-grandmother Mary Nolan. "She really, really liked me," he said. "We would go for long walks along the Long
Island shore. There was a small boat. My sister [Cynthia Ann] also had
fond memories of our great-grandmother."[779] Robert, born in 1943, had
no specific recollection of ever meeting his famous granduncle. However,
when watching his films, Robert connects the sound of Brent's resonant

voice with his childhood. Could there have been a rare occasion when Brent turned up at a family affair? Fletcher regrettably stated that any photos or memorabilia that he and his sister inherited had long been discarded. Fletcher acknowledged that his great-grandfather Nolan stayed behind in Ireland because, "He didn't want to come."

Brent's brother, John "Jack" Nolan, looked out for their mother, painting her cottage and keeping her company during her bouts with illness. In 1948, the *County Review* reported that Jack had been elected president of the Emergency Social Service Workers, Inc., a nonprofit organization. "His untiring efforts in taking care of children in distress for the past five years have finally been recognized," said the article. Nolan was also the owner/editor of *The Parent Teacher*, a newspaper devoted to the topic of juvenile delinquency.[780] It was also reported that Jack was a natural comedian, who enjoyed entertaining veterans and lending his comic talent to worthy causes. The winter of 1948–'49 found Mrs. Nolan "seriously ill most of the time," but she returned to her cottage, accompanied by Jack, who stayed on indefinitely. On July 22, she celebrated her seventy-fourth birthday.

While Brent was never mentioned being present at the Nolan gatherings, his sister Kathleen visited their mother in the summer of 1946. Kathleen was now going by the name China Marin. In the fall of 1942, she had married Hollywood agent Ned Marin in Phoenix. Marin was agent for such high-powered stars as John Wayne and Susan Hayward. After they separated in December 1950, Walter Winchell reported, "Pals are hoping the reconciliation chatter for Ned and China Marin is true. Two of Hollywood's best-liked people."[781] By 1953, the couple divorced. Columnists hinted that the problem in their marriage was Susan Hayward, who was looking for a strong shoulder to cry on. Hayward biographer, Beverly Linet, described Ned as a "white-haired bear of a bachelor."[782] When Ned passed away unexpectedly in 1955, it brought Hayward close to the brink of suicide.[783]

When I heard from China's grandson, Ian Watson, he laid the cards on the table regarding Ned Marin. "Her husband after Harris was a drunk and a gambler," said Ian. "He spent what China had inherited, although she was never good with money. China ended up broke in the actresses and actors guild home in Englewood, N.J.—that ironically, Harris set up years before. I remember all those birthday and Christmas cards with a neatly folded brand new $5 note in it for me. She was a very kind and good grandma."[784]

During interviews, George Brent's mother was consistently laid to rest by reporters. He persisted in repeating the myth, or a variation thereof, that he was "orphaned at eleven" and "sent to live with an aunt in New York."[785] Surprisingly, Brent broke the mold regarding his mother in a 1939 interview with Franc Dillon of the Screen Women's Press Club. Dillon had cornered Brent as he stalked back and forth along a tall hedge adjoining the set of *Dark Victory.* "He lays the blame for his early failures on his mother's shoulders," wrote Dillon. "She was always worrying about me," said Brent. "As a man reaches the age of long pants, their concern increases instead of diminishes … it becomes a burden. It acts as a damper and is a continual source of annoyance to the person who is being worried over. That's why men are always trying to escape."[786] Dillon noted that Brent was reluctant to talk any further. He changed the subject after stating,

> *When I was little I was invariably caught when I tried to escape, and … found myself on the receiving end of a good spanking. As I grew older … I wanted to be free—from what I don't know—but … I was never free because I knew that my mother was fretting about me.*

With the birth of Suzanne Brent on August 3, 1950, George's family life was centered at his Hidden Valley ranch.[787] Four years later, his son Barry was born. For a Christmas present, the bouncing boy received a broodmare from his proud papa.[788] When they moved from Hidden Valley in 1958, George explained, "We love it here. The move is more for the children."[789] He thought Suzanne and Barry would have "better schooling" in Rancho Santa Fe. Brent seemed determined that his own children wouldn't face the rough edges, hardships, "the worry"—the "need to escape," with which he had struggled while growing up.

FBI Girl (Lippert 1951) (l to r) Audrey Totter, Tom Drake,
Jan Kayne, Joi Lansing, Cesar Romero and Brent

14

Changing Channels

In the fall of 1951, Brent was reported to be changing channels when it came to making movies. "I won't have much time for them with TV," he said. Brent was scheduled to play the gentleman thief in thirty-nine episodes based on E. W. Hornung's *Raffles.* Nigel Bruce would costar. "I haven't been too busy about my film career," Brent admitted. "It's hard to get good material. In pictures today it's 'Print it' if they can see you and hear you. Ten years ago we took longer … but it was worth it. The result was beautiful and it paid off at the box office."[790] He overlooked the fact that aggressive shooting schedules were cost-effective—the life's blood of small studios. When *Raffles* ran into legal difficulties, Brent opted to make his British film debut instead. His foray into the new medium of television was postponed, temporarily.

Prior to leaving for England, Brent took second billing to Cesar Romero in the low-budget *FBI Girl.* That is, after both actors, as well as the entire film crew, were investigated. The FBI had tremendous influence in making what was essentially a B noir. Richard Hood, special agent overseeing the production, reported to Clyde Tolson, Associate Director of the FBI and companion/protégé of J. Edgar Hoover, that George Brent had "apparently kept himself fairly clean."[791] In other words, Brent had no affiliation with communist front organizations. The story's author, Rupert Hughes (uncle of Howard Hughes), had raged about Communist propaganda in Hollywood before the House Un-American Activities Committee investigations in 1947. Rupert went so far as to call UCLA a "Communist dominated institution."[792] He had the bureau's complete cooperation on *FBI Girl*.

Crack FBI agents Romero and Brent are all business and no personality as they unravel the murder of a female FBI employee who had tampered with the department's fingerprint files. Brent's character is at the beck and call of Romero. James Robert Parish described Brent "halfheartedly lumbering through a cops 'n' robbers tale in his attempt to capture crime lord Raymond Burr."[793] It is Burr who steals the show. He plays a brutal racketeer—the power behind an ambitious governor with an unsavory past. Burr's looks are both seductive and menacing. The film's (unintentional) romantic interlude has Burr board a plane then ask Romero if the seat next to him is occupied. "The lady up there is traveling with a baby," Burr explains. "Not that I don't like children." Romero chuckles, "Yeah, I know what you mean." They warm up to each other making plans for drinks at the luxury Mayflower hotel in D.C. Neither has a clue as to the other's identity. "If I'd only known," Romero reflects later. "We were going to get together alright, but not for a drink." Instead of quiet cocktails and conversation, Romero ends up filling Burr with lead from a machine gun.

The FBI "girl" in this case is played by Audrey Totter. The ads featured her packing a pistol—a "woman on a manhunt." Not so. Instead of pulling a trigger, Totter's fingers focus solely on her job as a bureau file clerk. Tom Drake offered a solid performance as Totter's fiancé. He's a Washington lobbyist tied in with Burr's syndicate—an opportunist who's out to make big money. Despite its patriotic pledge to promote Washington, D.C., as "the hope for the entire world," *FBI Girl* portrays D.C.'s corrupt political system as "hopeless." Commentary by Alan K. Rode, on the film's 2007

In the British Exclusive release *The Last Page/Man Bait* (1952),
Brent is blackmailed by Diana Dors (above).
Marguerite Chapman (below) comes to his rescue.

DVD release, correctly placed *FBI Girl* "under the old triangle: fast, good, and cheap." In 2012, author Laura Wagner rated the film to be a "fun, fast-paced docu-noir." Wagner enjoyed the film's absurdities, admitting "the roles aren't much of a stretch for any of the actors."[794] Brent's next role, in the British noir *Man Bait*, offered him an opportunity to really stretch. The question was—could he dig deep enough emotionally to pull it off?

Man Bait (*The Last Page* in Britain) was notches above *FBI Girl*. The atmospheric thriller, stimulated by a British cast and a good director, had dashes of Hitchcock—black humor, odd characters, and Brent as the innocent man on the run. He played the owner of an upscale London bookstore who finds himself being blackmailed by a very blonde, curvaceous invoice clerk (nineteen-year-old Diana Dors). In a moment of weakness, Brent made the mistake of kissing her eager, amply lipped mouth. Dors's boyfriend (Peter Reynolds), an ex-con, sees dollar signs when he learns of Brent's indiscretion—via extortion. After all, Brent has an invalid wife. What if she found out? A chain of events lead to the deaths of the wife and the guilt-ridden Dors. Brent is accused of murder. His loyal secretary (Marguerite Chapman) inadvertently helps Scotland Yard solve the grisly crime. Brent and Chapman end up together, which is what he wanted all along. Produced by Hammer Films, *Man Bait* held a few neat surprises for audiences when released in the U.S.

Diana Dors and Peter Reynolds effortlessly walk away with the picture. *Man Bait* helped launch Dors's career as Britain's blonde bombshell. A Cleveland critic observed, "Brent convincingly depicts the battle-shocked bookman who runs away in a moment of panic." The same critic qualified his praise by admitting "George Brent … can't quite compete against the sultry charms of Diana Dors in this murder tale."[795] Even so, Brent fills the shoes of a stoic gentleman in a rut. When Dors persists in her accusations of sexual assault, he finally lashes out, slamming down her payoff in bundles of cash. "One hundred, two hundred, there!" he shouts. "Now take the lot and get out!" When Brent receives news of his wife's sudden death, the camera cuts him off. His somber response feels disingenuous—his display of grief, minimal. The psychological aspect of Brent's emotionally scarred war veteran was also left unexplored. Nonetheless, *Man Bait* still manages to register as Brent's last strong performance. When he commented on the film in 1960, he said, "It was so bad I don't even remember the name of it."[796] Director Terence Fisher would later claim fame for horror genre hits (*The Curse of Frankenstein, Horror of Dracula*) starring Christopher Lee and Peter Cushing.

Hedda Hopper reported that after completing *Man Bait* Brent planned to visit a chum in Ireland named Hubert Hardigan. Hardigan, a horse trainer, was responsible for numerous Irish Classic Winners. He ran a stud farm for Aly Kahn (married to Rita Hayworth). Upon Brent's return to the U.S., Hopper mentioned that he had also met a young playwright in Ireland named Thomas Poole. Brent purchased Poole's story *Woman Hater*, as a possibility for the screen. The plot eliminated all bachelors in the world except one—a confirmed woman hater. Brent abandoned the idea. It would be a year before he made another film.

Brent arrived home from London on August 23, 1951. In October he began plugging *FBI Girl* by guest appearances on such popular programs as Mutual radio's *Queen for a Day*. He was also reunited with Bette Davis for her Mutual series *Woman of the Year*. "Bette Davis put in a big pitch to have George Brent costar," reported Sheilah Graham.[797] *All About Eve* (1950), with 14 Academy Award nominations, had boosted Davis's career. When columnist Erskine Johnson asked Brent about Davis's comeback, Brent snapped, "It's not a question of a comeback for an actress of her caliber. Just because a person has had bad pictures doesn't mean they're supposed to hang you out to dry and run you out of town."[798]

Reunited with Bette Davis for Mutual radio's *Woman of the Year* in 1952

Woman of the Year debuted December 31. Davis starred as Tess Harding, an international news columnist. Brent, as Sam Craig, played a sports reporter for the same paper. By February, after ratings went up twenty-seven percent, Tess and Sam were married. In May, national news carried a photo of Brent and Davis happily chatting over coffee and cigarettes during rehearsal. They had a hit on their hands. Davis later recalled, "We had fun when we did *Woman of the Year* on radio. [Brent's] one of my few lovers whom I've remained friends with."[799] Pleased with the series' success, Mutual asked Brent for an extension of his option. Brent opted to bow out. Aside from making another film, he was celebrating his success with thoroughbreds, having just sold 16 of them to a Japanese racing syndicate for a cool $60,000.[800]

Brent filmed his first teleplay in early 1952. *A Fond Farewell* was a love triangle costarring Gertrude Michael and Donald Woods. The thirty-minute drama would finally air in 1953 as an episode of *Crown Theatre* hosted by Gloria Swanson. Brent also appeared on the small screen as an angry city editor in *Double Exposure*—a comedy for *Ford Television Theatre* costarring Dan Duryea. *Variety* only gave praise to supporting player Marvin Kaplan. "He so completely dominates this effervescent comedy," said the review, "that the others become almost mere puppets."[801] Shortly before *Double Exposure* aired, Brent's Allied Artists' release *Tangier Incident* hit theatre screens.

Filmed in the fall of 1952, *Tangier Incident* fueled the paranoia surrounding atomic scientists selling "secret information" to Communist Russia. Brent easily adapted to his role as a government CIA operative posing as a black market kingpin in Morocco. While trying to foil the scheme of three rogue scientists, he becomes a man marked for murder. Not that the film took itself too seriously. Brent finds ample time to lock lips with a Soviet spy (Mari Aldon) and a couple of other shapely blondes. More tomfoolery emerges when Brent discovers that his room is being wiretapped. Using a thick Brooklyn accent, Brent invents "Louie," an imaginary accomplice. For those listening in, Brent tells "Louie" that whoever is doing the "bugging" will have to pay for it. "Louie" offers to track 'em down and "give 'em da boom-boom treatment!" Brent pulls off this hokum with surprising panache. Nonetheless, *Tangier Incident* was destined to be lowercase filler for the movie marquee.

"Uninspired writing and unconvincing incidents combine to make film an also-ran," warned *Variety*. "Brent walks through his rather unbelievable role. American outwits the Commies for a conventional climax."[802] There would be numerous B-films fueling the dangers of atomic information getting into the hands of the wrong people. Meanwhile, the U.S. government spent millions testing nuclear weapons in Utah, Nevada, New Mexico, Texas, and the Pacific islands, deliberately exposing thousands of troops (and citizens) to radioactivity—leaving behind a legacy of leukemia, cancers, birth defects, infertility and miscarriages. Who needed enemies?

Tangier Incident (Allied Artists 1953) with Benny Rubin and Mari Alden

Surprisingly, Brent made a return to the stage after twenty-three years. In early 1952, playwright Clifford Odets had negotiated with Brent for the male lead in the national company tour of *The Country Girl*. The role of the alcoholic, down-on-his-luck actor eventually went to Robert Young. A year later, Brent signed to tour in *Affairs of State*. Louis Verneuil's topical comedy set in Washington, D.C., had a successful run on Broadway (1950–'52). *Variety* reported that Brent "wasn't able to get up in the part on time" for the March 4 Kansas City opening.[803] Harry Bannister (Ann Harding's ex) substituted for Brent, who was battling the flu. Ten days later, Brent made his debut in Minneapolis. The unusual triangle in *Affairs of State* included an elderly senator (Brent) who marries his mousy secretary (Haila Stoddard) in order to cover up his affair with the wife (Irene Hervey) of an ex-Secretary of State (Bannister). *Variety* said the cast did "first rate justice to the play. George Brent is top-starred. A bit too youthful and vigorous for his supposed 70 years, he's handsome, while bringing a fine speaking voice, ease and assurance for his none-too-demanding task."[804]

Mexican Manhunt (Allied Artists 1953) with Morris Ankrum and Karen Sharpe Kramer

Brent's stage "comeback" was short lived. Twelve days to be exact. While playing the Cox Theatre in Cincinnati, "ailing" George was replaced by veteran Otto Kruger. The flu was blamed for his withdrawal prior to an extended Chicago run. Brent took a three month break from acting, before returning to the big screen for his film swan song, a serviceable programmer titled *Mexican Manhunt*. In this, Brent played an upbeat crime novelist who receives a "hot" tip on the whereabouts of a reporter who had been missing for 15 years. Brent is one step ahead of the bad guys, while assisting the reporter (Morris Ankrum) and his daughter (Karen Sharpe) across the Mexican border and back into the U.S. In this game of cat-and-mouse, Brent smells a rat when glamour puss Hillary Brooke shows up in a shiny convertible, asking for directions. "She's pretty," he cautions, "in an unpleasant kind of way." *Mexican Manhunt* allowed a dash of offbeat humor. Scene stealer Alberto Morin, playing Ankrum's hired hand, insists that he is Ms. Sharpe's "mother"—which places his relationship with Ankrum, a heavy drinker, into question. But, basically, it's Brent's show. Leslie Halliwell noted that the film "coasts along on the strength of its star."[805]

Settling for the small screen, Brent guest starred on *Revlon Mirror Theatre*. The teleplay, *Key in the Lock*, directed by Peter Godfrey (*Christmas in Connecticut*), had Brent as a jealous husband who drives his wife (Marguerite Chapman) into the arms of her lover, before killing him. Brent frames his wife for the murder. *Variety* wasn't impressed, finding the "highly contrived situations ... disappointing." "Brent," said the review, "performs his chores automatically and expressionless."[806] On this note, Brent took a sabbatical from acting for over a year.

1954 found Brent taking time out to turn fifty—staying close to home in Hidden Valley. The ranch community bordered Lake Sherwood and the Santa Monica Mountains (where Doug Fairbanks, Sr., had filmed scenes for the 1922 film *Robin Hood*). "You don't see George Brent in Hollywood much anymore," commented Sheilah Graham. "But here's some news about Brent's family life—his wife is expecting their baby any minute.[807] Taking a year off had proved productive. On November 26, George, Janet, and Suzanne welcomed a new addition to their family. Barry Brent weighed in at six pounds, nine ounces at St. John's Hospital in Oxnard.

Shortly before Barry's birth, Brent returned to television for three episodes of the popular *Fireside Theatre*. Angela Lansbury offered a vigorous turn as his paranoid wife in *The Indiscreet Mrs. Jarvis*. Brent, the head of Jarvis Chemicals, wants to promote a man (William Lundigan) whose wife (Martha Vickers) had known Lansbury years ago. The panic-stricken Lansbury foils Lundigan's promotion by saying his wife was a troublemaker. Brent realizes that something's amiss. In a sensitively played scene he reassures Lansbury, "There's very little that you can say that I don't already know. I didn't have to be clairvoyant to know that you had been hurt before we met." While Lansbury desperately tries to

Climax! featured Sylvia Sidney, Brent and Diana Lynn in
The Leaf Out of the Book (1955). Below, Bobby Clark is seen with
Brent in a Crossroads episode *The Kid Had a Gun* (1956)

conceal her youthful fling with a married man, Brent smoothly earns the acting palm as the husband who possesses profound understanding.

Respected director Bretaigne Windust signed Brent, Sylvia Sidney, and Diana Lynn for TV's *Climax!* In *The Leaf Out of the Book* the star trio tore the executive world of big business apart driving home the theme that money and ambition can't buy happiness. Boston critic, Joseph Purcell, felt that the teleplay was "quite a few notches above the usual TV fare." "Sylvia Sidney was convincing," said Purcell, "Mr. Brent's performance was the only weak link in the entire presentation ... stiff and unyielding throughout. We got the idea that a lot more could have been done with the role."[808] One possible excuse for Brent's belly flop was that it was his "live" TV debut. Viewers could hear an occasional offstage whisper leaking into the audio, prompting actors to keep on script. *Variety* indicated that "all the cast toppers were guilty of frequent dialogue fluffs."[809] Thereafter, Brent avoided "live" telecasts. "I tried just one live show, a *Climax!*" he grimly told *TV Guide*, "and that was my first and last one. How they ever get a show on the air with all those cameras and cables is beyond me. I suppose they get used to it, but I'm not about to."[810]

Brent had his hopes up for a TV pilot titled *Jody and Me*. Like many pilots that failed to find a sponsor, it was eventually slotted into an anthology series—in this case, *Stage 7*. Rechristened *The Magic Hat*, Brent came across as relaxed and perfectly at home as the widowed father of a precocious daughter (Lydia Reed) who has her eye on purchasing a ladies' hat much too sophisticated for her nine years. "I'm not sure that I see you in that hat, exactly," he advises tenderly. "That hat seems to me more of the Ava Gardner type." Reed persists, "It would do a lot for me." "Well," he ponders, "that's a very important consideration." She gets the hat and together they suffer the consequences. Reed and the silver-haired Brent were an amicable duo and, together, they create a warm-hearted tale that champions being an individual. Lydia Reed would later find success playing Hassie on ABC's popular sitcom, *The Real McCoys*. Brent indicated to columnist Vernon Scott that he preferred the half-hour family comedy show to a dramatic series. This was after his experience as a globe-trotting reporter on the first hour-long, weekly televised series, *Wire Service*.

Prior to signing on for *Wire Service*, Brent appeared on *The George Gobel Show*. Gobel and his guest star spoofed popular TV drug commercials in the evening's funniest sketch. Brent was on a variety of programs during 1955–'56, including the religious anthology, *Crossroads*, in which he played Father Raymond, a Jesuit priest in rural China. Enter Po Ling, a blind boy. Father Raymond trains Po Ling in the art of smuggling sacred wine from a Communist controlled city. He tells him that the wine is good for Chinese souls—and a profitable business career. *Variety* nodded, "George Brent on the whole gives a very sympathetic and understanding performance."[811] The story, written by the fervent anti-Communist journalist Irene Corbally Kuhn, was purported to be true, and about as plausible as Brent's visit on *Science Fiction Theatre*. In *The Long Day*, we learn that the government is quietly launching a radium-infused missile ("Operation Torch") that will produce a vast amount of artificial light at night. Scenarists George and Gertrude Fass had enough savvy in writing this Cold War tale to include a Congressman telling the physicist in charge, "All Washington can do is keep assuring residents that they're in no danger, whether they believe it or not." The scenario also tackled discrimination. Brent played an unscrupulous realtor whose vengeful nighttime plan against a struggling new home owner, an ex-con (*Star Trek's* DeForest Kelly), is thwarted by "the light."[812] Concerned about property values, Brent complained, "Decent folk won't want to buy!" After witnessing "Operation Torch" (as if it were an act of God), he declares, "I will not sit in judgment of my fellow man!" The reality of mushroom-shaped clouds continued to rise along western skies until the Limited Test Ban Treaty of 1963.

Brent was romantically teamed with Ann Harding in *The Fleeting Years*—an episode of *Celebrity Playhouse*. *Variety* wasn't impressed with the story but commented, "in the capable hands of a four-star cast it develops an engrossing quality."[813] Widow Harding takes a fast shine to Brent, a wealthy meat-packer, after breaking off her affair with a fortune hunter. Apparently, Harding took a shine to Brent off camera as well. For her following "live" appearance on *Playwrights '56*, she insisted on having Brent as her costar in the controversial story *Center of the Maze* penned by Sam Hall. They were in mid-rehearsals when Harding put her foot down. When I talked with Hall in 2009, he elaborated on a sticky situation. "At one point Harding wanted us to fire the leading man. She wanted us to get George Brent who was … in Mexico. She had checked with him and he would have gladly come to New York. She was very taken with him."[814] Ann didn't get her wish and vowed never to do another "live" telecast. "That glazed look you see in the eyes of actors on 'live' TV," she said, "is not histrionic emotion, but inner panic. They're in a mental turmoil to remember their next lines."[815] When it came to "live" television, Harding and Brent were on the same page.

Wire Service

Wire Service, filmed on location in Mexico, Los Angeles, and England, debuted on ABC in October 1956. When questioned about being in a regular series, Brent said that he wanted to "get out amongst 'em again just for the fun of it. And," he stressed, "I have a percentage of the series."[816] Brent came across as focused and comfortable in his role as Dean Evans, an investigative reporter for the *Trans-Globe*. His first episode, *Campaign Train*, based on a crime novel by a former FBI agent, involved a would-be political assassin. *Variety* observed, "George Brent, still a suave figure, played his role as sleuth-newsman with the dignified aplomb of a White

House news ferret not content with mere handouts."[817] George reveled in the fact that he no longer dyed his hair. "There [is] really only one, small interesting thing about me," he mused, "and the studio publicity people would never let me mention it. This white hair of mine—why, it started turning when I was only 15. But in the *Wire Service* series they're letting me be myself. My hair is all my own and it's pure white. I like it."

There was a humanitarian side to Dean Evans that Brent admirably utilized as he dug deeper than the law to protect the innocent. His underlying compassion comes across in *Four Minutes to Shot*, penned by the husband-wife team of Frank and Doris Hursley. In August 1945, nineteen hours after the atom bomb fell on Hiroshima, the Hursleys had hastily scripted a radio broadcast, *Atomic Bombs*, theorizing that the new weapon would force mankind to be peaceful. They soon realized they were mistaken. *Four Minutes to Shot* targeted nuclear testing as well as the military brass in charge. Brent joins 200 other correspondents for ringside seats at the latest atom bomb test seventy miles from Las Vegas. When the test is temporarily called off due to wind shifts, Brent's off-the-cuff remark, "You can't blame them for being careful with the public screaming the dangers of fallout" foreshadows decades of controversy, compounded by nuclear reactor disasters—Chernobyl, Three Mile Island, etc. The Hursleys add to this mix the sudden appearance of a pregnant Hispanic woman named Consuelo Perez. When she shows up, atomic bomb tests and the men who oversee them are put under even closer scrutiny.

In *Wire Service*, Dean Evans never allows protocol to get in the way of "doing the right thing." In *Four Minutes to Shot* Brent is cordial with the thick-skinned General Saxon (Edward Binns) but not intimidated. At a crucial moment, Brent hijacks Saxon's jeep to locate Consuelo's husband, an illegal alien construction worker who is hiding in the restricted test area. When Brent asks to postpone the next scheduled test, the General is outraged. "The American people can't afford to wait," he puffs. Brent argues,

"A human being's life is at stake … here and *now*." The situation is cushioned with a dash of humor when General Saxon begrudgingly offers his rare blood type to save Consuelo's life. A male nurse reminds Saxon that no man is indispensable in the army. "It might help you to think about that," he calmly advises while drawing the blood. Exasperated, Saxon rolls his eyes in disbelief just as the hospital windows fill the room with immense light from the nuclear test. Consuelo has her baby and all is well. Or, is it? Brent's narrative concludes, "Even as man's most destructive weapon spewed its 35 kiloton force flame and radioactive poison … a new life was born." In a subsequent episode, *Run Sheep, Run*, the writers went so far as to call uranium "manna from hell" that fed America's mania for profiteering.

Dane Clark and Mercedes McCambridge also had solo-starring roles on *Wire Service*. Despite a few farfetched stories, and actors puffing away on the sponsor's Camel cigarettes, the series provided meaty TV fare. As writer Cary O'Dell points out, "The series' unique rotation of talent was the first of its kind. *Wire Service* remains a hard-hitting, well-produced, well-acted drama, anchored by an impressive trio of lead stars."[818] Brent impressed viewers as he tackled other hard-hitting issues such as prison reform in *The Night of August Seventh*. During a riot in a maximum security area, the instigators demand to see reporter Dean Evans. They want him to print their side of the story. At one point, bad-boy Lee Van Cleef gets a stronghold on Brent, pulls a knife, and threatens to send him out in a sack. Brent exudes an inner strength and confidence that counters all odds—even psychopaths. O'Dell commented, "Brent's character … and the prison's warden each wonder aloud about the humanity of holding '4,000 men in a place designed for 2,000' and of the inevitable conflicts that arise from warehousing rather than rehabilitating"—or, as Evans puts it, the manufacture of "habitual criminals to turn loose on the state." In Brent's hands, Dean Evans is always believable, and he easily carries each episode unhampered by a leading lady. Unfortunately, *Wire Service*,

**Brent offered excellent work as a crusading newsman on
TV's first hour-long dramatic series *Wire Service* (1956-57)**

playing opposite the popular *Climax!* time slot, never broke into the top
twenty-five Nielsen ratings. Brent offered some of his best work in the
series, but years later he commented,

> *When I saw the first rushes of the show—I knew it wouldn't go. It
> lasted only 39 weeks. When I signed to do it, it sounded great. We
> were to go all over the world filming it. As it turned out we only
> did a week's work in Mexico. The rest was shot in Los Angeles. I
> didn't like the formula for the shows. I was always acted upon in
> the part. Everyone else knew where it was going to end but me.
> That's very frustrating.[819]*

It was an odd assessment, considering that Brent's character was truly engaged, intrepid, taking the initiative to right the wrongs and turn things around. Perhaps the real rub was that Brent had opted for a percentage of the series' profits, rather than residuals from reruns.

As *Wire Service* invaded American homes, Brent appeared on the large screen, but briefly. Due to an attack of laryngitis, he was dismissed from his role in *Death of a Scoundrel* (1956). Producer/director Charles Martin left a glimpse of Brent in the final print—a costly scene involving hundreds of extras. Dorothy Kilgallen noted in her column, "There's a sudden gasp from the audience at the sneak preview of the new suspense film, *Death of a Scoundrel*, when viewers recognize George Brent. A big star of a couple of decades ago, Brent appears in a party scene—for only a second or two—his hair white and his role no more important than that of a dress extra."[820] Kilgallen's sensational report—the tragic demise of Brent's career—didn't bother with the *real* truth. In late 1955, producer Martin had signed George Sanders for the lead, Zsa Zsa Gabor, Yvonne DeCarlo, and Brent for supporting roles. Sanders played the scoundrel (echoing the real-life of notorious manipulator Serge Rubenstein). All the players had good reason to kill Sanders—"the most hated man on earth." Brent, as his business partner, an opportunistic stockbroker, was to fire the fatal shot that puts an end to Sanders's ruthless escapades.

After completing a couple of scenes, Brent came down with a severe case of laryngitis. "I couldn't talk—nothing would come out," he recalled. "They couldn't wait around until I got better."[821] Production closed down on January 25, 1956. *Variety* reported that doctors could not promise Brent's complete recovery within a month. Brent spent six weeks in the hospital. He was replaced by John Hoyt. "That was the very first time I was unable to finish a film," Brent recalled sadly. "One of those things, I guess."[822] An hour into this excessively long film, the debonair-looking Brent walks up behind Sanders and Gabor at a gala ball. Sanders mo-

Brent lost his voice, but took home $25,000 for his 58-second spot in *Death of a Scoundrel* (RKO 1956) with Zsa Zsa Gabor, George Sanders and Coleen Gray

tions for Brent to take the dazzling Zsa Zsa onto the dance floor. Brent holds Gabor in his arms and waltzes away. This bit is followed by a subsequent spot in which Brent looks on while Gabor humiliates her female secretary in front of the other guests. Brent was on screen for a total of fifty-eight seconds. Hedda Hopper commented on Brent's elaborate ballroom scene, saying, "George Brent claims to be the highest paid extra in the world. They left in the one sequence that he shot and he received his $25,000."[823] According to the critics, Brent didn't miss out on much. Only the easily duped would have taken *Death of a Scoundrel* seriously. *Variety* thought the film went "from real-to-ridiculous" and would "need selling."[824] Author Richard B. Jewell (*The RKO Story*) calls it "the epitome of lurid trash."[825] Jeff Stafford, managing editor for the Turner Classic Movies site, qualified *Scoundrel* as "enormously entertaining trash." He also

c. 1957 Sharing his passion for horses with daughter Suzanne
(courtesy of Brian Reddin)

felt that Sanders's lead role reflected the actor's own misanthropic nature. Sanders's last top billing in a major film was rumored to be his favorite.

George and Janet contemplated relocating to San Diego County. Surely, the series of raging fires that ravaged the Santa Monica Mountains during the winter of 1956–'57 influenced their decision. Much of the picturesque scenery was left a smoldering wasteland. Fires around Lake Sherwood placed Brent's home on the "endangered" list.[826] "If I sell," said Brent, "I retain all oil and mineral rights to the property. Just a mile down the way, a guy's been sinking an oil well for the last two-and-a-half years. Persistent cuss. He's put at least $400,000 into it and gone down more than 7,000 feet. If he hits oil—and he's convinced he will someday—no telling what will happen around here."[827] By the spring of 1958, the Brent family made the move to Rancho Santa Fe—a high income community and home to the Del Mar Race Track. They purchased a hilltop two-story Monterey-styled home resting on forty acres from John W. Rice, Jr., a brick manufacturer. Brent quickly converted the acreage into a breeding farm for thoroughbreds, adding a 5,000 square foot barn. A tree boarded lane, off the Rambla de los Flores, led to the picturesque residence that overlooked a guest house, barn and fences—all painted gleaming white in contrast to the lush green pastures.

Living 100 miles south of Los Angeles, Brent was often curious to know what was going on in good old Hollywood. He cornered one reporter and asked, "Tell me, how has Loretta been doing? How is her health? What's old Bill Boyd up to these days? How much longer does Lucille figure on going on with *I Love Lucy*? Have another beer."[828] Brent and Loretta Young were patients at St. John's when he had emergency surgery of an "undisclosed nature." Brent was discharged, but Loretta, tired and underweight, had to endure a three-month stay. The reporter for *TV Guide* indicated that George and Janet were avid television viewers. "Gleason kills me," George confessed. "Isn't that Audrey Meadows great? I don't see how Brod Crawford stands the gaff, turning out those *Highway Patrol* shows every week. Good show, too." It wasn't long before Brent decided to "stand the gaff" of another series, *El Coyote*. Showman Ken Murray filmed a pilot costarring Brent and Muriel Davis—champion gymnast at the 1956 Olympic Games. Despite his long record of alcohol/drug abuse, former child star Scotty Beckett also signed on. Beckett had played with Brent in *The Case Against Mrs. Ames* in 1936. In *El Coyote*, Brent was the editor of a frontier newspaper, and young Davis, as his daughter, masqueraded as a female Zorro-like avenger. Despite the popularity of TV Westerns, producer Murray never managed to get *El Coyote* on the air.

It was inevitable that Brent would eventually end up as a guest star on one of the Westerns that populated TV screens during the late '50s and '60s. Former costars Bette Davis (*Wagon Train*) and Myrna Loy (*The Virginian*) made the sojourn, while Barbara Stanwyck had a huge success in her popular *The Big Valley* series. *Rawhide*, starring Eric Fleming and Clint Eastwood, focused on the challenges of cattle drives in the Old West. Guest stars included Stanwyck, Mary Astor, Cesar Romero, Brian Aherne—"Every kind of person imaginable came through," recalled Eastwood.[829] During its first season, Brent joined the cast in an episode titled *Incident at Chubasco* (1959). For this 'round 'em up, shoot 'em up, he dyed his hair black, although he wore a Stetson in most scenes. As one review put it, "The best thing about this episode … is the familiar face of George Brent. He plays a sour old man determined to find his runaway wife, and gives trail boss Gil Favor [Fleming] all the trouble he can muster."[830] Shortly after the episode aired, Brent was acting once again, but this time as a real-life jury foreman on a petty larceny case in Encinita. It was reported that the defendant fondly shook Brent's hand after being acquitted of stealing nine chickens at the county fair.[831] It prepped Brent to face the camera for producer Norman Herman's proposed series *You and the Law.* In the fall of 1959, Brent breezed into Hollywood for a two-day shoot of the five-minute pilot. It failed to find a sponsor.

In 1960, Brent's swan song for television was on the *Chevy Mystery Show*, a summer replacement for *The Dinah Shore Show*. Director Marc Daniels (*I Love Lucy, Gunsmoke, Star Trek*) was at the helm of a gripping episode involving a high school teacher (Brent) who refuses to help a woman pleading outside his front door late at night. She claims to be a victim of assault by two men she had picked up at a bar. Brent strongly registers his frustration, then remorse as he grasps the gravity of the situation. The woman is murdered, and Brent becomes a target of scorn by the local media. One syndicated critic found the teleplay to be a "fairly entertaining hour."[832] Brent told columnist Vernon Scott,

> *I rarely come [to Hollywood], and I didn't even have an agent when this job came along. I'm content to stay down in Rancho Santa Fe on the ranch keeping an eye on my stock. I have about 18 brood mares that have turned out some mighty useful horses. I've never produced a top flight stakes winner, but our ranch has come up with a lot of thoroughbreds who have earned $30-50,000 dollars in two years of racing. And that's pretty good.*[833]

George gave up acting as a hobby to devote all his time to his string of racehorses. In 1961, he appeared on TV's *Sports Unlimited*, offering a preview of the Rancho Santa Fe horse show. That same year, Brent took out a license as a trainer. He had no trouble passing the exam. "One of the questions they asked me," he said, "is how long does it take to get a horse ready for the races? It's one of those trick questions. The right answer is— it depends on the horse."[834] Brent told *The Los Angeles Times*, "I love the atmosphere of racing, the life around horses and the friendships I have made. All my horses are young and have promise." "They do not know

**July 1962. George Brent, horse trainer,
with his two-year-old thoroughbred Court Tower**

what meanness is," he emphasized. "No one is allowed to shout or curse at them around this barn. I have hopes of getting a winner soon."[835] Being a trainer meant getting up at 4:30 a.m., training until 10:30 a.m., and after a break, back at the track for the afternoon races. Feeding time began at 4 p.m. "With hours like that," George admitted, "you don't stay up late often, and I'm in bed by 9:30 each evening." And, George meant it when he told Hedda Hopper, "Horses are more interesting than people."[836]

In 1966, Brent surprised everyone when he decided to relocate his horse breeding business to Ireland. The Emerald Isle's proverbial "forty shades of green" seemed ideal turf. Or, was it that George was swept into a wave of nostalgia—a case of . . .

"Eire go Brach"[1]

In May 1966, Brent retired as a board member of Del Mar Charities. He was considered one of the organization's "most colorful members." At an informal luncheon in his honor at San Diego's landmark Lubach's Restaurant, Brent handed over his beloved shillelagh to John Quimby, a labor and civic leader, who was also president of the Friendly Sons of St. Patrick. George had announced plans that he and Janet were headed for Ireland. Along with Suzanne (age sixteen) and Barry (age eleven) they planned to reside on the outskirts of Dublin. "Ireland is a great country for raising horses and racing them," he explained. "And that is my main occupation now. I have six brood mares and yearlings that I will be taking with me."[837] After pooh-poohing the prospect of Ireland's damp, chilly climate, he put in a plug for two of his horses: Shimmering Star, winner of Las Flores Stakes at Santa Anita, and Kimberly Queen, who had placed in the Princess Stakes at Hollywood Park. "[They] should take well to the grass there," he added.[838]

Before the move, Brent donated autographed first editions from his personal book collection to the San Diego library. Some predicted he was contemplating a permanent stay on the old sod. By August, the Brents had closed up their ranch house, flown to Ireland, and settled into Foxrock, a suburb south of Dublin, where they rented an older home. Suzanne and Barry would attend boarding schools. Suzanne had previously attended Chateau Mont-Choisi in Switzerland. Barry had been at a military academy.

Sheilah Graham reported that George and Janet had settled not far from director (and horse enthusiast) John Huston. According to Irish director Brian Reddin, it was Huston who had encouraged Brent to move

---

1 The standard Irish version of the anglicized "Erin go Bragh"—expressing allegiance to Ireland. Often translated as "Ireland Forever."

to Ireland in the first place, telling him that he would "love it."[839] George was, in fact, about two hours away from Huston, an Irish citizen, living in County Galway. Huston had left the U.S. in the early 1950s during what he referred to as the "obscene game of blackmail" that transpired during the House Un-American Activities Committee investigations.[840] By the spring of 1967, Brent indicated that although he was focused on horse breeding, he could be lured back to movies. "If the right role came along," he said, "maybe something from John Huston, I might just fly out of the starting gate and act again."[841]

While mixing the best of Irish bloodstock with California horses, Brent made his debut at The Curragh, Ireland's racing headquarters in County Kildare. His entry was Sharp Tack, trained by Paddy Prendergast—winner of seventeen Irish classics. Brent also had a horse entered in England's Epsom Derby. While his horses fared well on Irish soil, Brent did not. "We almost froze to death," he said afterwards. "And you couldn't get anybody to do anything, everything was *mañana*. I shipped my Rolls-Royce over and they scratched the doors; they thought it belonged to a British official. I had a helluva time getting it repaired."[842] Daughter Suzanne noted one definite highlight for her father during their stay. It occurred one afternoon while dining at Dublin's Shelbourne Hotel. A member of the IRA came up to Brent and said, "Mr. Brent … we want to let you know that we haven't forgotten."[843] "He was really honored that they remembered him," recalled Suzanne. Brian Reddin stressed that Brent was very popular in Ireland. "He was always referred to as 'Our man in Hollywood,' " said Reddin. "The release of his movies was always met with some fanfare. There was a huge appetite for all things Hollywood and having one of our own out there was a big deal."[844]

Before a year was out, Brent and family returned to Rancho Santa Fe. When James Cagney phoned Brent to find out what had happened,

Brent replied, "It's still a wonderful country, but, oh, Jim—those Irish mornings! You freeze. So the wife and I decided that the only place to be was where it was sunshine most of the time."[845] George Raft also got in touch. He coaxed Brent into a joint venture filming a TV automobile commercial for the '69 Pontiac. Raft had assumed it would be an easy day's work. "It was the hardest *two* days I've ever worked in my life," Brent complained afterward. "Never—*Never* again."[846]

While Brent's Pontiac commercial was airing in the fall of 1968, Janet took ill. Specialists diagnosed that it was cancer and gave her two years to live. In an about turn, George opted to sell his horses in order to devote full time to his ailing wife.

15

Wind at His Back

T he two years that doctors had predicted for Janet went by slowly. In the interim, the Brents relocated from their Rancho Santa Fe horse farm to Solana Beach. Their residence was a short walk from the Pacific Ocean. Janet was confined at home, enduring rest and medication. Her condition remained the same for five years. While taking care of his wife, Brent gave up smoking. In so doing, he gained forty pounds indulging in cakes and cookies. By the spring of 1973, he cut out sweets and began swimming to keep his weight down. Barry Brent, age nineteen, was on active duty with the U.S. Army. Suzanne was employed as a designer for J.C. Penney. It was around this time that George cooperated with the authors of *The Debonairs* to offer comments on his acting career. "I'm afraid most people think I'm dead or not interested," he told them. "There are a great many now in the industry who have never heard of me. But, I'll tell you one thing. I may have been around since Christ was a corporal, but most of us in those days were professionals. We didn't get by on looks alone, like so many of them do nowadays."[847]

On March 24, 1974, Janet passed away at the age of fifty-three, just nine days after George's seventieth birthday. They had been married twenty-six years. A few months later, he told a local columnist, "I don't know what I want to do, but I have a friend, a former navy commander living in Guadalajara, and I'll probably go there. I disposed of the horses. I couldn't afford to keep them."[848] It wasn't long before Brent gave up on the idea of Guadalajara, saying there was too much political unrest. Protests, driven by poverty, drug gang violence, and religious disputes, didn't make an ideal location to be sporting around in his new green Cadillac.

In early 1976, Brent decided to find consolation by writing his memoirs. "I can't paint and I hate gardening," he indicated. "I've never been any good with my hands."[849] From his home in Solana Beach, he talked about his new venture. "I'm remembering everything I can and making notes. I want to be ready before I start to write."[850] By late summer, Brent ditched the entire idea. He complained to San Diego columnist Frank Rhoades, "This thing would be an endless project. I don't see how Niven remembered it all." Brent was referring to David Niven's recent best seller, *Bring on the Empty Horses.* Niven's humor and writing skill (coupled with a dash of creative license) offered a firsthand account of Hollywood's Golden Age. Brent didn't feel he could measure up. Besides, he would have to confront all the blarney that he had dished out over the years. Instead, George contented himself with his regular Tuesday luncheon dates with actors Milburn Stone and George Lewis, along with David Miller, a noted artist/archivist on Native American history. The foursome met regularly at Solana Beach's Jolly Roger Restaurant. Stone, known for his "Doc" on TV's *Gunsmoke*, hosted a reunion at his ranch that spring for James Cagney and producer A. C. Lyles. Following the festivity, it was reported that they visited with Brent, who was thinking about accepting some acting offers. This caught the attention of director Irving Rapper.

George and Jane Powell on the set of MGM's
Luxury Liner in summer of 1947. A bittersweet
reunion took place in the fall of 1977

In the fall of 1977, Brent yielded to romantic sentiment after learning that Jane Powell, who played his daughter in *Luxury Liner*, had brought her road show of *South Pacific* to San Diego's Fox Theater. After the opening, he sent flowers and a note asking if his daughter Suzanne could meet Jane back stage. Powell was delighted. Upon their meeting, Jane asked about making arrangements to see George. Suzanne mentioned that he was struggling with emphysema and rarely left home. This made Powell all the more determined. She phoned Brent and encouraged him to take the train up from Solana Beach. After several more phone chats, she could tell he was warming up to the idea. Powell offered these details in her 1988 autobiography:

He came to a Sunday matinee. I reserved a house seat for him.
Everybody in the cast kept peeking through the curtain to catch a
glimpse of him; so did I. He looked like an El Greco painting—
thin face, white hair, small goatee. Very slender. Straight as a ram-
rod. Don Quixote. So handsome. He saw the show and left.[851]

The following day, Powell met Brent at his suite at the Beverly Wilshire Hotel. After inviting her in, he led her toward the couch where he had placed a framed photograph of the two of them, laughing together, on the set of *Luxury Liner.* Jane had signed it to him all those years ago. He remarked that he always kept it in his possession. In her book, Powell went on to say, "George told me that he had always loved me. He couldn't pursue me when I was a girl, he said—someone was always with me, but he had never forgotten me. We had dinner and I left feeling warm and excited."

Powell had prefaced these recollections by recapping her huge crush on George while they were filming at MGM. Of course, at that time, he was dating Janet almost exclusively. Powell was flattered and surprised by Brent's attentiveness. She began to wonder if she had been too flirtatious. She could see that he was lonely. As she resumed her tour, he continued to send her flowers. In turn, she sent him vitamins and encouraged him to gain weight. They talked long distance. People told Jane that Brent had a new sparkle. Shortly before Christmas, Brent called Jane, telling her, "I have to see you." She flew down to San Diego. "I finally met Skipper, his too fat little dog, and saw his house. It was sparsely decorated, almost bare, with a few pictures on the wall, but he had scrapbooks. Although George said we weren't going to exchange presents, I had brought Skipper a silver bowl. Then ... George asked me to marry him."[852]

Brent explained that he and Jane could have their own separate lives. "You can live in Hollywood," he said. "And I can live here." Powell was in shock. She finally declared, "I just can't George." He wasn't discouraged.

George kept hoping. In the meantime, Irving Rapper, who had directed Bette Davis in the classic *Now, Voyager* and Brent and Stanwyck in *The Gay Sisters*, talked George into making a screen comeback.

Born Again

George stayed in good spirits while fulfilling director Irving Rapper's offer to play the role of U.S. Federal Judge Gerhard Gesell, who presided over the Watergate Seven trials in 1974. The film was based on a memoir written by Charles Colson, former attorney and special advisor to President Richard Nixon. Colson had conspired to cover-up the Watergate burglary. It was Judge Gesell who sentenced Colson, famously known as Nixon's "hatchet man," to prison. Rapper told reporters, "George said he would never return to Hollywood, but when I discovered him out in Oceanside, I said, 'Look, here, George, I'm not asking you to play this role, I'm *telling* you to.'"[853]

Prior to filming *Born Again*, Barry drove his father the 100-plus miles from Solana Beach to Los Angeles. The studio arranged to pick them up for a quick trip to a local courtroom for Brent's cameo appearance in the three million dollar production. He was paid $75,000 for one day's work. The original casting had included Alice Faye, as one of Colson's secretaries.[854] She eventually reneged on Rapper's offer, but he successfully coaxed other veterans into the production, among them Dana Andrews. Andrews played Tom Phillips, CEO of Raytheon—a big arms company making billions in defense contracts. Phillips was the catalyst for Colson's religious conversion. Also on board was Anne Francis, as Colson's wife. The exploitive subject matter in *Born Again* was familiar territory for Rapper, whose previous release, *The Christine Jorgensen Story*, was based on the autobiography of the celebrity transsexual.

"When I got down to the court building," said Brent, "they put me in a side room to rest. It had been twenty years since I'd picked up a script. Then someone said, 'Ready, Mr. Brent,' and when I walked into the courtroom the applause began."[855] With a shy, triumphant flourish, Brent added, "They gave me a standing ovation for about five minutes and I didn't know what to say. I damned near died. It caught me flat-footed, you know. I asked the director, 'Did you fix this?' But he assured me that he didn't. I was flabbergasted."[856] Son Barry, who had decided on an acting career, was among the extras in the courtroom scene.

In *Born Again*, Brent's no-nonsense Judge Gesell stands out for several reasons. The moment he enters court, his disposition, demeanor, and imposing attitude fill the room. He is prepared, poised, and takes charge of the situation. He motions for Colson (Dean Jones) and his attorney, David Shapiro (Jay Robinson, who had worked with Brent on *Wire Service*) to come forward. He asks Colson if he has anything to say before sentence is passed. In reality, Colson spoke for twelve minutes. Onscreen, he is allotted eighteen seconds. Attorney Shapiro spent a full half hour pleading on Colson's behalf. In *Born Again*, Brent indicates that he's heard enough from Shapiro after 20 seconds. "Mr. Shapiro," he says resolutely, "you're barking up the wrong tree. No man is above the law. Morality is a higher force than expediency. This court will impose a sentence of one to three years." An air of "let's get this over with" makes Brent's character all the more interesting to watch. He offers a solid impression to the proceedings.

In his memoirs, Colson details his religious conversion from the White House to the "big house." Producer Frank Capra, Jr., said of Colson, "He isn't merely mouthing some lofty platitudes, but putting into practice his firm convictions. And that was why I wanted to produce this unique film."[857] Former Disney star Dean Jones, who played Colson, had recently become a devout born-again Christian. Capra commented that Jones's participation added a dimension of realism to the film. Most critics didn't agree. Onscreen, Rapper was deterred from detailing the crimes of

Colson and focused on his redemption. A jailed felon, Colson emerges as a convicted innocent—a pawn of political machinations. A Dallas critic thought Jones gave a "conscientious, believable performance" despite the pious subject matter. "The movie radiates spiritual, but not cinematic inspiration," said the review. "*Born Again* is (a) not very subtle ... long trip down the straight and narrow path. George Brent, as a stern judge, and Dana Andrews, as the business executive who solidifies Colson's faith, perform like the veterans they are."[858] Critic Bruce Medville thought sixth-billed Brent the "highlight" of the film, saying, "After banging down his gavel, [Brent] takes one last, disgusted look around him and retires to his chambers. He looks for all the saved world like an actor resolved not to come back for another 22 years."[859] A Cleveland critic complained about the film's "clumsiness" but agreed that the roles of Andrews and Brent were "effectively done."[860] At the film's premiere, Colson's mother, Inez, perplexed by her son's Christian contrition, told reporters, "I born him first. I had him baptized as a baby. I don't understand this 'Born Again' business."[861]

Anne Francis's slant on her role was influenced by her lifelong pursuit of metaphysics. To Francis, being "born again" was a simple matter of an individual realizing their own spiritual nature—or, as she put it, "letting the love of life move through you."[862] When I contacted Dana Andrews's biographer, Carl Rollyson, he told me, "*Born Again* was done as a favor to Irving Rapper. The part that Dana plays is directly contrary to his own beliefs. But he was an actor, you know, and that meant taking all sorts of roles."[863] For Brent, it was mostly a matter of money. He was asked to return the following day to do publicity. Brent replied, "Sure I will—if you pay for the second day's work!"[864]

The thirtieth anniversary release of *Born Again* in 2008 was "updated" by the Prison Fellowship Ministries, which Colson had founded in 1976. This version "bleeps" out twenty-two "offensive" words spoken by various characters, including Colson. It makes about as much sense as removing every "damned," "hell," "ass," "bastard," and "dung" in the Bible. You may not be able to hear the word, but you can easily figure out what it is. This tactic shortchanges the film and lessens the intended intuitive experience for the viewer. Since Brent had been around "since Christ was a corporal" he most likely would respond to the Fellowship as Judge Gessel himself: "You're barking up the wrong tree." The "redeemed" Colson, an evangelical conservative, subsequently championed the death penalty and didn't hesitate to say that homosexuals were "lower than the animal species."[865] Ironically, *Born Again* was the last film Irving Rapper, a homosexual, directed.[866]

When the Associated Press carried a story that George Brent was about to celebrate his seventy-fourth birthday, it didn't go unnoticed. "People drove me nuts with phone calls from all over the country," he said. "I loved it. My daughter came in and cooked me some corn beef and cabbage."[867] Daughter Suzanne was still pursuing a career in interior design, and son Barry, after four years in the Army, was a drama student at Palomar College in San Marcos. As Brent put it, he only saw them "when I want to."[868] He made a point to brag about Barry. "He's 6 feet 4 and very good looking," boasted Brent. "And he's so talented. He's just done *The King and I* in college. One day soon you're going to hear of him. He's going to be a star."[869] After interviewing Suzanne and Barry in 2012, Irish director Brian Reddin told me that they enjoyed their Dad and his eccentricities.[870] Brent's daily routine included walks with his fourteen-year-old dog Skipper (who ate half the morning bacon) and driving his Cadillac to a nearby restaurant for a small steak and tea. George enjoyed swapping stories with his Tuesday lunch bunch (which now included James Cagney, who spent winters in the Los Angeles area). "I felt like a junior member of the club," recalled artist David Miller in 1981. "The conversation between Brent and Cagney was fascinating. They had been at Warner Brothers together and knew all the other great stars of that era."[871]

Prior to the release of *Born Again*, George was generous with his opinions on how Hollywood had changed. "The labor problems. The lack of discipline," he observed. "Nothing like the old days." He told Copley News reporter Nancy Anderson, "Hollywood desperately needs beautiful people. I'm glad that I don't have to put up with some of the ugly people who are working now. I don't understand the dirty-shirt crowd you see in pictures today."[872] Brent claimed he hadn't seen a movie since *Dr. Zhivago* in 1965. When asked why he quit, Brent put it bluntly. "I must have made a hundred pictures," he said. "Hell, I was sick of it."[873]

George still received fan mail. "Some of the most beautiful, most charming letters," he commented. "But I never answer them. I'm rather shy of people. I've had so much of them all my life."[874] He admitted that he preferred his own company. "Maybe something's wrong with me," he explained, "but I've always been a fellow to back off from crowds. I'm very shy of people-strangers. Always was, and that's the way it is! Some people misconstrue that for being anti-social, but that's too damn bad."[875]

When asked about Senator Joseph McCarthy and the Communist scare in the 1950s, Brent answered, "I never got my nose into politics, it's hopeless. Bogart stuck his nose in, and a few others got in trouble. Larry Parks was a good actor and was doing quite well … But, he hasn't worked since. People have been locked out of the picture business for less. If you say the wrong thing to the right schmo up front and he picks up the phone … you might as well shove off."[876] Brent was referring to the power-hungry movie moguls of yesteryear. He mentioned his own suspension in 1933–'34. "You couldn't work anywhere in the world. I couldn't work in a gas station—they would stop you. That's how tough they were. They would just pick up the phone and say, 'Brent, that (obscenity), don't touch him. But the dough runs out, you see."[877]

San Diego reporter, Carla DeDominicis, categorized Brent as an endangered species, a remnant of Hollywood's heyday of glitter and gold. She still found him to be charismatic and charming—carrying the "culture of class and kings." "He's perfected these qualities that brought him his glory," DeDominicis observed. "Even one too young to remember the star is left standing in awe of him. His dress is impeccable. Wrinkles line his face, but that famous glint in his hazel eyes shows no sign of fading."[878]

Whenever Brent spoke of his wife, Janet, his voice hollowed. He admitted filling the void with books, drawing sketches, long walks with Skipper, and the daily paper. "I read that thing from cover to cover," he told reporter Bill Kelly. "That usually knocks off two or three hours a day."[879] Kelly found Brent "a heck of a nice guy … opinionated, but gracious." For the Irishman, Brent paid the lunch tab, and opened up a bit more.

> *I have problems, sure. I've got some arthritis in my upper spine. It's painful at times. I have a bronchial condition. I get short of breath. I quit smoking for ten months, but something upset me one day. I've forgotten what now: but I started smoking again. Another time I quit for a year and gained 40 pounds. I ate candy and every damn cookie I could get my hands on—jellybeans. As they say, the water will kill you. Sanka will kill you. Coffee is going to kill me—cigarettes.*

Kelly interrupted Brent's train of thought: "A car can kill you." Brent laughed, "Sure! So what the hell's the use of worrying about it?" As far as missed acting opportunities, Brent mentioned one in particular. "I would have like to have gone out with the role of Hemingway—the last half of his life. Because I loved the man, and of course his books. What must have been going through that man's mind in his final days? What a picture that would make, and I'd love to do it."[880]

Brent also arranged a reunion with Bette Davis, whose one-woman show had arrived in San Diego's Civic Theater in May 1978. It had been over twenty-five years since they had teamed on radio. George sent her a dozen orchids backstage with a note attached asking to see her before the show. Davis recalled,

> *I had half my makeup on when the orchids arrived. In spite of myself, I felt a rush of excitement. I said to my hairdresser, "Let's make me look as good as possible before George arrives." The George Brent of my past … walked into my dressing room. He had changed a lot. Why not? So had I. I might have felt a little sad and a little cheated except for one rather nice reminder. As he left, George giggled. He still had the same crazy, infectious giggle I remembered so well.[881]*

Brent usually paid homage to his most frequent costar, Bette Davis, and made a point to put in a good word for Jane Powell. "Another little girl who was very charming to work with," he cheered, "was little Janie Powell. She could sing the birds out of the trees."[882] In October 1978, his tune changed. Powell remarried. "When I did get married again," said Powell, "[George] was furious. He was cold when we talked after that. George was a sad man, but not because of me."[883] Powell herself faced emotional challenges during the year she reconnected with Brent. She was recovering from a loveless marriage. Her son was heavily involved with drugs and had distanced himself. When I chatted with Jane Powell backstage during her show at San Francisco's "Bimbo's 365" (1968), she was a gracious, very present, engaging personality. A good listener. On stage, she had opened up about her son's drug problem, followed by a heartfelt rendition of the

Jimmy Rogers song, "Child of Clay." It's easy to understand Brent's rejuvenated spirit after Jane Powell came back into his life.

Powell explains in her autobiography that when she reconnected with Brent, she was already seeing writer David Parlour. When she got married, Brent followed suit. *Variety* reported that he had married Mary Costa, the opera singer.[884] This erroneous news flub was repeated in gossip columns until the soprano diva refuted it.[885] The

Jane Powell thought Brent in his 70's looked like an El Greco painting

Mary Costa who Brent married lived in Hawaii. The ceremony took place in Long Beach, November 13, 1978. According to Jane Powell, Brent didn't want to live in Hawaii, and his new wife didn't want to live in California. "So I presume they lived separate lives," said Powell, "as he said we would have."

Powell was mostly correct in her assumption. George and Mary lived separate lives. Their marriage lasted two weeks. Divorce proceedings were soon underway. Mary Costa Brent returned to Hawaii where she resumed managing Kula Lodge on the island of Maui. In November 2013, I talked with Mary's daughter, Cherie Meade Frakes. "My mother and George Brent had known each other for a long, long time," she said. "I really don't remember all the details, but they met at the Royal Hawaiian."[886] Cherie confirmed that her mother was born in Philadelphia.

Mary Hall Meade Costa Brent

The marriage license of George Brent and Mary M. Costa indicated that she was fifty-seven years old. Mary was born on January 16, 1921, to Clifford and Ruth James Hall. Mary's grandfather, Dr. William Francis James, had relocated his family from San Antonio to the Hawaiian Islands in 1904. A U.S. Army physician, Dr. James became one of the islands' first territorial doctors. In 1918, Mary's parents married in San Diego. They raised their family in Philadelphia. In 1938, Mary married Hugh Meade. The couple had three children: Robert, Helen (Cherie), and Dale. There were frequent trips to Hawaii to visit relatives during the 1940s. It is most likely that on one of these sojourns Mary had the opportunity to meet George Brent at the Royal Hawaiian on Oahu. Brent frequently stayed at the Waikiki landmark hotel since his first trip there in 1938.

By the 1960s, Mary had remarried and was going by Mary M. Costa. She became the manager of Kula Lodge on the Western Slopes of Haleakala Crater. The rustic hideaway, with sweeping ocean views, was originally built in the 1940s as a private home for Mary's uncle, Frank James. In 1973, she purchased the lodge from him. During Mary's tenure, the lodge gained a reputation. One local resident mused that of all the managers at Kula, "the best or the worst was Mary Costa because you could hear the rock-and-roll music … a mile and a half away."[887] Three years after her marriage to Brent, Mary put the Lodge up for public auction. She remained in Hawaii and died in Honolulu at the age of eighty-two in 2003. She kept the name Mary Costa Brent.

Jane Powell's marriage to David Parlour also fell apart. In a matter of months her unemployed producer/husband was taking legal action, asking *her* for alimony. Powell's glimpse into George Brent's life during his final months was telling. He was in the back of her mind the day he died. "The day before he passed away," she wrote, "I … thought, *I've got to give George a call.* But I didn't. Oh, how I wish I had. He passed away that night. My sweet George. I hope he died a happy man, but I have my doubts."[888] Brent died on May 26, 1979, at his Solana Beach home. Producer A. C. Lyles informed the press that Brent's body was discovered by actor George Lewis and Suzanne, who had been unable to reach her father by phone. In 2012, Suzanne Brent recalled that they "had no warning" that their father was near the end. Apparently, Brent had collapsed while preparing for bed. It was mentioned that he had suffered from emphysema. News reports included only Brent's children and his sister, China Marin, as survivors.[889] Private services were held at his home on May 28.

Author Lawrence J. Quirk observed about Brent,

> *For all his rueful realism, sophisticated awareness of the female psyche, and a feet-on-the-ground cynicism doubtless born of his stark and brutal experiences during the Irish rebellion, Brent had a steadying influence on the ladies in his life and met their problems with a kind of rough compassion that they found healing—while it lasted.*[890]

Leading ladies Chatterton, Garbo, Davis, and Sheridan fit into this category—Bette Davis in particular. Brent frequently mentioned his teaming with Davis in *Dark Victory* as being his best film. Their offscreen affair had fueled onscreen simpatico. Out of all his leading ladies, Davis was more likely to bring up Brent's name. While on a three-day personal appearance tour of *Hush ... Hush, Sweet Charlotte* in 1965, Davis and costar Olivia de Havilland faced 4,000 fans at Loew's Kings Theatre in New York. One audience member asked de Havilland, "Does George Brent always have a twinkle in his eye?" Without hesitation, de Havilland answered, "I think Miss Davis knows more about his twinkle than I do."[891] During her speaking tours in the 1970s, Davis, without hesitation, would invariably answer "George Brent" when asked to name her favorite leading man. Audiences would murmur, "Who?"

Ruth Waterbury, editor for *Photoplay* who covered the film industry for over fifty years, recalled, "George always kept—at least on the surface—that quizzical, detached attitude toward women that they took to like catnip. Bette Davis was no exception."[892] Waterbury always felt that Davis was more emotional about Brent than he was about her. While Davis completed her final film, *Wicked Stepmother* (1989), director Larry Cohen recalled, "Whenever a plane flew over the house ... ruining the take, Bette murmured 'George Brent.' I asked her what she meant." Davis explained that when Brent was on suspension at Warners he had circled his plane over the sound stages until he was rehired. Cohen played along. "I would shout 'George Brent' every time a plane passed over our location," he said, "and Bette would crack up."[893]

While preparing a biography on Bette Davis, author Quirk asked Waterbury about Brent. Aside from socializing with George in Los Angeles, she had hobnobbed around New York with him in the late 1930s. "George never thought much of his acting abilities," said Waterbury, "and told me once he was afraid people would find out how lousy he was and fire him—so he seldom made waves."[894] Whether spoken in jest or no, Brent's modesty regarding his talent wasn't necessary. While he may have walked through some of his less memorable roles in order to get a paycheck, an innate, stabilizing solidity defined his better film portrayals. Following Brent's death, Bette Davis reflected, "George was marvelous in *Dark Victory*. He was always very good when he liked the script. When he didn't like it, he was a lazy, lazy, lazy Irishman."[895] Over the years, audiences have often equated good acting with overacting. Brent stood out because of his moderation. His trademark understatement and effortless truth onscreen was often overlooked—by critics and Academy Awards.

In 1940, Brent admonished *Photoplay*, saying that their preoccupation with stars was misguided. "Your readers are naturally concerned with everything pertaining to the movies and movie stars," he explained. "Therefore, why not devote a little more effort toward covering the Hollywood scene from every point of interest. We forget that there are millions of people who have never seen the inside of a studio. A prop room or makeup department may appear to be a commonplace thing to the average writer who visits the studios. Yet, there is just as much drama that goes on … as there is on a sound stage where pictures are shooting."[896] Brent saw his connection to the *whole* process that created cinema magic. Under close scrutiny, as Brent suggested, are the stars any different from the rest of the cast and crew? Apparently not. Brent's costar Mary Astor came to a similar conclusion. After receiving her Oscar for *The Great Lie*, Astor became introspective. "I began to think, more than ever," she recalled, "'What's so damned important about being an actress?' I saw my little world, insulated, self-absorbed, limited. It was a partial acceptance of reality."[897] In my correspondence with Astor's daughter, Marylyn Roh, she recounted, "Mom used to tell me, 'It's just a job.'"[898]

On November 2, 1979, Suzanne and Barry held an estate sale of their father's belongings. Brent's tuxedos, cummerbund and tie sets, silk handkerchiefs, ascots, antique furnishings, German beer steins, and autographed records were on display. The first fifty customers received glossy movie stills from the actor's collection.[899] Columnist Frank Rhoades stated that Brent's clothing articles sold in a hurry, but other personal effects showed "lagging interest."[900]

Brent's treasure trove of movie stills had provided hours of reminiscing for the actor after his wife died. "Every now and then I go out into my garage and open a box and go through them," he told a reporter shortly before his death. "And say, 'Oh boy!'"[901] The dashing, young face staring back at him in the photographs left him in a wave of nostalgia … but, only momentarily. He wasn't craving for yesterday. Brent's impulsive nature may have been hampered as his body aged, but that was to be expected. "Why fear or worry about the inevitable?" Brent mused. "Death is merely the end. Some people reach it like a lazy river, slowly, evenly, uninterestingly. Others rush to it like a mountain torrent, plunging forward impulsively, joyously. I prefer that way, because it's a fuller and richer life."[902] He had discovered this simple truth while dispatching in Ireland, trouping on stage through the 1920s, soaring his plane through the skies, and sailing *Southwind* in the decades that followed. Brent's attitude regarding death allowed him to be immersed in the moment at hand. What else is living for?

Brian Reddin's documentary *Reabhloidithe Hollywood* confirms that after the real life horror George Nolan had witnessed during the Irish Revolution, he was beyond the reach of life's usual intimidations. Following death, Brent's body was cremated and its ashes scattered at sea.[903]

It would take an Irish poet to best describe the inherent quality that George Brent brought to the screen—the unique "something" that made him different from the others—his quiet reassurance and emotional support that allowed numerous leading ladies to shine brighter as he graciously basked in the glow of their stellar luminescence.

> *We can make our minds so like still water that beings gather about us that they may see, it may be: their own images, and so live for a moment with a clearer, perhaps even with a fiercer life because of our quiet* – W. B. Yeats [904]

"Brentie" on a bike c. 1940

Acknowlegements

The Emerald Isle

May 30, 1994. As I leaned backward to kiss Cork County's famous Blarney Stone, I had no inkling that twenty years later I would pen the first biography on George Brent. And, little did I know, as I puckered my lips and looked down through the 300 foot crevice, that many a drunken Irish prankster had relieved himself on that same stone. Couldn't they read? The sign next to it clearly spelled out that it's kissing with a "K" not a "P."

The closest I got to Brent's birthplace, Ballinasloe, was Galway Bay—sixty kilometers to the west. The proverbial forty shades of green that bless Ireland made a lasting impression. In 2012, Irish filmmaker Brian Reddin surprised me by requesting an interview about Brent's career. A wave of nostalgia took me back to the Emerald Isle. I could easily understand George Brent's affection for his homeland. As I researched his life, I could also appreciate Brent's gift for blarney regarding his troubled Irish family and ambiguous past. It was through Reddin's encouragement that I tackled George as a subject after completing *Ruth Chatterton – Actress, Aviator, Author.* And on that note, one must acknowledge Chatterton for making Brent's film career a reality. Director Reddin shared what he had discovered while visiting Ballinasloe and the local townsfolk. He provided me with a copy of George's birth certificate.

The Debonairs (1975) by James Robert Parish and Don E. Stanke proved to be an indispensable guide to Brent's career. Coincidentally, it was Parish who had suggested that Brian Reddin contact me for his documentary on Brent. Parish has been a real champion, encouraging me every step of the way with each of the five film biographies I have written. He suggested contacts and located numerous rare films. Publisher G. D. Hamann graciously printed a special edition of *George Brent in the 1930s* (2013). This publication provided extensive coverage from the Los Angeles press.

In 2012, when I contacted Brent's daughter Suzanne, she mentioned that she and her brother Barry were working on a project of their own about their father. Suzanne offered a short recap of what she knew about the Nolan family. She mentioned that her aunt China had passed away in April 2000 "at nearly 100 years old." "Her son Patrick," added Suzanne, "our first cousin, just passed this January 2012, but his son Ian is married and lives in Boston."[905] Ian was especially helpful in sharing memories of his grandmother China, Brent's sister. He generously forwarded me the log book from George and Patrick's "unforgettable" voyage on *Southwind* during the 1947 San Pedro-Honolulu yacht race. He also provided a copy of the marriage certificate of Brent's parents. Ian detailed the life of his own father. Patrick graduated from Princeton (Class of 1944) and became a stockbroker. Patrick always spoke fondly of his uncle George from whom he had acquired a lifelong passion for sailing. The input from Brent's grandnephew Robert E. Fletcher was also helpful, as was my conversation with Cherie Frakes, the daughter of Brent's last wife (Mary Costa Brent).

Others who pitched in with this project include Larry Smith and Jenny Paxson, archivists at the Library of Congress facility in Culpeper, Virginia.

As they had with my books on Ann Harding and Ruth Chatterton, Jenny and Larry were generous with providing me with photos from their private collection. Thanks also to fellow author Charles Tranberg for sharing sources that covered Brent's stay at Elitch Gardens in the summer of 1929. Tranberg has received excellent notices for his biographies on Brent's contemporaries: Fred MacMurray, Robert Taylor, and Fredric March.

When I contacted author and noted film scholar Jeanine Basinger about contributing a foreword for the book, she willingly complied. "We have a deal!" she wrote. "I think it's so wonderful that someone cares and writes seriously and joyously about the stars you are writing about. They deserve it … and it encourages new generations to explore their work."[906] In a few paragraphs Basinger summed up what made Brent, not only unique and successful, but in demand for so many years. I have been a fan of Basinger's work ever since reading her perceptive *A Woman's View – How Hollywood Spoke to Women 1930–1960* (Knopf, 1993).

Dan and Darlene Swanson (Van-garde Imagery, Inc.) are due heartfelt thanks—Dan for designing a striking Irish-themed cover, and Darlene for the attractive layout of photos and text. I also owe a very special thank you to fellow writer Graceann Macleod of London. This is the third book that the talented Graceann has proofed and edited for me. Her fine-tuning and input have been invaluable.

My career as a writer was initially nudged forward by the late Doug Mc-Clelland, and Mick LaSalle, both respected authors in the classic film genre. In 1995, McClelland wrote to me praising Kay Francis—her "great presence" and "beautiful speaking voice." He agreed that she was deserving of a major biography. In a follow-up letter McClelland explained that sometimes it was "a matter of connecting with an editor who happens to personally like your subject," which is exactly what happened when he tried to find a publisher for *Susan Hayward: The Divine Bitch* (1973).[907]

I took McClelland's cue a few months later and wrote the article "Kay Francis – Portrait on Silk" for *Films of the Golden Age*.[908] Not long afterward, Mick LaSalle contacted me regarding the Pre-Code film research he was doing. He was interested in viewing some of Kay's early Paramount films that I had in my collection. We met for lunch and I urged him to write a book on her, mentioning that Kay's personal diaries were held at Wesleyan University. He looked directly at me and said, "No Scott. You should write a book about Kay Francis." I wasn't ready for that kind of undertaking.

Several years passed before I found myself at Wesleyan consuming each of Kay's diary entries (1922–1953). My partner, Joel, happily brought along his laptop to help. The end result: *Kay Francis – I Can't Wait to be Forgotten*. BearManor Media publisher Ben Ohmart was the editor (as McCelland put it) "who happens to personally like your subject." Author and TCM host Robert Osborne enthusiastically got on board to write the book's introduction. Ohmart has been a godsend in helping to resurrect forgotten stars of the past who deserve to be rediscovered.

In 2011, I began in earnest to research the life of George Brent. In the Chatterton biography I included a seven-page profile of his early life. I suspect I was trying to answer the question she asked Perc Westmore upon seeing Brent's 1931 screen test: "Where has he been all my life?"

I see no reason to demonize or lionize the actors I write about. To sensationalize a star's private life is a poor excuse for a book. In the process of delving into the personal stories of film stars, I have discovered that they are people just like you and me. The phenomenon of celebrity, relentless publicity, overblown "scandals," and outrageous salaries distort this simple fact. As Mary Astor's daughter put it to me, "Yes – 'movie stars' are just like everyone else – except there's a point where equality dims – and that's with the excruciatingly enormous salaries they get. Think of the hundreds of working people in the studios plus the fans they must climb up over to reach their sometimes short-lived celluloid fame."[909]

I must add that when I first grew my moustache in 1971, my mother's reaction was, "You look like George Brent." As I was a blonde, I didn't pay much attention to her remark. However, she started calling me "George." The nickname stuck. She called me that until she passed away in 2005. Call it a mother's uncanny presentiment.

Credits

Stage Credits
(**List of known plays for George Nolan/George Brent**)

1921–'22

The Dover Road (by A. A. Milne) Bijou Theatre, New York City, premier December 23, 1921 (ran ten months - 305 performances); Guthrie McClintic (producer/director) Cast: Charles Cherry, George Riddell, Reginald Mason, Winifred Lenihan, Molly Pearson, Lyonel Watts, Phyllis Carrington, Ann Winslow, Edwin H. Morse, George Nolan (staff/servitor)

The Dover Road – On tour September–December 1922: Philadelphia, Chicago (four weeks), Cleveland, Canton, Harrisburg, Wilkes-Barre, Boston (four weeks), New York (off-Broadway)

1923

Blaney Stock Players, Gotham Theatre, Brooklyn, New York. (J.V. McShea, manager) Plays included:

The Sheik's Love (by Wilson Collison) February; Dan Malloy (director) Cast: Frances Gregg, Clifford Alexander, Miami Campbell, H.J. Montgomery, Stanley Andrews, Albert Vees, George Nolan (Ben Ali)

George Gatts Productions:

The Unwanted Child (by Florence Edna May) Play dates included: Murat Theatre, Indianapolis, September 12–17; Grand Theater, Canton, Ohio, September 24–26; Park Theater, Youngstown, Ohio, September 27–29; Trent Theatre, Trenton, N.J., October 2–3; Orpheum, Reading, Pennsylvania, November 1–4; Cast: George B. Nolan (as the young husband), Winifred Gilmore, Edwin Dudley, Fred Harvey, Violet Deane, Gertrude Boyes, Jeanette Cass

F. James Carroll Players:

Why Men Leave Home (comedy by Avery Hopwood) November 12–?, Halifax, Nova Scotia; Bennett Finn (director) Cast: Foster Williams, Frances Woodbury, George Nolan, Shirley Gray, Cecilia Frank, Emma Deweal, Walter Marshall, John E. Hinds, James Swift

1924–'26

Abie's Irish Rose (by Anne Nichols) on tour (Brent joined the cast in Cincinnati during its 13 week run February–April 1924) Augustus Thorne (director) Cast: George B. Nolan (Abie), Peggy Parry, Leo Hoyt, James R. Waters, Bella Pogany, Frederick Forrester, Billy Fay, Alice Dudley, Charles W. Guthrie, John F. Webber

> Play dates included: Cincinnati, Omaha (four weeks – August 1925), Joplin, St. Louis, Pittsburgh, Dayton, Lexington, Baltimore (twelve weeks), Columbus (thirteen weeks), Dayton (eight weeks), Indianapolis (eight weeks), Louisville (eight weeks), Washington, D.C. (twelve weeks), Kansas City (fifteen weeks), Rockford, Ill. (January 1926)

The Bat (by Mary Roberts Rinehart) three-act play, on tour; unknown play dates

1926

George B. Nolan Stock Company, Nashville, North Carolina (managed by George Nolan) plays and dates unknown (cast included James Linehan)

1927

George B. Nolan Stock Company, Star Theatre, Pawtucket, Rhode Island (managed by George Nolan) summer of 1927

1927

Academy Players, Academy of Music, Northampton, MA (managed by George Nolan) Plays included:

Seventh Heaven (by John Golden) September 5–10 Cast: Helen Louise Lewis, George B. Nolan (Chico), James A. Bliss, William H. McDougal, Mike McMahon, Bettie Wilkes

New Brooms (by Frank Craven) September 13–17 Cast: Helen Louise Lewis, George B. Nolan

Dancing Mothers (by Edgar Selwyn and Edmund Goulding) September 20–25 Cast: Helen Louise Lewis, George Nolan, Grace O'Leary

The Last of Mrs. Cheney (by Frederick Lonsdale) September 26–October 1 Cast: Helen Louise Lewis, George Nolan, Maxwell Driscoll, James A. Bliss

The Bride (by Stuart Olivier and George Middleton) October 10–15 Cast: Helen Louise Lewis, George B. Nolan

The Family Upstairs (by Harry Delf) October 17–22 Cast: George Nolan, Helen Louise Lewis

The Brat (by Oliver Morosco) October 25–29 Cast: Helen Louise Lewis, George Brent, John Linehan, Grace O'Leary, Maxwell Driscoll, Grace Kern

Silence (by Max Marcin) October 31–November 5 Cast: Helen Louise Lewis, George Nolan

Stella Dallas (by Gertrude Purcell and Harry Wagstaff Gribble) November 14–19 Cast: Helen Louise Lewis, George B. Nolan (Richard Grosvenor)

Loose Ankles (by Sam Janney) November 21–26 Cast: George Nolan, Helen Louise Lewis

The Patsy (by Barry Conners) November 28–December 3 Cast: Helen Louise Lewis, George B. Nolan, Edward R. Davidson, Grace O'Leary, James Linehan

The Man on the Roof (by Howard Irving Young) December 5–10 Cast: George Nolan

Within the Law (by Bayard Veiller) December 19–24 Cast: Helen Louise Lewis, George Nolan (Gilder), William H. MacDougall, Grace O'Leary

1928

Plaza Players, Plaza Theater, St. Petersburg, Florida (George Nolan, manager) (George Earle, director) Plays included:

Why Men Leave Home (by Avery Hopwood) January 2 George Earle (director) Cast: George Nolan (Tom Morgan), Helen Louise Lewis, Lyman Hayes, Lynda Earle, Helene Pierlot, James Linehan, Vera Painter, Eleanor Likely, Bert Keller, Marion Mulligan, Eloise Eaton, William Pendexter

The Patsy (by Barry Conners) January 9 Cast: Helen Louise Lewis, George Nolan (Tony), Vera Painter, Lynda Earle, George Earle

The Hottentot (by Victor Mapes and William Collier) January 16 George Earle (director) Cast: Bert Keller, George Nolan (Sam Harrington), Helen Louise Lewis

The Dividing Line (by Will Cressy) January 23 Cast: Will Cressy, Helen Louise Lewis, George Nolan, Helene Pierlot

The Girl From Childs (by Archie Colby and Alfred Jackson) January 30 Cast: William Pendexter, George Nolan, Helen Louise Lewis

Up in Mabel's Room (by Wilson Collison and Otto Hauerbach) February 6 Cast: George Nolan (Garry), Helen Louise Lewis, James Linehan, Bert Keller, Vera Painter, Helene Pierlot, Lynda Earle, William Pendexter

Tiger Rose (by Willard Mack) February 13 Cast: Helen Louise Lewis, George Nolan, Bert Keller, James Linehan, Arlan R. Thorley

The Family Upstairs (by Harry Delf) February 20 Cast: George Nolan (Mr. Heller), James Linehan, Helen Louise Lewis, Lynda Earle

The Girl in the Limousine (by Wilson Collison and Avery Hopwood) February 27 Cast: George Nolan, Bert Keller, Helen Louise Lewis

Rolling Home (by John Hunter Booth) March 5 (reviews agreed that this pay was the worst offered by the Plaza Players) Cast: George Nolan, James Linehan, William Pendexter, Bert Keller

Square Crooks (by James P. Judge) March 12 Cast: George Nolan, James Linehan, William Pendexter, Helen Louise Lewis, Vera Painter, Bert Keller

Peg O' My Heart (by J. Hartley Manners) March 19 Cast: Helen Louise Lewis, James Linehan, James Bliss, George Nolan (Jerry), Lynda Earle, Vera Painter, William Pendexter, Helen Pierlot, Bert Keller

Dancing Mothers (By Edgar Selwyn and Edmund Goulding) March 26 Cast: Helen Louise Lewis, William Pendexter, George Nolan (Jerry Naughton), Helen Pierlot, Lynda Earle, Vera Painter, James Linehan, James Bliss

1928

Mountain Park Casino, Holyoke, MA (summer) plays unknown

Night Hostess (by Philip Dunning) tryout Metropolitan Theatre, Minneapolis (August 26– September 8, 1928) John Golden (producer) Winchell B. Smith (director) Cast: Marguerite Churchill, Norval Keedwell, Norman Foster (replaced Ross Alexander), Porter Hall, John L. Kearny, Gail De Hart, Averell Harris, Katharine Hepburn (billed as Katherine Burns), George Nolan (winner and loser)

Night Hostess Martin Beck Theatre, New York (Opened September 12, 1928 - 117 performances – Nolan left production before closing) John Golden (producer) Winchell B. Smith (director) Cast: Norman Foster, Porter Hall, John L. Kearny, Gail De Hart, Averell Harris, Maurice Freeman, Ruth Lyons, Charles Laite, Katharine Hepburn (billed as Katherine Burns), George Nolan (winner and loser)

K-Guy (by Walter DeLeon and Alethea Luce) tryout Syracuse, Wieting Theatre (October 8–13, 1928) Cast: Ralph Murphy, Constance McKay, Alan Ward, George Nolan (Reggie Manville), Jeanne Greene, Jessamine Newcombe, Francis Compton, Edward Keane

K-Guy Biltmore Theatre, New York (Opened October 15, 1928 – eight performances) Melville Burke (director) Cast: Ralph Murphy, Constance McKay, Alan Ward, George Nolan (Reggie Manville), Jeanne Greene, Jessamine Newcombe, Francis Compton, Edward Keane

1928–'29

Sherman Brown Players, Milwaukee, Pabst Theatre; Albert Mack (director) Russell Hicks was leading man; George Brent was second man; productions included:

Baby Cyclone (by George Cohan) November 25–30 Cast: Helene Dumas, George Brent (Joseph Meadows), Russell Hicks, Lorraine Barnard

Elmer the Great (by Ring Lardner) December 2–7 Cast: Russell Hicks, George Brent

Interference (by Roland Pertwee and Harold Dearden) December 9–14 Cast: Carolyn Humphreys, George Brent

Outward Bound (by Sutton Vane) December 17–23 Cast: Russell Hicks, Mabel Montgomery, Alfred Layne, Edward Butler, George Brent (Duke), Franklin H. Allen, Carolyn Humphreys, Jane Kane

Old Heidelberg (by Wilhelm Mayer-Foerster) December 24–30 Cast: Katherine Standing, Alfred Layne, Russell Hicks, Edward Butler, John Kane, George Brent, Edward Owens

Mary's Other Husband (by Larry E. Johnson) December 31, 1928–January 6, 1929 Cast: Katherine Standing, Russell Hicks, George Brent, Lorraine Bernard

In Love With Love (by Vincent Lawrence) January 7–12 Cast: Katherine Standing, Russell Hicks, George Brent, John Kane

The Dove (by David Belasco) January 14–19 Cast: George Brent (Johnnie Powell), Edward Butler, Katherine Standing, Joseph Reed

Crime (by Samuel Shipman and John B. Hymer) January 22–26 Cast: George Brent (Eugene Fenmore), Katherine Standing, Carolyn Humphreys, John Kane, Alfred Layne, Rodney Hildebrand, Edward Butler

Under Cover (by Roi Cooper Megrue) January 27–February 1 Cast: William Courtenay, Katherine Standing, Rodney Hildebrand, George Brent (Monty Vaughan), Mabel Montgomery, Alfred Layne

The Spider (by Fulton Oursler and Lowell Bretano) February 3–8 Cast: William Courtenay, George Brent (police inspector), John Kane

Aren't We All (by Frederick Lonsdale) February 10–16 Cast: Raymond Hitchcock, Katherine Standing, George Brent, Rodney Hildebrand, Mabel Montgomery, Frank McDonald, Sumner Gard

The Sap (by William A. Grew) February 17–23 Cast: Raymond Hitchcock, George Brent, Katherine Standing, Carolyn Humphreys, Mabel Montgomery, Edward Butler

Crashing Through (by Saxon Kling) February 24–March 2 Cast: Henrietta Crosman, George Brent (Chris), Katherine Standing, Carolyn Humphreys, John Kane

1929
Elitch Gardens, Denver, Colorado (seventeen plays) April–August 1929 Melville Burke (director) Players included: George Brent, Madge Evans, Victor Jory, Kenneth MacKenna, C. Henry Gordon

Seven Year Love (by John D. Haggert) Ford Theatre, Baltimore October; National Theatre, Washington, D.C., October 28–November 2, 1929 Cast: Catherine Willard, Horace Pollack, Frank Elliott, George Brent (Keyes), Guido Nadzo

1930
Those We Love (by George Abbott and S.K. Laurens) Boulevard Theatre, Jackson Heights, February 3, 1930; Flatbush Theatre, Brooklyn, February 10, 1930; Philip Dunning (producer) George Abbott (director) Cast: Helen Flint, Josephine Hull, George Brent (Frederick Williston), Charles Waldron, Armina Marshall, Edwin Phillips

Love, Honor and Betray (a.k.a. *The Fatal Woman* - adapted from the French of Audre-Paul Antoine, by Frederic and Fanny Hatton) Apollo Theatre, Atlantic City, tryout February 23–28, 1930; Flatbush Theatre, New York, tryout March 3, 1930; Eltinge Theatre, New York, opened March 12, 1930; Al H. Woods (producer) Lester Lonegran (director); Cast: Alice Brady, Robert Williams, Clark Gable, George Brent (Chauffeur), Glenda Farrell, Wilton Lackaye

1953
Affairs of State (by Louis Verneuil) March 14–26, 1953; Minneapolis & Cox Theatre, Cincinnati Cast: George Brent (George Henderson), Haila Stoddard, Harry Bannister, Irene Hervey

Note: Brent also mentioned favoring his lead roles (dates unknown) in such popular plays as: *White Cargo* and *Lilac Time*

Film Credits

(in order of release dates)

1) *The Big Trail* (Fox 1930) 108/122 M – filmed April–May 1930 (released October 1930); Director, Raoul Walsh; Story, Hal G. Evarts; Camera, Lucien Andriot (35mm version), Arthur Edeson (70mm version); Cast: John Wayne, Marguerite Churchill, El Brendel, Tully Marshall, Tyrone Power, Sr., David Rollins, Frederick Burton, Ian Keith, Charles Stevens, Louise Carver, Ward Bond, Iron Eyes Cody, George Brent (uncredited extra)

2) *Under Suspicion* (Fox 1930) 64 M – filmed July–August 1930 (released December 1930); Director, A.F. Erickson; Story-Screenplay, Tom Barry; Camera, Ross Fisher; Cast: Lois Moran, J. Harold Murray, J.M. Kerrigan, Edwin Connelly, Marie Saxon, Lumsden Hare, George Brent (Inspector Turner), Erwin Connelly, Herbert Bunston

3) *Once A Sinner* (Fox 1931) 71 M – filmed October 1930 (released January 1931); Director, Guthrie McClintic; Story-Screenplay, George Middleton; Camera, Arthur L. Todd; Cast: Dorothy Mackaill, Joel McCrea, John Halliday, C. Henry Gordon, Ilka Chase, Clara Blandick, Myra Hampton, George Brent (James Brent), Sally Blane, Nanette/Nadia Faro, Bill Elliot

4) *Fair Warning* (Fox 1931) 74 M – filmed July 1930 (released February 1931); Director, Alfred L. Werker; Screenplay, Ernest L. Pascal (novel The Untamed by Max Brand); Camera, Ross Fisher; Cast: George O'Brien, Louise Huntington, Mitchell Harris, George Brent (Les Haines), Nat Pendleton, John Sheehan, Erwin Connelly

5) *Charlie Chan Carries On* (Fox 1931) 76 M – filmed December 1930 (released March 1931); Director, Hamilton MacFadden; Screenplay, Philip Klein (story by Earl Derr Biggers); Camera, George Schneiderman; Cast: Warner Oland, John Garrick, Marguerite Churchill, Warren Hymer, Marjorie White, C. Henry Gordon, William Holden, George Brent (Captain Ronald Keane), Lumsden Hare, Zeffie Tilbury

6) *Ex-Bad Boy* (Universal 1931) 66 M – filmed April–May 1931 (released July 1931); Director, Vin Moore; Screenplay, Dale Van Every (play The Whole Town's Talking by Anita Loos and John Emerson); Camera, Jerome Ash; Cast:

Robert Armstrong, Jean Arthur, Jason Robards, Sr., Spencer Charters, Grayce Hampton, Lola Lane, George Brent (Donald Swift), Mary Doran

7) *Homicide Squad* (Universal 1931) 69 M – filmed June 1931 (released August 1931); Director, George Melford; Screenplay, John Thomas Neville (story by Henry LaCossitt); Camera, George Robinson; Cast: Leo Carrillo, Noah Beery, Mary Brian, Russell Gleason, George Brent (Jimmy), Walter C. Percival; J. Carroll Naish, Pat O'Malley

8) *Lightning Warrior* (Mascot 1931) 250 M, 12 Chapters – filmed October 1931 (released November 1931); Directors, Armand Schaefer, Ben Kline; Screenplay, Wyndham Gittens, Ford Beebe, Helmar Bergman, Colbert Clark; Camera, Tom Galligan, Ernest Miller, William Nobles; Cast: Rin Tin Tin, Frankie Darro, Georgia Hale, George Brent (Alan Scott), Pat O'Malley, Theodore Lorch, Lafe McKee, Bob Kortman, George Magrill, Frank Lanning, Frank Brownlee, Hayden Stevenson, Dick Dickinson, Kermit Maynard, Yakima Canutt

9) *So Big* (WB 1932) 82 M – filmed January–February 1932 (released April 1932); Director, William Wellman; Screenplay, J. Grubb Alexander (novel by Edna Ferber); Camera, Sid Hickox; Cast: Barbara Stanwyck, George Brent (Roelf), Dickie Moore, Bette Davis, Mae Madison, Hardie Albright, Alan Hale, Earle Foxe, Robert Warwick, Dorothy Peterson, Noel Francis, Dick Winslow, Elizabeth Patterson, Anne Shirley

10) *The Rich Are Always With Us* (WB First National 1932) 71 M – filmed February 1932 (released May 1932); Director, Alfred E. Green; Screenplay, Austin Parker (novel by E. Pettit); Camera, Ernest Haller; Cast: Ruth Chatterton, George Brent (Julian Teirney), Bette Davis, John Miljan, Adrienne Dore, John Wray, Robert Warwick

11) *Week-End Marriage* (WB First National 1932) 65 M – filmed March 1932 (released June 1932); Director, Thornton Freeland; Screenplay, Sheridan Gibney (novel by Faith Baldwin); Camera, Barney McGill; Cast: Loretta Young, Norman Foster, Aline MacMahon, George Brent (Peter Acton), Grant Mitchell, Vivienne Osborne, Sheila Terry, J. Farrell MacDonald, Louise Carter, Roscoe Karns, Herman Bing

12) *The Purchase Price* (WB 1932) 68 M – filmed April–May 1932 (released July 23, 1932); Director, William Wellman; Screenplay, Robert Lord (story

"The Mud Lark" by Arthur Stringer); Camera, Sid Hickox; Cast: Barbara Stanwyck, George Brent (Jim Gilson), Lyle Talbot, Hardie Albright, David Landau, Murray Kinnell, Leila Bennett, Matt McHugh, Clarence Wilson, Anne Shirley

13) **Miss Pinkerton** (WB First National 1932) 66 M – filmed February–March 1932 (released July 30, 1932); Director, Lloyd Bacon; Screenplay, Lillian Hayward and Niven Busch (story by Mary Roberts Rinehart); Camera, Barney McGill; Cast: Joan Blondell, George Brent (Inspector Patten), Ruth Hall, John Wray, Elizabeth Patterson, C. Henry Gordon, Holmes Herbert, Lyle Talbot

14) **The Crash** (WB First National 1932) 58 M – filmed May 1932 (released September 1932); Director, William Dieterle; Screenplay, Earl Baldwin (novel Children of Pleasure by Larry Barretto); Camera, Ernest Haller; Cast: Ruth Chatterton, George Brent (Geoffrey Gault), Paul Cavanagh, Barbara Leonard, Henry Kolker, Lois Wilson, Ivan Simpson, Helen Vinson, Hardie Albright, Edith Kingdon, Richard Tucker, Virginia Hammond, Herman Bing

15) **They Call It Sin** (WB First National 1932) 69 M – filmed June 1932 (released November 1932); Director, Thornton Freeland; Screenplay, Lillian Hayward and Howard J. Green (novel by Alberta Stedman Eagan); Camera, James Van Trees; Cast: Loretta Young, George Brent (Dr. Tony Travers), Una Merkel, David Manners, Helen Vinson, Louis Calhern, Joseph Cawthorn, Nella Walker, Elizabeth Patterson, Roscoe Karns

16) **Luxury Liner** (Paramount 1933) 68 M – filmed November 1932 (released February 1933); Director, Lothar Mendes; Screenplay, Gene Markey (novel by Gina Kaus); Camera, Victor Milner; Cast: George Brent (Dr. Thomas Bernhard), Zita Johann, Vivienne Osborne, Alice White, Verree Teasdale, C. Aubrey Smith, Frank Morgan, Henry Wadsworth, Wallis Clark, Billy Bevan, Barry Norton, Christian Rub

17) **42nd Street** (WB 1933) 89 M – filmed October–November 1932 (released March 11, 1933); Director, Lloyd Bacon (musical numbers directed by Busby Berkeley); Screenplay, Rian James and James Seymour; Camera, Sol Polito; Cast: Warner Baxter, Bebe Daniels, George Brent (Pat Denning), Una Merkel, Ruby Keeler, Guy Kibbee, Ned Sparks, Dick Powell, Ginger Rogers, Allen Jenkins, Henry B. Walthall, Edward J. Nugent, Al Dubin, Harry Warren, George E. Stone, Jack LaRue, Lyle Talbot (Academy Award nominations: Best Picture; Nathan Levinson – Best Sound, Recording)

18) *The Keyhole* (WB 1933) 69 M – filmed December 1932 (released March 25, 1933); Director, Michael Curtiz; Screenplay, Robert Presnell (story *The Adventuress* by Alice D.G. Miller); Camera, Barney McGill; Cast: Kay Francis, George Brent (Neil Davis), Glenda Farrell, Allen Jenkins, Monroe Owsley, Helen Ware, Henry Kolker, Ferdinand Gottschalk, Irving Bacon

19) *Lilly Turner* (WB First National 1933) 63 M – filmed February 1933 (released May 1933); Director, William Wellman, Screenplay, Gene Markey and Kathryn Scola (play by Philip Dunning); Camera, Sid Hickox; Cast: Ruth Chatterton, George Brent (Bob Chandler), Frank McHugh, Ruth Donnelly, Guy Kibbee, Gordon Westcott, Marjorie Gateson, Arthur Vinton, Robert Barrat, Grant Mitchell, Margaret Seddon, Hobart Cavanaugh, Mayo Methot

20) *Private Detective 62* (WB 1933) 62 M – filmed March–April 1933 (released June 1933); Director, Michael Curtiz; Screenplay, Rian James (story by Raoul Whitfield); Camera, Tony Gaudio; Cast: William Powell, Margaret Lindsay, Ruth Donnelly, Gordon Westcott, James Bell, Arthur Byron, Natalie Moorehead, Sheila Terry, Arthur Hohl, Hobart Cavanaugh, Theresa Harris, Renee Whitney, Ann Hovey, Irving Bacon, Georges Renavent, Eddie Phillips, Toby Wing, George Brent (Club Extra), Bill Elliott [Note: This film is listed as a George Brent credit in *The Debonairs* (Arlington House, © 1975). 30 minutes into the film Brent (or his lookalike) walks behind William Powell and Margaret Lindsay near at a nightclub hatcheck]

21) *Baby Face* (WB 1933) 70 M – filmed January 1933 (released July 1933); Director, Alfred E. Green; Screenplay, Gene Markey and Kathryn Scola (story by Mark Canfield, pseudonym for Darryl F. Zanuck); Camera, James Van Trees; Cast: Barbara Stanwyck, George Brent (Mr. Trenholm), Donald Cook, Arthur Hohl, John Wayne, Henry Kolker, James Murray, Robert Barrat, Margaret Lindsay, Douglass Dumbrille, Theresa Harris, Renee Whitney, Nat Pendleton

22) *Female* (WB First National 1933) 60 M – filmed July-August 1933 (released November 1933); Director, Michael Curtiz; Screenplay, Gene Markey and Kathryn Scola (novel by Donald Henderson Clark); Camera, Sid Hickox; Cast: Ruth Chatterton, George Brent (Jim Thorne), Johnny Mack Brown, Ruth Donnelly, Lois Wilson, Ferdinand Gottschalk, Phillip Reed, Rafaela Ottiano, Gavin Gordon, Kenneth Thomson, Huey White, Douglass Dumbrille, Wal-

ter Walker, Charles Wilson, Edward Cooper, Spencer Charters, Irving Bacon, Charley Grapewin, Jean Muir, Dick Winslow

23) *From Headquarters* (WB 1933) 63 M – filmed September 1933 (released December 1933); Director, William Dieterle; Screenplay, Robert N. Lee, Peter Milne (story by Robert N. Lee); Camera, William Reese; Cast: George Brent (Lieutenant J. Stevens), Margaret Lindsay, Eugene Pallette, Hugh Herbert, Dorothy Burgess, Theodore Newton, Hobart Cavanaugh, Robert Barrat, Henry O'Neill, Edward Ellis, Ken Murray, Kenneth Thomson, Robert Homans

24) *Stamboul Quest* (MGM 1934) 86M – filmed May–June 1934 (released July 1934); Director, Sam Wood; Screenplay, Herman J. Mankiewicz (story by Leo Birinski); Camera, James Wong Howe; Cast: Myrna Loy, George Brent (Douglas Beall), Lionel Atwill, C. Henry Gordon, Rudolph Amendt, Mischa Auer

25) *Housewife* (WB 1934) 69M – filmed April–May 1934 (released August 1934); Director, Alfred E. Green, Screenplay, Manuel Seff (story by Robert Lord, Lillie Hayward); Camera, William Rees; Cast: George Brent (William Reynolds), Bette Davis, Ann Dvorak, John Halliday, Ruth Donnelly, Hobart Cavanaugh, Robert Barrat

26) *Desirable* (WB 1934) 68M – filmed July 1934 (released September 1934); Director, Archie Mayo; Story–Screenplay, Mary C. McCall, Jr.; Camera, Ernest Haller; Cast: Jean Muir, George Brent (Stuart McAllister), Verree Teasdale, John Halliday, Charles Starrett, Russell Hopton, Virginia Hammond, Joan Wheeler, Arthur Treacher, Nella Walker, Jane Darwell

27) *The Painted Veil* (MGM 1934) 85M – filmed July–August 1934 (released November 1934); Director, Richard Boleslawski; Screenplay, John Meehan, Salka Viertel, Edith Fitzgerald (novel by W. Somerset Maugham); Camera, William Daniels; Cast: Greta Garbo, Herbert Marshall, George Brent (Jack Townsend), Warner Oland, Jean Hersholt, Bodil Rosing, Katharine Alexander, Cecilia Parker

28) *The Right to Live* (WB 1935) 69M – filmed October 1934 (released January 1935); Director, William Keighley; Screenplay, Ralph Block (play The Sacred Flame by W. Somerset Maugham); Camera, Sid Hickox; Cast: Josephine Hutchinson, George Brent (Colin Trent), Colin Clive, Peggy Wood, Henrietta Crosman, C. Aubrey Smith, Leo G. Carroll, Claude King, Nella Walker, Halliwell Hobbes

29) *Living On Velvet* (WB 1935) 75M – filmed November–December 1934 (released March 1935); Director, Frank Borzage; Story-Screenplay, Jerry Wald, Julius Epstein; Camera, Sid Hickox; Cast: Kay Francis, Warren William, George Brent (Terrence Clarence Parker), Helen Lowell, Henry O'Neill, Samuel S. Hinds, Russell Hicks, Maude Turner

30) *Stranded* (WB 1935) 72M – filmed March–April 1935 (released June 1935); Director, Frank Borzage; Screenplay, Delmar Daves (story Lady with a Badge by Frank Wead, Ferdinand Reyher); Camera, Sid Hickox; Cast: Kay Francis, George Brent (Mack Hale), Patricia Ellis, Donald Woods, Barton McLane, Robert Barrat, June Travis, Henry O'Neill, Ann Shoemaker, Frankie Darro, William Harrigan, Gavin Gordon, Mary Forbes, Zeffie Tilbury

31) *Front Page Woman* (WB 1935) 82M – filmed May 1935 (released July 1935); Director, Michael Curtiz; Screenplay, Roy Chanslor, Lillie Hayward, Laird Doyle (story Women Are Bum Newspapermen, by Richard Macaulay); Camera, Tony Gaudio; Cast: Bette Davis, George Brent (Curt Devlin), Roscoe Karns, Winifred Shaw, Joseph Crehan, Joseph King, J. Farrell Macdonald

32) *Special Agent* (WB 1935) 76M – filmed July 1935 (released September 14, 1935); Director, William Keighley; Screenplay, Laird Doyle, Abem Finkel (story Martin Mooney); Camera, Sid Hickox; Cast: Bette Davis, George Brent (Bill Bradford), Ricardo Cortez, Joseph Sawyer, Joseph Crehan, Henry O'Neill, Irving Pichel, Jack La Rue, Robert Strange, Joseph King, William B. Davidson, J. Carroll Naish, Paul Guilfoyle, Robert Barrat

33) *The Goose and the Gander* (WB 1935) 65M – filmed January–February 1935 (released September 21, 1935); Director, Alfred E. Green; Story-Screenplay, Charles Kenyon; Camera, Sid Hickox; Cast: Kay Francis, George Brent (Bob McNear), Genevieve Tobin, John Eldredge, Claire Dodd, Helen Lowell, Ralph Forbes, William Austin, Spencer Charters

34) *In Person* (RKO 1935) 87M – filmed July–August 1935 (released November 1935); Director, William A. Seiter; Screenplay, Allan Scott (based on the novel by Samuel Hopkins Adams); Camera, Edward Cronjager; Cast: Ginger Rogers, George Brent (Emory Muir), Alan Mowbray, Grant Mitchell, Samuel S. Hinds, Joan Breslau, Louis Mason, Spencer Charters, William B. Davidson

35) *Snowed Under* (WB First National 1936) 63M – filmed November–December 1935 (released April 1936); Director, Raymond Enright; Screenplay, F. Hugh Herbert (story by Lawrence Saunders); Camera, Arthur Todd; Cast: George Brent (Alan Tanner), Genevieve Tobin, Glenda Farrell, Patricia Ellis, Frank McHugh, John Eldredge, Porter Hall, Helen Lowell, Olin Howland, Joseph King, Mary Treen

36) *The Case Against Mrs. Ames* (Paramount 1936) 85M – filmed March 1936 (released May 8, 1936); Director, William A. Seiter; Screenplay, Gene Towne, Graham Baker (story by Arthur Somers Roche); Camera, Lucien Andriot; Cast: Madeleine Carroll, George Brent (Matt Logan), Arthur Treacher, Alan Baxter, Beulah Bondi, Alan Mowbray, Brenda Fowler, Esther Dale, Edward Brophy, Richard Carle, Scotty Beckett, Mayo Methot, Guy Bates Post, Ward Bond

37) *The Golden Arrow* (WB First National 1936) 68M – filmed January–February 1936 (released May 23, 1936); Director, Alfred E. Green; Screenplay, Charles Kenyon (play by Michael Arlen); Camera, Arthur Edeson; Cast: Bette Davis, George Brent (Johnny Jones), Carol Hughes, Eugene Pallette, Dick Foran, Catharine Doucet, Craig Reynolds, Hobart Cavanaugh, Henry O'Neill, Ivan Lebedeff, G. P. Huntley, Jr., Rafael Storm, E. E. Clive, Bess Flowers, Mary Treen

38) *Give Me Your Heart* (WB 1936) 88M – filmed May–June 1936 (released September 1936); Director, Archie Mayo; Screenplay, Casey Robinson (play Sweet Aloes by Jay Mallory (Joyce Carey)); Camera, Sidney Hickox; Cast: Kay Francis, George Brent (Jim Baker); Roland Young, Patric Knowles, Henry Stephenson, Frieda Inescort, Helen Flint, Halliwell Hobbes, Zeffie Tilbury, Elspeth Dudgeon, Bess Flowers

39) *More Than A Secretary* (Columbia 1936) 77M – filmed September–October 1936 (released December 1936); Director, Alfred E. Green; Screenplay, Dale Van Every, Lyn Starling (story by Ethel Hill and Aben Kandel from Safari in Manhattan by Matt Taylor); Camera, Henry Freulich; Cast: Jean Arthur, George Brent (Fred Gilbert); Lionel Stander, Ruth Donnelly, Reginald Denny, Dorothea Kent, Charles Halton

40) *God's Country and the Woman* (WB 1937) Technicolor - 84M – filmed June–August 1936 (released January 1937); Director, William Keighley; Screenplay, Norman Reilly Raine (novel by James Oliver Curwood and adapted

by Peter Milne, Charles Belden); Camera, Tony Gaudio; Cast: George Brent (Steve Russett), Beverly Roberts, Barton MacLane, Robert Barrat, Alan Hale, Addison Richards, El Brendel, Roscoe Ates, Billy Bevan, Bert Roach, Joseph Crehan, Mary Treen

41) *Mountain Justice* (WB 1937) 82 M – filmed September–November 1936 (released April 1937); Director, Michael Curtiz; Story-Screenplay, Norman Reilly Raine, Luci Ward; Dialogue Director, Irving Rapper; Camera, Ernest Haller; Cast: George Brent (Paul Cameron), Josephine Hutchinson, Guy Kibbee, Mona Barrie, Robert Barrat, Elisabeth Risdon, Margaret Hamilton, Edward Pawley, Marcia Mae Jones, Fuzzy Knight, Robert McWade, Granville Bates, Russell Simpson, Sibyl Harris, Joseph King

42) *The Go-Getter* (WB 1937) 90M – filmed December 1936–January 1937 (released May 1937); Director, Busby Berkeley; Screenplay, Delmer Daves (story from Peter B. Kyne's Cappy Ricks Comes Back); Camera, Arthur Edeson; Cast: George Brent (Bill Austin), Anita Louise, Charles Winninger, John Eldredge, Henry O'Neill, Willard Robertson, Eddie Acuff, Mary Treen, Craig Reynolds, Carlyle Moore, Jr., Gordon Oliver, Ward Bond

43) *Submarine D-1* (WB 1937) 98M – filmed July–August 1937 (released November 1937); Director, Lloyd Bacon; Screenplay, Frank Wead, Warren Duff, Lawrence Kimble (story by Frank Wead); Camera, Arthur Edeson; Cast: Pat O'Brien, George Brent (Lieutenant Commander Matthews), Wayne Morris, Doris Weston, Frank McHugh, Henry O'Neill, Dennie Moore, Veda Ann Borg, Regis Toomey, John Ridgely, Owen King, Elliott Sullivan, Don DeFore (Ronald Reagan was billed sixth in the original print, but his scenes were deleted)

44) *Gold Is Where You Find It* (WB 1938) Technicolor – 90M – filmed August–October 1937 (released February 1938); Director, Michael Curtiz; Screenplay, Warren Duff, Robert Buckner (story by Clements Ripley); Camera, Sol Polito; Cast: George Brent (Jared Whitney), Olivia de Havilland, Claude Rains, Margaret Lindsay, John Litel, Tim Holt, Barton MacLane, Henry O'Neill, Marcia Ralston, George F. Hayes, Sidney Toler, Robert McWade, Clarence Kolb, Harry Davenport, Russell Simpson, Willie Best, Moroni Olsen, George "Gabby" Hayes

45) *Jezebel* (WB 1938) 104M – filmed October 1937– January 1938 (released March 1938) Director, William Wyler; Screenplay, Clement Ripley, Abem Fin-

kel, John Huston (play by Owen Davis, Sr.); Camera, Ernest Haller; Cast: Bette Davis, Henry Fonda, George Brent (Buck Cantrell), Margaret Lindsay, Fay Bainter, Richard Cromwell, Donald Crisp, Henry O'Neill, John Litel, Gordon Oliver, Janet Shaw, Spring Byington, Irving Pichel, Eddie Anderson, Stymie Beard (Academy Awards: Bette Davis – Best Actress; Fay Bainter – Best Supporting Actress) (Academy Award nominations: Best Picture; Ernest Haller – Best Cinematography; Max Steiner – Best Music Scoring)

46) *Racket Busters* (WB 1938) 71M – filmed April–May 1938 (released July 1938) Director, Lloyd Bacon; Story-screenplay, Robert Rossen, Leonardo Bercovici; Camera, Arthur Edeson; Cast: George Brent (Denny Jordan), Humphrey Bogart, Gloria Dickson, Allen Jenkins, Walter Abel, Penny Singleton, Henry O'Neill, Oscar O'Shea, Elliott Sullivan, Fay Helm

47) *Secrets of an Actress* (WB 1938) 70M – filmed February–March 1938 (released September 1938) Director, William Keighley; Screenplay, Milton Krims, Rowland Leigh, Julius J. Epstein; Camera, Sidney Hickox; Cast: Kay Francis, George Brent (Dick Orr), Ian Hunter, Gloria Dickson, Isabel Jeans, Penny Singleton, Dennie Moore, Selmer Jackson, Herbert Rawlinson, Clayton Moore

48) *Wings of the Navy* (WB 1939) 89M – filmed July–September 1938 (released February 1939) Director, Lloyd Bacon; Story-screenplay, Michael Fessier; Camera, Arthur Edeson, Elmer Dyer; Cast: George Brent (Cass Harrington), Olivia de Havilland, John Payne, Frank McHugh, John Litel, Victor Jory, Henry O'Neill, John Ridgely, John Gallaudet, Don Briggs, Regis Toomey, Edgar Edwards

49) *Dark Victory* (WB 1939) 104M – filmed October–November 1938 (released April 1939) Director, Edmund Goulding; Screenplay, Casey Robinson (play by George Emerson Brewer, Jr., Bertram Block); Camera, Ernest Haller; Cast: Bette Davis, George Brent (Dr. Frederick Steele), Humphrey Bogart, Geraldine Fitzgerald, Ronald Reagan, Henry Travers, Cora Witherspoon, Virginia Brissac, Dorothy Peterson, Charles Richman, Fay Helm (Academy Award nominations: Best Picture; Bette Davis – Best Actress; Max Steiner – Best Music, Original Score)

50) *The Old Maid* (WB 1939) 95M – filmed March–May 1939 (released August 1939) Director, Edmund Goulding; Screenplay, Casey Robinson (based on the play by Zoe Akins as adapted from Edith Wharton's novel); Camera, Tony

Gaudio; Cast: Bette Davis, Miriam Hopkins, George Brent (Clem Spender), Jane Bryan, Donald Crisp, Louise Fazenda, James Stephenson, Jerome Cowan, William Lundigan, Cecilia Loftus, Rand Brooks, Janet Shaw, William Hopper

51) ***The Rains Came*** (20th-Century Fox 1939) 103M – filmed April–July 1939 (released September 1939) Director: Clarence Brown; Screenplay, Philip Dunne, Julien Josephson (based on the Louis Bromfield novel); Camera, Arthur Miller; Cast: Myrna Loy, Tyrone Power, George Brent (Tom Ransome), Brenda Joyce, Nigel Bruce, Maria Ouspenskaya, Joseph Schildkraut, Mary Nash, Jane Darwell, Marjorie Rambeau, Henry Travers, H. B. Warner, Laura Hope Crews, William Royle, Montague Shaw, Harry Hayden, Herbert Evans, Lal Chand Mehra (Academy Awards: Fred Sersen, Edmund H. Hansen – Best Effects, Special Effects; Arthur C. Miller – Best Cinematography, black-and-white; William S. Darling, George Dudley – Best Art Direction) (Academy Award nominations: Edmund H. Hansen – Best Sound Recording; Barbara McLean – Best Film Editing; Alfred Newman – Best Music, Original Score)

52) ***The Fighting 69th*** (WB 1940) 89M – filmed September–October 1939 (released January 1940) Director, William Keighley; Screenplay, Norman Reilly Raine, Fred Niblo, Jr., Dean Franklin; Camera, Tony Gaudio; Cast: James Cagney, Pat O'Brien, George Brent (Wild Bill Donovan), Jeffrey Lynn, Alan Hale, Frank McHugh, Dennis Morgan, William Lundigan, Dick Foran, Guinn "Big Boy" Williams, Henry O'Neill, John Litel, Sammy Cohen, Harvey Stephens, William Hopper, Tom Dugan, George Reeves

53) ***Adventure in Diamonds*** (Paramount 1940) 76M – filmed July–August 1939 (released March 1940) Director, George Fitzmaurice; Screenplay, Leonard Lee, Franz Schulz (based on story by Frank O'Connor); Camera, Charles Lang; Cast: George Brent (Captain Stephen Bennett), Isa Miranda, John Loder, Nigel Bruce, Elizabeth Patterson, Matthew Boulton, Rex Evans, Cecil Kellaway, Walter Kingsford, Ernest Truex, Ralph Forbes, Bess Flowers

54) ***'Til We Meet Again*** (WB 1940) 99M – filmed December 1939–January 1940 (released April 1940) Director, Edmund Goulding (Anatole Litvak shot about 26% of the film), Screenplay, Warren Duff (based on story by Robert Lord); Camera, Tony Gaudio; Cast: Merle Oberon, George Brent (Dan Hardesty), Pat O'Brien, Geraldine Fitzgerald, Binnie Barnes, Frank McHugh, Eric

Blore, George Reeves, Henry O'Neill, Frank Wilcox, Doris Lloyd, John Ridgely, Marjorie Gateson, Regis Toomey, William Halligan

55) *The Man Who Talked Too Much* (WB 1940) 75M – filmed April–May 1940 (released July 1940) Director, Vincent Sherman; Screenplay, Walter DeLeon, Tom Reed (based on the play The Mouthpiece by Frank J. Collins); Camera, Sid Hickox; Cast: George Brent (Stephen Forbes), Virginia Bruce, Brenda Marshall, Richard Barthelmess, William Lundigan, John Litel, George Tobias, Henry Armetta, Alan Baxter, Marc Lawrence, Clarence Kolb, John Ridgely, David Bruce

56) *South of Suez* (WB 1940) 86M – filmed September–October 1940 (released November 1940) Director, Lewis Seiler; Screenplay, Barry Trivers; Camera, Arthur Todd; Cast: George Brent (John Gamble/John Bradley), Brenda Marshall, George Tobias, Lee Patrick, James Stephenson, Eric Blore, Miles Mander, Cecil Kellaway, Mary Forbes, Stanley Logan

57) *Honeymoon For Three* (WB 1941) 77M – filmed July–August 1940 (released January 1941) Director, Lloyd Bacon; Screenplay, Earl Baldwin (based on the play Goodbye Again by Alan Scott, George Haight); Camera, Ernest Haller; Cast: Ann Sheridan, George Brent (Kenneth Bixson), Charles Ruggles, Osa Massen, Jane Wyman, William T. Orr, Lee Patrick, Walter Catlett, Herbert Anderson, Johnny Downs

58) *The Great Lie* (WB 1941) 102M – filmed October–December 1940 (some sources say filming went into February 1941) (released April 1941) Director, Edmund Goulding; Screenplay, Lenore Coffee (based on the novel January Heights by Polan Banks); Camera, Tony Gaudio; Cast: Bette Davis, George Brent (Pete Van Allen), Mary Astor, Lucile Watson, Hattie McDaniel, Grant Mitchell, Jerome Cowan, Sam McDaniel, Thurston Hall, Charles Trowbridge, Russell Hicks, Doris Lloyd (Academy Award – Mary Astor – Best Supporting Actress)

59) *They Dare Not Love* (Columbia 1941) 76M – filmed January–February 1941 (released April 1941) Director, James Whale; Screenplay, Charles Bennett, Ernest Vajda (story by James Earl Grant); Camera, Franz F. Planer; Cast: George Brent (Prince Kurt von Rotenburg), Martha Scott, Paul Lukas, Egon Brecher, Roman Bohnen, Edgar Barrier, Kay Linaker, Frank Reicher, Gregory Gaye, Peter Cushing, Lloyd Bridges, Bodil Rosing

60) *International Lady* (UA 1941) 102M – filmed April–June 1941 (released September 1941) Director, Tim Whelan; Screenplay, Howard Estabrook (story, E. Lloyd Sheldon, Jack De Witt); Camera, Hal Mohr; Cast: George Brent (Tim Hanley), Ilona Massey, Basil Rathbone, Gene Lockhart, George Zucco, Francis Pierlot, Martin Kosleck, Charles D. Brown, Marjorie Gateson, Clayton Moore

61) *Twin Beds* (UA 1942) 85M – filmed September–October 1941 (released April 1942) Director, Tim Whelan; Screenplay, Curtis Kenyon, Kenneth Ear, E. Edwin Moran (based on the play by Margaret Mayo, Salisbury Field); Camera, Hal Mohr; Cast: George Brent (Mike Abbott), Joan Bennett, Mischa Auer, Una Merkel, Glenda Farrell, Ernest Truex, Margaret Hamilton, Charles Coleman, Charles Arnt, Cecil Cunningham

62) *In This Our Life* (WB 1942) 97M – filmed October–December 1941 (released May 1942) Director, John Huston; Screenplay, Howard Koch (based on the novel by Ellen Glasgow); Camera, Ernest Haller; Cast: Bette Davis, Olivia de Havilland, George Brent (Craig Fleming), Dennis Morgan, Charles Coburn, Frank Craven, Billie Burke, Hattie McDaniel, Lee Patrick, Mary Servoss, Ernest Anderson, William Davidson, Edward Fielding, John Hamilton, William Forrest, Elliott Sullivan, Eddie Acuff, Walter Huston

63) *The Gay Sisters* (WB 1942) 110M – filmed January–March 1942 (released August 1942) Director, Irving Rapper, Screenplay, Lenore Coffee (based on the novel by Stephen Longstreet); Camera, Sol Polito; Cast: Barbara Stanwyck, George Brent (Charles Barclay), Geraldine Fitzgerald, Donald Crisp, Gig Young, Nancy Coleman, Gene Lockhart, Larry Simms, Donald Woods, Grant Mitchell, William T. Orr, Anne Revere

64) *You Can't Escape Forever* (WB 1942) 77M – filmed May–July 1942 (released October 1942) Director, Jo Graham; Screenplay, Fred Niblo, Jr., Hector Chevigny (story by Roy Chanslor); Camera, Tony Gaudio; Cast: George Brent (Steve Mitchell), Brenda Marshall, Paul Harvey, Roscoe Karns, Gene Lockhart, Charles Halton, Eduardo Ciannelli, George Meeker, Joseph Downing, Don De-Fore, Erville Alderson, Fay Helm

65) *Silver Queen* (UA 1942) 80M – filmed April–May 1942 (released November 1942) Director, Lloyd Bacon; Screenplay, Bernard Schubert, Cecile Kramer; Camera, Russell Harlan; Cast: George Brent (James Kinkaid), Priscilla Lane,

Bruce Cabot, Lynne Overman, Eugene Pallette, Janet Beecher, Guinn "Big Boy" Williams, Roy Barcroft, Eleanor Stewart, Arthur Hunnicutt, Sam McDaniel, Spencer Charters, Cy Kendall, Georges Renavent, Francis X. Bushman (Academy Award nominations: Ralph Berger, Emil Kuri – Best Art Direction-Interior Decoration, black-and-white; Victor Young – Best Music, Scoring of a Dramatic or Comedy Picture)

66) *Experiment Perilous* (RKO 1944) 91M – filmed July–October 1944 (released December 1944) Director, Jacques Tourneur; Screenplay, Warren Duff (based on the novel by Margaret Carpenter); Camera, Tony Gaudio; Cast: Hedy Lamarr, George Brent (Dr. Huntington Bailey), Paul Lukas, Albert Dekker, Carl Esmond, Olive Blakeney, George Neise, Margaret Wycherly, Stephanie Bachelor, Mary Servoss, Julia Dean, William Post, Jr., Billy Ward, Alan Ward, Nolan Leary, Larry Wheat, Sam McDaniel (Academy Award nomination – Albert S. D'Agostino, Jack Okey, Darrell Silvera, Claude E. Carpenter – Best Art Direction-Interior Decoration, black-and-white)

67) *The Affairs of Susan* (Paramount 1945) 110M – filmed October–December 1944 (released January 1945) Director, William A. Seiter; Screenplay, Thomas Monroe, Laszlo Gorog, Richard Flournoy; David Abel; Cast: Joan Fontaine, George Brent (Roger Berton), Dennis O'Keefe, Walter Abel, Don DeFore, Rita Johnson, Mary Field, Byron Barr, Francis Pierlot, Lewis Russell, Vera Marshe, James Millican, Crane Whitley, Warren Hymer, Ruth Roman, Bess Flowers (Academy Award nomination – Laszlo Gorog, Thomas Monroe – Best Writing, Original Story)

68) *The Spiral Staircase* (RKO 1946) 83M – filmed August–October 1945 (released early January 1946) Director, Robert Siodmak; Screenplay, Mel Dinelli (based on the novel Some Must Watch by Ethel Lina White); Camera, Nicholas Musuraca; Cast: Dorothy McGuire, George Brent (Professor Warren), Ethel Barrymore, Kent Smith, Rhonda Fleming, Gordon Oliver, Elsa Lanchester, Sara Allgood, Rhys Williams, James Bell, Charles Wagenheim, Ellen Corby, Richard Tyler, Erville Alderson (Academy Award nomination – Ethel Barrymore – Best Supporting Actress)

69) *My Reputation* (WB 1946) 96M – filmed November 1943–January 1944 (released overseas for servicemen, February 1945) (general U.S. release early January 1946) Director, Curtis Bernhardt; Screenplay, Catherine Turney (based on the novel Instruct My Sorrows by Clare Jaynes); Camera, James Wong Howe; Cast: Barbara Stanwyck, George Brent (Major Scott Landis),

Warner Anderson, Lucile Watson, John Ridgely, Eve Arden, Esther Dale, Jerome Cowan, Leona Maricle, Scotty Beckett, Bobby Cooper, Ann Todd

70) *Tomorrow Is Forever* (RKO-International 1946) 105M – filmed March–June 1945 (released mid-January 1946) Director, Irving Pichel; Screenplay, Lenore Coffee (based on the novel by Gwen Bristow); Camera, Joseph Valentine; Cast: Claudette Colbert, Orson Welles, George Brent (Larry Hamilton), Lucile Watson, Richard Long, Natalie Wood, Sonny Howe, John Wengraf, Ian Wolfe, Douglas Wood, Joyce MacKenzie, Tom Wirick

71) *Lover Come Back* (Universal 1946) 90M – filmed February–April 1946 (released June 1946) Director, William A. Seiter; Screenplay, Michael Fessier, Ernest Pagano; Camera, Joseph Valentine; Cast: George Brent (Bill Williams), Lucille Ball, Vera Zorina, Charles Winninger, Carl Esmond, Raymond Walburn, Elisabeth Risdon, Louise Beavers, Wallace Ford, Franklin Pangborn, William Wright, George Chandler, Joan Shawlee, Ellen Corby, Bess Flowers

72) *Temptation* (Universal-International 1946) 98M – filmed April–June 1946 (released December 1946) Director, Irving Pichel; Screenplay, Robert Thoeren (based on the novel Bella Donna by Robert Hichens and the play by James Bernard Fagan); Camera, Lucien Ballard; Cast: Merle Oberon, George Brent (Nigel Armine), Charles Korvin, Paul Lukas, Lenore Ulric, Arnold Moss, Ludwig Stossel, Gavin Muir, Ilka Gruning, Robert Capa, John Eldridge

73) *The Corpse Came C.O.D.* (Columbia 1947) 87M – filmed December 1946–late January 1947 (released June 1947) Director, Henry Levin; Screenplay, George Bricker, Dwight Babcock (based on the novel by Jimmy Starr); Camera, Lucien Andriot; Cast: George Brent (Joe Medford), Joan Blondell, Adele Jergens, Jim Bannon, Leslie Brooks, John Berkes, Fred Sears, William Trenk, Grant Mitchell, Una O'Connor, Marvin Miller, Gregory Gaye

74) *Slave Girl* (Universal-International 1947) Technicolor 79M – filmed July–October 1946 (released August 1947) Director, Charles Lamont; Screenplay, Michael Fessier, Ernest Pagano; Camera, George Robinson, W. Howard Greene; Cast: Yvonne De Carlo, George Brent (Matt Clairbourne), Broderick Crawford, Albert Dekker, Lois Collier, Andy Devine, Carl Esmond, Arthur Treacher, Philip Van Zandt, Dan Seymour, Don Turner, Humpy the Camel (voice of Buddy Hackett)

75) *Out of the Blue* (Eagle Lion 1947) 86M – filmed March–April 1947 (released October 1947) Director, Leigh Jason; Screenplay, Vera Caspary, Walter Bullock, Edward Eliscu; Camera, Jackson Rose; Cast: George Brent (Arthur Earthleigh), Virginia Mayo, Turhan Bey, Ann Dvorak, Carole Landis, Elizabeth Patterson, Julia Dean, Richard Lane, Charles Smith, Paul Harvey, Alton E. Horton, Hadda Brooks

76) *Christmas Eve* (UA 1947) 90M – filmed November 1946–early January 1947 (released late October 1947) Director, Edwin L. Marin; Screenplay, Laurence Stallings, Richard H. Landau; Camera, Gordon Avil; Cast: George Raft, George Brent (Michael Brooks), Randolph Scott, Joan Blondell, Virginia Field, Dolores Moran, Ann Harding, Reginald Denny, Carl Harbord, Clarence Kolb, John Litel, Joe Sawyer, Douglass Dumbrille, Dennis Hoey, Molly Lamont, Walter Sande, Konstantin Shayne, Marie Blake

77) *Luxury Liner* (MGM 1948) Technicolor 98M – filmed August–September 1947 (released September 1948) Director, Richard Whorf; Screenplay, Gladys Lehman, Richard Connell; Camera, Ernest Laszlo; Cast: George Brent (Captain Jeremy Bradford), Jane Powell, Lauritz Melchior, Frances Gifford, Marina Koshetz, Xavier Cugat, Thomas E. Breen, Richard Derr, John Ridgely, The Pied Pipers, Connie Gilchrist, Lee Tung Foo, Juanita Quigley, May McAvoy

78) *Angel On The Amazon* (Republic 1948) 86M – filmed April–May 1948 (released December 1948) Director, John H. Auer; Screenplay, Lawrence Kimble (story by Earl Felton); Camera, Reggie Lanning; Cast: George Brent (Jim Warburton), Vera Ralston, Brian Aherne, Constance Bennett, Fortunio Bonanova, Alfonso Bedoya, Gus Schilling, Richard Crane, Walter Reed, Ross Elliott, Konstantin Shayne

79) *Red Canyon* (Universal 1949) 84M – filmed June–July 1948 (released April 1949) Director, George Sherman; Screenplay, Maurice Geraghty (based on the novel Wildfire by Zane Grey); Camera, Irving Glassberg; Cast: Ann Blyth, Howard Duff, George Brent (Mathew Bostel), Edgar Buchanan, John McIntire, Chill Wills, Jane Darwell, Lloyd Bridges, James Seay, Edmund MacDonald, Denver Pyle

80) *Illegal Entry* (Universal 1949) 84M – filmed December 1948–January 1949 (released June 1949) Director, Frederick de Cordova; Screenplay, Joel Malone (based on a story by Ben Bengal, Herbert Kline, Dan Moore); Camera, William Daniels; Cast: Howard Duff, Marta Toren, George Brent (Dan Col-

lins), Gar Moore, Tom Tully, Paul Stewart, Richard Rober, Joseph Vitale, James Nolan, Clifton Young

81) *The Kid from Cleveland* (Republic 1949) 89M – filmed May–June 1949 (released September 1949) Director, Herbert Kline; Screenplay, John Bright (story by Herbert Kline, John Bright); Camera, Jack Marta; Cast: George Brent (Mike Jackson), Lynn Bari, Rusty Tamblyn, Tommy Cook, Ann Doran, Louis Jean Heydt, K. Elmo Lowe, John Berardino, Tris Speaker, Leroy 'Satchel' Paige, Bob Lemon, and other members of the Cleveland Indians Baseball Team

82) *Bride For Sale* (RKO 1949) 87M filmed February–April 1949 (released November 1949) Director, William D. Russell; Screenplay, Bruce Manning, Islin Auster (story by Joseph Fields, Frederick Kohner); Camera, Joseph Valentine; Cast: Claudette Colbert, Robert Young, George Brent (Paul Martin), Max Baer, Gus Schilling, Charles Arnt, Ann Tyrrell, Paul Maxey, Burk Symon, Stephen Chase, Anne O'Neal, Eula Guy, John Michaels, Georgia Caine, William Vedder, Thurston Hall, Hans Conried

83) *FBI Girl* (Lippert 1951) 71M filmed June 1951 (released November 1951) Director, William Berke; Screenplay, Richard Landau, Dwight Babcock (story by Rupert Hughes); Camera, Jack Greenhaigh; Cast: Cesar Romero, George Brent (Jeff Donley), Audrey Totter, Tom Drake, Raymond Burr, Raymond Greenleaf, Tom Noonan, Pete Marshall, Margia Dean, Alexander Pope, Richard Monohan, Don Garner, Jan Kayne, Joy (Joi) Lansing, Walter Coy, Byron Foulger, Joel Marston, Marie Blake

84) *The Last Page* (Exclusive 1952) U.S. release title: Man Bait (Lippert, 1952) 84/80M filmed July 1951 (in England) (released January 1952) Director, Terence Fisher; Screenplay, Frederick Knott (story by Terence Fisher, James Hadley Chase); Camera, Walter Harvey; Cast: George Brent (John Harman), Marguerite Chapman, Raymond Huntley, Peter Reynolds, Diana Dors, Eleanor Summerfield, Meredith Edwards, Harry Fowler, Conrad Phillips, Isabel Dean

85) *Montana Belle* (RKO 1952) Color – 81M filmed October–November 1948 (released November 1952) Director, Allan Dwan; Screenplay, Horace McCoy, Norman S. Hall (story by M. Coates Webster, Howard Welsch); Camera, Jack Marta; Cast: Jane Russell, George Brent (Tom Bradfield), Scott Brady, Forrest Tucker, Andy Devine, Jack Lambert, John Litel, Ray Teal, Rory Mallinson, Roy Barcroft, Holly Blane, Iron Eyes Cody

86) *Tangier Incident* (Allied Artists 1953) 77M filmed September 1952 (released February 1953) Director, Lew Landers; Screenplay, George Bricker; Camera, William Sickner; Cast: George Brent (Steve Gordon), Mari Alden, Dorothy Patrick, Bert Freed, Dan Seymour, Dayton Lummis, Alix Talton, John Harmon, Richard Karlan, Shepard Menken, Benny Rubin, Mike Ross

87) *Mexican Manhunt* (Allied Artists 1953) 71M filmed June 1953 (released September 1953) Director, Rex Bailey; Screenplay, George Bricker; Camera, William Sickner; Cast: George Brent (Dave Brady), Hillary Brooke, Morris Ankrum, Karen Sharpe, Marjorie Lord, Douglas Kennedy, Alberto Morin, Carleton Young, Stuart Randall, Marvin Press

88) *Death of a Scoundrel* (RKO 1956) 119M filmed January–February 1956 (released November 1956) Producer/Director/Screenplay, Charles Martin; Camera, James Wong Howe; Cast: George Sanders, Yvonne De Carlo, Zsa Zsa Gabor, Victory Jory, Nancy Gates, Coleen Gray, John Hoyt, Lisa Ferraday, Tom Conway, Celia Lovsky, Werner Klemperer, Justice Watson, John Sutton, Curtis Cooksey, Gabriel Curtis, Morris Andrum, George Brent (originally slated for the role of Mr. O'Hara, but was replaced by John Hoyt)

89) *Born Again* (AVCO Embassy Pictures 1978) 110M filmed January–February 1978 (released September 1978) Producer, Frank Capra, Jr.; Director, Irving Rapper; Screenplay, Walter Bloch (based on the autobiography by Charles W. Colson); Camera, Harry Stradling, Jr.; Cast: Dean Jones, Anne Francis, Jay Robinson, Dana Andrews, Raymond St. Jacques, George Brent (Judge Gerhard Gesell), Harold Hughes, Billy Graham, Harry Spillman, Scott Walker, Robert Gray, Arthur Roberts, Ned Wilson, Dean Brooks, Christopher Conrad, Peter Jurasik, Stuart Lee, Richard Caine, Brigid O'Brien, Robert Broyles, Anthony Crane, Corinne Comacho, Danny Bonaduce, Morton Downey, Jr., Corey Feldman

Short Subjects:

Hollywood on Parade (No. A-13) (Lewis Lewyn Prod. 1933) 11M Cast: Buster Keaton, Warner Baxter, Joan Bennett, Joan Blondell, George Brent, Clive Brook, Ruth Chatterton, Maurice Chevalier, Ronald Colman, Gary Cooper, Marlene Dietrich, Carole Lombard, Bessie Love, Tim McCoy, Adolphe Menjou, Louella Parsons, William Powell, Lois Wilson

A Dream Comes True (WB 1935) 8M All-star short promoting *A Midsummer's Night Dream.* Brent is seen escorting Marion Davies to the event. Appearing as themselves: Ross Alexander, James Cagney, Sybil Jason, Max Reinhardt, Virginia Bruce, Freddie Bartholomew, Bette Davis, Olivia de Havilland, Errol Flynn, Hugh Herbert, Joe E. Brown, Margaret Lindsay, Anita Louise, Pat O'Brien, Dick Powell, Lili Damita, Lyle Talbot, Warren William, Donald Woods, Jack Warner, Dolores del Rio, Hal Wallis, Frank McHugh, Grace Moore, William Dieterle, Jean Muir, Gladys Swarthout, Cesar Romero, Erich Wolfgang Korngold, Louise Fazenda, Paula Stone, Hobart Cavanaugh

Breakdowns of 1935 (a.k.a. Things You Never See on the Screen) (WB 1935) All-star short with Brent in scene from *Living On Velvet* with Kay Francis

Breakdowns of 1937 (WB 1937) All-star short with Brent in scene from *Give Me Your Heart* with Helen Flint

Breakdowns of 1938 (WB 1938) All-star short with Brent in a scene from *Jezebel* where he forgets his lines

Out Where the Stars Begin (WB 1938) Technicolor short that includes a scene from *Gold is Where You Find It* with George Brent and Olivia de Havilland. Guest appearances by: Ann Sheridan, Pat O'Brien, Wayne Morris, Dick Foran; Director, Bobby Connolly Cast: Evelyn Thawl, Jeffrey Lynn, Armida, Fritz Feld

Swingtime in the Movies (WB 1938) 20M Technicolor short in which various Warner stars make cameo appearances: George Brent, Humphrey Bogart, John Garfield, Priscilla Lane, Rosemary Lane, Pat O'Brien, Marie Wilson, Bobby Jordan, Billy Halop, Huntz Hall, Leo Gorcey; Director, Crane Wilbur; Cast: Fritz Feld, Kathryn Kane, John Carroll, Charley Foy, Jerry Colonna, Irene Franklin (Nominated in 1939 for Best Live Action Short)

Land of Liberty (1939) A contribution to 1939's New York World's Fair and San Francisco Exposition, this 138 minute feature included a scene from *Jezebel* (1938) with Bette Davis, George Brent, and Henry Fonda. It premiered in June, 1939. Edited by Cecil B. DeMille, the original release also had footage from *Cimarron* (1931), *Showboat* (1936), *San Francisco* (1936), et al., before being cut for further showings. By 1941, *Land of Liberty* had been reduced to ninety-eight minutes.

Breakdowns of 1940 (WB 1940) All-star short with Brent in scenes from *The Old Maid* (with Miriam Hopkins), *The Fighting 69th*, *'Til We Meet Again* (paired with Pat O'Brien, Merle Oberon)

Breakdowns of 1944 (WB 1944) All-star short with Brent in scene from *You Can't Escape Forever* with Brenda Marshall

*Note – on February 8, 1960, George was awarded two stars on the Hollywood Walk of Fame—one for motion pictures and one for his TV work. Both are located on Vine Street.

Radio Credits
(alphabetically arranged selected programs)

Abbott & Costello (NBC):

April 20, 1944
GB (guest), Connie Haines, Mel Blanc

November 2, 1944
GB (guest) gives speech on behalf of Thomas Dewey campaign

Cavalcade of America (NBC):

November 1, 1943
Burma Surgeon with GB

The Doctor Fights (CBS):

September 4, 1946
Hero Without Medals with GB (Lt. Commander A. Duane Bean); Dee Engelbach (director) (The week prior to Brent's appearance, announcer Jimmy Wallington broke up the cast during rehearsal when he stepped to the mike for the promo spot and blurted, "George Brent in a thrilling true story, *His Brother Uses a Bagel.*")

Edgar Bergen and Charlie McCarthy Show (NBC):

May 28, 1939
GB (guest), Billy Gilbert

George Fisher (CBS):

November 15, 1951
GB (guest) promoting his new film *FBI Girl*

Hallmark Playhouse (CBS):

April 14, 1949
One Foot in Heaven with GB

Hollywood Hotel (CBS):

January 4, 1935
Living on Velvet with GB, Kay Francis

May 15, 1936
The Case Against Mrs. Ames with GB, Madeline Carroll, James Melton (guest host)

September 25, 1936
Give Me Your Heart with GB, Kay Francis (Burns and Allen guest hosts)

January 22, 1937
God's Country and the Woman with GB, Beverly Roberts, Fred MacMurray (guest host)

May 14, 1937
The Go-Getter with GB, Anita Louise, Charles Winninger

March 25, 1938
Jezebel with GB, Bette Davis, Henry Fonda

Hollywood Star Time (CBS):

June 2, 1946
Second Honeymoon with GB, Lynn Bari, Mary Jane Croft

August 17, 1946
Conflict with GB, Sidney Greenstreet

Hollywood Theatre (ABC):

September 3, 1948
The Next Chapter with GB

Jack Colon (sportscaster):

March 18, 1949
GB (guest), Max Baer

Kate Smith (CBS):

February 2, 1939
GB (guest)

Kraft Music Hall (NBC):

March 24, 1938
Bing Crosby, GB (guest)

Leave It To The Girls (Mutual):
March 12–August 6, 1948 (Friday nights)
Female panel show with GB (moderator), Constance Bennett, Sylvia Sidney, Binnie Barnes (Rudy Vallee replaced Brent beginning with the August 13 broadcast)

Lux Radio Theatre (CBS):

May 16, 1938
The Girl From 10th Avenue with GB, Loretta Young, Beulah Bondi, Mona Barrie

July 4, 1938
I Found Stella Parish with GB, Constance Bennett, Herbert Marshall, Lucile Watson

October 3, 1938
Another Dawn with GB, Madeleine Carroll, Franchot Tone

June 26, 1939
Mrs. Moonlight with GB, Janet Gaynor,

September 25, 1939
She Married Her Boss with GB, Ginger Rogers, Edith Fellows

November 6, 1939
Only Yesterday with GB, Barbara Stanwyck

March 18, 1940
The Rains Came with GB, Kay Francis, Jean Parker, Jim Ameche, Jack Lewis, Lal Chand Mehra (produced and directed by Cecil B. DeMille)

June 10, 1940
'Til We Meet Again with GB, Merle Oberon, Pat O'Brien

November 7, 1940
Wings of the Navy with GB, Olivia de Havilland, John Payne

April 28, 1941
Wife, Husband and Friend with GB, Priscilla Lane, Gail Patrick

March 2, 1942
The Great Lie with GB, Loretta Young, Mary Astor

June 15, 1942
You Belong to Me with GB, Merle Oberon

November 9, 1942
Sullivan's Travels with George Brent, Veronica Lake, Ralph Bellamy

March 1, 1943
The Lady is Willing with GB, Kay Francis, Ann Doran, Lillian Randolph, Arthur Q. Bryan, Edward Marr, Fred MacKaye

June 7, 1943
My Friend Flicka with GB, Roddy McDowell, Rita Johnson

September 20, 1943
Flight for Freedom with GB, Rosalind Russell, Chester Morris

September 10, 1945
Experiment Perilous with GB, Virginia Bruce, Paul Henreid, Howard McNear

October 29, 1946
The Affairs of Susan with GB, Joan Fontaine, Don DeFore

April 21, 1947
My Reputation with GB, Barbara Stanwyck, Jeff Chandler, William Keighley (host)

June 16, 1947
The Other Love with GB, Barbara Stanwyck, Richard Conte

Mary Pickford-Parties at Pickfair (CBS):

March 24, 1936
GB (guest), Helen Gahagan, Melvyn Douglas

Meet the Missus (CBS):

October 6, 1951
GB (guest)

Queen for a Day (Mutual):

October 17, 1951
GB (guest)

Radio Hall of Fame (NBC):

February 4, 1945
Experiment Perilous with GB, Hedy Lamarr, Andy Russell, Marjorie Main

Rudy Vallee Varieties (NBC):

September 26, 1935
GB (guest), Lionel Atwill

Screen Guild Players/Theatre (CBS):

March 29, 1943
This Thing Called Love with GB, Alice Faye, Allyn Joslyn, Robert Young

October 14, 1946
Experiment Perilous with GB, Joan Bennett, Adolph Menjou

November 4, 1946
Experiment Perilous with GB, Ruth Hussey, Adolph Menjou

May 11, 1950
Mad About Music with GB, Alan Mowbray, Joan Evans

Silver Theatre (CBS):

January 21, 1940
Meet Mr. Tompkins with GB, Florence Baker

June 18, 1944
The Lady's Name Was Paris with GB, Ida Lupino

Stardom (Mutual):

June 6, 1948
GB (guest)

Stars Over Hollywood (CBS):

February 28, 1953
Meet the Hero with GB (Uncle Andy)

Suspense (CBS):

March 14, 1946
No More Alice with GB

This is Hollywood – The Hedda Hopper Show (CBS):

October 26, 1946
Lover Come Back with GB, Louise Allbritton

February 15, 1947
The Spiral Staircase with GB, Ann Todd

March 15, 1947
The Best Years of Our Lives with GB (in the Fredric March screen role), Dana Andrews, Harold Russell, Cathy O'Donnell, Margaret Muse (in the Myrna Loy screen role)

WGY Players

November 13, 1925
The Dover Road (by A. A. Milne) Ten Eyck Clay (director) Cast: Maurice Randall, Edward E. St. Louis, Rosaline Greene, Marjorie Tyler, Frank Oliver, George Nolan (staff), Phyllis Carrington

Woman of the Year (Mutual):

December 31, 1951–June 16, 1952 and September 29, 1952–October 20, 1952
Series starring Bette Davis and GB. Fred MacKaye (director), Peter Rugelo (orchestra conductor)

Your Hollywood Parade (NBC):

February 16, 1938
Gold Is Where You Find It (sketch) with GB, Olivia de Havilland, Dick Powell (host)

TELEVISION CREDITS

1953:

Crown Theatre with Gloria Swanson (ABC) (filmed February 1952) (aired September 1953)

> *A Fond Farewell* (by Arthur Ross) Host: Gloria Swanson; Director: Bernard Girard; Cast: GB (Robert Jenssen), Gertrude Michael, Donald Woods

Schlitz Playhouse (CBS) (filmed January 1953) (aired May 1953)
Medicine Woman Host: GB; Cast: GB (Sam Bentley), Andrea King, William Fawcett, Frank Jenks, Mary Ellen Kay, Donny Hyatt

Ford Television Theatre (NBC) (aired March 1953)
Double Exposure (adapted from a Ben Hecht story) Cast: GB, Dan Duryea, Marvin Kaplan, Jean Willes

Revlon Mirror Theatre (CBS) (filmed August 1953) (aired November 1953)
Key in the Lock (by James Gunn, Harold Goldman, Frederick Kohner) Director: Peter Godfrey; Cast: GB, Marguerite Chapman, Walter Coy, Dick Simmons, Byron Keith, Lois Austin

1954:

Ford Television Theatre (NBC) (filmed October 1954) (aired December 1954)
The Unbroken Promise Cast: GB, Frances Dee, Gigi Perreau, Sara Haden, Doreen Brewster

1955:

Fireside Theatre (NBC)
The Indiscreet Mrs. Jarvis (filmed September 1954) (aired January 1955) (by Frank Burt); Director, Alan Smithee; Camera, Floyd D. Crosby; Cast: GB (Paul Jarvis), Angela Lansbury, William Lundigan, Martha Vickers

Return in Triumph (aired March 1955) Cast: GB (Horatio Thomas), Gertrude Michael, Kathleen Crowley, Tyler MacDuff

It's Easy to Get Ahead (aired March 1955) Director, Frank Wizbar; Cast: GB, Marilyn Erskine, Gene Raymond, Irene Hervey

Climax! (CBS) (aired "live" February 3, 1955)

The Leaf Out of the Book (by Morton Fine, David Friedkin from book by Margaret Cousins) Director: Allen Reisner; Cast: Diana Lynn, Sylvia Sidney, GB (Harrison Winters), Hugh Beaumont, Louis Jean Heydt, Tom Powers, Linda Williams

Stage 7 (CBS) (filmed March 1955) (Originally a pilot for the series Jody and Me; aired April 1955)

The Magic Hat (by Irving Gaynor Neiman) Director, Louis R. Foster; Camera, George E. Diskant; Cast: GB (Prof. Michael Balsam), Kristine Miller, Lydia Reed, Nora Marlowe

Studio 57 (Dumont)

Death Dream (aired November 1955) Cast: GB (Paul Winterton), Lorne Greene, Lorna Thayer

Diagnosis of a Selfish Lady (aired October 1955) Cast: GB (Williams), Marguerite Chapman, Carolyn Jones, Jeanne Wood, Jerry Glick

Science Fiction Theater (ZIV)

The Long Day (aired December 1955) (by George and Gertrude Fass) Director, Paul Guilfoyle; Assistant Director, Erich von Stroheim, Jr.; Camera, Monroe Askins; Host, Truman Bradley; Cast: GB (Sam Gilmore), Steve Brodie, Jean Byron, Michael Winkelman, Michael Garth, Brad Jackson, DeForest Kelley, Addison Richards, Raymond Bailey, Carol Thurston

George Gobel Show (NBC) (aired October 1955)

GB (guest star)

1956:

Celebrity Playhouse (Syndicated) (filmed February 1956) (aired May 1956)

The Fleeting Years (from a story by Rosamund Du Jardin) Director, Danny Dare; Cast: Ann Harding, GB, May Wynn, Tristam Coffin, William Leslie

Crossroads (ABC)
The Inner Light – (filmed November 1955) (aired February 1956) Teleplay, George Bruce (from story by Irene Corbally Kuhn) Director, George Waggner; Camera, William Whitley; Cast: GB (Father Raymond), Benson Fong, Marya Marco, Keye Luke, Joseph Kim, Frank Tang, Judy Dan, George Chan

The Kid Had a Gun – (aired December 1956) Cast: GB (Father George B. Ford), Pat Conway

1956–'57:

Wire Service (ABC) Cast: GB (Dean Evans), Mercedes McCambrige, Dane Clark; Brent appeared in 13 episodes:
Campaign Train (aired October 11, 1956) (from the novel by Mildred and Gordon Gordon) Director, Tom Gries; Cast: GB, Dayton Lummis, Bartlett Robinson, Sidney Smith, Robert Burton, Harry Shannon

The Night of August 7 (aired November 1, 1956) Screenplay, Al C. Ward; Director, Alvin Ganzer; Camera, Joe Novak; Cast: GB, Paul Richards, Lee Van Cleef, Malcolm Atterbury, Virginia Gregg, Ralph Moody, Thomas Browne Henry, Joe Perry

Deported (aired November 22, 1956) Director, Tom Gries; Cast: GB, Peter Mamakos, Anthony Caruso

Deep End (aired December 13, 1956) Screenplay, Edward Miston (from a novel by Fredric Brown); Director, Tom Gries; Camera, Joe Novak; Cast: GB, Margaret Hayes, Larry Pennell, S. John Launer, Marion Burns, Robert B. Williams, Edward (Edd) Byrnes

Chicago Exclusive (aired January 3, 1957) Screenplay, Steve Fisher; Director, Alvin Ganzer; Camera, Joe Novak; Cast: GB, Fay Spain, Vaughn Taylor, Ainslie Pryor, Craig Hill, Phillip Terry

Flowers for the General (aired January 24, 1957) (Filmed in Mexico) Screenplay, Laszlo Gorog; Director, Alvin Ganzer; Camera, Carlos Carbajal; Cast: GB, Julio Villarreal, Angelica Ortiz Hartman, Pedro Galvan, Reinaldo Rivera, Andrea Palma

El Hombre (aired February 18, 1957) (Filmed in Mexico) Screenplay, Frederic Brady (from story by Richard Bluel and M.L. Lynn); Director, Alvin Ganzer; Camera, Carlos Carbajal; Cast: GB, Eduardo Noriega, Rafael Alcayde, Elvira Quintana, Claudio Brook, Pedro Galvan, Larry Gray

Forbidden Ground (aired March 11, 1957) Director, Tom Gries; Cast: GB, Barton MacLane, Terry Becker

Misfire (aired April 1, 1957) Screenplay, Daniel Mainwaring; Director, Tom Gries; Camera, Joe Novak; Cast: GB, Roy Roberts, Don Kelly, Rebecca Welles, John Hoyt, Robert Burton, James Anderson

The Oil Man (aired April 22, 1957) Cast: GB, Harry Carey, Jr., Emlen Davies, Harry Shannon

Violence Preferred (aired May 13, 1957) Screenplay, Lowell Barrington (from story by Stanley Niss); Director, Tom Gries; Camera, Joe Novak; Cast: GB, Royal Dano, Louis Jean Heydt, Paul Fix, Helen Westcott, Jean Inness

Four Minutes to Shot (aired June 3, 1957) Screenplay, Frank and Doris Hursley; Director, Tom Gries; Camera, Joe Novak; Cast: GB, Edward Binns, Gina Core, Bartlett Robinson, Peter Hansen, Victor Millan, John Sorrentino

The Nameless (aired September 9, 1957) Screenplay, Gabrielle Upton; Director, Alvin Ganzer; Camera, Joe Novak; Cast: GB, Audrey Totter, Richard Jaeckel, Philip Pine, Dennis Holmes, Judith Ames, Jack Albertson, Jim Nolan

1958:

El Coyote – (produced in 1958 – never aired) Producer: Ken Murray; Pilot and several segments for a series costarring GB (Colonel Bart Edwards), Muriel Davis, Billy Gilbert, Scotty Beckett

1959:

Rawhide (CBS – Filmed at MGM) (aired April 3, 1959)

Incident of the Chubasco – by Al C. Ward; Director, Buzz Kulik; Camera, John M. Nickolaus, Jr.; Cast: GB (Jefferson Devereaux), Eric Fleming, Clint Eastwood, Sheb Wooley, Paul Brinegar, James Murdock, Steve Raines, Rocky Shahan, John Ericson, Noah Beery, Olive Sturgess, Stacy Harris

You and the Law – (produced in 1959 - never aired) Producer, Norman Hermann; GB starred in a pilot for the five-minute series

1960:

The Chevy Mystery Show (NBC) (aired July 24, 1960)
I Know What I'd Have Done – by Charles Larson; Director, Marc Daniels; Host, Walter Slezak; Cast: GB (Fred Girard), Maggie Hayes, Nancy Rennick, Peter Walker, Ann Seymour, Charles Meredith, Susan Davis, Paul Mazursky, Vanessa Brown

1961:

Sports Unlimited (NBC San Diego, Channel 10) (aired June 1, 1961)
Host, Lute Mason; GB (guest) gives preview of the Rancho Santa Fe horse show

2013:

Reabhloidithe Hollywood – "Hollywood Rebels" (TG-4 Ireland) (aired December 28, 2013)
Irish television documentary juxtaposing the careers of Irish actors associated with the IRA: George Brent and Arthur Shields. Director, Brian Reddin; Interviews (in order of appearance): Ruth Barton, Briona Nic Dhiarmada, Adrian Frazier, Aindria O'Cathasaigh, Scott O'Brien, Suzanne Brent, Barry Brent, Fiach Mac Conghail, Sean O'Mahoney, Christine Shields, Robert McMillen, Leonard Maltin, Marc Wannamaker; includes scenes from *Female* (1933), *Baby Face* (1933), *Jezebel* (1938), *Dark Victory* (1939), *'Til We Meet Again* (1940), *The Great Lie* (1941), and *Mexican Manhunt* (1953)

Photo Credits

Every effort has been made to trace the copyright holders of photographs in this book; if any have been inadvertently overlooked, the author and publisher will be pleased to make the necessary changes.

All Warner Bros./First National photos © Warner Bros. Entertainment Inc. Co. All Rights Reserved

All MGM and Eagle-Lion photos © Metro-Goldwyn-Mayer Studios Inc. All Rights Reserved

All 20th Century-Fox photos © 20th Century-Fox Film Corp. All Rights Reserved

All Paramount and Republic photos © Paramount Pictures. All Rights Reserved

All Columbia photos Columbia Pictures-Sony Entertainment. All Rights Reserved

All Universal photos © Universal Studios. All Rights Reserved

All RKO photos © RKO Pictures LLC. All Rights Reserved

All Allied Artists photos © Allied Artists Int. Inc. All Rights Reserved

All Lippert photos © Lippert Productions. All Rights Reserved

All other photos, unless otherwise noted, are from the author's collection. The author would like to express his thanks to the following individuals: Brian Reddin, Ian Watson, Jenny Paxon and Larry Smith, Howard Mandelbaum (of Photofest).

(Front cover – top row) Claudette Colbert, Barbara Stanwyck, Merle Oberon, Bette Davis, Myrna Loy, Kay Francis

(Front cover – bottom row) Greta Garbo, Olivia de Havilland, Ann Sheridan, Hedy Lamarr, Loretta Young, Ruth Chatterton

About the Author

Scott O'Brien has written four film biographies on Hollywood leading ladies: Kay Francis, Virginia Bruce, Ann Harding, and Ruth Chatterton. He has contributed articles for *Films of the Golden Age, Classic Images,* and *Filmfax.* O'Brien has done interviews for classic cinema blogs: TCM's *Movie Morlocks, Silver Screen Oasis, Let's Misbehave,* and *Close-Ups and Long Shots.* His guest appearances include the San Francisco Silent Film Festival, KRCB's *Outbeat Radio* and *A Novel Idea, Yesterday USA Radio,* as well as Jan Wahl's "Inside Entertainment" for KRON-TV in the Bay Area. He has introduced the film classics *Trouble in Paradise* (1932) and *Double Harness* (1933) at the Library of Congress's Packard Theater in Culpeper, Va. Scott has appeared in two film documentaries: *Queer Icon – the Cult of Bette Davis* (2009) and *Reabhloidithe Hollywood* (2013) chronicling the careers of Irish actors George Brent and Arthur Shields. Scott lives with his partner Joel Bellagio in Sonoma County. (website: www.scottobrienauthor.com)

(Endnotes)

Endnotes: Introduction

1   George Brent, "Without a Shirt," *The Milwaukee Journal*, June 12, 1938

2   One of the first studio generated publicity stories, "The Real-Life Story of George Brent," appeared as a two-part series in *Screenland* (September-October 1932). It was written by Warner press agent Carlisle Jones. Filled with misinformation, the article refers to George's deceased parents as John and Mary Brent and extends his position as a dispatcher for the IRA from a few months to two years.

3   Barry Paris, *Garbo: A Biography*, Alfred A. Knopf, NY © 1995, p. 313

4   Ted Magee, "What George Brent Thinks of Women," *Hollywood*, March 1936

5   James Robert Parish, *Hollywood's Great Love Teams*, Arlington House, NY, p. 196

6   Kay Francis, diary, January 5, 1935, Kay Francis collection, Wesleyan Cinema Archives, Wesleyan University, Middletown, CT

7   ⁷ Clifford Terry, "Domesticated Ladies – Why the Often Sappy 'Woman's Film' Wasn't Such a Bad Thing," *Chicago Tribune*, October 10, 1993

8   Nancy Anderson, "Brent, Still Debonair, Coaxed Back to Work," *North Tonawanda Evening News*, June 2, 1978

9   Samuel Richard Mook, "Liar, Pest and Nitwit," *Picture Play*, January 1936

10   Samuel Richard Mook, "Liar, Pest and Nitwit," *Picture Play*, January 1936

11   Dan Camp, "Take Me Away From It All!" *Motion Picture*, November 1938

12   Elizabeth Wilson (a.k.a. "Liza"), "Why the Sheridan-Brent Marriage Failed," *Screenland*, January 1943

13   Elizabeth Wilson (a.k.a. "Liza"), "Why the Sheridan-Brent Marriage Failed," *Screenland*, January 1943

Endnotes: Chapter 1

14   Gladys Hall, "They told George Brent that he was going *blind!*" *Movie Classic*, September 1932

15   Brent's birth certificate #4666252. Born: George Patrick Nolan, March 15, 1904, to John and Mary McGuiness Nolan, Ballinasloe. Brendan was added later on.

16   New York Passenger Lists-arrival September 20, 1915, *S.S. Philadelphia*

17   Brent's mention of his dead parents was in many articles. A partial list includes:

September 1932 (*Movie Classic*) "My father, a newspaperman, had died when I was two ..."

December 1939 (*Modern Screen*) "George and his sister Peggy had been sent here when they were orphaned ..."

February 1940 (*Motion Picture*) "When he was 7, his father died ... When he was 15, his mother died."

April 1940 (*Silver Screen*) "Orphaned at eleven ... sent to live with an aunt in New York"

September 13, 1942 (*Ogden Standard Examiner*) "His father died when he was seven years old and his mother, when he was 11"

October 1972 (*Film Fan Monthly*) "He was eleven when his parents died ..."

1975 (*The Debonairs*) "When George was seven his father died suddenly. Four years later his mother passed away."

18   Birth Certificate, registered April 21, 1904, #4666252, Ballinasloe (Birth date: March 15, 1904, Main Street)

19   Marriage Certificate #36: February 11, 1892, in Ballinasloe, Roscommon. John Nolan (a farmer, age 26), Mary McGuinness (age 16 ½) both resided in Shannonbridge, Cloonfad.

20   The U.S. Census of 1920 confirms that Mary Nolan, age 44, immigrated to the U.S. in 1905. She had been accompanied by her daughter Mary and son John (Jack).

21   Email from Brian Reddin, dated May 9, 2012

22   Email from Brian Reddin, dated May 27, 2012

23   Barry Lally, "The Story of Three Georges," *Ballinasloe Life*, October/November 2012 [note: George's sister Lucy indicated on her 1913 passenger list that her Grandfather McGuinness lived in Clonfad, Roscommon, Ireland—however, Clonfad is in County Offaly; Cloonfad is in County Roscommon]

24   Alien Passenger List for the United States, November 6, 1913, sailing on the *S.S. Cedric* from Liverpool, arriving in New York on November 15, 1913

25   James Reid, "Hollywood's Champion Lone Wolf," *Motion Picture*, February 1940

26   Thornton Sargent, "The Nine Hectic Lives of George Brent," *Oakland Tribune*, May 19, 1935

27   "Brent Wants Race Winner More Than He Wants Oscar," *Los Angeles Times*, May 6, 1962

28   "De Mar's Loss Is Ireland's Gain," *San Diego Union*, May 20, 1966

29   James Robert Parish and Don E. Stanke, *The Debonairs*, Arlington House, NY, © 1975, p. 56

30   New York Census (June 1, 1915) John J. Nolan, age 20 was listed in the U.S. Army; Mary, age 22, a telephone operator, Lucy, age 17, a checker, and head of the household, Mary Nolan, age 39, a housekeeper

31   "'Strong, Silent Man' Brent Refuses to be Drawn," *Salt Lake Tribune*, February 14, 1937

32   Charles Grayson, "Is George Brent Another Gable?" *Motion Picture*, June 1932 (The *American National Biography* lists the schools that George Nolan attended as: Dwight School, High School of Commerce, and Rand School of Social Science. It also states that Nolan attended the National University of Ireland, which is untrue)

33   Alice Pardoe West, "Irish Adventures Prime Brent for Soldier Role," *Ogden Standard Examiner*, September 13, 1942

34   Helen Louise Walker, "If I Had My Life To Live Over," *Silver Screen*, April 1940 (*Film Daily* in 1963 reported that Brent had attended Dwight Preparatory School in New York)

35   Gladys Hall, "They told George Brent that he was going *blind!*" *Movie Classic*, September 1932

36   U.S. census of 1920 (January). Lucile Nolan was listed as being a model. Robert Fletcher, age 1 year, 3 months, was listed as being the grandson of Mary Nolan, age 44; George Nolan, age 15, was neither in school nor working

37   In the 1940 U.S. Census, Mary, age 46, a widow. Son Robert, age 21, a laborer, was residing with her in a rental on Seventh Avenue, Brooklyn. There was also a lodger, David Fox, age 48, a native Irishman

38   In the 1940 U.S. Census Mary listed herself as a widow

39   Helen Louise Walker, "If I Had My Life To Live Over," *Silver Screen*, April 1940

40   A.I. Tobin, Elmer Gertz, *Frank Harris: A Study in Black and White*," Ardent Media, © 1931, p. 234

41   A.I. Tobin, Elmer Gertz, *Frank Harris: A Study in Black and White*," Ardent Media, © 1931, p. 118

42   John Dos Passos, "Frank Harris – The Bomb," © 1963, The Anarchist Library, http://theanarchistli-brary.org/library/frank-harris-the-bomb

43   "Frank Harris," obituary, *Springfield Republican*, September 3, 1931

44   Alice Pardoe West, "Irish Adventures Prime Brent for Soldier Role," *Ogden Standard Examiner*, September 13, 1942

45   Alice Pardoe West, "Irish Adventures Prime Brent for Soldier Role," *Ogden Standard Examiner*, September 13, 1942

46   Gladys Hall, "They told George Brent that he was going *blind!*" *Movie Classic*, September 1932

47   William Butler Yeats, "Nineteen Hundred and Nineteen," *The Tower*, Scribner edition, © 2004, p. 37

48   UK Incoming Passenger List, New York to Liverpool, February 7, 1921- George lists his age as 22

49   Buck Herzog, "Along Amusement Row," *Milwaukee Sentinel*, July 19, 1934

50   Brain Reddin, email sent May 27, 2012

51   Herbert Cruikshank, "The Inside Story of the Ruth Chatterton-George Brent Romance," *Modern Screen*, October 1932

52   Charles Grayson, "Is George Brent Another Gable?" *Motion Picture*, June 1932

53   Brian Reddin, email sent February 7, 2013

54   James Robert Parish and Don E. Stanke, *The Debonairs*, Arlington House, © 1975, p. 24

55   Alice L. Tildesley, "Best Slappers Become Rivals of Clark Gable," *Oakland Tribune*, August 14, 1932

56   Gwen Dew, "A Spy In Hollywood," *Picture Play Magazine*, October 1938

57   Thornton Sargent, "The Nine Hectic Lives of George Brent," *Oakland Tribune*, May 19, 1935

58   Gwen Dew, "A Spy In Hollywood," *Picture Play Magazine*, October 1938

59   Thornton Sargent, "The Nine Hectic Lives of George Brent," *Oakland Tribune*, May 19, 1935

60   Joseph McKenna, *Guerilla Warfare in the Irish War for Independence*, McFarland, © 2011, p. 107

61   David Thomson, *The New Biographical Dictionary of Film*, Random House, © 2008, p. 117

62   Gwen Dew, "A Spy In Hollywood," *Picture Play Magazine*, October 1938

63   Lowell Thomas, "Hollywood's Soldiers of Fortune," *Photoplay*, October 1938

64   Lucie Neville, "What Can They Say About A Nice Guy Like Me?" *Seattle Daily Times*, July 16, 1939

65   Alice Pardoe West, "Irish Adventures Prime Brent for Soldier Role," *Ogden Standard Examiner*, September 13, 1942

66   Thornton Sargent, "The Nine Hectic Lives of George Brent," *Oakland Tribune*, May 19, 1935

67   Gwen Dew, "A Spy In Hollywood," *Picture Play Magazine*, October 1938

68   U.S. Petition for Naturalization #55766, District Court of U.S. at Los Angeles 1937 (Brent designated the August 22, 1921, date as his last entry into the U.S. for permanent residency)

69   (August 1921) Border Crossing information Class B Seaport of landing: Montreal; border crossing: Rouses Point. He then headed to St. Albans, Vermont; for more processing; Kathleen was residing at 540 West 157th Street, NY; George Nolan noted that he was born in Ballinasloe, Ireland. In 1935, the U.S. Department of Labor wired information (#23-35183) re: Brent's 8/22/1921 arrival at Rouse's Point for naturalization purposes; to confuse matters, Brent also indicated on his naturalization papers that he immigrated from the port of Cherbourg, France, and that his last foreign residence was Paris.

70   Barry Lally, "The Story of the Three Georges," *Ballinasloe Life*, October/November 2012

71   Barry Brent, *Hollywood Rebels* (2013), Irish TV documentary

72   Fred Watkins, "George Brent," *Film Fan Monthly*, October 1972

73   U.S. Census, Los Angeles (April, 1930) Brent listed as "George B. Nolan" lodger, born in the "Irish Free State;" U.S. Census, Los Angeles (April, 1940) Brent again said he was born in the "Irish Free State"

74   Helen Louise Walker, "If I Had My Life To Live Over," *Silver Screen*, April 1940

75   George Brent, "Without a Shirt," *The Milwaukee Journal*, June 12, 1938

76   Frank Gordon, *The Irish Digest*, Volume 68, 1960, p. 156 (Costello also fought on the anti-treaty side of the Irish Civil War, driving cars loaded with arms and ammunition)

77   Ruth Waterbury, "Close-Ups and Long Shots," *Photoplay*, May 1939

78   Duncan Underhill, "Hollywood Newsreel," *Hollywood*, April 1941

Endnotes: Chapter 2

79   Alice L. Tildesley, "Best Slappers Become Rivals of Clark Gable," *Oakland Tribune*, August 14, 1932

80   "College Graduates with 'The Dover Road,' " *Evening Telegram*, March 31, 1922

81   Marsh, review of *The Dover Road*, *Plain Dealer*, November 8, 1922

82   Hart, review of *The Sheik's Love*, February 15, 1923

83   Arthur J. Busch comment, *Variety*, September 13 & 20, 1923

84   Jack Grant, "Shooting at Hollywood," *Movie Classic*, March 1935

85   "St. Louis Company," *Variety*, May 20, 1925

86   Ralph De Toledano, *Frontiers of Jazz*, Pelican, © 1994, p. 129 (reissue of 1947 publication)

87   Jack Grant, "Shooting at Hollywood," *Movie Classic*, March 1935

88   Jack Grant, "Shooting at Hollywood," *Movie Classic*, March 1935

89   Evelyn F. Scott, *Hollywood When Silents Were Golden*, McGraw-Hill, © 1972, p. 185 (Evelyn's mother was screenwriter Beulah Marie Dix)

90   Review for *Abie's Irish Rose*, *World-Herald* (Omaha), August 3, 1925

91   *Abie's Irish Rose*, *Variety*, May 20, 1925

92   "Long Runs Wear Off Atmosphere of Stage," *Sunday World-Herald* (Omaha), August 23, 1925

93   "A Leading Man's Kiss," *Variety*, May 11, 1927

94   Fred Watkins, "George Brent," *Film Fan Monthly*, October 1972

95   Helen Louise Walker, "If I Had My Life To Live Over," *Silver Screen*, April 1940

96   "Marriages," *Variety*, October 26, 1927 (The announcement of George and Helen's wedding mentioned his position at the Strand, which featured both stage shows and movies until 1929)

97   Review of *Seventh Heaven*, *Springfield Weekly Republican*, September 8, 1927

98   "Marriages," *Variety*, October 26, 1927

99   James Robert Parish and Don E. Stanke, *The Debonairs*, Arlington House, © 1975, p. 24

100 A.R.D. review for *Up in Mabel's Room*, *The Evening Independent*, February 7, 1928

101   K.L.J., "Plaza Show is Solid Laughter," *St. Petersburg Times*, February 21, 1928

102   Thornton Sargent, "The Nine Hectic Lives of George Brent," *Oakland Tribune*, May 19, 1935

103   Fred Watkins, "George Brent," *Film Fan Monthly*, October 1972

104   "No Comedy Company Shall Advertise Its Wares In My Church," *Cleveland Leader*, April 22, 1903

105   U.S. Census 1910 shows Helen Campbell (Cambell) living with her grandparents Mr. and Mrs. W.T. Lewis in Zanesville, Ohio

106   "Helen Lewis, Guest Star at Weller, is Zanesville Girl," *Times Recorder* (OH), January 3, 1930

107   George A. Benson, "Helen Lewis Fine Actress," *Grand Forks Herald*, January 25, 1921

108   "She Should Worry," *The Baltimore Sun*, January 5, 1919

109   Ruth Biery, "Two New Screen Personalities," *Photoplay*, June 1932

110   Gladys Hall, "They told George Brent that he was going *blind*!" *Movie Classic*, September 1932

111   U.S. Census Los Angeles 1930 (April) listed George B. Nolan, motion picture actor, as still being married. Several news items mention that his divorce was finalized in Los Angeles 1929-30 ("George Brent First Married In This City," *Hartford Courant*, August 21, 1932)

112   William J. Mann, *Kate: The Woman Who Was Hepburn*, Macmillan, © 2007, p. 131

113   Sheridan Morley, *Katharine Hepburn: A Celebration*, Hal Leonard Corp., © 1999, p. 17

114   Richard S. Davis, "Elmer Found Full of Humor," *The Milwaukee Journal*, December 3, 1928

115   C. Pannill Mead, "Miss Crosman Alone Makes Finished Play-Thin Plot Is Saved by Acting of Star and George Brent," *Milwaukee Sentinel*, February 25, 1929

116   Cyrus F. Rice, "Town Talent Parade," *Milwaukee Sentinel*, March 4, 1951

117   "Stocks Opening," *Variety*, April 10, 1929

118   Elza Schallert, "'The Royal Family of Hollywood' Now," *Motion Picture*, September 1932

119   Gladys Hall, "They told George Brent that he was going *blind*!" *Movie Classic*, September 1932

120   Charles Denton, "Stars of TV's *Wire Service* Naturals," *Mansfield News Journal*, March 17, 1957

121   Jack Gurtler, *The Elitch Gardens Story*, Rocky Mountain Guild, © 1982 p. 69

122   "All Kinds of Shows are Preparing to Descend Upon Broadway," *New York Times*, October 27, 1929

123   Evelyn F. Scott, *Hollywood When Silents Were Golden*, McGraw-Hill, 1972, p. 185

124   California Birth Index: Patrick's birth name was Marcel Draguseianu (his director/father used De Sano as a professional name), born September 21, 1923

125   "Wedding Bells Ring When She Says 'Yes'," *Brooklyn Daily Eagle*, August 5, 1928

126   Joseph E. Greenidge, review of *Those We Love*, *Daily Star*, February 4, 1930

127   Review for *Those We Love*, *Brooklyn Daily Eagle*, February 4, 1930

128   Charles Grayson, "Is George Brent Another Gable?" *Motion Picture*, June 1932

129   Weintraub, review of *The Fatal Woman*, *Variety*, February 26, 1930

130   J. Brooks Atkinson, review of *Love, Honor and Betray*, *New York Times*, March 13, 1930

131   Arthur Pollock, review of *Love, Honor and Betray*, *Brooklyn Daily Eagle*, March 4, 1930

132   Betty L. Hull, *Denver's Elitch Gardens: Spinning a Century of Dreams*, Big Earth Pub., © 2003, p. 86

133   "Woods Recalls Brent," *Variety*, August 6, 1930

134   "Sheehan's Unique Record for Handling All Fox's Production Work ," *Variety*, April 16, 1930

135   "Along the Rialto," *Film Daily*, April 10, 1930

136   U.S. Census (April 9, 1930) George Brent listed his profession as "Motion Picture Actor"

137   George Brent, handwritten letter sent to Jane Broder c/o Roosevelt Hotel, New York (no date given) (copy from author's collection)

138   George Brent Western Union Cable sent to Jane Broder August 15, 1930 (copy from author's collection)

139   "Woods Recalls Brent," *Variety*, August 5, 1930

Endnotes: Chapter 3

140   Fred Watkins, "George Brent," *Film Fan Monthly*, October 1972

141   Perc Westmore, "Secrets of the Make-Up Room," *Modern Screen*, May 1934 (Chatterton's remark was actually, "Perc, where has this man been all my life?" Westmore had done Brent's makeup for the test. It was Westmore who would accompany Brent to Chatterton's dressing room for their first meeting)

142   Red Kann, review of *Under Suspicion*, *Motion Picture News*, November 22, 1930

143   Review for *Under Suspicion*, *Chicago Daily Tribune*, February 2, 1931

144   Don Ashbaugh, review of *Fair Warning*, *Motion Picture News*, November 1, 1930

145   Louella Parsons column, *Rochester Evening Journal*, November 1, 1930

146   *Charlie Chan Carries On* is a lost film. Lines taken from the shooting script, dated December 23, 1930

147   "Gilda to Wed," *Capital Times* (WI), December 13, 1930

148   "Von Stroheim Says Ideal Picture Embraces, Color, Width, Dimension," *Film Daily*, October 8, 1930

149   Ruth Biery, "Two New Screen Personalities," *Photoplay*, June 1932

150   Mae Tinee, "Movie College Girl Prefers 'Ex-Bad Boy'," *Chicago Daily Tribune*, August 1, 1931

151   *Hollywood Citizen News*, June 4, 1931

152   John Scott, "Police Win In Picture At R.K.O.," *Los Angeles Times*, October 24, 1931

153   U.S. Census (April 21, 1910) Mary Michalski (Gilda's adopted name) gave her age as 14 (her birthday was October 24, 1895)

154   Karl K. Kitchen, "What Are 'The Blues?' Ask Gilda Gray," *New Orleans State*, September 21, 1919

155   Gilbert Seldes, "True to Type," *Syracuse Journal*, July 1, 1931

156   U.S. World War I Draft registration (June 3, 1917) Gilda's first husband, John Gorecki, listed their son Martin as being four years old

157   "Gilda Gray's Husband Accuses the Actress," *Omaha World Herald*, December 22, 1928

158   "Gilda Gray Wins Divorce, Calling Gil Ungrateful Sot," *Standard Union* (NY), January 14, 1929

159   "Gilda Gray Near Death," *Plain Dealer*, June 28, 1931

160   Gilda Gray, "My Soul Danced," *San Antonio Light*, December 30, 1945

161   James Robert Parish and Don E. Stanke, *The Debonairs*, Arlington House, © 1975, p. 26

162   Charles Grayson, "Is George Brent Another Gable?" *Motion Picture*, June 1932

163   "Coming and Going," *Film Daily*, October 15, 1931

164   Gilda Gray, "My Soul Danced," *San Antonio Light*, December 30, 1945

165   Walter Winchell, "On Broadway," June 30, 1931

166   John Tuska, *The Vanishing Legion: A History of Mascot Pictures*, McFarland, © 1999, p. 47

167   Susan Orlean, *Rin Tin Tin: The Life and the Legend*, Simon and Schuster, © 2012, p. 110 (Rumor had it that Rin Tin Tin died in the arms of Jean Harlow. In his memoirs, his owner, Lee Duncan, simply stated that he found the dying canine star lying on the ground.)

168   Georgia Hale, *Charlie Chaplin: Intimate Close-Ups*, Scarecrow Press, © 1995, p. 150

169   Fred Watkins, "George Brent," *Film Fan Monthly*, October 1972

170   Cruikshank, "The Inside Story of the Ruth Chatterton-George Brent Romance," *Modern Screen*, October 1932

171   James Robert Parish, "George Brent" from *The Debonairs*, Arlington House, NY, © 1975, p. 26

172   Norbert Lusk, review of *So Big*, *Picture Play*, July 1932

173   Emma Keats, review of *So Big*, *Richmond Times-Dispatch* (VA), April 30, 1932

174   Elizabeth Yeaman column, *Hollywood Citizen News*, March 10, 1932

175   James Spada, More than a *Woman: An Intimate Biography of Bette Davis*, Bantam, © 1993, p. 90

176   Margaret Talbot, *The Entertainer*, Riverhead Books, © 2012, p. 194

177   Lawrence J. Quirk, *Fasten Your Seat Belts: The Passionate Life of Bette Davis*, William Morrow, © 1990, p. 53

178   Cruikshank, "The Inside Story of the Ruth Chatterton-George Brent Romance," *Modern Screen*, October 1932

179   Ralph Wilk, "A Little From the Lots," *Film Daily*, February 8, 1932

180   Bette Davis, *The Lonely Life*, Putnam, © 1962, pp. 124-125

181   James Spada, *More than a Woman: An Intimate Biography of Bette Davis*, Bantam, © 1993, p. 90

182   Bette Davis, *The Lonely Life*, Putnam, © 1962, pp. 124-125

183   Whitney Stine, *Mother Goddam*, Hawthorne Books, © 1974, p. 28

184   James Spada, *More Than a Woman: An Intimate Biography of Bette Davis*, Bantam, © 1993 p. 90

185   Norbert Lusk, review of *The Rich Are Always With Us*, *Picture Play*, August 1932

186   Mordaunt Hall, review of *The Rich Are Always With Us*, *The New York Times*, May 16, 1932

187   Elizabeth Yeaman, review of *The Rich Are Always With Us*, *Hollywood Citizen News*, May 13, 1932

188   Review of *The Rich Are Always With Us*, *Screenland*, July 1932

189   William K. Everson, *The Detective in Film*, Citadel Press, © 1972, p. 132

190   Jerry Hoffman, review of *Miss Pinkerton*, July 1, 1932

191   Review of *Weekend Marriage*, *Motion Picture*, August 1932

192   Elsie Randall, "Ruth Marries George And Everybody's Happy," *Movie Classic*, October 1932

193   Elsie Randall, "Ruth Marries George And Everybody's Happy," *Movie Classic*, October 1932

194   "Eats Her Meat Raw," *Seattle Daily Times*, August 12, 1932

195   Elsie Randall, "Ruth Marries George And Everybody's Happy," *Movie Classic*, October 1932

196   "Gilda Gray Talks Back to Father," *Seattle Daily Times*, August 12, 1932

197   Mordaunt Hall, review of *They Call It Sin*, *New York Times*, October 21, 1932

198   James Roy Fuller, "Ask Chatterton," *Picture Play*, November 1932

199   Faulkner's book was filmed as *The Story of Temple Drake* (1933) starring Miriam Hopkins

200   Dorothy Manners, "What Has Marriage Done to George Brent?" *Motion Picture*, February 1933

201   Charles Grayson, "Is George Brent Another Gable?" *Motion Picture*, June 1932

202   Charles Grayson, "Is George Brent Another Gable?" *Motion Picture*, June 1932

203   Ben Maddox, "George Brent from Dublin," *Silver Screen*, May 1932

204   Cruikshank, "The Inside Story of the Ruth Chatterton-George Brent Romance," *Modern Screen*, October 1932

205   Jerry Lane, "Loretta Young's Romantic Secrets," *Movie Classic*, July 1935

Endnotes: Chapter 4

206   "Warner Bros. for 1932-33!" *Film Daily* insert, June 7, 1932

207   "News and Gossips of the Studios," *Motion Picture*, September 1932

208   Mark Dowling, "They Name Their Next Mates Before They're Free From Ex-Mates," *Motion Picture*, November 1932

209   "Ruth Chatterton Marries George Brent on Same Day She Hears of Divorce," *Syracuse Herald*, August 13, 1932 (in this article Ruth claimed her rendezvous with Rex Smith was arranged three years beforehand, but Smith's assignment to Madrid wasn't until 1931. His previous assignment was in France.)

210   Jessie Royce Landis, *You Won't Be So Pretty*, W.H. Allen, London, © 1954, pp. 121-123

211   Adela Rogers St. Johns, "The Men in Ruth Chatterton's Life," *Liberty*, January 20, 1934

212   "Ruth Chatterton Weds George Brent," *New York Times*, August 14, 1932

213   Gladys Hall, "Ruth Chatterton's Own Story of Her Second Marriage," *Motion Picture*, January 1933

214   Gladys Hall, "Ruth Chatterton's Own Story of Her Second Marriage," *Motion Picture*, January 1933

215   Adela Rogers St. Johns, "The Men in Ruth Chatterton's Life," *Liberty*, January 20, 1934

216   Andre Sennwald, review of *The Purchase Price*, *New York Times*, July 16, 1932

217   Sheilah Graham, *San Francisco Chronicle*, October 14, 1936

218   Norbert Lusk, review of *The Purchase Price*, *Picture Play*, October 1932

219   Elizabeth Yeaman, review of *The Crash*, *Hollywood Citizen News*, October 21, 1932

220   Norbert Lusk, review of *The Crash*, *Picture Play*, December 1932

221   Review of *The Crash*, *Film Daily*, September 9, 1932

222   Nancy Pryor, "Yankee Doodle Dandy is in the Movies Now," *Movie Classic*, September 1932

223   Ann V. Masters, "Ruth Chatterton Steps Again Before the Footlights," *Bridgeport Post*, August 21, 1955

224   James Robert Parish and Don E. Stanke, *The Debonairs*, Arlington House, © 1975, p. 29

225   Review of *Luxury Liner, Hollywood Reporter,* January 14, 1933

226   James Reid, "Hollywood's Champion Lone Wolf," *Motion Picture,* February 1940

227   James Robert Parish and Don E. Stanke, *The Debonairs,* Arlington House, © 1975, p. 31

228   Eric L. Ergenbright, "The Strange Case of George Brent," *Picture Play,* December 1933

229   Jerry Lane, "He's Jinx-Proof Now," *Photoplay,* November 1934

230   Review of *The Keyhole, Film Daily,* March 31, 1933

231   Elizabeth Yeaman, review of *The Keyhole, Hollywood Citizen News,* April 14, 1933

232   Jerry Hoffman, review of *The Keyhole, Los Angeles Examiner,* April 14, 1933

233   Margaret Talbot, *The Entertainer,* Riverhead Books, © 2012, p. 190

234   "Ruth Chatterton Revising 'West of Broadway,' " *Boston Herald,* March 13, 1939

235   Harry Lang, "Why George Brent Shuns Romance," *Movie Classic,* August 1936

236   Louella Parsons, "Chatterton Brent," *Syracuse Herald,* June 7, 1933

237   Ben Maddox, "The Lady Talks Back," *Screenland,* January 1936

238   Louis Sheaffer, "Curtain Time," *Brooklyn Eagle,* May 22, 1951

239   "Ruth Chatterton Seriously Ill," *Montana Butte Standard,* June 17, 1933

240   Walter Addiego, "A Wealth of Pre-Code Wellman," *San Francisco Chronicle,* April 12, 2009

241   Conversation with William Wellman, Jr., San Francisco Silent Film Festival, July 21, 2013

242   Review of *Lilly Turner, Hollywood Reporter,* April 20, 1933

243   Review of *Lilly Turner, Film Daily,* June 15, 1933

244   Harriet Parsons, review of *Lilly Turner, Los Angeles Examiner,* June 2, 1933

245   Eleanor Barnes, review of *Lilly Turner, Illustrated Daily News,* June 2, 1933

246   Review of *Baby Face, Film Daily,* June 24, 1933

247   James Robert Parish and Don E. Stanke, *The Debonairs,* Arlington House, © 1975, p. 29

248   "Goldwyn After Brent," *Film Daily,* June 10, 1933

249   Review of *From Headquarters, Photoplay,* December 1933

250   Review of *From Headquarters, Los Angeles Evening Herald Express,* December 15, 1933

251   James Robert Parish and Don E. Stanke, *The Debonairs,* Arlington House, © 1975, p. 31

252   Ralph Wilk, "A 'Little' from Hollywood 'Lots,' " *Film Daily,* October 16, 1933

253   "Brent-Warner Trial Technical Battle," *Hollywood Reporter,* February 24, 1934

254   Dickson Morley, "Parts They Craved—and Lost," *Picture Play,* August 1934

255   Eric L. Ergenbright, "The Strange Case of George Brent," *Picture Play,* August 1933

256   Eric L. Ergenbright, "The Strange Case of George Brent," *Picture Play,* December 1933

257   "Brent Suspended In Row With Warners," *Hollywood Reporter,* January 5, 1934

258   Jack Grant, "Why the Chatterton-Brent Love Died," *Movie Mirror,* June 1934

259   Jack Grant, "Why the Chatterton-Brent Love Died," *Movie Mirror,* June 1934

Endnotes: Chapter 5

260　"Shivering Fans Get An Icy Turndown From Ruth Chatterton," *Albuquerque Journal*, March 19, 1934

261　"Ruth Chatterton Denies Separation," *Corsicana Daily* (TX), March 20, 1934

262　"Ruth Chatterton and George Brent Separate," *Telegraph-Herald and Times Journal*, March 27, 1934

263　"George Brent Blames Career For Discord," *Nevada State Journal*, March 29, 1934

264　Lucie Neville, "What Can They Say About A Nice Guy Like Me?" *Seattle Daily Times*, July 16, 1939

265　Jerry Lane, "He's Jinx-Proof Now," *Photoplay*, November 1934

266　Larry Cohen, "I Killed Bette Davis," *Film Comment*, 2012

267　Mordaunt Hall, review of *Female*, *New York Times*, November 4, 1933

268　Jimmy Starr, review of *Female*, *Los Angeles Evening Herald Express*, October 14, 1933

269　Mick LaSalle, *Complicated Women*, St. Martin's Press, © 2000, p. 81

270　Conversation with William Wellman, Jr. (his father's notebooks indicate he completed approximately 17 scenes – mostly exterior shots), San Francisco Silent Film Festival, July 21, 2013

271　James Robert Parish and Don E. Stanke, *The Debonairs*, Arlington House, © 1975, p. 31

272　"Ruth Chatterton Granted Divorce From Geo. Brent," *Lewiston Daily Sun*, October 3, 1934

273　Walter Clausen, "Noted Actress Given Divorce in Los Angeles," *Schenectady Gazette*, October 5, 1934

274　"Ruth Chatterton Granted Decree, Says Actor Domineering," *The Border Cities Star*, October 4, 1934

275　Eric L. Ergenbright, "The Strange Case of George Brent," *Picture Play Magazine*, December 1933

276　Franc Dillon, "George Brent Is On His Own Now—And Likes It," *Movie Classic*, October 1934

277　"George Brent Sues Film Company," *Los Angeles Evening Herald Express*, January 6, 1934

278　Jerry Lane, "He's Jinx-Proof Now," *Photoplay*, November 1934

279　Clive Hirschhorn, *The Warner Bros. Story*, Crown Pub., © 1979, p. 144

280　Review of *Housewife*, *Film Daily*, August 11, 1934

281　Bill Kelly, "George Brent in 'Born Again' Role," *Santa Ana Orange County Register*, May 28, 1978

282　James Robert Parish and Don E. Stanke, *The Debonairs*, Arlington House, © 1975, p. 32

283　Myrna Loy, James Kotsilibas-David, *Myrna Loy-Being and Becoming*, Alfred A. Knopf, 1987, p. 93

284　Ted Magee, "What George Brent Thinks of Women," *Hollywood*, March 1936

285　Norbert Lusk, review of *Stamboul Quest*, *Picture Play*, October 1934

286　Review of *Stamboul Quest*, *Hollywood Filmograph*, July 7, 1934

287　"Automobile Crash Followed By Suit," *The Van Nuys News*, June 14, 1934

288　"Hollywood Day By Day," *New Movie*, July 1934

289　"Telling on Hollywood," *San Antonio Express*, July 10, 1934

290　Thornton Sargent, "The Nine Lives of George Brent," *Oakland Tribune*, May 19, 1935 (article was a collection of several incidents where fate had stepped into Brent's life)

291　Mae Tinee, "George Brent Outshines Muir in Desirable," Chicago *Daily Tribune*, December 18, 1934

292　Mollie Merrick, "George Brent Doesn't Talk and Neither Does Greta Garbo," *Dallas Morning News*, November 11, 1934

293   Louella Parsons column, *Los Angeles Examiner*, August 10, 1934

294   Hal Hall, "Garbo Fear," *Motion Picture*, April 1935

295   Andre Sennwald, review of *The Painted Veil*, *New York Times*, December 7, 1934

296   Mollie Merrick, "George Brent Doesn't Talk and Neither Does Greta Garbo," *Dallas Morning News*, November 11, 1934

297   Ted Magee, "What George Brent Thinks of Women," *Hollywood*, March 1936

298   Fred Watkins, "George Brent," *Film Fan Monthly*, October 1972

299   Madge Kelly, "From the Desk," *Filmograph*, September 15, 1934

300   Elizabeth Yeaman column, *Hollywood Citizen News*, September 6, 1934

301   Franc Dillon, "George Brent Is On His Own Now—And Likes It," *Movie Classic*, October 1934

302   Mollie Merrick, "George Brent Doesn't Talk and Neither Does Greta Garbo," *Dallas Morning News*, November 11, 1934

303   Barry Paris, *Garbo*, Alfred A. Knopf, © 1995, p. 315

304   Smith, Alex D., "Lonely Garbo's Love Secret is Exposed," *The Observer* (London), September 10, 2005 (note on MGM paper written 1929-30)

305   Smith, Alex D., "Lonely Garbo's Love Secret is Exposed," *The Observer* (London), September 10, 2005

306   Harry Lang, "Why George Brent Shuns Romance," *Movie Classic*, August 1936

307   Jack Oakie, "The One Time I Saw Garbo," *Hollywood Studio Magazine*, May 1978

308   Myrna Loy, James Kotsilibas-David, *Being and Becoming*, Alfred A. Knopf, NY, © 1987, p. 121

309   "Ay Tank Ay Stay Here Now," *Mason City Globe-Gazette*, December 20, 1934, and *Manitowoc Herald Times*, December 27, 1934

310   Mollie Merrick, "George Brent Doesn't Talk and Neither Does Greta Garbo," *Dallas Morning News*, November 11, 1934

311   Lawrence J. Quirk, *Fasten Your Seatbelts: The Passionate Life of Bette Davis*, Morrow, © 1990, p. 100

312   F.S.N. review of *Living on Velvet*, *New York Times*, March 8, 1935

313   Kent Jones, *Film Comment*, September/October, 1997

314   Harrison Carroll, review of *Living On Velvet*, *Los Angeles Evening Herald Express*, March 2, 1935

315   Samuel Richard Mook, "Liar, Pest and Nitwit," *Picture Play*, January 1936

316   Myrtle Gebhart, "What Price Glory," *Picture Play*, November 1936 (stand-in information: George Schaffer article, *Times-Picayune*, March 1, 1935)

317   Barry Paris, *Garbo*, Alfred A. Knopf, © 1995, p. 315

318   W. Ward Marsh, "Hollywood's Forgotten Actors," *Cleveland Plain Dealer*, November 22, 1936

319   W. Ward Marsh, "Hollywood's Forgotten Actors," *Cleveland Plain Dealer*, November 22, 1936

320   Gladys Hall, "They've Had Brent All Wrong!" *Motion Picture*, December 1940

Endnotes: Chapter 6

321   James Robert Parish and Don E. Stanke, *The Debonairs*, Arlington House, © 1975, p. 33

322   Kay Francis Diaries, Wesleyan University, January 4, 1935

323   Harry Lang, "Why George Brent Shuns Romance," *Movie Classic*, August 1936

324   "Ex Husbands of Same Woman," *Seattle Daily Times*, February 10, 1935

325   Jimmy Starr, review of *The Goose and the Gander*, *Los Angeles Evening Herald Express*, August 3, 1935

326   Andre Sennwald, review of *The Goose and the Gander*, *New York Times*, September 12, 1935

327   Samuel Richard Mook, "Liar, Pest and Nitwit," *Picture Play*, January 1936

328   George Eells, *Ginger, Loretta and Irene, Who?* G. Putnam and Sons, © 1976 pp. 218, 224

329   Kay Francis Diaries, Wesleyan University, March 16, 1935, March 25, 1935

330   W.E. Oliver column, *Los Angeles Evening Herald Express*, June 29, 1935

331   W.E. Oliver column, *Los Angeles Evening Herald Express*, June 29, 1935

332   Ted Magee, "What George Brent Thinks of Women," *Hollywood*, March 1936

333   Louella Parsons column, *Syracuse Journal*, July 11, 1935

334   "George Brent is Commander of Aerial Group," *Illustrated Daily News*, April 17, 1935

335   Harrison Carroll, *Los Angeles Evening Herald Express*, April 13, 1935

336   "Women Ask to Join Brent Escadrille," *San Diego Union*, June 9, 1935

337   Larry Ceplair, Stephen Englund, *The Inquisition of Hollywood: Politics in the Film Community, 1930-1960*, University of California Press, © 1983, p. 97

338   Samuel Richard Mook, "Liar, Pest and Nitwit," *Picture Play*, January 1936

339   Alan L. Gansberg, *Little Caesar: a Biography of Edward G. Robinson*, Scarecrow Press, © 2004, p. 73

340   Jeanne Adelman, "Hollywood's 'Heroes' Heil Hearst," *The Student Advocate*, March 1936

341   "Brent 'Bails Out' of Airplane By Way of Practice," *Seattle Daily Times*, December 13, 1935 (This studio publicity release states that Brent's parachute jump was his first and occurred shortly after completing *Special Agent* – a film that wrapped shooting in July 1935.)

342   Maude Cheatham, "George Brent Tells 'Why Ann Sheridan and I Won't Marry,' " *Photoplay*, September 1941

343   Gladys Hall, "They've Had Brent All Wrong!" *Motion Picture*, December 1940

344   Lawrence J. Quirk, *Fasten Your Seatbelts: The Passionate Life of Bette Davis*, Morrow, © 1990, p. 105

345   Lawrence J. Quirk, *Fasten Your Seatbelts: The Passionate Life of Bette Davis*, Morrow, © 1990, p. 107

346   Mary Gilmore, review of *Front Page Woman*, Rochester Evening Journal, July 27, 1935

347   Mae Tinee, review of *Front Page Woman*, *Chicago Daily News*, August 3, 1935

348   Daniel Bubbeo, *The Women of Warner Brothers*, McFarland, © 2002, p. 36

349   Jimmy Starr, review of *Special Agent*, *Los Angeles Evening Herald Express*, August 17, 1935

350   Mary Gilmore, review of *Special Agent*, *Rochester Journal*, October 19, 1935

351   Harrison Carroll, review of *Special Agent*, *Los Angeles Evening Herald Express*, September 26, 1935

352   Ed Sikov, *Dark Victory: The Life of Bette Davis*, Macmillan, © 2008, p. 111

353   Frank Westmore and Muriel Davidson, *The Westmores of Hollywood*, J.B. Lippincott, © 1976, p. 82

354   Notes, *In Person*, AFI Catalogue, afi.com (Under the working title, *Tamed*, Astaire had been the studio's first choice for the male lead)

355   Ginger Rogers, *Ginger: My Story*, G.K. Hall, © 1992, p. 206

356   Ted Magee, "What George Brent Thinks of Women," *Hollywood*, March 1936

357   Ernest Hemingway, "Million Dollar Fright: A New York Letter," *Esquire*, November 1935

358   "Notables View Stadium Fight," *Poughkeepsie Daily Eagle*, September 25, 1935

359   Richard Bak, *Joe Louis: The Great Black Hope*, Da Capo Press, © 1996, p. 93

360   "Ruth Chatterton, Divorce Final," *New York Times*, October 15, 1935

361   W. E. Oliver column, *Los Angeles Evening Herald Express*, September 19, 1936

362   Harrison Carroll column, *Los Angeles Evening Herald Express*, December 7, 1935

363   John H. Reid, *Hollywood Classic Movies 1*," Lulu.com, © 2004, p. 97

364   Frank S. Nugent, review of *Snowed Under*, New York Times, March 30, 1936

365   Clive Hirschhorn, *The Warner Bros. Story*, Crown Pub., © 1979, p. 164

366   Ed Sikov, *Dark Victory: The Life of Bette Davis*, Macmillan, © 2008, p. 79

367   Review of *The Golden Arrow*, Montreal Gazette, June 1, 1936

368   James Robert Parish and Don E. Stanke, *The Debonairs*, Arlington House, © 1975, p. 36

369   Review of *The Case Against Mrs. Ames*, Film Weekly, October 24, 1936

370   James Robert Parish, *Hollywood's Great Love Teams*, Arlington House, © 1974, p. 184

371   Madeleine Carroll, "George Brent," *Film Weekly*, October 24, 1936

372   Ethel Harmel, "He's a Fool for Cupid," *Movie Classic*, December 1936

373   Frank S. Nugent, review of *Give Me Your Heart*, New York Times, September 17, 1936

374   Irene Thirer, "George Brent Says Actor Benefits By a 'Past,' " *New York Post*, April 27, 1936

375   W.E. Oliver column, *Los Angeles Evening Herald Express*, September 19, 1936

Endnotes: Chapter 7

376   "George Brent Seeks U.S. Citizenship," *Oakland Tribune*, August 18, 1934

377   Information taken from copy of United States of America – Petition For Naturalization #55766 (District Court of U.S. – Los Angeles) July 16, 1937

378   U.S. – Petition For Naturalization #55766 (District Court of U.S. – Los Angeles) July 16, 1937

379   "George Brent Takes Oath as U.S. Citizen," *Omaha World Herald*, November 27, 1937

380   "The Talk of Hollywood," *Motion Picture*, March 1938

381   Robert Osborne, "Dedication at 17-film salute to Jean Arthur," TCM broadcast, January 2007

382   Review of *More Than A Secretary*, Film Daily, December 11, 1936

383   Bette Davis, *The Lonely Life*, Putnam, © 1962, p. 156

384   Frank S. Nugent, review of *God's Country and the Woman*, *New York Times*, January 11, 1937

385   Sharon Hatfield, *Never Seen the Moon-The Trials of Edith Maxwell*, Univ. of Illinois Press, © 2005 p. 205

386   Ralph Wilk, "A 'Little' From the 'Lots,' " *Film Daily*, May 18, 1936

387   Sharon Hatfield, *Never Seen the Moon-The Trials of Edith Maxwell*, Univ. of Illinois Press, © 2005 p. 208

388   Harrison Carroll column, *Los Angeles Evening Herald Express*, October 9, 1936

389   Joe Tennis, "Did Edith Maxwell Murder Her Father in 1935?" *Blue Ridge Country*, March 1, 2006

390   Harrison Carroll, "Lights! Camera! Action!" *Los Angeles Evening Herald Express*, September 26, 1936

391   Review of *Mountain Justice*, *Film Daily*, May 16, 1937

392   Frank S. Nugent, review of *Mountain Justice*, *New York Times*, May 13, 1937

393   Sheilah Graham, "On The Sets," *San Francisco Chronicle*, October 14, 1936

394   Ankerich, Michael G., *The Sound of Silence*, McFarland, © 2011, p. 146

395   Matthew Kennedy, *Joan Blondell-A Life Between Takes*, University of Mississippi, © 2007, pp. 80-81

396   Review for *The Go-Getter*, *The Sun*, June 7, 1937

397   Fred Watkins, "George Brent," *Film Fan Monthly*, October 1972

398   Jeffrey Spivak, *Buzz: The Life and Art of Busby Berkeley*, Univ. Press of Kentucky, © 2011, pp. 125-128

399   Michael Barson, *The Illustrated Who's Who of Hollywood Directors*, Noonday Press, © 1995, p. 29

400   Vernon Hoagland, "Few Film Extras Make a Living," *Repository* (OH), June 25, 1940

401   "On and Off the Set," *Picture Play*, February 1937

402   George Shaffer, "Here's Garbo News Straight from Mr. Brent," *Chicago Daily Tribune*, February 16, 1937

403   Carol Craig, "The Girl George Brent Married," *Motion Picture*, September 1937 (Another source says it was RKO producer Edward Small who offered Constance her first Hollywood screen test)

404   "Romance With Brent Told By Film Actress," *Los Angeles Examiner*, August 20, 1937

405   "Weddings Okeh Across Border," *Ogden Standard Examiner*, September 14, 1937

406   "Court Rules Marriages In Mexico Valid," *San Francisco Chronicle*, September 14, 1937

407   James Robert Parish and Don E. Stanke *The Debonairs*, Arlington House, © 1975, p. 38

408   James Robert Parish and Don E. Stanke, *The Debonairs*, Arlington House, © 1975, p. 38

409   "Births," *Sydney Morning Herald*, August 26, 1911 (daughter of Moffatt Howarth born August 19)

410   "Jocelyn Howarth," *The Longreach Leader* (Queensland), September 28, 1935

411   "In Divorce," Howarth v Howarth, *Sydney Morning Herald*, September 21, 1921 (Mary Ellen Howarth accused her husband Moffatt of "having had improper relations with a woman named Molly McGann.")

412   Carol Craig, "The Girl George Brent Married," *Motion Picture*, September 1937

413   "Romance With Brent Told By Film Actress," *Los Angeles Examiner*, August 20, 1937

414   "Brent Trial Thrown in Confusion," *Los Angeles Examiner*, August 22, 1937

415   "Divorces George Brent," *New York Times*, December 8, 1937

416   James Reid, "Hollywood's Champion Lone Wolf," *Motion Picture*, February 1940

417   "Film Actress Saved By Veteran Player," *Trenton Evening Times*, August 4, 1936

418   "Saved By Phone," *Hagerstown Daily*, August 7, 1936

419   "Secret Wedding for Star Says Hollywood," *Sunday Times* (Perth), February 20, 1944

420   "George Brent's Marriage Discussed in Australia," *Lethbridge Herald*, January 12, 1938

421   Review for *Submarine D-1*, *Evansville Courier*, December 13, 1937

422   John Hobart, "Undersea Plot," *San Francisco Chronicle*, November 26, 1937

423   John Meredyth Lucas, *Eighty Odd Years in Hollywood*, McFarland, © 2004, pp. 108-109

424   Frank S. Nugent, review of *Gold Is Where You Find It*, *New York Times*, February 14, 1938

425   "Comments on Current Movies," *Register-Republic*, March 26, 1938 (excerpts from various reviews)

426   William K. Everson, *A Pictorial History of the Western Film*, Citadel Press, © 1969, p. 176

427   Harlan Fiske, review of *Gold Is Where You Find It*, *Portsmouth Times*, February 21, 1938

428   John C. Tibbetts, James M. Welch, *American Classic Screen Interviews*, Scarecrow Press, © 2010, p. 26

Endnotes: Chapter 8

429   Tony Martin, *The Two of Us*, Mason/Charter, © 1976, p. 66

430   Harry Lang, "Talkie Town Tattler," *Motion Picture*, December 1938

431   Gwen Dew, "A Spy In Hollywood," *Picture Play*, October 1938

432   Mason Wiley and Damien Bona, *Inside Oscar*, Ballantine Books, © 1996, p. 85

433   Brad Darrach, "Grand Dame, Grande Dame," *Time*, October 23, 1989

434   Mason Wiley and Damien Bona, *Inside Oscar*, Ballantine Books, © 1996, p. 85

435   Fred Watkins, "George Brent," *Film Fan Monthly*, October 1972

436   Jimmy Starr, review of *Jezebel*, *Los Angeles Evening Herald Express*, March 12, 1938

437   Frank S. Nugent, review of *Jezebel*, *New York Times*, March 11, 1938

438   Mark van Doren, review of *Jezebel*, *Nation*, March 26, 1938

439   Review of *Jezebel*, *Variety*, March 16, 1938

440   Mae Tinee, review of *Jezebel*, *Chicago Daily Tribune*, April 4, 1938

441   Paul Harrison, "News and Gossip of Stage and Screen," *Repository* (OH), February 1, 1938

442   Philip K. Scheuer, review of *Jezebel*, *Picture Play*, June 1938

443   Elisabeth Weis, *The National Society of Film Critics on The Movie Star*, Viking, © 1981, p. 185

444   "Entertains Orphans," *Reno Evening Gazette*, November 27, 1937

445   James Robert Parish and Don E. Stanke, *The Debonairs*, Arlington House, © 1975, p. 40

446   James Robert Parish, *Hollywood's Great Love Teams*, Arlington House, © 1974, p. 194

447   Glenn C. Pullen, "Kay Francis Gets a Bad Break Again," *Cleveland Plain Dealer*, September 10, 1938

448   Clive Hirschhorn, *The Warner Bros. Story*, Crown Publishers, © 1979, p. 193

449   Bosley Crowther, review of *Racket Busters*, *New York Times*, August 11, 1938

450   Bosley Crowther, review of *Wings of the Navy*, *New York Times*, February 4, 1939

451   James V. Griffin, "West Coast Chatter," *National Aeronautics*, V. XVII, Number 2, 1939

452   Edward Churchill, "It's Not All Hokum!" *Flying Magazine*, July 1939

453   "No Love Losses," *Reno Evening Gazette*, November 9, 1938

454   Adele Fletcher, "How George Brent Brought New Faith to Bette Davis," *Photoplay*, April 1939

455   Ed Sikov, *Dark Victory: The Life of Bette Davis*, Macmillan, © 2007, p. 138

456   Fred Watkins, "George Brent," *Film Fan Monthly*, October 1972

457   James Robert Parish and Don E. Stanke, *The Debonairs*, Arlington House, © 1975, p. 41

458   Ed Sikov, *Dark Victory: The Life of Bette Davis,* Macmillan, © 2007, p. 138

459   Matthew Kennedy, *Edmund Goulding's Dark Victory: Hollywood's Genius Bad Boy*, Terrace Books, © 2004, p. 184

460   Adele Fletcher, "How George Brent Brought New Faith to Bette Davis," *Photoplay*, April 1939

461   Jack Wade, "We Cover the Studios," *Photoplay*, January 1939

462   Adele Fletcher, "How George Brent Brought New Faith to Bette Davis," *Photoplay*, April 1939

463   Adele Fletcher, "How George Brent Brought New Faith to Bette Davis," *Photoplay*, April 1939

464   Ed Sikov, *Dark Victory: The Life of Bette Davis*, Macmillan, © 2007, p. 141

465   Adele Fletcher, "How George Brent Brought New Faith to Bette Davis," *Photoplay*, April 1939

466   Lawrence J. Quirk, *Fasten Your Seatbelts: The Passionate Life of Bette Davis*, William Morrow, © 1990, p. 181

467   Bernard F. Dick with Casey Robinson, *Dark Victory*, University of Wisconsin Press, © 1981, p. 24

468   Bette Davis, *This 'N That*, G.P. Putnam, © 1987, p. 2

469   Charlotte Chandler, *The Girl Who Walked Home Alone*, Hal Leonard Corp., © 2007, p. 137

470   Ronald Reagan, Richard G. Hubler, *Where's the Rest of Me?* Duell, Sloan and Pearce, © 1965, p. 102

471   Jimmy Starr, review of *Dark Victory*, *Los Angeles Evening Herald Express*, March 8, 1939

472   Ruth Waterbury, "Close Ups and Long Shots," *Photoplay*, January 1940

473   Adele Fletcher, "Reborn! How George Brent Brought New Faith to Bette Davis," *Photoplay*, April 1939

474   Harrison Carroll, column, *Los Angeles Evening Herald Express*, October 13, 1938

475   Manifest of inbound passengers, *S.S. Matsonia*, December 28, 1938 (Brent and Turner were listed together on the passenger list)

476   Jimmy Starr column, *Los Angeles Evening Herald Express*, January 19, 1939

477   "Film Stars at Capitol for FDR Birthday Ball," *Film Daily*, January 31, 1939

478   James Robert Parish and Don E. Stanke, *The Debonairs*, Arlington House, © 1975, p. 41

479   Matthew Kennedy, *Edmund Goulding's Dark Victory: Hollywood's Genius Bad Boy*, Terrace Books, © 2004, p. xv

480   Lawrence J. Quirk, *Fasten Your Seatbelts: The Passionate Life of Bette Davis*, William Morrow, © 1990, p. 224

481   Matthew Kennedy, *Edmund Goulding's Dark Victory: Hollywood's Genius Bad Boy*, Terrace Books, © 2004, p. 185

482   Ed Sikov, *Dark Victory: The Life of Bette Davis*, Macmillan, © 2007, p. 150

483   Philip K. Scheuer, "'Old Maid' Poignant Drama," *Los Angeles Times*, September 8, 1939

484   "Ten Best Eyed Critically," *Film Daily*, January 12, 1940

485   Helen Louise Walker, "Is George Brent a Wallflower?" *Hollywood*, March 1941

486   George Brent, "Without a Shirt," *Milwaukee Journal*, June 12, 1938

487   Molly Hollywood, "Turns His Back," *San Antonio Light*, August 29, 1937

488   Harold Heffernan, "Out Hollywood Way," *Repository* (OH), May 17, 1948

489   W. Ward Marsh, "One Moment, Please!" *Cleveland Plain Dealer*, August 2, 1939

490   George Brent as told to Frank Dillon, "Women Worry Men," *Hollywood*, February 1939

491   "Vants To Be Alone," *Motion Picture*, February 1939

492   Harrison Carroll column, *Los Angeles Evening Herald Express*, September 19, 1938

Endnotes: Chapter 9

493   "Bright-Eyed Girl No. 1," *Sydney Times* (Australia), October 20, 1940

494   James Reid, "Hollywood's Champion Lone Wolf," *Motion Picture*, February 1940

495   Harrison Carroll, column, *Los Angeles Evening Herald Express*, March 23, 1939

496   Bette Davis, *This 'N That*, G.P. Putnam, © 1987, p. 2

497   Whitney Stine, *"I'd Love to Kiss You . . ." Conversations with Bette Davis*, Thorndike, © 1990, p. 98

498   Katharine Hartley Flings, "Will the Oomph Title Hurt Her?" *Motion Picture*, August 1939

499   Daniel Bubbeo, *The Women of Warner Brothers*, McFarland, © 2002, p. 196

500   Jimmy Fidler, "In Hollywood," *State Times Advocate*, January 26, 1940

501   Charles Higham, *Hollywood Cameramen*, Garland, © 1986, p. 146

502   "The Truth About Stars' Salaries," *Photoplay*, January 1942

503   Louis Bromfield, "And It All Came True," *Photoplay*, October 1939

504   Louis Bromfield, "And It All Came True," *Photoplay*, October 1939

505   Harrison Carroll column, *Los Angeles Evening Herald Express*, April 17, 1939

506   Harrison Carroll, "Lights! Camera! Action!" *Los Angeles Evening Herald Express*, April 29, 1939

507   Louella Parsons column, *Los Angeles Examiner*, March 15, 1939

508   Sheilah Graham, "Hollywood in Person," *Dallas Morning News* , October 18, 1939

509   Jimmy Fidler, "In Hollywood," *Richmond Times*, June 29, 1939

510   "Indian Scholar Of U.C. Extension Lectures In City," *San Diego Union*, December 5, 1934

511   Myrna Loy, John Kotsilibas-Davis, *Myrna Loy: Being and Becoming*, Knopf, © 1987, p. 248

512   Philip Ziegler, Mountbatten, Knopf, © 1985, p. 53

513   Francis Wheen, *Tom Driberg: The Soul of Indiscretion*, Chatto & Windus, © 1990, p. 211

514   Prem Chowdry, *Colonial India and the Making of Empire Films*, Manchester Univ., © 2000, p. 196

515   Jeannine Woods, *Visions of Empire and Other Imaginings*, Peter Lang, © 2011, p. 231

516   Myrna Loy, James Kotsilibas-Davis, *Myrna Loy-Being and Becoming*, Knopf, © 1987, p. 159

517   Review of *The Rains Came*, *Film Daily*, September 11, 1939

518   "Rains Keeps Up Record," *Film Daily*, October 3, 1939

519   Ruth Waterbury, "Close-Ups and Long Shots," *Photoplay*, November 1939

520   Review of *The Rains Came*, *Sydney Morning Herald* (Australia), December 25, 1939

521   Frank S. Nugent, review of *The Rains Came*, *New York Times*, September 9, 1939

522   Harrison Carroll, review of *The Rains Came*, *Los Angeles Evening Herald Express*, September 15, 1939

523   Brent and Forbes left California February 16, 1940 (SS Lurline) arriving in Honolulu February 21. They returned March 8, 1940 (SS Lurline) arriving home March 15

524   B. R. Crisler, review of *Adventure in Diamonds*, *New York Times*, April 4, 1940

525   Clive Hirschhorn, *The Warner Brothers Story*, Crown Pub., © 1979, p. 211

526   Bill Kelly, "George Brent in 'Born Again' Role, *Santa Ana Orange County Register*, May 28, 1978

527   Douglas Waller, *Wild Bill Donovan*, Simon & Schuster, © 2012, p. 54

528   James Cagney, *Cagney on Cagney*, Doubleday, © 1976

529   James Cagney, *Cagney on Cagney*, Doubleday, © 1976

530   John McCabe, *Cagney*, Da Capo, © 1998, p. 183

531   Sheilah Graham column, *Plain Dealer*, July 28, 1939

532   James Robert Parish and Don E. Stanke, *The Debonairs*, Arlington House, © 1975, p. 43

533   Herbert Cohn, review of *'Til We Meet Again*, *Brooklyn Eagle*, April 20, 1940

534   W. Ward Marsh, review of *'Til We Meet Again*, *Cleveland Plain Dealer*, April 29, 1940

535   Vincent Sherman, *Studio Affairs: My Life as a Film Director*, Univ. of Kentucky, © 1996 pp. 87-88

536   Review of *The Man Who Talked Too Much*, *Time*, July 15, 1940

537   Review of *South of Suez*, *Photoplay*, March 1941

538   Eileen Creelman, review of *South of Suez*, *New York Sun*, December 19, 1940

539   T.M.P., review of *South of Suez*, *New York Times*, December 19, 1940

540   "Hollywood Parties," *Motion Picture*, November 1940

541   Helen Louise Walker, "Is George Brent a Wallflower?" *Hollywood*, March 1941

542   "Brent Will Quit, Grow Pineapples," *Omaha World Herald*, May 14, 1940

543   Irving Wallace, "Brent's New Design for Living," *Modern Screen*, September 1940

544   Dan Camp, "Take Me Away From It All!" *Motion Picture*, November 1938

545   Frederick C. Othman column, *Omaha World Herald*, May 8, 1941

546   *The Rudder*, Volume 67, p. 17, 1951

547   Gladys Hall, "They've Had Brent All Wrong!" *Motion Picture*, December 1940

548   Howard Sharpe, "Categorically Speaking," *Photoplay*, September 1940

549   Howard Sharpe, "Categorically Speaking," *Photoplay*, September 1940

550   Harrison Carroll column, *Los Angeles Evening Herald Express*, May 10, 1940

Endnotes: Chapter 10

551   James Robert Parish and Don E. Stanke, *The Debonairs*, Arlington House, © 1975, p. 23

552   Daniel Bubbeo, *The Women of Warner Brothers*, McFarland, © 2002, p. 191

553   Sheilah Graham, "Ann Sheridan Hangs Up Mistletoe, Complains," *Plain Dealer*, December 21, 1940

554   W. E. Oliver, review of *Honeymoon For Three*, *Los Angeles Evening Herald Express*, January 17, 1941

555   Herbert Cohn, review of *Honeymoon For Three*, *Brooklyn Daily Eagle*, February 8, 1941

556   "'Oomph Girl,' Brent Break Record With 56-Second Kiss," *Omaha World Herald*, August 8, 1940

557   Archer Winsten, review of *Three On A Honeymoon*, *New York Evening Post*, February 8, 1941

558   "Cruising After Film Rift," *Trenton Evening Times*, October 20, 1940

559   Maude Cheatham, "George Brent Tells 'Why Ann Sheridan and I Won't Marry,'" *Photoplay*, September 1941

560   Jack Holland, "Bette Davis Turns Softie," *Hollywood*, May 1941

561   Lawrence J. Quirk, *Fasten Your Seatbelts: The Passionate Life of Bette Davis*, William Morrow, © 1990, p. 224

562   Mary Astor, *A Life on Film*, Dell, © 1967, p. 153

563   Mary Astor, *A Life on Film*, Dell, © 1967, p. 152

564   Review of *The Great Lie*, *Film Daily*, April 4, 1941

565   Ruth Barton, *Acting Irish in Hollywood: From Fitzgerald to Farrell*, Irish Academic Press, © 2006, p. 57 (taken from Bette Davis' *The Lonely Life*)

566   Robyn Karney, *The Movie Stars Story*, Crescent Books, © 1984, p. 48

567   Gladys Hall, "They've Had Brent All Wrong!" *Motion Picture*, December 1940

568   "Mayer's Salary Tops Industry," *Film Daily*, July 1, 1940

569   Tom Weaver, *Eye On Science Fiction: 20 Interviews With Classic SF and Horror Filmmakers*, McFarland, © 2007, p. 229

570   Leonard J. Kohl, "Formerly Kate Linaker: Part 3" (Interview), *Scarlet Street*, 2004

571   Dennis R. Smith, "Nazi Drama Without Hate," *Canton Repository*, May 2, 1941

572   Review of *They Dare Not Love*, *Photoplay*, July 1941

573   "Good News," *Modern Screen*, September 1941

574   Ruth Waterbury, "Close-Ups and Long-Shots," *Photoplay*, August 1941

575   Harrison Carroll column, *Times-Picayune*, April 2, 1941

576   Bosley Crowther, review of *International Lady*, *New York Times*, November 11, 1941

577   Grace Morphy-Hulst, "Out of the Past," *Photoplay*, December 1942

578   Alex Ben Block, Lucy Autrey Wilson, *George Lucas's Blockbusting*, HarperCollins, © 2010, p. 273

579   John Huston, *An Open Book*, Da Capo, © 1994, p. 81

580   Lawrence J. Quirk, *Fasten Your Seatbelts: The Passionate Life of Bette Davis*, William Morrow, © 1990, p. 241

581   James Baldwin, *The Price of the Ticket*, Macmillan, © 1985, p. 593

582   Bosley Crowther, review of *In This Our Life*," *New York Times*, May 9, 1942

583   Lawrence J. Quirk, *Fasten Your Seatbelts: The Passionate Life of Bette Davis*, William Morrow, © 1990, p. 238

584   Maude Cheatham, "George Brent Tells 'Why Ann Sheridan and I Won't Marry,' " *Photoplay*, September 1941

585   John Meredyth Lucas, *Eighty Odd Years in Hollywood*, McFarland, © 2004, p. 128

586   "Ann Sheridan is Wed to Brent in Surprise Rites," *Fresno Bee*, January 6, 1942 (reporters concocted a story that the mantilla Sheridan wore had belonged to her grandmother)

587   "Noted Editor, a Suicide, Once Resided in Pawling," *News-Chronicle*, November 3, 1938

588   Frederick C. Othman, "Ann Takes Oomph to the Army," *Repository*, March 21, 1942

589   "Sheridan is Favorite of Service Men," *Seattle Daily Times*, May 25, 1942

590   "Nitery Rewards Buyers of $100 Bonds with Phone Talks to Picture Stars," *Variety*, March 25, 1942

591   "Tired, Sheridan May Pull Out of 'Slept,' " *Variety*, April 6, 1942

592   Ray Hagen, Laura Wagner, *Killer Tomatoes*, McFarland, © 2002, p. 168

593   Anita Blake, "What Ann Sheridan Learned in Exile," *Photoplay*, June 1941

594   John B. Merriman, "School-Marm From Texas," *Register-Republic* (IL), July 7, 1937

595   Ruth Rankin, "From Ranch to Riches," *Photoplay*, June 1939

596   Gladys Hall, "Confessions of a Contest Winner," *Motion Picture*, December 1938

597   Ray Hagen, Laura Wagner, *Killer Tomatoes*, McFarland, © 2002, p. 172

598   "Metro Studio Moving to Dallas to Discover Girl and Child Talent," *Dallas Morning News*, January 7, 1935

599   Keith Wilson, "Spotlight and Reel," *Omaha World Herald*, October 6, 1938

600   Walter Winchell, "On Broadway," *Syracuse Journal*, March 25, 1938

601   Ray Hagen, Laura Wagner, *Killer Tomatoes*, McFarland, © 2002, p. 176

602   Harrison Carroll, "Behind the Scenes in Hollywood," *Times-Picayune*, September 9, 1939

603   Ray Hagen, Laura Wagner, *Killer Tomatoes*, McFarland, © 2004, p. 176

604   Ruth Rankin, "From Ranch to Riches," *Photoplay*, June 1939

605   Lawrence J. Quirk, *Fasten Your Seat Belts: The Passionate Life of Bette Davis*, William Morrow, © 1990, p. 236

606   Paul Harrison, "Brent Blamed In Ann's Strike," *Canton Repository*, November 19, 1940

607   Helen Weller, "The Jinx Behind Filming *Kings Row*," *Hollywood*, January 1942

608   Gladys Hall, "Ann Sheridan's Surprise Marriage," *Photoplay*, March 1942

609   Lawrence J. Quirk, *Fasten Your Seatbelts: The Passionate Life of Bette Davis*, William Morrow, © 1990, p. 55

610   Richard Bard, "We Didn't Part Friends," *Hollywood*, February 1943

611   *Variety*, September 24, 1942

612   Louella Parsons, "Sheridan, Brent Split Up," *San Diego Union*, September 29, 1943

613   Liza, "Why the Sheridan-Brent Marriage Failed!" *Screenland*, January 1943

614   Liza, "Why the Sheridan-Brent Marriage Failed!" *Screenland*, January 1943

615   Richard Bar, "We Didn't Part Friends," *Hollywood*, February 1943

616   Jimmy Fidler, "In Hollywood," *Oregonian*, October 10, 1942

617   "Flynn Denies Plans to Wed Ann Sheridan," *Augusta Chronicle*, January 1, 1943

618   "Ann Sheridan Gets Divorce in Mexico," *Dallas Morning News*, January 12, 1943

619   Rosalind Leigh, "'Oomph' Can't Hold Husbands," *Sunday Times* (Perth), June 6, 1943

620   Stuart Jerome, *Those Crazy Wonderful Years When We Ran Warner Bros.*, Lyle Stuart, © 1983, p. 225

621   James Robert Parish and Don E. Stanke, *The Debonairs*, Arlington House, © 1975, p. 48

622   "To The Colors!" *Film Daily*, September 25, 1942

623   Louella Parsons column, *Waterloo Daily Courier*, October 7, 1942

Endnotes: Chapter 11

624   "Hollywood Salutes Volunteer Americans," *Hollywood*, July 1939

625   Gladys Hall, "Ann Sheridan's Surprise Marriage," *Photoplay*, March 1942

626   Alice Pardoe West, "Irish Adventures Prime Brent for Soldier Role," *Ogden Standard Examiner*, September 13, 1942

627   "George Brent Civilian Air Instructor," *The Mercury*, September 26, 1942

628   Alice Pardoe West, "Irish Adventures Prime Brent for Soldier Role," *Ogden Standard Examiner*, September 13, 1942

629   John Truesdell, "Close-Up on Brent," *Long Island Daily Press*, November 19, 1942

630   Review of *The Gay Sisters*, *Time*, July 27, 1942

631   Paul Harrison, "Harrison in Hollywood," *Advocate*, March 31, 1942

632   T.S., review of *The Gay Sisters*, *New York Times*, August 15, 1942

633   Review of *The Gay Sisters*, *Film Daily*, June 3, 1942

634   Charlotte Chandler, *The Girl Who Walked Home Alone: Bette Davis*, Hal Leonard Corp., © 2007, pp. 136-137.

635   T.S., review of *Silver Queen*, *New York Times*, January 11, 1943

636   Review of *Silver Queen*, *Film Daily*, November 10, 1942

637   Review of *You Can't Escape Forever*, *Variety*, September 21, 1942

638   Jimmy Fidler column, *State Times*, August 7, 1943

639   Louella Parsons column, *San Antonio Light*, December 19, 1942

640   Sheilah Graham, "In Hollywood," *Dallas Morning News*, January 10, 1943

641   Louella Parsons column, *Fresno Bee Republican*, December 23, 1942

642   "Whiskey Fraud Is Laid to 13," *Omaha World Herald*, February 27, 1943

643   Hedda Hopper column, *Kansas City Star*, April 2, 1943

644   Jeanine Basinger, *A Women's View*, Alfred A. Knopf, © 1993, p. 44

645   Axel Madsen, *Stanwyck*, Harper Collins, © 1994, p. 224

646   Wood Soanes, review of *My Reputation*, *Oakland Tribune*, February 15, 1946

647   Review of *My Reputation*, *Variety*, January 8, 1946

648   "Just For Variety: Call Sheet," *Variety*, May 16, 1943

649   "Lampooned," *San Francisco Chronicle*, February 2, 1941

650   "Hollywood Inside," *Variety*, April 10, 1944

651   James Robert Parish and Don E. Stanke, *The Debonairs*, Arlington House, © 1975, p. 49

652   T.M.P., review of *Experiment Perilous*, *New York Times*, December 30, 1944

653   W. Ward Marsh, review of *Experiment Perilous*, *Plain Dealer*, February 15, 1945

654   Doug McClelland, "Joan Fontaine – A Recent Interview," *American Classic Screen Magazine*, May/June 1978

655   Ruth Roman, "Beware of Experts," *Modern Screen*, November 1950

656   D.U., review of *The Affairs of Susan*, *Milwaukee Journal*, May 30, 1945

657   Lawrence J. Quirk, *Claudette Colbert: An Illustrated Biography*, Crown, © 1985, p. 148

658   Suzanne Finstad, *Natasha: The Biography of Natalie Wood*, Three Rivers Press, © 2002, p. 38

659   Dorothy Raymer, review of *Tomorrow Is Forever*, *The Miami News*, April 11, 1946

660   Richard E. Hays, review of *Tomorrow Is Forever*, *Seattle Daily Times*, April 24, 1946

661   Bosley Crowther, review of *Tomorrow Is Forever*, *New York Times*, February 22, 1946

662   Suzanne Finstad, *Natasha: The Biography of Natalie Wood*, Three Rivers Press, © 2002, p. 53

663   Louella Parsons column, *Omaha World Herald*, September 20, 1943

664   "Radio Department," *Geneva Daily Times*, November 2, 1944

665   James Robert Parish and Don E. Stanke, *The Debonairs*, Arlington House, © 1975, p. 50

Endnotes: Chapter 12

666   Florabel Muir, "Just For Variety," *Variety*, September 22, 1947

667   James Robert Parish and Don E. Stanke, *The Debonairs*, Arlington House, © 1975, p. 52

668   Virginia MacPherson, "Writer Lists Films That Won't Get This Year's Oscar," *Register-Guard*, January 11, 1948

669   "Schary Rolls *Some Must Watch* Tomorrow," *Variety*, August 15, 1945

670   James Kotsilibas-Davis, *The Barrymores: The Royal Family In Hollywood*, Crown, © 1981, p. 255

671   Doug McClelland, *Forties Film Talk*, McFarland, © 1992, p. 122

672   Review of *The Spiral Staircase*, *Variety*, January 4, 1946

673   Bosley Crowther, review of *The Spiral Staircase*, *New York Times*, February 7, 1946

674   Anthony Slide, *Selected Film Criticism*, Scarecrow Press, © 1983, pp. 225, 227

675   Douglas Brode, *Edge of Your Seat: The One Hundred Greatest Movie Thrillers*, Citadel, © 2003, p. 146

676   Amy Lawrence, *Echo and Narcissus*, University of California Press, © 1991, p. 113

677   Leslie Halliwell, *Halliwell's Harvest*, Scribner, © 1986, p. 252

678   Lucille Ball, *Love, Lucy*, Boulevard Books, © 1996, p. 147

679   Paul Rosenfield, "Compulsively Lucy," *Los Angeles Times*, October 12, 1986

680   Review of *Lover Come Back, Film Daily*, June 26, 1946

681   Bosley Crowther, review of *Lover Come Back, New York Times*, June 20, 1946

682   Leonard Maltin, *Leonard Maltin's 2009 Movie Guide*, Penguin, © 2008, p. 841

683   "What the Picture Did For Me," *Motion Picture Herald*, October 18, 1947

684   Evelyn Schloss, review of *Temptation, Audio-Visual Guide*, Vol. 13, 1946, p. 57

685   Bosley Crowther, review of *Temptation, New York Times*, December 25, 1946

686   Donald Kirkley, review of *Temptation, The Sun*, January 16, 1947

687   Kaspar Monahan, review of *Temptation, Pittsburgh Press*, February 6, 1947

688   "Brent to Enter Honolulu Race," *San Diego Union*, June 23, 1946

689   "Screen Morgan Not Real Thing," *Portland Sunday Telegram*, January 19, 1947

690   "34 Yachts in Pacific Race," *Winona Republican-Herald*, July 5, 1947

691   Erskine Johnson, "With the Stars," *Abilene Reporter News*, July 2, 1949

692   "Sleek Yachts Begin Voyage to Honolulu," *San Diego Union*, July 5, 1947

693   *Southwind* log book, Friday, July 4, 1947 (entry by Carl Cook)

694   *Southwind* log book, Tuesday, July 22, 1947 (entry by Carl Cook)

695   "Actor Morgan Wins Coast-Hawaii Race," *Richmond Times-Dispatch*, July 22, 1947

696   "Morgan Wins Hawaiian Race," *Seattle Times Daily*, July 21, 1947

697   Bob Thomas, "Life in Hollywood," *San Mateo Times*, August 14, 1947

698   T.M.P., review of *The Corpse Came C.O.D., New York Times*, August 19, 1947

699   A.W., review of *Christmas Eve, New York Times*, November 28, 1947

700   Wood Soanes, review of *Christmas Eve, Oakland Tribune*, December 4, 1947

701   Sheilah Graham column, *Hollywood Citizen News*, January 15, 1947

702   Review of *Out of the Blue, Variety*, August 26, 1947

703   E.L., review of *Out of the Blue, Richmond Times Dispatch*, December 18, 1947

704   John Rosenfield, review of *Out of the Blue, Dallas Morning News*, October 23, 1947

705   David Bleiler, *TLA Video and DVD Guide 2005*, Macmillan, © 2004, p. 468

706   Note: *Slave Girl*, AFI.com

707   Sheilah Graham column, *Kingsport News*, August 10, 1946

708   E.L., review of *Slave Girl, Richmond Times Dispatch*, November 13, 1947

709   George Brent, "This is My Side of It," *Motion Picture*, December 1946

710   Brian Doyle, "Emotional Support," *Classic Images*, December 2002

711   Viola MacDonald, "Tropical Island Life Ahead for George Brent," *Women's Weekly*, November 1, 1947

712   John Todd, "Brent Ready for Run-Out," *Oregonian*, August 17, 1947

713   Sheilah Graham column, *Hollywood Citizen News*, December 1, 1947

714   Florabel Muir, "Just For Variety," *Variety*, April 27, 1948

715   Bob Thomas, "Hollywood News," *Corpus Christi Times*, April 23, 1948

716   Sheilah Graham, "Brent Loves Horses?" *Plain Dealer*, July 28, 1946

717   "Just For Variety," *Variety*, April 23, 1947

718   Louella Parsons column, *San Diego Union*, September 1, 1947

719   "George Brent Marries," *Dallas Morning News*, December 18, 1947

720   Florabel Muir, "Just For Variety," *Variety*, February 25, 1948

721   California Birth Index (1905-1995)

722   Hyman Weintraub, *Andrew Furuseth*, University of California, © 1959, pp. 61-63

723   Robert Edward Lee Wright, *Industrial Relations in the San Francisco Bay Area, 1900-1918*, University of California Press, © 1960, pp. 66-67

724   1930 U.S. Federal Census (California)

725   "Gave Dinner Party," *San Francisco Chronicle*, January 31, 1937

726   "Ride Neptune's Chariot," *San Francisco Chronicle*, August 23, 1937

727   "Let It Rain!" *Berkeley Daily Gazette*, January 26, 1940

728   Herb Caen, "It's News to Me," *San Francisco Chronicle*, January 4, 1941

729   "Artists Choose Glamor Gals," *The News-Dispatch*, January 14, 1947

730   Frank Rhodes column, *San Diego Union*, July 28, 1974

731   Herbert L. Larson, "*Luxury Liner* Unloads Hit," *Oregonian*, September 29, 1948

732   Jane Powell, *The Girl Next Door—and How She Grew*, William Morrow, © 1988, p. 112

733   Bosley Crowther, review of *Luxury Liner*, *New York Times*, September 10, 1948

734   A.R.D., "*Luxury Liner* Pleases Crowds at the Florida," *Evening Independent*, October 7, 1948

735   John Rosenfield, "Notes on the Passing Show," *Dallas Morning News*, September 26, 1948

736   Jimmy Fidler, "In Hollywood," *Oregonian*, January 4, 1949

Endnotes: Chapter 13

737   Gene Handsaker, "In Hollywood," *Ironwood Daily Globe*, September 6, 1946

738   Florabel Muir, "Just For Variety," *Variety*, April 27, 1948

Sheilah Graham column, *Hollywood Citizen News*, May 14, 1948

739   Article in *Southwind-The Yachting News Magazine*, May 1983

740   "Thieves Rob Mrs. George Brent," *Long Beach Independent*, October 10, 1948

741   "Why George Brent Came Out of Retirement," *TV Guide*, March 16-22, 1957

742   James Robert Parish and Don E. Stanke, *The Debonairs*, Arlington House , © 1975, p. 53

743   James Robert Parish, *The RKO Gals*, Arlington House, © 1974, p. 95

744   Edith Lindeman, "*Angel on the Amazon* Rates Vote as One of the Year's Worst," *Richmond Times-Dispatch*, December 20, 1948

745   "What the Picture Did For Me," *Motion Picture Herald,* January 1, 1949

746   H.H.T., review of *Angel on the Amazon, New York Times,* December 27, 1948

747   George H. Jackson, review of *Angel on the Amazon, Los Angeles Evening Herald,* February 10, 1949

748   Article in *Variety,* April 23, 1948

749   Sheilah Graham column, *Hollywood Citizen News,* May 15, 1948

750   "Actor Edgar Buchanan Dies At 76," *San Diego Union,* April 5, 1979

751   T.M.P., "Zane Grey Story as New Film," *New York Times,* April 28, 1949

752   Sara Hamilton, review of *Red Canyon, Los Angeles Examiner,* April 2, 1949

753   Turner Classic Movie notes on *Montana Belle*

754   Richard B. Jewell, Vernon Harbin, *The RKO Story,* Octopus Books, © 1982, p. 267

755   Frederic Lombardi, *Allan Dwan and the Rise and Fall of the Hollywood Studios,* McFarland, © 2013, p. 274

756   Jane Russell, *Jane Russell: My Paths and My Detours,* Franklin Watts, © 1985, p. 97

757   Marjorie Turner, review of *Montana Belle, Syracuse Herald Journal,* December 11, 1952

758   Report from *Hollywood Citizen News,* December 23, 1948

759   Bosley Crowther, review of *Illegal Entry, New York Times,* June 11, 1949

760   Richard E. Hays, review of *Illegal Entry, Seattle Daily Times,* June 16, 1949

761   W.E. Oliver, review of *Illegal Entry, Los Angeles Evening Herald Express,* June 13, 1949

762   David Maciel and Maria Herrera-Sobek, *Culture Across Borders: Mexican Immigration and Popular Culture,* University of Arizona Press, © 1998, p. 168

763   Note in *Variety,* January 10, 1949

764   Lowell E. Redelings, "One Minute Interviews," *Hollywood Citizen News,* March 4, 1949

765   "Film Work a Hobby to Busy George Brent," *The Capital* (MD), July 14, 1949

766   Harrison Carroll column, *Los Angeles Evening Herald Express,* December 24, 1948

767   Lawrence J. Quirk, *Claudette Colbert: An Illustrated Biography,* Crown, © 1985, p. 158

768   J.R., review of *Bride for Sale, Dallas Morning News,* November 24, 1949

769   Lawrence J. Quirk, *Claudette Colbert: An Illustrated Biography,* Crown, © 1985, p. 158

770   Lawrence J. Quirk, *Claudette Colbert: An Illustrated Biography,* Crown, © 1985, p. 157

771   Joseph T. Moore, *Pride Against Prejudice: the Biography of Larry Doby,* ABC-CLIO, © 1988, p. 91

772   Michelle Nolan, *Ball Tales,* McFarland, © 2010, p. 259

773   W. Ward Marsh, review of *Kid from Cleveland, Plain Dealer,* September 1, 1949

774   Bosley Crowther, review of *The Kid from Cleveland, New York Times,* September 5, 1949

775   Longislandgenealogy.com (Mount Pleasant) site indicates that tombstone #1397 is shared by Mary Nolan (1875-1950) and her daughter Mary N. Fletcher (1893-1943)

776   "Legal Notice," *Suffolk County News,* January 9, 1953

777   "Mastic," *The County Review,* May 14, 1942

778   "Mastic," *The County Review,* January 4, 1945

779   Conversation with Robert E. Fletcher, February 2, 2014

780   "Mastic," *The County Review*, April 15, 1948

781   Walter Winchell column, *Springfield Union*, June 22, 1951

782   Beverly Linet, *Susan Hayward, Portrait of a Survivor*, Atheneum, © 1980, p. 154

783   Doug McClelland, *Susan Hayward: The Divine Bitch*, Pinnacle Books, © 1973, p. 62

784   Email from Ian Watson, March 31, 2014

785   Helen Louise Walker, "If I Had My Life to Live Over," *Silver Screen*, April 1940

786   George Brent (as explained to Franc Dillon), "Women Worry Men," *Hollywood*, February 1939

787   "Daughter is Born to George Brents," *Richmond Times*, August 4, 1950

788   Frank Colley, "The Morning Herald Sports," *Morning Herald*, February 1, 1955

789   "George Brent Sells Ranch in Hidden Valley," *Oxnard Press Courier*, June 3, 1958

Endnotes: Chapter 14

790   Erskine Johnson, "In Hollywood," *Harrisburg Daily Register*, July 28, 1951

791   Bob Herzberg, *FBI and the Movies*, McFarland, © 2007, p. 153

792   Edward Dmytryk, *Odd Man Out: A Memoir of the Hollywood Ten*, SIU Press, © 1996, p. 45

793   James Robert Parish and Don E. Stanke, *The Debonairs*, Arlington House, © 1975, p. 55

794   Laura Wagner, review of *FBI Girl*, "Laura's Miscellaneous Musings," laurasmiscmusings.blogspot.com, October 10, 2012

795   Glenn C. Pullen, "Diana Dors is Tower's Latest British Siren," *Plain Dealer*, May 24, 1952

796   Vernon Scott, "Matinee Idols Do Fade," *Eureka Humboldt Standard*, July 25, 1960

797   Sheilah Graham column, *Deseret News*, December 22, 1951

798   Erskine Johnson column, *Advocate*, September 16, 1951

799   Whitney Stine, *"I'd Love to Kiss You . . ."Conversations with Bette Davis*, Thorndike, © 1991, p. 99

800   Copp Collins, "So This is Hollywood," *Waycross Journal-Herald*, March 14, 1952

801   Review of *Double Exposure*, Variety, March 30, 1953

802   Review of *Tangier Incident*, Variety, February 4, 1953

803   *Variety*, March 4, 1953

804   Rees, review of *Affairs of State*, Variety, March 14, 1953

805   Leslie Halliwell, *Halliwell's Film Guide*, Harper Perennial, © 1996, p. 755

806   Review of *Key in the Lock*, Variety, November 25, 1953

807   Sheilah Graham, "In Hollywood," *Seattle Daily Times*, November 17, 1954

808   Joseph M. Purcell, "Last Night on TV," *Boston Daily Record*, February 4, 1955

809   Review of *A Leaf Out of the Book*, Variety, February 8, 1955

810   "Why George Brent Came Out of Retirement," *TV Guide*, March 16-22, 1957

811   Review of *The Inner Light*, Crossroads, February 6, 1956

812   Michael Winkelman, who played Brent's son in *The Long Day*, was Little Luke on *The Real McCoys*

813   Review of *The Fleeting Years*, *Variety*, May 10, 1956

814   Interview with Sam Hall, June 16, 2009

815   Hal Humphrey, "Viewing TV," *Oakland Tribune*, March 15, 1956

816   "Why George Brent Came Out of Retirement," *TV Guide*, March 16-22, 1957

817   Review of *Campaign Train*, *Variety*, October 15, 1956

818   Cary O'Dell, *Wire Service*, tvparty.com, 2013

819   Fred Watkins, "George Brent," *Film Fan Monthly*, October 1972

820   Dorothy Kilgallen, "Voice of Broadway," *Coshocton County Democrat*, October 14, 1956

821   Fred Watkins, "George Brent," *Film Fan Monthly*, October 1972

822   James Robert Parish and Don E. Stanke, *The Debonairs*, Arlington House, © 1975, p. 56

823   Hedda Hopper, "Looking Over Hollywood, *Springfield Union*, October 15, 1956

824   Review of *Death of a Scoundrel*, *Variety*, October 31, 1956

825   Richard B. Jewell, Vernon Harbin, *The RKO Story*, Arlington House, © 1982, p. 287

826   "Fire Ravaged Santa Monica Area Hit by Third Big Blaze," *Montana Standard*, December 29, 1956

827   "Why George Brent Came Out of Retirement," *TV Guide*, March 16-22, 1957

828   "Why George Brent Came Out of Retirement," *TV Guide*, March 16-22, 1957

829   Richard Schickel, *Clint Eastwood*, Alfred A. Knopf, © 1996, p. 120

830   TV Key, "Behind Your TV Screen," *The Miami News*, August 27, 1959

831   Frank Rhoades, "The High Road," *San Diego Union*, July 21, 1959

832   TV Key staff, review of *I Know What I'd Have Done*, *Salina Journal*, July 24, 1960

833   Vernon Scott, "Matinee Idols Do Fade," *Eureka Humboldt Standard*, July 25, 1960

834   Bob Hebert, "Brent Wants Race Winner More Than he Does Oscar," *Los Angeles Times*, May 6, 1962

835   Bob Hebert, "Brent Wants Race Winner More Than he Does Oscar," *Los Angeles Times*, May 6, 1962

836   James Robert Parish and Don E. Stanke, *The Debonairs*, Arlington House, © 1974, p. 56

837   "Del Mar's Loss is Ireland's Gain," *San Diego Union*, May 20, 1966

838   Nelson Fisher column, *San Diego Union*, June 2, 1966

839   Conversation with Brian Reddin, June 19, 2012

840   John Huston, *An Open Book*, Da Capo Press, ©© 1994, p. 137

841   Dorothy Manners' column, *Marietta Journal*, April 24, 1967

842   Fred Watkins, "George Brent," *Film Fan Monthly*, October 1972

843   Suzanne Brent, *Hollywood Rebels* (2013), Irish TV documentary

844   Brian Reddin, e-mail February 20, 1914

845   James Cagney, *Cagney by Cagney*, Doubleday, © 1976, p. 94

846   James Robert Parish and Don E. Stanke, *The Debonairs*, Arlington House, © 1974, p. 56

Endnotes: Chapter 15

847   James Robert Parish and Don E. Stanke, *The Debonairs*, Arlington House, © 1975, p. 58

848   Frank Rhoades column, *San Diego Union*, July 28, 1974

849   James Robert Parish and Don E. Stanke, *The Debonairs*, Arlington House, © 1975, p. 57

850   Frank Rhoades column, *San Diego Union*, February 1, 1976

851   Jane Powell, *The Girl Next Door and How She Grew*, William Morrow & Co., © 1988, pp. 113-114

852   Jane Powell, *The Girl Next Door and How She Grew*, William Morrow & Co., © 1988, p. 114

853   Guy Flatley, "At the Movies," *New York Times*, December 2, 1977

854   Guy Flatley, "At the Movies," *New York Times*, December 2, 1977

855   Nancy Anderson, "George Brent, Still One of Debonairs," *Rome News-Tribune*, July 2, 1978

856   Bill Kelly, "George Brent in 'Born Again' Role," *Santa Ana Orange County Register*, May 28, 1978

857   Robert Kendall, "Producer Frank Capra Jr. Talks About Hollywood Today," *Hollywood Studio Magazine*, October 1979

858   Philip Wuntch, "*Born Again* Cursed with Familiarity," *Dallas Morning News*, September 30, 1978

859   Bruce Medville, review of *Born Again*, *Encore American & Worldwide News*, V. 7, P. 31

860   Emerson Baldorff, "*Born Again* 'awkward' in its delivery," *Plain Dealer*, November 14, 1978

861   Jonathan Aitken, *Charles W. Colson: A Life Redeemed*, Random House, © 2010, p. 18

862   Laura Wagner, *Anne Francis: The Life and Career*, McFarland, © 2011, p. 114

863   Carl Rollyson, message via *Silver Screen Oasis*, December 10, 2012

864   Whitney Stine, "*I'd Love to Kiss You . . .*" *Conversations with Bette Davis*, Pocket Books, © 1990, p. 63

865   Max Blumenthal, "Born Again, Again," *Washington Monthly*, July/August, 2005

866   William J. Mann, *Behind the Screen: How Gays and Lesbians Shaped Hollywood 1910-1969*, Viking, © 2001, pp. 176-180

867   Frank Rhoades column, *San Diego Union*, March 16, 1978

868   Bill Kelly, "George Brent, In *Born Again*," *Santa Ana Orange County Register*, May 28, 1978

869   Nancy Anderson, "Brent, Still Debonair, Coaxed Back to Work," *North Tonawanda Evening News*, June 2, 1978

870   Conversation with Brian Reddin, June 19, 2012

871   Joyce Caufield, "Early Decision Leads Artist to Lifelong Love of Indians," *San Diego Union*, April 19, 1981

872   Nancy Anderson, "George Brent, Still One of Debonairs," *Rome News-Tribune*, July 2, 1978

873   Carla A. DeDominicis, "Golden Days, Silver Screens," *San Diego Union*, March 16, 1978

874   Dan Tedrick, "George Brent Finds Hollywood Changed," *Mobile Register*, February 10, 1978

875   Bill Kelly, "George Brent, In *Born Again*," *Santa Ana Orange County Register*, May 28, 1978

876   Carla A. DeDominicis, "Golden Days, Silver Screens," *San Diego Union*, March 16, 1978

877   Bill Kelly, "George Brent, In *Born Again*," *Santa Ana Orange County Register*, May 28, 1978

878   Carla A. DeDominicis, "Golden Days, Silver Screens," *San Diego Union*, March 16, 1978

879   Carla A. DeDominicis, "Golden Days, Silver Screens," *San Diego Union*, March 16, 1978

880   Bill Kelly, "George Brent, In *Born Again*," *Santa Ana Orange County Register*, May 28, 1978

881   Bette Davis, *This 'N That*, Putnam, © 1987, p. 46

882   Carla A. DeDominicis, "Golden Days, Silver Screens," *San Diego Union*, March 16, 1978

883   Jane Powell, *The Girl Next Door and How She Grew*, William Morrow & Co., © 1988, p. 114

884   "Marriages," *Variety*, December 20, 1978

885   Liz Smith column, *Plain Dealer*, December 31, 1978

886   Conversation with Cherie Meade Frakes, November 26, 2013

887   "Minutes – County of Maui Government," March 17, 2010, p. 34

888   Jane Powell, *The Girl Next Door and How She Grew*, William Morrow & Co., © 1988, p. 115

889   Social Security Death Index: China H. Marin passed away on May 7, 2000. She had resided for over 20 years at the Actors Fund Home in Englewood, New Jersey

890   Lawrence J. Quirk, *Fasten Your Seatbelts: the Passionate Life of Bette Davis*, William Morrow, © 1990, p. 55

891   Vincent Canby, "With Bette and Olivia into Brooklyn, Making Bally Noises for 'Hush … Hush,' " *Variety*, March 10, 1965

892   Lawrence J. Quirk, *Fasten Your Seatbelts: the Passionate Life of Bette Davis*, William Morrow, © 1990, p. 107 (Waterbury had ghostwritten an article for Brent that appeared in the January 6, 1940 issue of *Liberty* magazine, titled "Not a Feminine Woman in Hollywood")

893   Larry Cohen, "I Killed Bette Davis," *Film Comment*, July/August 2012

894   Lawrence J. Quirk, *Fasten Your Seatbelts: the Passionate Life of Bette Davis*, William Morrow, © 1990, p. 107

895   Harry Haun, "Bette Davis Reflects on Illustrious Career," *Austin American Statesman*, April 30, 1989

896   George Brent, "Star Reporting," *Photoplay*, May 1940

897   Mary Astor, *Mary Astor – A Life on Film*, Dell, © 1967, p. 157

898   Email from Marylyn Roh, July 21, 2010

899   "Antiques & Art," *San Diego Union*, November 3, 1979

900   Frank Rhoades column, *San Diego Union*, November 7, 1979

901   Bill Kelly, "George Brent, In *Born Again*," *Santa Ana Orange County Register*, May 28, 1978

902   Thornton Sargent, "The Nine Lives of George Brent," *Oakland Tribune*, May 19, 1935

903   George Brent @ findagrave.com

904   William Butler Yeats, "Earth, Fire and Water," *The Celtic Twilight*, Dover Pub., © 2011, p. 69

Footnotes: Acknowledgements

905   Email from Suzanne Brent, November 10, 2012

906   Jeanine Basinger, email, February 7, 2014

907   Doug McClelland, letters dated April 29, 1995, and May 6, 1995

908   Scott O'Brien, "Kay Francis – Portrait on Silk," *Films of the Golden Age*, Winter 1995/1996, pp. 56-62

909   Email from Marylyn Roh, July 21, 2010

INDEX

Made in the USA
Las Vegas, NV
17 April 2021